Destiny of

Dragons

PRAISE FOR THE PILLARS OF REALITY SERIES

"Campbell has created an interesting world... [he] has created his characters in such a meticulous way, I could not help but develop my own feelings for both of them. I have already gotten the second book and will be listening with anticipation."

–Audio Book Reviewer

"I loved *The Hidden Masters of Marandur*...The intense battle and action scenes are one of the places where Campbell's writing really shines. There are a lot of urban and epic fantasy novels that make me cringe when I read their battles, but Campbell's years of military experience help him write realistic battles."

–All Things Urban Fantasy

"I highly recommend this to fantasy lovers, especially if you enjoy reading about young protagonists coming into their own and fighting against a stronger force than themselves. The world building has been strengthened even further giving the reader more history. Along with the characters flight from their pursuers and search for knowledge allowing us to see more of the continent the pace is constant and had me finding excuses to continue the book."

–Not Yet Read

"*The Dragons of Dorcastle*... is the perfect mix of steampunk and fantasy... it has set the bar to high."

–The Arched Doorway

"Quite a bit of fun and I really enjoyed it. . .An excellent sequel and well worth the read!"

–Game Industry

"The Pillars of Reality series continues in *The Assassins of Altis* to be a great action filled adventure. . .So many exciting things happen that I can hardly wait for the next book to be released."

—Not Yet Read

"The Pillars of Reality is a series that gets better and better with each new book. . .*The Assassins of Altis* is a great addition to a great series and one I recommend to fantasy fans, especially if you like your fantasy with a touch of sci-fi."

—Bookaholic Cat

"Seriously, get this book (and the first two). This one went straight to my favorites shelf."

—Reanne Reads

"[Jack Campbell] took my expectations and completely blew them out of the water, proving yet again that he can seamlessly combine steampunk and epic fantasy into a truly fantastic story. . .I am looking forward to seeing just where Campbell goes with the story next, I'm not sure how I'm going to manage the wait for the next book in the series."

—The Arched Doorway

"When my audiobook was delivered around midnight, I sat down and told myself I would listen for an hour or so before I went to sleep. I finished it in almost 12 straight hours, I don't think I've ever listened to an audiobook like that before. I can say with complete honesty that *The Servants of The Storm* by Jack Campbell is one of the best books I've ever had the pleasure to listen to."

—Arched Doorway

PRAISE FOR THE LOST FLEET SERIES

"It's the thrilling saga of a nearly-crushed force battling its way home from deep within enemy territory, laced with deadpan satire about modern warfare and neoliberal economics. Like Xenophon's Anabasis – with spaceships."

–The Guardian (UK)

"Black Jack is an excellent character, and this series is the best military SF I've read in some time."

–Wired Magazine

"If you're a fan of character, action, and conflict in a Military SF setting, you would probably be more than pleased by Campbell's offering."

–Tor.com

". . . a fun, quick read, full of action, compelling characters, and deeper issues. Exactly the type of story which attracts readers to military SF in the first place."

–SF Signal

"Rousing military-SF action… it should please many fans of old-fashioned hard SF. And it may be a good starting point for media SF fans looking to expand their SF reading beyond tie-in novels."

–SciFi.com

"Fascinating stuff … this is military SF where the military and SF parts are both done right."

–SFX Magazine

PRAISE FOR THE LOST FLEET: BEYOND THE FRONTIER SERIES

"Combines the best parts of military sf and grand space opera to launch a new adventure series … sets the fleet up for plenty of exciting discoveries and escapades."

—Publishers Weekly

"Absorbing…neither series addicts nor newcomers will be disappointed."

—Kirkus Reviews

"Epic space battles, this time with aliens. Fans who enjoyed the earlier books in the Lost Fleet series will be pleased."

—Fantasy Literature

"I loved every minute of it. I've been with these characters through six novels and it felt like returning to an old group of friends."

—Walker of Worlds

"A fast-paced page turner … the search for answers will keep readers entertained for years to come."

—SF Revu

"Another excellent addition to one of the best military science fiction series on the market. This delivers everything fans expect from Black Jack Geary and more."

—Monsters & Critics

Destiny of Dragons

The Legacy of Dragons
Book 3

JACK CAMPBELL

JABberwocky Literary Agency, Inc.

Destiny of Dragons

First paperback edition in 2018 by JABberwocky Literary Agency, Inc.

Published as an ebook in 2018 by JABberwocky Literary Agency, Inc.

Originally published in 2018 as an audiobook by Audible Studios

This is a work of fiction. Names, characters, businesses, places, events and incidents are either the products of the author's imagination or used in a fictitious manner. Any resemblance to actual persons, living or dead, or actual events is purely coincidental.

Cover art by Dominick Saponaro

Map by Isaac Stewart

ISBN 978-1-625673-64-0

To Elizabeth Moon,
U.S. Marine, Mother, Chronicler of Paksenarrion and Vatta, Keeper of
Horses No Matter How Difficult, Captain of Musketeers, and Friend

For S, as always

ACKNOWLEDGMENTS

I remain indebted to my agents, Joshua Bilmes and Eddie Schneider, for their longstanding support, ever-inspired suggestions and assistance, as well as to Krystyna Lopez and Lisa Rodgers for their work on foreign sales and print editions. Many thanks to Betsy Mitchell for her excellent editing. Thanks also to Robert Chase, Kelly Dwyer, Carolyn Ives Gilman, J.G. (Huck) Huckenpohler, Simcha Kuritzky, Michael LaViolette, Aly Parsons, Bud Sparhawk and Constance A. Warner for their suggestions, comments and recommendations.

CHAPTER ONE

Kira of Dematr woke from a dark dream of being pursued through an endless maze of boulders by faceless, implacable Imperial legionaries, dragons whose eyes glowed with mindless hate, and a mysterious figure in Mage robes who shadowed her every move with silent menace.

She looked up at the ceiling of her room, calming her breathing and her racing heart. Seventeen years old seemed too young to be having such nightmares built from real memories. For some inexplicable reason the twin scars made by a dragon's claws on her left shoulder were itching but the marks of newer injuries from swords and a bullet were not.

Who had the Mage been, though? The lightning Mage who had tried to kill her and Jason in Kelsi? But Kira had been certain that Mage was a man, whereas the Mage in her dreams had felt like a woman.

From the morning twilight visible through her window, she could tell it was very early, dawn still a little way off. The house was silent with the peace of undisturbed sleep for her mother and father, and for her fiancé Jason in the room next to hers.

Kira's eyes stayed on the door to her room. Sighing, she finally got up and walked to the door, turning the latch to assure herself that she wasn't locked in. The fear was silly, here safe at home, but at the same time as real as the memories of her imprisonment a few months ago on an Imperial warship whose burned-out hulk now rested half-submerged in the harbor at Caer Lyn.

Knowing that sleep would not come again, Kira went to the window to look out on the still, dark fields around the house. Several hundred lances off she could see a group of riders, Lancers on patrol around the house. Sentries and bodyguards like that had been part of her life for as long as Kira could remember, protecting her mother, and Kira, from the enemies who wished them dead.

Acting on a sudden impulse, Kira grabbed her clothes, slipping into her trousers and buttoning up her shirt. Strapping on the shoulder holster was a task as familiar as pulling on her socks. She checked her pistol to ensure the magazine was full and the safety set before holstering it. Pulling on her jacket, she paused to make sure the loose cartridge was still in one pocket.

She'd brought that cartridge with her from the Northern Ramparts. During the night when she and Jason had nearly died, it would have been her last shot. She wasn't sure of everything that it symbolized for her. Hope, definitely. Not giving up. Jason's love. There were plenty of reasons why she kept it close.

Not wanting to disturb anyone else, she opened the door quietly before going down the stairs carefully and as silently as possible, carrying her boots until she reached the front door. Once out on the front porch she pulled on the boots, then headed for the barn, grateful for her jacket in the predawn chill. The air held a faint scent of seawater borne by the breeze from the coast south of the house. The outskirts of the growing city of Pacta Servanda were still far enough off that no sight or sound of it intruded on the countryside here.

Her new horse wasn't in the barn, instead standing outside in the fenced field, looking toward the north. "Good morning, Suka," Kira said, walking up to stroke the gelding's neck. "Do you miss the mountains?"

Suka tossed his head in what might have been a nod before turning to nuzzle Kira affectionately. Obviously eager for exercise, the gelding waited patiently as Kira saddled and bridled him, not playing any tricks as she tightened the girth. Draping the reins across the saddle, Kira walked back to the gate, Suka following without any need for direction. Once outside the gate, Kira swung herself up into the saddle, leaving the reins loose as she directed Suka with her seat and her legs, falling quickly into the familiar rhythm of the horse's movement.

She headed out across the fields. Suka broke into a tentative canter, and when Kira indicated it was all right her horse went to a full gallop, racing across the grass, wind blowing back his mane as Kira leaned forward, enjoying the feeling of freedom.

As they approached one of the patrols, several Lancers on their own mounts, Kira shifted her seat to the back of the saddle and broke with the rhythm of Suka's movement, deliberately moving against it as she also lightly squeezed with both legs. Suka slowed to a walk again, almost prancing as he neared the other horses. The stocky mountain breed was shorter than the tall horses bred on the wide plains of Tiae, but the other horses gave him careful looks that testified to their wariness around the tough northern mount. Kira turned Suka by pressing lightly with one leg while opening the other slightly, so that she and Suka were riding alongside the patrol.

"Is there anything wrong, Captain Kira?" asked the corporal in charge of the patrol, saluting.

"No," Kira said, returning the salute and realizing they had misinterpreted Suka's gallop as a sign of urgency. "Sorry. My mount just wanted to stretch his legs. Is it all right if we ride along with you for a while?"

"Of course, Captain." The corporal looked Suka over. "He's pretty fast."

"Your mount could probably beat him in a dash," Kira said, "but Suka can outrun most in a long race."

"He's a Free Cities mount?"

"Yes. From the Fourth Lancers of Alexdria. I rode him when I was up there. His original rider had to retire because of injuries, so the Fourth Lancers were kind enough to send Suka to me."

The corporal nodded, smiling. "Any veteran of fighting the legions, woman or man or horse, is always welcome with the Lancers of Tiae."

Kira nodded in reply, feeling embarrassed by the praise. She'd heard people calling her a hero, but heroes were supposed to be brave and she didn't remember feeling brave. All she recalled of the long days and nights in the Northern Ramparts was being tired and hungry and scared, fighting to keep herself and Jason alive. The cartridge in her jacket pocket was a reminder of that, too, of how close they'd both come to dying, and how great a treasure it was to be alive and seeing a new day dawn.

Kira dropped back slightly, riding just to one side of the patrol, far enough out that Suka wouldn't be tempted to nip playfully at any of the other horses. Trained cavalry mount though he was, Suka had a mischievous streak that could surface without warning. But this morning Suka behaved himself, letting her relax.

The patrols never followed fixed routes and times, avoiding any predictable patterns that enemies could exploit. Occasionally the corporal ordered the patrol to a trot for a minute or so before dropping back to a walk. The reins loose before her, Kira directed her well-trained mount without having to think about it, enjoying the open spaces about her, the open sky above, and the growing light as the sun rose into view in the east. Riding with the other Lancers was also pleasant, giving her a feeling of belonging that Kira had often missed when she was younger and hemmed in by bodyguards. For their part, the Lancers were comfortable around her, seeing Kira as one of their own, though being careful to treat her as an officer.

Captain. It still felt weird, to be respectfully addressed that way by men and women who in some cases had been soldiers longer than Kira had been alive. She had been only an honorary lieutenant in the Queen's Own Lancers of Tiae, but after the fighting in the Northern Ramparts she had been field-promoted to Captain of Lancers by the Alexdrian forces, a rank that seemed to mysteriously follow her wherever she went.

The patrol met up with their reliefs, another group of Lancers.

"Patrols are going to be doubled starting today," the leader of the new group informed the others.

They all turned to look at Kira, but all she could do was shake her head in ignorance. "I haven't heard anything yet." As the two groups of Lancers turned over duties Kira saluted in farewell and guided Suka in a walk back toward the barn.

When Kira got close enough, she saw her mother—Master Mechanic Mari of Dematr, the daughter of Jules—waiting outside the house in her dark jacket, trousers, and boots. Kira had once bridled at her close resemblance to her mother, the greatest hero the world of Dematr had ever known, but these days seeing Mari as an older image of herself felt immensely comforting. So did knowing that under her jacket her mother wore the same sort of holster and carried the same kind of pistol. Because the patrols couldn't stop every threat.

Kira swung down off of Suka as she neared her mother. "Good morning!"

"You're in a good mood," Mari observed, falling in to walk alongside Kira as Suka followed. "Of course you didn't wake up to find your daughter missing."

"I'm sorry. I didn't want to bother anyone."

"Next time leave a note, all right?" Mari grimaced as memories flitted across her face. "I worry."

"You have every right to," Kira said, leading Suka into the barn and removing his tack. "I worry, too. That's why I had to get out this morning."

"Bad dreams?"

"Yes. And . . . I felt . . . confined."

"I know all about nightmares like that," her mother said, and for a moment her eyes went distant and Kira knew that Mari was once again on the walls of Dorcastle as the city burned and the Imperial legions attacked. It had taken Kira a long time to realize that part of her mother had never left those walls. She would always be there, forever fighting to free the world.

But then Mari's eyes cleared and she was here again. "I'm glad you went out," she told Kira. "Is there anything you need to talk about?"

"Not right now," Kira said. "Riding is great therapy."

Her mother helped as Kira rubbed down and brushed Suka. Kira enjoyed the shared work, feeling closer to Mari at such times. "Suka likes you, you know."

Mari laughed. "I'm glad we finally found one horse in the world of Dematr who likes me."

"I'm serious. If you ever want to ride him, I'm sure Suka would be fine. You'd just have to be very light on the rein. He's used to being guided by a Lancer."

"Thank you, but I'm going to try to avoid riding until this little guy is with us safe and sound," her mother replied, patting the swell of her body where the pregnancy was now easy to see.

Neither one of them said anything about the last time, when Kira herself had still been very little, but yesterday Kira had noticed fresh flowers on the grave of her little brother, who had died during birth. She paused in her work with her horse to give her mother a long, wordless embrace. Some things didn't have to be spoken.

Kira poured out some grain for Suka before giving him a final pat and walking back to the house with her mother.

Inside, the delicious aroma of coffee met them. "Mother, out of all the things you've done, teaching a Mage how to make good coffee has to be your greatest achievement."

In the kitchen, her father Alain of Ihris, Master of Mages, offered them each a cup, even his Mage training at concealing emotions unable to hide his pride in being able to make coffee. Kira gave him a smile, knowing that even the simple workings of a coffee maker were beyond a Mage's comprehension and that her mother made up everything and set the brewer over the heat. All her father had to do was take the pot off at the proper time, but for a Mage that was neverthe-less something special. Alain could do things considered scientifically impossible, making parts of objects disappear for a while or creating intense heat anywhere he desired, but he couldn't work any piece of technology more complicated than a knife even if his life depended on it.

"Where's Jason?" Kira asked as she sat down at the kitchen table and grabbed a piece of buttered toast.

"He is still in bed," her father said.

"You're kidding. People from Urth must need lots of sleep." Kira turned her head toward where the guest bedroom lay. "HEY, JASON! GET DOWN HERE FOR BREAKFAST!"

Her mother rubbed her ear. "Next time maybe you could go knock on his door. The security patrols probably heard that and went to high alert."

"The security patrols should be used to me by now." Kira sipped her coffee, watching her mother. "Speaking of high alert, I just heard that patrols around the house are being doubled starting today."

Mari raised her eyebrows in surprise at the news. "I didn't think they'd react that quickly to what are still vague warnings of trouble."

"Care to share?" Kira asked. "I saw that courier come in late last night with a half-troop of cavalry as an escort. Those must have been some pretty hot dispatches."

Mari nodded, smiling at Alain as he sat down next to her, then turning a serious face to Kira. "Yes. Something's up, but we still don't have enough pieces to see the picture. Queen Sien's security services here in Tiae are worried that the pieces they do have seem to point at us. There are reports of odd activity involving Mages in the Empire and the Western Alliance, and we still haven't located the former leaders of the Mechanics Guild since they went into hiding after the Empire cracked down on them. And the Empire itself is a source of concern as always, but especially now. Prince Maxim is safely out of the way, but his former followers blame you for his death and his failures."

Kira shrugged. "It's not my fault that cowardly, arrogant jerk was stupid enough to kidnap me."

"That's right, dearest, but that also means next time they'll just try to kill you right off rather than take any chances."

"Why are those followers still running around freely, anyway?" Kira demanded, letting her worries come through as irritation. "I thought the Empire was really good at locking up people and killing its enemies."

Her father smiled slightly. "That is usually true, except where this family is concerned."

"Which is no grounds for complacency," Kira's mother warned. "The latest secret dispatches from Palandur say the old emperor is very sick. With his grip on power fading, the empire is already feeling some turmoil. He could die at any time, which could render the empire unstable until the emperor's successor solidifies control."

"Princess Sabrin is securely positioned to become empress, isn't she?"

"Yes, but nothing is certain with Imperial politics. Nor can we be certain what Empress Sabrin would do."

"Mother, I talked personally to Sabrin. She was sincere in offering to ally with me. With us. And she did help me escape."

"I know." Her mother took a drink of coffee, her eyes hooded with thought. "But Sabrin is a pragmatist. She'll do whatever seems best for her and the Empire, and if that means changing her attitude toward me and you, she'll do that." Mari turned a sardonic look on Kira. "And for some reason Sabrin is concerned that the two of us may be what Imperial gossip claims."

Kira tried to make a joke of the Imperial superstition that she and her mother were what Jason said were called vampires on Urth. "They probably think we start the morning with hot mugs of blood."

"You'd almost think someone had encouraged the Imperials, and Sabrin in particular, to believe that we craved the blood of young men," her mother said, still looking at Kira.

"Excuse *me*. I was trying to survive." Kira took a bite of toast, reveling in the crunch of the bread and the rich taste of the butter. In the time since her ordeal in Imperial captivity and escaping at sea and through the mountains, she had been forced to fight a compulsion to squirrel away food. At times it still felt odd to know she wouldn't have to go hungry today.

But that brought up memories of the Ramparts, and her night-mare.

"What is wrong?" her father asked, having instantly seen the sudden tension in Kira. Mages were like that; their training allowed them to spot any emotion in others, no matter how well hidden.

"Nothing," she said. "I just had a nightmare before I woke up, that's all. The usual dragons and Imperial soldiers and . . ."

"And?"

"I don't know," Kira said, feeling irritable again at having to talk about it. "Some female Mage."

"A female Mage?" Mari asked. "One of those who attacked you in Kelsi?"

"I don't know. She had her hood up so I couldn't see her face, but everywhere I went in that dream she was right there, watching me." Kira took a sip of coffee to give herself time to think. "It was just another nightmare." She decided to change the subject so she could divert the unpleasant memories that had been brought up. "Wasn't the Western Alliance threatening to do something about the pirates hitting their shipping in the Jules Sea? Has that settled out?"

"No," Mari said, accepting without comment Kira's sudden change of topic. She leaned forward toward Kira, her arms on the table. "The pirates are still a problem. The Western Alliance is certain they're based out of Syndar, and I'm sure they're right. But Syndari officials are sure to be getting a cut of what the pirates are bringing in, and Syndar knows the Alliance isn't eager to start hostilities, so they keep stalling, and for now Alliance warships remain outside of Syndari territorial waters, playing cat and mouse with the pirates. But at some point Alliance patience will give out and they'll move against Syndar, unless the situation gets resolved first. What do you think I should do, Kira?"

Kira paused to think. When she was fifteen, she'd been terrified by the idea of trying to be her mother. Mari had done the impossible, defeating the Great Guilds to free Dematr. Mari had slain dragons and raised an army. Mari had changed the world. Kira had thought it ridiculous that she could ever step into her mother's shoes, responsible for trying to resolve disputes between nations and if necessary rallying armies and navies to fight for her. And her mother had never pushed for that, trying to shield her daughter from the responsibilities and burdens that came with being the daughter of Jules.

But Jason had come to this world and Kira had been forced to face her legacy, discovering that she did have something of her mother inside her. And not so long ago Kira had experienced first-hand what could happen without her mother resolving disputes between nations. Kira had seen war up close. She knew what could happen, and how many could die. A still-fresh scar on one side of her neck told of an Imperial bullet that had come too close to ending her life, and when she moved quickly a lingering tightness in her side reminded her of the Imperial sword that had ridden along her ribs. She had survived, but others had not.

Kira hadn't said anything directly to her mother since then about someday taking on at least some of the responsibilities of her mother. But she had asked questions, and cautiously offered opinions, waiting to hear her mother's reactions and advice. And Mari, not without a certain sadness sometimes apparent, had accepted that her daughter was subtly volunteering to step up. Because when there was a job to be done, the women and the men in her family did it.

"Could you let the Syndaris know that Queen Sien is preparing to hit them because of the damage the pirates are doing to trade between Tiae and the Alliance?" Kira asked. "Syndar has been terrified of Sien ever since the War of the Great Guilds."

"No," Mari said. "I can't threaten action, even indirectly, on behalf of Sien. That would commit her to following through if the bluff failed. One of the reasons the queen and I have remained on good terms is because I don't presume to throw my weight around inside her kingdom. And Sien isn't going to want to threaten action until she's prepared to follow through on it if necessary."

"Oh." That made sense. Kira frowned down at her coffee, thinking. "What if . . . the Syndaris heard that Queen Sien was . . . thinking about . . . joint action with the Western Alliance against the pirates?"

Her mother smiled and nodded. "Which Sien would agree to me saying, because it doesn't commit her to any action. And it is likely to get Syndar's attention."

"Is that what you're going to do?" Kira asked.

"I've already sent a message to Sien asking if I can inform Syndar of that. I think the queen will agree. As a matter of fact, one of those dispatches last night told me she is going to open some secret talks with the Alliance in case action does have to be taken." Mari hoisted her coffee cup in a salute to Kira. "Good job."

Kira felt her face growing warm at the praise. "Thank you. Um, what about the librarians? Has Urth told us anything yet?"

"No." Mari glanced at the sky outside the kitchen window as if the far-off star that warmed Urth was somehow visible during the day. "I haven't heard anything new, which means that Urth still refuses to tell us anything about what might be buried under Pacta Servanda. As soon as Jason is fully recovered, we need to go take a look at it."

Jason came in, smiling sheepishly, his hair still rumpled from sleep and walking a little stiffly because the bullet wound to his leg was still healing. "Hey, dragon slayer," he said.

Both Kira and her mother turned to look. "Which one?" Mari asked dryly.

"Ummm, Kira. Sorry. Good morning, Lady Mari, Sir Alain."

"Stop being so formal," Mari said. "We're going to be your parents whenever Kira gets around to setting the date."

"Good morning, my love," Kira said to Jason. "Want to get married today?"

"Sure," Jason said, getting some coffee.

Her father shook his head. "You ask him every morning as a joke, but once you both turn eighteen, Kira, you might say that and find that Jason has turned the joke on you by having the papers all prepared and ready to say his promise to you."

"Oh, Father, Jason wouldn't ambush me into getting married without me even knowing what was happening! Who would do something like that?"

Mari bent a sharp look Kira's way. "Very funny. Your father never complained . . . once he realized what had happened. I'll remind you that after the wedding your father and I barely escaped before the harbor of Caer Lyn was locked down. There wasn't any time to waste on explanations."

"Maybe Jason and I will do the same thing," Kira suggested. "A very quick wedding with just the two of us and then dash away before anyone can catch us."

"You're not allowed," her mother said. "In part because there are still too many people who want to get their hands on you and too many assassins waiting to get a shot at you. But also because a lot of people want to be there when you and Jason exchange promises. Queen Sien would not take it well if you two eloped instead."

"It's not like Sien is still my queen," Kira grumbled. "She never really was."

"She's always treated you like a daughter of her own, young lady. And she's one of our best friends, who fought alongside your father and me to reforge the kingdom and defeat the Great Guilds. Even if she wasn't the Queen of Tiae we'd want to give her wishes some consideration. But, speaking of the wedding, exactly when do you turn eighteen, Jason?"

"That's a good question," Jason said, sitting down beside Kira. "Relativity kind of messed that up. I mean, there's my birthday back on Earth. If we did a straight count of Earth standard days, I'd be twenty-eight now. I think legally, on Earth, I am twenty-eight, if anyone still cares about me back there. But during my ten-year-long trip to this world, only about two months passed inside the ship because of how fast we were going most of that time. So in terms of how much I've aged, I'm really close to eighteen. I think I'm a little over eighteen. But your days aren't exactly the same length as days on Earth, and your years aren't exactly the same length, so . . . I don't know. I doubt anyone knows."

"If the date is so uncertain," Alain said, "why not choose the birthday date on this world that feels right to you? No one can call you wrong."

"A Mage's answer," Mari said, smiling. "Just make something up!"

"Not so," Kira's father objected. "If I understand Jason right, then the date of his birth on Urth cannot be used to determine his age here on Dematr. His exact age is not a fixed illusion like a wall, but something uncertain and ever changing, like the flow of a river. Pick any spot on that river, then, and say his journey began *here*."

Jason scratched his head. "So, I can say I'm eighteen now?"

"Nice try," Kira's mother said, offering him some toast. "But you don't get to marry Kira until she's also eighteen, and we know exactly when that will be. You've got another month before she'll be of legal age."

"We're really not in a rush," Kira said, grabbing another piece of toast. "I mean, we've already got each other."

Mari nodded. "That's what counts. But the promises count, too. You may not believe that, but when you say them, it matters, and you know it in your heart."

"All right! I'll try to decide when. Maybe we'll do it in a couple of years," Kira added.

"Fine," her mother said.

"It's almost like you don't want to argue about it."

"Almost."

"Just remember that Jason knows he can back out any time before the wedding if he decides he isn't comfortable always worrying about being killed by our family's enemies."

"I've survived everything so far. I'm sort of used to it by now," Jason said. "Did I hear something about going to Pacta Servanda?"

"Yes," Mari said. "We've been waiting for Urth to relent and actually tell us something, but so far they've simply ignored the last two messages about it that the librarians sent through the Feynman unit. I'm uncomfortable continuing to wait. Even if the weapons that might be buried there are still stable after all this time, there's still the chance that someone might find references to them in the old files of the Mechanics Guild, and if they do that they might come up with some scheme to try to get them and use them. If you feel up to it, I can see how soon Queen Sien and the others can get here, and we'll see what we can see of whatever's buried under Pacta."

"Okay," Jason said. "I hope I'm wrong. But we do know the crew of the colony ship that brought your ancestors to Demeter—"

"Dematr," Kira said.

"To Dematr," Jason continued, "they broke a lot of rules. Suppressing most technology and knowledge of where you guys had come from, and putting themselves in control of everything as the Mechanics Guild. If they really did bury beta field generators and other weapons at Pacta, it could be a real mess to deal with. A scary mess."

"We've dealt with scary messes before," Mari replied. "But I agree with you. One less scary mess would be a nice thing."

It should have a nice moment, one where Kira could relax with those she loved, but as she thought about the dangers of what might be under Pacta her Mage powers abruptly surged past the bonds she had placed on them. Kira, alarmed, concentrated on once again suppressing them as much as possible.

But her father had sensed the outburst, of course, and was watching her intently. Her mother picked up on that. "What happened?" Mari asked.

"Kira's Mage powers suddenly became easy to sense," Alain said.

Jason was watching her now as well. Kira tried to control a burst of annoyance fed by her own worries. "It's all right. I'm fine. I just needed to reinforce the barriers I've built to keep them suppressed. Sometimes they break free."

"Is that normal?" Mari asked Alain, her voice carefully neutral.

Kira's father shook his head, his eyes fixed on Kira. "Many Mages work to hide their presence from other Mages. I know of none who seek to suppress their powers."

"Well, I'm kind of unique, aren't I?" Kira replied, her voice growing sharp. "I'm not supposed to have any Mage powers! It should be impossible for anyone who can do Mechanic work to have Mage powers, as I keep being reminded! So what's the big deal if I try to suppress them? Maybe if I suppress them long enough and hard enough they'll go away and I'll be a little less of a—" She bit off the last word with a guilty glance toward Jason.

But he knew what she'd been about to say. "You're not a freak," Jason said in a low voice.

"Those Mage powers have saved your life," her mother said, keeping her voice calm.

Her father nodded. "Kira, it is impossible to say what will happen if you continue to suppress the powers."

She glared at them and shoved the toast and coffee away, her appetite and her happiness both vanished. "I can tell you what happens when I don't suppress them! How do you think it feels to realize you've been blacked out and doing things without even being aware of them? Why would my powers do that to me if they weren't trying to hurt me?"

"We understand your worries," Mari began.

"No, Mother, you don't! You can't! None of you can! Because there's never been anyone else who could be a Mechanic and also have Mage powers. It's not natural! Everybody who knows has been worried about it since those powers first manifested, so don't try to tell me this is something *I* shouldn't worry about! And the fact that my powers keep fighting me is proof they want to take over! That's not going to happen! They will either listen to me, they will stay completely under my control, or I will find a way to make them go away for good!" Kira jumped to her feet, trying not to glare at everyone. "Excuse me."

She went out to the front porch and sat down, glowering at the sky, her insides churning with unhappiness. One hand went into her jacket pocket, her fingers feeling the loose cartridge and gaining comfort from that.

After a while, Jason came out as well, sitting down a little distance away but saying nothing.

"What do you want?" Kira finally asked.

"Nothing. I just thought you might want some company."

"I'm fine."

"Yeah," Jason said. "But we've got each other's back, right? No matter what, we're there for each other. Like in the Ramparts."

Kira covered her face with one hand, trying to calm herself. "How upset are my parents?"

Jason shrugged. "Your mom and dad aren't happy. They're worried."

"And so are you. So why doesn't everybody say, 'You're right, Kira. Suppressing those powers until they go away is a great idea!'"

"They *hope* you're right."

This time Kira buried her face in both hands. "I can't believe I went off on Mother like that when she's expecting. What's wrong with me?"

"You're seventeen," Jason said. "Seriously. It's a crazy time, even when you haven't had to deal with kidnappings and war and dragons and stuff. Or so my life science classes back on Earth warned me."

"The only good thing that ever came from Urth is you!"

"You guys all originally came from there. I mean, your ancestors did."

"I'm trying to vent and you're being logical," Kira grumbled.

"Sorry."

She looked over at him, feeling guilty for snapping at him earlier, old doubts forcing their way to the surface. "Jason, did you say yes to my proposal because it looked like we were going to die soon?"

His expression shifted rapidly from incomprehension to puzzlement to cautious humor. "That's a joke, right?"

"I'm serious. We spotted the legions entering the Northern Ramparts and I asked you to promise yourself to me and you said yes and I can't help wondering if you thought you had to so I wouldn't lose all hope."

He acted puzzled again. "You're serious?"

"Just answer the question. Why aren't you answering the question?" Kira pressed, a tight feeling growing inside her.

"Because . . ." Jason paused before speaking slowly and earnestly. "The happiest moment of my life was when you asked me that. The second happiest moment was when I asked you back and you said yes to me. I really don't understand why you'd think . . . I felt obligated."

Kira frowned at the boards of the porch under her feet. "I'm not the easiest person to live with, Jason. I have my mother's temper. I'm as stubborn as my mother and my father combined. I tend to . . .

attract trouble. And assassins. We heard this morning there's more trouble brewing! I've had those blackouts and have Mage powers I'm not supposed to have. I wake up screaming sometimes because of stuff that's happened."

"You don't wake up screaming very often," Jason said, looking like he realized how weak that assurance was.

"I'm not beautiful—"

"Yes, you are!"

"Jason, even you called me 'exotic,' whatever that is." Kira's hand went up, two of her fingers stroking the long mark under her jaw. "I'm seventeen years old and I've already got scars! What do people think when they look at me?"

She heard him laugh and looked over, perplexed, to see Jason shaking his head.

"Kira, do you know what I think when I see that scar on your neck?" Jason asked. "I think it's even more beautiful than the rest of you. Because I think about me lying there, I've lost a lot of blood, not sure how much longer I have to live, and you standing between me and the legionaries who want to finish killing me. I see you fighting like the toughest valkyrie out of Valhalla, determined to die before you let those legionaries get to me and kill me. Fighting like that for me. And I think, what did I ever do to deserve a girl like that? Maybe I have to do a lot more before I deserve her. Maybe I have to spend my life trying to do enough that I deserve her. Because I'm no special prize. But for some crazy reason this amazing girl loves me and says she wants to marry me, and I'm so lucky I can't put it into words."

Kira had to look away again, smiling with embarrassment. "What's a valkyrie?"

"A type of female warrior," Jason said. "They're really brave and smart, and they never give up, and they believe in doing the right thing even when it's dangerous or hard, and there's no better friend anywhere, and exotic actually does mean a type of beautiful."

She couldn't quite stifle a laugh. "You're insane. Have I told you that?"

"Fairly often," Jason said.

She smiled at him. "I'm lucky, too. And I need to go in and apologize to Mother and Father."

"I've got your back."

"That's my man. Did I tell you I love you?"

"Not yet today."

"I love you," Kira said. "And I'm sorry for going off on you and . . . doubting. It all gets sort of scary sometimes."

He smiled at her. "I know you can handle it, dragon slayer."

"Jason, some things are much harder to slay than even dragons."

The house was simply too crowded, Kira decided. Her mother was working on some complicated diplomatic agreement in the kitchen with representatives from the Western Alliance and the Bakre Confederation, and her father was discussing wisdom with three other Mages in the living room. Mari had let her look over the dispatches from the night before, but just as her mother said, they offered only vague outlines of trouble. Somebody was preparing to act, but how and where remained frustratingly unclear. There were disturbing hints that Kira was the target of some of the threats, though. At least Kira's powers hadn't flared up again, but she had to devote attention to keeping them suppressed.

Feeling increasingly penned in, she made it until a hour after lunch before shutting her Mechanics studies book and walking the short distance to Jason's room.

"Are you up for a walk?" Kira asked. "Physical therapy, I mean."

Jason nodded, smiling. He had to take the stairs carefully before following Kira out the front door. Jason moved stiffly at first, his gait becoming more natural as the injured area loosened up. "Another week and I probably won't even notice this leg any more. Where are we going?"

"Those trees." Kira indicated a small patch of trees a few hundred lances from the house, their branches trimmed high to avoid offering cover for anyone trying to sneak up. "There's a special spot there."

As they walked, she looked around them for any signs of trouble, her eyes lingering on the pasture where Suka was grazing, seeing her horse gazing alertly, ears and head up, toward an empty field. Kira studied the field as well, but stopped worrying when a patrol rode through it without reacting to any trouble. Whatever had spooked Suka wasn't still there.

Reaching the trees, she pointed to a small depression in the ground. "See that? If you lie down in there, you can't see the house, or anyone around. And no one can see you. Unless they noticed you walking out here. When I was younger, I'd come out here and lie there and imagine I was all alone."

"That's, uh, cool," Jason said, giving her a curious look. "Why did you want to show it to me?"

"I want to see if it works for two people. Come on."

She helped him lie down in the depression so they were face to face on their sides.

"No one can see us?" Jason asked.

"That's right," Kira said, grinning. "We're all alone." She pulled off her jacket and shoulder holster, then closed her eyes as her lips sought his.

Almost lost in the experience, Kira felt an irritating tingle behind her forehead. She dismissed it, focusing on Jason, only to feel it return after a short time.

Kira opened her eyes as she continued to kiss Jason, remembering her mother's advice about keeping an eye out for trouble even at times like this. How had it gotten so dark so fast?

She realized the sky hadn't darkened. There was a black haze drifting across her vision. Her foresight, warning of serious danger approaching. "Blazes!" Kira shoved Jason away and lunged for her holster lying nearby. "Look out!"

CHAPTER TWO

After a moment of bafflement, Jason grabbed his knife and looked around. "What is it?"

"I don't know," Kira said, flipping off the safety and chambering a round. She steadied her pistol in both hands as she slowly studied the open area where the haze over her vision seemed darkest. "I'm going to let my Mage powers loose a little."

She flinched as her tentative loosing of her powers resulted in them swelling out, filling her with a jolt that felt physical. But Kira forgot about that instantly as she sensed something: not the glowing pillar that would mark a Mage bending light to remain unseen, but the absence of that. If not for the fact that her father and Mage Asha had demonstrated it for her, Kira never would've noticed that subtle trace that still existed when one Mage used the newly developed means to hide the presence and spells of another. What could be sensed was not a spell itself, but an absence where a spell ought to be.

That absence of something felt way too close. It also felt like it was getting closer very fast.

Kira aimed for the center of the absence and fired.

A female Mage appeared seemingly out of nowhere, not much more than a lance from Kira, reeling away under the impact of the bullet.

Kira swung her pistol to the right as a male Mage appeared next to Jason, swinging the hilt of his long knife at Jason's head.

She tried to target the Mage, but Jason was in the way. As Jason fell, the Mage shoved him at Kira, leaping to attack her and reversing his knife to strike at her with the blade.

Kira staggered as Jason's weight hit her. Shrugging him to one side, she got off another shot, the bullet going wide as the Mage grabbed her arm. Then she was locked in a hand-to-hand struggle as they fell to the ground, the Mage managing to stay on top. Pinned beneath the heavier and stronger Mage, she couldn't get enough leverage to break his grip on the gun hand. Her other hand grasped the Mage's wrist, trying to hold back the knife, but the Mage's superior strength was slowly forcing the blade closer to her throat. She drew up her leg and slammed her knee viciously into the Mage's groin, but he didn't flinch, staring at Kira with unfeeling eyes.

She gasped with relief as Jason appeared over the Mage's shoulder, his expression grim. Jason swung his own knife hilt hard against the Mage's head. The Mage fell to one side, wavering on his hands and knees as Jason, still wobbly from the hit on his head, also swayed and tried to regain his balance. Kira rolled up to her feet and swung the butt of her pistol down hard against the Mage's skull, dropping him to the dirt.

"Thanks," Kira gasped. "Tuck in your shirt," she ordered Jason, fixing her own shirt. "The nearest patrol will be here any second and I don't want them to be able to see what we were doing."

The thunder of hooves came from two directions as different groups of sentries came charging toward the sound of Kira's gunshots. She held up one hand as they approached, gesturing toward the two fallen Mages with her pistol.

"What were you doing out there alone?" Mari demanded.

Kira glared at her mother. The kitchen had gone from feeling like a warm, safe place this morning to having the aura of an interrogation cell this afternoon. "We wanted some privacy."

"Why—?" Mari paused, looking from Kira to Jason, then sighed and nodded. "Privacy. All right. I understand."

"No!" Kira said, embarrassed.

"No?"

"All right! Maybe! We just wanted to be alone for a little while!"

Her father came into the kitchen, where Kira, Jason, and her mother sat around the table. "The female Mage is badly hurt. Healers are seeing to her. The male Mage has not yet regained consciousness. Both carry the stench of Dark Mage about them."

"They seemed pretty tough for Dark Mages," Kira said.

"The lives of Dark Mages have grown more difficult since the fall of the Mage Guild," Alain said. "Only the least capable, who escape notice, and the most capable, who can survive if noticed, still follow that path."

"So we don't know who sent them?" Mari asked.

"Not yet. Perhaps they will not know, if an intermediary was used to hire them." Alain sat down next to Mari looking at Kira and Jason. "It is odd. I am told the male Mage did not attempt to kill Jason."

Jason nodded. "I barely had time to notice him swinging at me and start to dodge out of the way. It was enough that he only hit me a glancing blow, though. I was dazed but not knocked out."

"He did try to kill Kira," Mari said.

"Yes," Alain said. "Why attempt to kill Kira, but refrain from killing Jason?"

"They must have wanted him alive," Kira said. "Maybe for his knowledge?"

"Perhaps," her father said. "Why were you and Jason—"

"They had reasons," Mari interrupted. "Kira, you said your foresight warned you of the danger?"

"Yeah. So I opened my eyes and— Jason, don't give me that look. You know I do that sometimes even when we're . . . busy," she finished, trying not to look at her father.

"Thank the stars above for your foresight," Mari said. "And that you listened to your mother's advice on keeping your eyes open for danger even when you're . . . busy. Our own Mages guarding the security perimeter should have sensed those two approaching, though, before they activated those spells. Isn't that right, Alain?"

Her husband nodded. "Both Mages had been sweating heavily, as if nearly worn out from exertion. It is possible they activated the invisibility spell, and the spell to hide that spell, while still far off and held the spells until Kira spotted them. They should have both been nearly exhausted."

"That male Mage was old-school," Kira said. "You could see it in his scars and his eyes. I kneed him hard and he didn't even flinch."

Mari looked at Alain. "You're still tough from having gone through that brutal acolyte training the Mage Guild used to employ." She shifted a puzzled gaze to her daughter. "There's something that I don't understand, though. Kira, why doesn't foresight make you black out?"

"Ummm . . . I don't know."

"Foresight does not work like other Mage talents," Alain said. "It cannot be summoned on demand, no matter how much power is available in the world around a Mage."

"Mages must have some idea how it works," Mari insisted.

Kira shook her head. "No. It's not like that, Mother. Mage talents . . . it's like you knew how to drive and operate a locomotive, and knew how to feed fuel into it, but you had no idea how the locomotive worked to move itself and pull things. All you knew was how to make it work. I mean, it's all based on the *nothing is real* concept, but that's just sort of a starter key for an engine that works by unknown means."

Mari nodded in reply, intent on Kira's words. "You don't know how wonderful it is to have someone who can explain Mage things in Mechanic terms. You've got a unique perspective, Kira."

"Yeah," Kira said. "Great. Lucky me. Anyway, Mages have even less idea how foresight works than they do how their spells work. Foresight just happens to some Mages, as if knowing how to drive that locomotive suddenly enabled you to also . . . play a musical instrument. Only you couldn't play it when you wanted to. The ability would show up sometimes, and the rest of the time it wouldn't be there."

"Your Uncle Calu thinks it's somehow tied in with quantum-level probabilities," Mari said. "The foresight only kicks in when the probabilities line up, and even then you might be seeing something that is itself only a product of future probabilities. He thinks the minds of Mages can translate that into visions or sounds that make sense to us."

"Another form of illusion," Alain said. "Calu suggested that many people can on rare occasions experience such a thing in dreams."

"Déjà vu," Jason said. "That's what they call that on Earth. The sense that you're experiencing something again even though it seems to be the first time. It's still not considered real because it can't be proven. Maybe it isn't the same thing as Mage foresight, or maybe it's just too unpredictable to ever be provable."

"Unpredictable is the word for foresight," Mari said. "I'm glad it hasn't caused you to black out, Kira. As much as I complain about vague warnings from foresight, sometimes it is a life-saver."

"Are we sure you'll black out again if you use the other powers?" Jason asked Kira. "I mean, those two times you blacked out were under very stressful conditions."

"Two times?" Kira sighed, feeling awful. "I lied about the second time, when I had to hide us from the legionaries using the invisibility spell. I also blacked out that time even though I told you I didn't. You knew, Jason? I knew Father did. I couldn't . . . it was too much to deal with then and there. So I didn't tell you the truth. I'm sorry. I promise I'll never lie to you again."

Her father placed a reassuring hand on Kira's shoulder. "This was known. I had already told your mother. We knew you would tell us when you were able. What Jason says may be so. Perhaps the stress under which the spells were made caused the blackouts."

"How can we know?" Mari said.

"A small spell, Kira," Alain suggested. "Perhaps the invisibility spell again. Here. Surrounded by those who love you. Knowing that you are safe no matter what happens."

She felt a surge of fear and tried to control her breathing and heartbeat. "You want me to try a spell?"

"Only if you wish to."

Kira closed her eyes, attempting to calm herself. What if Jason was right? What if the blackouts had been triggered by stress? Wouldn't it be wonderful to learn that, to know that her Mage powers weren't dangerous to her?

Opening her eyes, she nodded to her parents and Jason. "I'll try. The invisibility thing." Kira shifted her chair about so she was looking out the window. Sitting with her eyes fixed on the sky, she tried to block out all distractions: her parents, Jason, the guards and sentries outside. No one else was here. And what she could see—the window, the counter beneath it, the world outside—was all an illusion. None of it was real. The light itself that streamed through the window was an illusion, an illusion that with access to enough power could be altered for a short time.

Kira cautiously lifted her controls on her Mage powers, feeling them immediately surge through her again like a powerful wave crashing through a seawall. She heard a sound from her father, and knew he must have been as startled to sense that rush of strength as she had been.

Block it out, block fear out, block everything out. Sense only the power available in the land around her to help her cast the spell. Not much, but enough. Invisibility didn't take a lot of power unless it had to be sustained for a long time. Her thoughts threatened to wander down Mechanic pathways of calculating power usage over time. Kira brought them back to concentrating on the Mage teachings. Calm. Illusion. Change the light, so it did not strike her, but flowed around her. She could—

Kira came to a sudden halt and stared at her mother, who was blocking the front door of the house, barricading it against her. She took a shaky breath, looking around before returning her gaze to Mari. "What happened?"

Her father answered from behind them. "We saw the spell take effect as you vanished from sight. I could still sense your presence, and saw you rise from your chair and head quickly for the back door.

I was able to get there first and stand across the door. You turned and I cautioned your mother to close off the front door."

Kira took in a deeper breath, trying to calm herself, her heart pounding from more than the exertion of the spell. "I tried to run away. That's what happened. Isn't that what happened?"

Her mother's eyes stayed on her, worried. "Yes. You don't remember anything?"

"No. I was sitting in the chair and then I was facing you."

"You have no idea why you tried to run out of the house?"

The word almost caught in her throat. "No." Kira closed her eyes, concentrating now on both hiding her Mage powers and suppressing them, layering on the strongest controls she could manage.

When she gazed around again, she saw the look in her father's eyes. "What?"

He spoke carefully. "I was surprised by the strength of your Mage presence, Kira."

"Yeah, well, so was I. That's just wonderful, isn't it? I want to get rid of it, and it just keeps getting stronger." Kira looked at Jason, who was standing to the side, looking miserable. "It's not your fault. You made a good suggestion."

"I want to help," Jason said. "What are you trying to run away from?"

"I don't know!" She took another look at him and suddenly understood the worries behind his words. "Not you. No. I don't want to leave you. Not ever."

"The blackouts didn't *start* until after you said you realized you loved me," Jason said. "That's what you told me."

Kira hesitated, not certain what to say or do. She saw her parents also uncertain. "That's not it," she finally said. Kira looked down at herself, seeing what looked like a single glowing strand of spider silk leading from her to Jason. "The thread is there, Jason! It's still there, running between us, just like it has ever since I realized that I loved you! I'm sorry you can't sense it. I'm sorry it's not really there, but it is there. Isn't it, Father?"

Alain nodded, speaking with the authority that only the sole Master of Mages could claim. "Just as the thread that runs between Mari and myself is there, and not there. Kira could not fake such a thing between you and her."

"But only Kira can see—" Jason began.

"When she speaks of it," Kira's father continued, "she speaks only truth. Kira sees it, and feels it."

Kira walked to Jason and held him. "The only time I have ever lied to you was about that second blackout. I haven't lied to you since then and I will never lie to you again. What I feel, what I sense, is real, and you are so very much what I want. And . . . " She looked at him, trying to sort out a sudden sensation. "I have this feeling that any solution will need you. I don't know why I feel that way. But I do."

He gave her a doubtful look. "All of a sudden you know that?"

"Yes! Suddenly I know that!" Kira insisted. "You're part of the answer. Somehow. Don't ask me to explain. But I *know* that's true."

"Then I'll be here," Jason said. "I promise."

Her mother put her arm around Kira. "When I ask Queen Sien to come up here for our look at what's under Pacta, I'll also ask her to bring along Doctor Sino. If there's something wrong, Kira, maybe she can find it."

"Yeah!" Jason agreed, nodding enthusiastically. "Doc Sino will find out what the problem is. The sooner the better."

"And we'll try to discover who sent those Mages and why."

"Isn't that obvious?" Kira asked . "Your enemies are still after me, Mother, as well as the enemies I've personally managed to acquire. Mechanics who want to return to the days when their Guild ruled the world, Mages who want to be able to do anything they want like they could when their Guild existed, former Dark Mechanics, disgruntled Imperials seeking revenge, and regular people hired to do the bidding of those others. That's not exactly the first time someone has tried to kill me."

"It is the first time since the ship from Urth left that someone might have tried to capture Jason," her father reminded her. "If so, that argues that something new is happening. We have to learn what it is."

Later, when Kira walked with Jason up to his room, she stopped at the door and looked away. "I'm sorry."

"For what?" Jason asked.

"You're not exactly getting a perfect girl. Jason, if you want to reconsider the engagement—"

"Why would I want to do that?"

"Because . . . because there might be something seriously wrong inside me!" Kira said, finally turning her head to meet his eyes.

He looked down, obviously uncomfortable and searching for words. Finally Jason looked back up at her. "Wouldn't that mean you needed me there all the more?"

She found herself smiling at him. "Yes, it would. I'm serious, though, Jason. You didn't agree to promise yourself to someone who might black out at any time and do things without having any memory of them."

He shrugged. "On Earth they say for better or worse at weddings. So . . . yeah . . . I was thinking that. For better or worse. We'll get through whatever it is. Together. That's how we've survived everything so far, right?"

"Right."

"You wouldn't leave me, Kira, even when I wasn't much fun to be around. I won't leave you."

"Thanks, my Urth demon." She held him tightly.

"Do you really think I'll help you find the answer?"

Kira nodded, still holding him and feeling that indefinable sense inside her again. "Yes. It's not foresight. I don't know where it's coming from. But it says you'll help me figure out what's happening. Jason, there's something else you want to say."

"Having a girl who can spot that sort of thing takes some getting used to. I was thinking . . . Kira, that guy tried to kill you."

"As I said to Mother, he's not the first person who's tried to kill me."

Jason looked away, frowning. "I bet Maxim isn't dead."

She stared at him, rattled by the sudden announcement. "Why do you say that?"

"Because in vids and games bad guys are always faking their deaths."

Kira drew back, exasperated. "Jason, how many times have we talked about this kind of thing? Those Urth vid and game things aren't real."

"Nothing is real," Jason said, holding up a forefinger for emphasis. "You and your dad keep saying that. So if that stuff isn't real, and nothing is real, that stuff is just as real as anything else."

"*Seriously?* That is what you've learned since coming to this world?"

"Kira," Jason said stubbornly, "you have a feeling you can't explain that I'll help you figure out what's going on with your powers. I have a feeling I can't explain that Maxim is still alive. And if he is, he's going to want you totally dead."

"Um, yeah," Kira agreed. "If he is. All right. I'm staying alert. And keeping my eyes open."

"Yeah," Jason said, rubbing the back of his neck with one hand. "Even when we're, um . . ."

"I'm sorry we keep getting interrupted," Kira grumbled. "You're my man. We're engaged. But every time we want to do something we end up being chased by legionaries or attacked by assassins or something. I'm pretty sure most couples don't have that problem."

"It's okay," Jason assured her.

"No, it's not! You're not the only one feeling frustrated! The Imperials think I'm a monster who's constantly seducing young men to drink their blood, but I can't even seduce my own man!" She forced herself to step away from him. "There's nothing we can do right now. After this latest attack we'll have a dozen bodyguards treading on our heels the instant we step outside."

He nodded, stepping back as well. "Don't forget what I said. Be careful."

"I'm always careful," Kira said. "All right, I'm usually careful. Don't worry too much. With the queen coming, security here and in Pacta Servanda is going to be as tight as a drum. Nobody's going to be able to get to her, or to me."

"Oh," Jason said as he realized that "nobody" included him. "Well . . . good. As long as you're safe."

She didn't have any trouble spotting the disappointment in the first part, but let it go both because of the truth in the second half of his statement and because she was as disappointed as he was, but also trying to hide it for his sake.

Jason shifted in his seat next to her in the armored coach taking them to Pacta Servanda. This section of road had been paved so the team of six horses drawing the coach didn't raise dust, and outriders on both sides and ahead were ensuring that no ambushers could strike, so the armored louvered windows were wide open, allowing clear views of the countryside as they neared the city. The fields lay green and sparkling under the sun, dappled with spots of water after a recent rain shower. The remaining rain clouds were fleeing to the west under the push of a brisk breeze. In the distance a rising column of smoke marked a steam locomotive on the main rail line through Tiae, Kira without even thinking about it analyzing the darkness of the smoke for how well the engineers on that locomotive were handling the fuel/air mixture.

Jason shifted in his seat again.

"Too slow?" Kira asked.

"I didn't say that!" Jan protested.

"But you were thinking it."

"All right, I'm used to forms of transportation that are a lot faster. But it's still cool to be in a horse-drawn vehicle."

"What are you thinking, Kira?" her mother asked. Mari and Alain sat together on the seat at the back of the enclosed coach, while Kira and Jason sat on the seat to the front facing them. "You seem pensive."

"I was thinking about illusions," Kira said as she looked out the window at the outskirts of the city beginning to appear along the road. "About how the way we see things reflects the illusion we expect to see. I've been to Pacta Servanda a lot when I was younger, but it looks different to me now that we know about those weapons buried under the city."

"We don't know for certain the weapons are there," Jason reminded her. "I thought you were isolated a lot as a kid?"

"Yeah. But for a while I went to a school in Pacta with other kids."

Her mother sighed. "What Kira isn't telling you is that we had to pull her out of that school when we discovered a plot to blow up the entire building in order to kill her. She wasn't happy about that, but we didn't have much choice."

"I gave you a pretty hard time, didn't I?" Kira said.

Mari nodded. "It was one of the many times that you told me I was ruining your life. I'm sorry. You were so unhappy to leave there."

Kira sighed, keeping her gaze out the window. "I acted unhappy to give you a hard time. The truth is, I was relieved I didn't have to go back." She heard the silence that followed her statement, a silence that felt baffled and maybe a little worried, and finally said more. "The others . . . treated me differently. At play period they often wanted to play Dorcastle. You know, one side plays the bad guys, the Imperials, and the other side plays the good guys. And they'd tell me I had to be one of the good guys, because I was your daughter, and then they'd tell me I had to die, because you did. Every time we played that blasted game I had to die, and then come back to life, while they all talked about my mother being dead when I was born."

Mari's voice held mixed outrage and sorrow. "Why didn't you tell me or your father? Or one of the teachers?"

"Because I was your daughter, and I was going to be as tough as you were, even if it killed me." Kira finally looked over at her mother. "One day they tried to make me play an Imperial. As a joke. They thought it was funny. That was the day I tried to walk home in the afternoon."

Mari unhappily shook her head at Kira. "I remember that. Half of Pacta Servanda got locked down while the police and the army searched for you and whoever might have kidnapped you. You refused to tell me why you'd walked away from your school that day."

Kira shrugged. "I didn't want anyone feeling sorry for me. I was tough enough to fight my own battles. Like my mother."

"During those years you kept insisting that you weren't anything like me!"

"I didn't think I was," Kira said. "But I wanted to be. I loved you so much and I resented you so much and I couldn't explain it to anyone. Not even to myself." She looked at Jason beside her. "And then I met you, and you were all amazed at how wonderful you thought I was because you had no idea how messed up I was inside."

Jason, who'd been listening with obvious distress, managed a smile. "If we're going to have a messed up when we met contest, I'd win. It wouldn't even be close."

"You were pretty hard to be around," Kira admitted. "Mother, it wasn't your fault. Not really. It's just the way things were, and I needed to learn how to live with that."

"I still feel guilty about it," Mari said. "But that's being a mother. Alain? What are you thinking and not saying?"

Mari's father bent a cautionary look towards Jason. "Your partner does learn how to know what thoughts you have," he said. "I believe that the promise rings focus the ability. I was thinking," he told Mari, "that there had been a time when I wondered if you and Kira would ever be able to talk without arguing."

"Do you miss that? We can start again. Right, Kira?"

"I don't want to!" Kira said in her old, put-upon voice, then laughed.

But when the carriage halted at a well-guarded hostel near the center of Pacta Servanda, Kira gave her mother a puzzled look. "We're not staying with Sien?"

"We will be," Mari said. "But you've got an appointment here first."

"Just me?" Kira asked. "What's going on?"

"Just a little surprise," her mother replied. "Come on."

Jason came with Kira as she followed Mari out of the carriage, past the sentries at the door, and into the hostel, where Kira saw Mechanic Calu waiting with an oddly impassive expression instead of his usual smile.

"I leave this Apprentice in your capable hands, Mechanic Calu," Kira's mother said, her voice also crisp and unemotional.

Kira frowned as Mari left. "I'm not big on surprises," she said to Calu, who to her surprise gave her another stern look. "Uncle Calu?"

"Mechanic Calu," he corrected her. "Follow me, Apprentice. Your friend can wait out here."

"Where are we going? And Jason is not my friend. He's my man. Anything that I do . . ." Kira's voice faltered under Calu's flat gaze.

"You sit there," Calu directed Jason. "And you come along," he told Kira, walking to a door leading deeper into the building.

Scowling, Kira followed Calu into a larger room. In the center was a desk with a stack of paper and some pens and pencils at the ready as well as some specialized drawing equipment. Beside the desk was a workbench equipped with a variety of tools and parts. Facing the desk and workbench was a long table, behind which already sat Master Mechanic Lukas, Master Mechanic Alli, and Mechanic Dav. All regarded her with the same cool, emotionless expression, as if they were total strangers. As Kira stared about her, Calu sat down next to Dav.

Kira's mouth fell open as she realized what the setup signified. "Is this an exam?"

Lukas, stern and stolid, rapped the surface of the desk before him. "This examination to test the qualifications, knowledge, and skills of the Apprentice Kira of Dematr is called to order."

Horrified, Kira stared at the impassive expressions of people she had called "uncle" and "aunt" for as long as she could remember. "A Mechanic qualifying exam? I'm not ready!"

Lukas frowned at her. "We were told that you were ready, Apprentice. Are you questioning the judgment of Master Mechanic Mari?"

"I'm her daughter! I've spent my whole life questioning her judgment!"

"*Sit down*, Apprentice," Mechanic Calu ordered in a voice that didn't leave any room for argument.

Kira dropped into the seat at the desk and the exam began.

She never could remember much of what followed, as questions came at her rapid fire and she fumbled to give correct responses or demonstrate her skills. Kira had always known that her examiners were among the most skilled and capable Mechanics in the world, but she had never before been made so painfully aware of how much more they knew than she did.

"The Apprentice will leave the room while the examiners discuss the results of her exam," Lukas said, his expression still stern.

Kira got up and stumbled out of the room, finding Jason waiting anxiously. "You were in there a long time," he said. "Are you okay?"

Kira dropped into the seat next to Jason, staring at nothing, feeling as though her life was over. "No."

"What happened?"

"A qualifying exam to be a Mechanic," she whispered.

"Really?" His initial enthusiastic reaction changed to wariness as Jason looked at her. "I'm sure you did great," Jason finally offered.

She groaned. "I didn't do great. I blew it. I forgot things and misstated things and fumbled around and must have sounded like a total idiot. To think I've been wondering for years if they'd go really easy on me because of Mother. I thought that, you know? She's Mari's girl, so let's just ask her some basic questions and then congratulate her. And I was all ready to be upset about *that*."

Kira dropped her face into her hands. "They took me apart. It was like facing a panel of Mages. I let everybody down. I'm such a failure."

"Kira, you're—"

"At least I have that Captain of Lancers thing to fall back on. Because I'm never going to be a Mechanic."

"But—"

"I always pretended I didn't want to be anything like my mother, but I really wanted to be a Mechanic like her and make her proud of me and now that's never going to happen."

"I don't—"

"I can't believe I messed up that badly!" Kira looked sorrowfully over at Jason. "Why aren't you saying anything?"

"I—"

"Because I could really use some words of comfort right now."

At least Jason seemed unhappy, too. Or maybe that was frustration? But before she could say anything else, Jason looked over to the side. "I think you're needed again."

Her heart sinking, Kira looked as well, seeing Calu standing in the doorway, beckoning to her, his visage still stern.

Kira's temper flared. She might have failed, but she wouldn't flinch from hearing the results. Standing up and squaring her shoulders, Kira gave Calu a look as stony as his own before following him back into the exam room.

And stared, uncomprehending, at the dark jacket on the exam table.

Master Mechanic Lukas spoke again. "As a result of her demonstrated knowledge and skills, the Apprentice Kira is hereby certified as a Mechanic, qualified in the areas of steam plant and locomotive operations, basic electronic repair and construction, as well as far-talker technology. Congratulations, Mechanic Kira."

Kira slowly realized that she was standing with her mouth hanging open, staring at the jacket. She finally looked up, seeing Lukas, Alli, Calu, and Dav smiling at her. "But . . . but . . ."

"You did pretty well," Lukas said, and even though she had trouble believing that Kira could see the truth in him as he spoke. Even if she hadn't had that skill Kira knew that Lukas would never say such a thing unless someone had earned it. Not even to the daughter of Master Mechanic Mari.

"I did?" Kira finally managed to say.

She realized that Calu had brought Jason in. "Help her put on the jacket," Calu told Jason. "It's traditional for a family member or engaged to be promised to do that."

"But . . . Mother . . ." Kira faltered.

"I'm here," the familiar voice came behind her.

"Both of you," Kira said. "Mother, you and Jason." They helped her pull off the jacket she'd been wearing, somewhat like a Mechanic jacket but not really one, and then Jason and Mari helped Kira put on a real Mechanic jacket. "How could you do this to me?" she whispered to her mother.

"You did fine. I'm proud of you," Mari said, smiling at her.

Kira nodded quickly, looking away, feeling dazed and uncomfortable. "All right. It's not a big deal, really."

Jason stared at her. "What about that stuff you were saying?"

"What stuff?" Kira asked, trying to signal Jason with her eyes.

"About how badly you thought you'd—ow! Why did you kick me?"

"We'll talk later." Kira looked at her examiners. "Thank you for pushing me so hard. I've been afraid that you'd go easy on me, but you didn't."

Master Mechanic Lukas frowned. "You thought *I'd* go easy on you?"

"That wasn't very smart was it?"

They all laughed at her, but that was all right. She was wearing, she had *earned*, the jacket of a Mechanic.

They didn't have a long ride the next morning to the site of the digging that had exposed the buried entry. As the armored carriage rolled through the streets of Pacta Servanda, its cavalry escort on alert in front and behind the vehicle, Kira peered out through the mostly closed armored louvers covering the windows, glimpsing the city only in thin strips. At another time she might have commented to her father on how that was sort of a metaphor for how every person viewed things, seeing only a small part of what was, limited by their own preconceptions and perspective.

But not today. The tension in the carriage, among everyone going to the site, was tight enough to feel confining to Kira. She would much rather have ridden a horse, alone with her thoughts, able to see everything around her instead of only those slim views visible between the armor. The carriage felt only a little like protection this morning, and much more like a cage.

Her mood troubled Kira. She should still be elated to have been qualified as a Mechanic, and to know she had truly earned that qualification. But something weighed on her even though she couldn't remember much of her dreams from last night. Her only strong sense was that the female Mage had been there again, watching her, face hidden in the cowl of her robes.

Maybe her tension was because of everyone's worries about whatever was buried under Pacta Servanda. The crew of the great ship that had brought people to this world, along with the animals and the plants and fish and birds they knew, had constructed that buried facility. Was what lay beneath Pacta as dangerous as the vague warnings passed down by the librarians claimed it to be?

Kira blinked in surprise as she abruptly seemed to see it before her, that entry to the buried place. The image just suddenly appeared, she standing a little back beside Jason, her mother talking to Queen Sien to Kira's right, Calu and Alli and Dav in a small group, and to Kira's left her father and Mage Asha. Master Mechanic Lukas stood farthest back, watching everything. The Mechanics all wore their usual dark jackets, Alain and Asha were in Mage robes, and Sien wore a Lancer uniform as she did sometimes. From their postures, Kira could tell that either Alain or Asha was preparing a spell. Perhaps both of them, if one was readying to deal with whatever the other might stir up.

She "saw" all that in a moment, an instant that ended as an opening appeared in the wall of the buried structure. One of the Mages must have made that, overlain the illusion of that hole on the illusion of the extremely tough material the crew had used.

She jerked, startled, as the image vanished in a flare of white light. What had happened? Not an explosion. There hadn't been any sense of force, just the light. But nothing remained of the odd picture she'd imagined seeing.

Kira bent her head a bit to peer between the armored louvers, searching for a large window or other shiny object that might have flashed the light of the rising sun into her eyes as the carriage passed.

She didn't see anything that might have done so, but it wasn't as if she had a good view of the street.

Could that have been a foresight vision such as Mages like her father had talked about? But there hadn't been any sense of warning to it, no feeling of danger such as she was used to feeling when her foresight went active. It had just felt like watching an anticipated event taking place. That must have been what it was, an exceptionally vivid image of something she was anticipating. No matter what else was wrong with her, her imagination seemed to be in great shape.

The site, in the basement of a building about as old as any human structure on Dematr, had guards all about. Kira, still troubled by the odd vision, felt her spirits lift at seeing the others already there.

Calu grinned at her. "Hey, Mechanic Kira. When's the wedding?"

"We haven't decided," Kira told him.

"Get married on a ship and you can honeymoon at sea," Alli said, smiling. "I highly recommend it, especially if you can work in a little piracy along the way."

Kira looked about the basement they were in, well lit by electric lights set up when the discovery had been made. The original basement had been expanded down and to one side as the digging exposed what it could reach, a wall of the incredibly hard and durable substance that Jason called permacrete. The room felt a little crowded, a little musty and earthy in that manner of somewhere underground where digging had been going on. Queen Sien and Kira's mother were talking. Mage Asha had gone over to speak with Kira's father, while Dav joined Alli and Calu. Master Mechanic Lukas was talking to Mari, their expressions serious as they regarded what could be seen of the permacrete.

Alli shook her head at the once-buried wall. "I know as much about weapons as anyone on this planet, but I really doubt that will help much if Jason is right about what could be inside there."

Calu put his arm around her shoulders. "Whatever you know is probably going to be more useful than the theory I know. Jason, you're the expert here."

Jason shrugged, nervous. "The real information about weapons like that is secret. All I know is what got put into games, which might be pretty close or might be totally wrong, and a few things from history."

"That still makes you our expert," Kira said. "So go solve this problem," she added with an encouraging smile.

"Okay." Jason walked to where a sheet of heavy cloth covered part of the permacrete, tugging the cloth aside and then staring in surprise. "Do you know what this is?" he asked Kira in a voice full of awe.

"Uh, no," Kira replied, feeling a growing sense of worry. Why did so much of this resemble the imagined vision that she'd seen in the carriage?

He pointed to three apparently identical panels set about a lance apart from each other. "It's a triple simul-cipher. Wow. I've seen these in games, but this is a real one!"

"What's a triple simul-cipher?" Mari asked, her businesslike voice snapping Jason out of his reverie.

Jason gestured toward the panels again. "A normal cipher lock has a panel where you enter the code to unlock it, right? Those can be broken, given enough time and enough tries, though good ones lock you out after several unsuccessful tries. But this is a triple." He pointed to each panel in turn. "You need three people, each one standing at one panel, each one entering their code at the same time as the other two. And all three codes have to be entered right the first time, or the lock doesn't open. You can't use 'bots to enter any of the codes, because of the sense pad above each panel. The person entering the code has to put one hand there. You need three humans."

Mari nodded, her eyes intent. "What's the purpose of that?"

"You need three people," Jason repeated. "Each person knows one of the codes. Unless all three are here and agree to open the door, it doesn't open. Hey. Pacta Servanda. It means *agreements must be honored*. So there was some agreement that required three different people to, um, agree to open this door, or it would stay locked."

Mechanic Dav gave a startled exclamation. "Mari, Alli, do you guys remember that I did some research into old Mechanics Guild records available at the Guild Hall in Altis? Back just before I met you, Mari?"

"What about that?" Alli asked.

"The oldest documents I saw described the Guild as having three grand masters, not one the way we were used to. Then after one of the gaps in the records that we figured indicated one of the purges, there was only one grand master. I didn't think that mattered much anymore, but . . ."

"Three grand masters," Queen Sien said. "Three panels. Three codes. As Jason says, once it would have required all three to agree to open this. What could require such extreme measures? It seems increasingly clear that the weapons Jason fears are indeed inside there."

"But we can get in, using the Mages," Calu said.

"The librarians were warned never to tamper with this structure," Mage Asha said, her eyes on the smooth gray surface. "That terrible things would occur if they did."

"Some sort of alarm system?" Mari speculated. "The librarians were also warned never to activate the Feynman unit, but as far as we can tell the Mechanics Guild wouldn't actually have been able to tell if they'd done that. That was a bluff."

"But we don't *know* this is a bluff. Should we risk trying to get in using Mages?" Dav asked.

Kira saw everyone turning to look at her mother. As they always did when such hard decisions needed to be made. When she was younger, Kira had thought that Mari enjoyed that attention, that deference to her opinions, but now she understood what a burden it was for her mother.

Mari sighed. "We can't disarm those weapons if we can't get at them, and they might already be dangerously unstable after centuries unattended. Does anyone disagree?"

Now eyes went to Queen Sien, because this was Tiae and the final decision had to be hers. Sien's mouth tightened as she gazed at the wall of the buried structure. Then she nodded. "We should try to get inside. It would be irresponsible to let the sort of dangers Jason says may exist in there go unexamined."

Kira watched Asha and her father move slightly farther to her left, facing the permacrete wall. She was standing with Jason, to their right her mother and Queen Sien. Then Alli, Calu, and Dav. Lukas back a little, watching everything. .An odd feeling came over Kira, a sense of having been here at this moment before this. What had Jason called it? Deshavu?

She could see her father and Asha concentrating, preparing their spells. Just like—

"*Stop!*"

CHAPTER THREE

Everyone turned to look at Kira, who realized she was shaking. "Don't," she gasped in a lower voice, grasping Jason's hand tightly.

Mari, Alain, and Asha came close to her, watching with concern and curiosity. "Why not?" her father asked, his dispassionate Mage voice calming amid the tension.

"On the way here," Kira explained, the words tumbling out, "I saw . . . I don't know what it was. I saw us. All of us. Just like this."

"You saw us? Including yourself? As clearly as if viewing the scene from not far away?"

"Yes!"

"That has never happened to you before?" Alain asked.

"No! Was that a foresight vision? Is that what they're like? But there wasn't any sense of warning to it!"

"The sensation is different for every Mage," Asha told her in a similarly Mage calm voice. "What did you see that frightens you now?"

"It only lasted a couple of seconds. You and Father were getting ready to do spells, and a hole appeared in that wall when you or Father did the spell, and then . . . just this light."

"Light?" Mari questioned.

"Yes. A bright white light everywhere. I thought the sun might have been reflected into my eyes." Kira looked over at Jason, startled to see his eyes wide with fear.

The others noticed as well, waiting as Jason swallowed and took a deep breath. "A bright, white light?" he asked Kira, his voice strained. "Not an explosion?"

"No. That's why I thought it was some sun glare. There wasn't any feeling of . . . of violence. Just the white light."

Jason drew in another shaky breath. "When a beta field generator dissolves atomic bonds, there is some energy released. A lot of it takes the form of visible light. Bright, white light."

No one said anything for a long moment.

"A trap," Lukas finally said. "They linked one of those beta fields to an alarm system that senses any breaks in the wall. If anyone breaks in, it goes off."

"And we'd just be gone," Jason said, his voice trembling. "Dissolved into component atoms. Us and who knows how much of the city."

"I don't understand," Kira said. "If that was foresight I experienced, why was I able to change things? Why didn't it happen?"

"You saw yourself, you said," Alain told her. "That meant you were seeing something that *could* happen, not something that *would* happen."

"How fortunate for us," Queen Sien said, running a hand across her forehead. "Jason, how much of the city would been destroyed?"

"I don't know, Your Majesty," Jason said. "That's not something they tell kids like I was when I left Earth. It's secret. But in games, the radius is usually up to fifty kilometers. That'd be, uh, twenty-five thousand lances."

"What would have been left?" Calu asked.

"Nothing," Jason said. "There'd be a bowl in the surface here, like something had scooped out a big, perfect sphere above and below the surface. Everything, and everyone, inside that sphere would just be gone."

Mari pressed both palms against her eyes. "All right. We know not to try to break into that place. How do we keep someone else from trying?"

Mage Asha answered. "A Mage must be able to touch or see a surface to overlay the illusion of an opening. Cover it again, and Mages would have to dig."

"I'll give orders for that to be done immediately," Sien said. "And here, I'll have two, no, three walls built before this section, each wall with a locked door. And guards. But how do we explain this in a way that neither causes panic nor undue curiosity?"

Kira's mother ran one hand through her hair. "Lukas? What's a good Mechanic explanation?"

The old master mechanic frowned as he considered the problem. "If you don't want anybody trying to get in, you tell them there's something toxic in there. Chemicals of some sort. Safe as long as it's confined, but if you open that up it'll kill anyone exposed."

Dav nodded. "We could say we opened a tiny hole to sample the inside and discovered that."

"Mages will see the lie," his wife Asha cautioned.

"We need to say it right enough that it's not a lie," Mari said. "We learned there's something inside that is confined safely, but if anyone opens this they'll die. That's completely true. We can say that and Mages will see we're not lying."

"Other Mages may see that we are not saying some of what we know," Alain cautioned. "But if it is described as a Mechanic thing, they will believe you are withholding Mechanic secrets of some kind."

"Why didn't *your* foresight warn us?" Mari said. "I admit I've come to depend on that."

"I do not know. Perhaps Kira received the warning because her Mechanic knowledge helped her grasp the danger. Perhaps it was because of her ties to Jason."

"We don't know how it works." Kira snapped. "Didn't we go over this?" She flinched. "I'm sorry. I didn't mean to sound like that. I'm still really freaked out."

Her mother came closer, peering at her. "You are. You're still trembling."

"Sorry!" Kira saw them all staring at her. "What's the matter with everyone? Don't I ever get to be afraid?"

Sien came close, nodding, her expression solemn rather than concerned. "Yes, Kira. You experienced something you could only describe to the rest of us. We all know how that feels."

Kira nodded, biting her lip and not trusting herself to speak. Why was she so scared? It didn't feel right. An overreaction. But why?

She abruptly realized that she was sensing the Mage presence of both her Father and Asha. Startled, Kira concentrated on completely controlling her own Mage powers again.

At least she hadn't blacked out.

"So what do we do now?" Alli asked the group. "Besides burying this again? That stuff is still there."

"A pair of Mages apparently tried to kidnap Jason and kill Kira a week ago," Mari told the others. "We know why they might have been after Kira. But why someone would want to kidnap Jason is another story."

Calu's gaze went from Jason to the gray wall of permacrete and back to Jason. "Someone who thinks he can help them get at something or use something?"

Jason made an angry gesture. "You know, sometimes in games there's like a signal you can send to deactivate something remotely. I mean, over distance, like, um, using a far talker signal to turn off something. Sort of a fail-safe. I heard that might be real, because if something goes wrong you don't want it to be impossible to deactivate your own bomb. Or some sort of energy pulse, an electro-magnetic pulse or something, that could fry the circuitry safely from a distance. Even permacrete shouldn't be able to stop a strong enough pulse. Earth might know how to do something like that!"

"But they won't tell us," Mari said. "They refuse to tell us anything." Her gaze on Jason sharpened. "Every time we've asked, it's been the librarians relaying a message from me. Maybe the librarians aren't saying it right. Jason, do you think there's any chance that Urth would respond differently if you asked them?"

"You mean if I wrote the next message for the librarians to send?"

"No. I mean if you spoke to Urth. Able to listen to their reply and make the appropriate response and ask the right questions for this level of technology."

Alli nodded approvingly. "That's a good idea."

"I agree as well," Queen Sien said. "If there might be a means to stop the threat of those weapons, and Jason can convince Urth to provide it, it would be a great service to the entire world."

"Hold on," Jason said, looking alarmed. "Why should Earth listen to me?"

"You're one of them," Calu pointed out. "You speak their language, not just in a technical sense but because you've got the same sort of accent. And you've been to Altis before. I forget, did you use the Feynman unit to talk to Urth then?"

"No," Jason said. "I didn't really want to. That's . . . another life, you know? I wanted to focus on my life here."

"*Here* needs you," Alli told him.

Jason nodded. "Yeah. If you guys want me to, I'll go."

"Wait!" Kira tightened her grip on Jason's hand. "Didn't we just talk about people wanting to kidnap Jason? And you want to send him to Altis?"

"He'll have a strong guard," Sien told her.

"Yes, he will, because he's not going alone. I'm going with him!"

"Kira," her mother began, "there are people trying to kill you. There's no need to expose yourself—"

"He's my man. My partner in life!"

"You're not married yet."

"What difference does that make? My man will not go to Altis unless I'm with him to help him and help protect him."

"Kira," her father started to say.

"Would you have let Mother go to Marandur alone? Mother, would you have let Father go to the Northern Ramparts alone? Oh, wait, you did! And look what almost happened! But you went to him and you saved him. Just like I'll go with Jason and keep him safe."

"The girl has a point," Alli said.

"The girl," Mari said, "is still seventeen. And there are . . . medical concerns."

"Kira's expecting, too?"

"Aunt Alli!"

"I take it the answer is no," Alli said. "What medical concerns?"

"It's up to Kira whether she wants those discussed," Mari said. Her mother looked at Kira.

Kira almost quailed before the focus on her, but steeled herself. "I've been having some blackouts," she said in as calm a voice as she could manage. "We don't know why. The Mage powers may be involved . . . *are* involved. Dr. Sino is going to be looking at me later."

"How dangerous is this?" Master Mechanic Lukas asked, his concern for Kira obvious.

"We don't know," Mari replied. "Hopefully Doctor Sino can tell us. If it turns out to be dangerous—"

"It doesn't matter," Kira insisted. "I'm the daughter of the daughter, and I will not sit home safe while my man faces danger. I *will* be with him." She turned a stubborn gaze on her mother, who glared back just as stubbornly.

"Perhaps," Kira's father said in the manner of someone who had witnessed many such stand-offs in the past between his wife and his daughter, "whatever Doctor Sino tells us will resolve the disagreement."

Queen Sien didn't have a palace in Pacta Servanda. What she had was an old building that had been her home and her headquarters during the dark days when what was then a fortified town had been the last portion of Tiae in which the kingdom still existed. The sole surviving member of the royal family, Sien had been leading Tiae's last stand against the chaos that had swallowed the rest of the broken kingdom. Kira had never been able to visit this building without thinking about

how her mother and father had arrived in Tiae with their first followers and given hope to Tiae while also beginning the revolution against
the Great Guilds.

The room set aside for Doctor Sino to examine her had a plaque on
the door announcing that it had been the bedroom and office of The
Daughter of Jules in those days. Kira couldn't help wondering if that
signified any special meaning for her.

Dr. Peggy Sino, who'd been left on Dematr by the same ship that
Jason had come on, smiled at her. "How are you, Kira?"

"I was hoping you could tell me how I am. That maybe some of
your equipment from Urth could find the problem."

"We'll see!"

"How's your horse Twilight?"

"She's almost as happy as I am." Doctor Sino smiled again. "I never
thought I'd have a horse. They can't keep them on orbital habitats,
you know."

"No, I didn't. You're not having any trouble with her?"

"Oh, Twilight has a mind of her own! Horses are like that, aren't
they? Now stop trying to distract me, Kira. Please, sit down and relax."

Kira took a seat in the indicated chair, trying to will herself into
a calm state. But every time Doctor Sino did anything Kira found
herself jerking nervously.

Sino took some of her devices, small things whose technology was
far beyond that still available on Dematr, and moved them around
Kira's head while asking her to think about various feelings or events
or people. Having to summon up memories of the fight in the Northern Ramparts was particularly unnerving, but Kira did her best.

"What about a spell, Kira?" Sino finally asked. "Can you try to do
a spell for me?"

"I . . ." Kira swallowed and tried again. "I'd rather not. The last time
I tried one I . . . tried to escape."

"Escape?" Doctor Sino pursed her lips in thought. "Can you go
part way to a spell? Start preparing yourself but not go through with
it?"

"I can try. Ummm, making something go away. The corner of that table," Kira said, pointing. "That's hardest for me, so I should be able to stop myself." She composed herself, trying to summon up the belief that all was an illusion, feeling for the power available in this place, willing herself toward the state in which the spell should occur . . . and abruptly pulled back, breathing heavily, her heart pounding. "I'm sorry. I don't want to do any more."

"That's all right, Kira." Sino pulled over a chair and sat down before Kira. "Tell me about the blackouts. Everything you can."

"Come on in," Sino urged those waiting outside.

Kira, feeling miserable, her stomach churning with anxiety, jumped to her feet as Queen Sien entered along with her parents. "Why is Queen Sien here?"

"You're under eighteen," Doctor Sino said, "so by the laws of this world your parents need to be here."

"Queen Sien isn't my parent. She isn't my queen. Not anymore. Never was."

"I will leave," Sien said, turning to go.

"No!" Kira looked at Sien, who was still wearing the same Lancer uniform that Kira had once taken pride in, feeling tears start. "I meant that oath of allegiance. I meant it with all my heart. But you cancelled it out, and I didn't even know."

"I'm sorry, Kira," Sien said. "I made a big mistake there. I should have let the oath stand until you had to be freed from it."

"I wanted you to be my queen. I was proud that you were my queen. But . . ."

"But I cast that loyalty aside?" Sien asked. "I did not, Kira. I swear to you that I always knew, as I know today, that I could have no truer friend aside from your mother and father. All I cast aside was your *obligation* to be a loyal friend. Because I knew I would never need that obligation. I'm here today because I care very deeply for you. Not because you are my subject, but because of who you are. But I will not remain if—"

Kira blinked away tears, rubbing at her eyes. "Please stay."

"All right." Sien sat down.

"What about Jason?" Kira said, looking around. "Isn't Jason coming in?"

"We didn't know whether you wanted him here," her mother said gently.

"He needs to be here. Jason needs to know. He has a right to know. Whatever's wrong with me."

Her father got up, stepping outside the room, and brought back Jason. Jason sat down as well, staring at Kira with a worried expression.

Without really thinking about it, her hand went into her pocket and grasped the loose cartridge, her thumb rubbing the tip as Kira waited nervously.

Doctor Sino looked around with a gentle smile. "We're all okay, then. Here's the good and the bad news, Kira. I can't find anything."

"There's nothing wrong?" Kira blurted out.

"No, I think it's pretty clear that there's something wrong. But I can't find it." Sino pointed to Kira's head. "We figured out a while back that the electrical impulses we can track inside a human brain are just the surface activity. There's a lot of other stuff going on beneath that. Some people say that's the soul down there playing with quantum foam. I don't know about that, but a lot of things happen down deep. That means monitoring the brain impulses can be like trying to diagnose a stomach ailment by looking at your abdomen."

Kira's mother leaned forward. "What about the blackouts?"

"Something caused that," Sino agreed. "There's a problem. But it's not a problem within the physical parts of the brain I can examine. The equipment that I have with me can't look down beneath that. Further complicating the problem is that it appears to be related to the Mage powers, which my equipment can only pick up traces of.

If you did a spell in front of me, I might be able to see more, but I understand Kira's reluctance to try that."

"If the powers are the problem," Kira said, "then as long as I keep them suppressed doesn't that solve the problem?"

Doctor Sino shook her head. "It might control things, like putting a bandage on a wound to stop bleeding. But, if there's an infection and all you do is slap a bandage on, you're covering up something that's going to fester and get worse."

"You don't know that, though."

"No, I don't," Sino admitted. "Whatever this is very likely doesn't match any neurological disorder known to my science. Maybe you're doing what you need to do. But if you have the slightest sign that those problems are still there you need to let people know. Does this world have the concept of disassociative personality disorders? What sometimes is called multiple personalities?"

"No," Mari answered. "Do you think that's behind Kira's problem?"

Sino made a face. "Even now there's considerable debate as to the nature of that disorder, and even whether it's real. Kira's inability to remember anything when she's employing her Mage powers is consistent with that kind of ailment, but there's something important about what she does during those blackouts. Or rather what she doesn't do."

"I don't understand," Kira said.

"There have been three blackouts," Sino said, looking from Kira to her parents. "In the first, you escaped from the room where you were imprisoned and incapacitated two guards. Kira, could you have killed those guards instead of merely knocking them out?"

"One was bleeding," Kira said. "I'd stabbed him."

"But not a fatal injury. You had a dagger, you said. How hard would it have been for you to kill both of them with a stab in the right place?"

Kira shook her head. "Doctor Sino, I don't kill unless I absolutely have to. And I wish I never had to."

Sino nodded. "So you didn't kill them?"

"I don't remember any of it. If you're asking could I have killed them, the answer is yes," Kira said. "I know how to strike the right blows in the right places."

"Exactly. The second blackout came when you needed to hide from Imperial searchers. You became impossible to see. You led Jason to safety."

"Yes, and then I stared at him like . . ."

Jason spoke up, his voice subdued. "Like I was someone you could never have."

"As if he was unattainable to you," Sino said to Kira. "You didn't attack him, though. You didn't abandon him. You didn't do anything except look at him. Then the third blackout. You became invisible, tried to exit one door that your father blocked, then tried to exit the other door that your mother blocked. Kira, if you wanted to, could you have gotten past either one of your parents?"

"What do you mean?" Kira asked. "They were standing in the doorways."

"Could you have attacked them and forced your way out either of those doors?"

Kira stared at Sino. "I don't . . . Physically attacking my parents? Doctor Sino, I've never even thought about doing that."

"If you had, could you have gotten past one of them?"

"Maybe," Kira said. "I guess. It wouldn't be easy, but if I surprised them I might've been able to."

"But you didn't even try, did you?"

"No! I wouldn't do that!"

Sino smiled. "That's my point, Kira. When you've been blacked out, you haven't done anything that you wouldn't normally do. You didn't kill either of those guards. You didn't abandon Jason or attack him for being unattainable, if that is indeed what you were thinking while blacked out. And you didn't even try to physically get past your mother or your father. That's *important*. Even when blacked out, you're still Kira. In the first two blackouts you did exactly what you needed to do with the spells, and apparently nothing else. Your other actions while blacked out are what you would have done while aware of your actions. That's right, isn't it?"

"Yes," Kira said. "Except the unattainable thing. And trying to run away."

"Those may represent something else. Kira, whatever is happening is not causing you to be a different person, a different personality. You're still you, doing what you would do. You're just not aware of it."

"But why aren't I aware of it?"

"I don't know," Sino admitted. "Kira, what's in your pocket?"

"My pocket?"

"There's something there that you seem to grasp harder whenever you're particularly tense."

Kira saw the others watching her and sighed in surrender. She brought her hand out, showing the object grasped in it.

"A cartridge?" her mother asked. "Why do you have a bullet in your pocket?"

"It's a special one," Kira said, finding it easier to explain as she went on. "When Jason and I were fighting the legionaries, and . . . we were down. to three shots. That's all I had left. I knew I couldn't stop the next attack. This one was the last of the cartridges in my pistol. This one," she repeated, holding it up.

Mari nodded, her eyes on Kira's.

"So, I . . ." Kira swallowed, looking down. "Knowing that Jason would be killed by the Imperials, I was going to use the third shot, my last one, this one, to kill myself." She paused, hearing the deep, deep silence that followed her words. "I didn't want to face being captured again, and losing Jason."

"But the Alexdrian Lancers arrived in time," her mother said, her voice soft and full of pain for what might have been.

"No, Mother, that's not why I didn't use it," Kira insisted, looking at her mother. "Jason convinced me to promise not to. Not to kill myself. To keep fighting even if I got captured again, to stay alive and keep trying no matter what. I would have kept that promise! He said . . . he told me that a world with me in it was much better than one without me." She held up the unfired cartridge again. "That's what this is. Not the bullet that I would have used to kill myself. It's the bullet that represents my promise to keep fighting and never give up. Because there's always hope, and because Jason loves me, and so do you guys. And . . . and it reminds me what Jason said, that having me here makes the world better, even when it doesn't feel like that to me."

Her mother sighed, then reached over to hug Jason. "You're still planning on marrying this guy, right?"

"If he's still interested in a walking mess like me."

"Yeah," Jason said, looking down, embarrassed. "I just hope I don't wake up before then."

"Wake up?" Doctor Sino asked.

"I've got to be dreaming all of this."

"Jason," Sino said, looking at him intently. "I know you feel very fortunate to have come to this world. You've told me that coming here was very important for you, and I've seen the proof of that. But maybe you didn't come to this world for you. Maybe you came here for Kira." She sighed. "I'm sorry I can't offer you any more than I have, Kira. Are you resting well? How's the post trauma?"

"I don't wake up screaming very often," Kira said with a smile at Jason.

"And we're talking," Mari said.

"That's good. For both of you! Your healers have some pills and teas made from herbs and other things, for easing tension and aiding sleep. Those contain some natural components which actually are pretty effective."

"I don't need drugs," Kira said.

"Kira—" her mother began.

"Maxim tried to drug me, Mother!"

"Drugs are a tool," Doctor Sino said in a calming voice. "They can be used for good or for ill. I don't think anyone in here wants to do you harm, Kira."

"But—"

"Kira, one of your healers could approach you with something that is a knife, and cut into your body. They'd be doing that to help you. It's not the same as using that knife to try to harm you. Knives, like drugs, are tools. No one here would use either if they thought it would hurt you."

Kira sighed. "I know. I'm sorry."

"Considering what you've been through, you have nothing to apologize for. Be careful when trying to employ those Mage powers until we learn more."

"I'm not going to use them again, Doctor Sino," Kira said. "It's too dangerous."

"Is it?" Doctor Sino looked at everyone before focusing back on Kira. "Kira, twice when you blacked out you did something very important, and did not do anything you would regret. If an emergency arises, one where your Mage powers could once again make a positive difference, I would urge you to keep that in mind."

Mari sat in a familiar chair in a familiar room in a very old building, looking at her friend Sien seated nearby. The sounds of the city outside came only faintly through the closed window. Except for those noises of busy commerce and normal life, it might have been twenty years ago when the sounds of the besieged town were those of war and hardship. "Sometimes," Mari said, "it feels like everything was yesterday, that the first time you and I sat here and talked was just last night. Other times it feels like so long ago in a different world."

"The world is different," Sien replied. "You made it different."

Mari felt the old sense of rejection of the idea that she was somehow special. "I couldn't have done anything without friends like you."

"Nonetheless, you're the daughter of Jules," Sien said, eying Mari. "And speaking of daughters . . ."

"Sien, how can I let her go?" Mari felt a tightness inside that seemed to hold more to it than just this one decision. "Kira is still all that Alain and I have. You know how dangerous the world is for her."

"Kira knows how dangerous that world is," Sien said, sitting back in her chair. "She's experienced it. And she doesn't want her man facing those dangers alone. Can you blame her?"

"No," Mari said, still fighting that tension inside her.

"What would you have wanted your parents to tell you?"

"My parents?" Mari laughed at the memories that question brought up. "My mother and father saw me taken from them by the Mechanics Guild as a little girl, and more than ten years later the daughter of Jules showed up at their doorstep with a Mage in tow who she planned to marry. My mother was smart enough to step out of the way of the avalanche that was me. My father tried to get control of it, and that didn't work at all."

She sighed, looking at her old friend, the Queen of Tiae. "You're trying to tell me that Kira is also an avalanche, right? That she's going to go where she needs to go, and trying to stand in her way would be foolish? Sien . . ." Mari couldn't speak for a moment as emotion choked her. "Letting go is so hard," she finally whispered, feeling tears threatening. "Seeing her go, knowing I'm going to become less and less in her life, being oh so proud of who she is and who she's becoming, but also so scared of what might happen. I swear, I'd rather refight the siege of Dorcastle than see her hurt."

"Alain feels that, too," Sien said.

"Oh, Alain feels it worse than I do! If not for his Mage training he'd be a total wreck these days. All those years when Kira and I couldn't talk, he was the one she could share things with. Now he's losing her, too. Jason's a fine man. But . . . he's taking her away from us."

Sien got up, walking over to embrace Mari. She hugged her friend back, remembering shared losses and trials. But the awkwardness of the hug caused by Mari's pregnancy reminded her that things were already changing, had been changing. The world would never be what it had been. "Why does changing the world always have to be so hard?" Mari murmured.

"You went to Dorcastle," Sien murmured in reply. "You can face your daughter."

Mari reached the door to the room her daughter was staying in, braced herself, then knocked gently.

"What?" Kira answered, the single word as sharp as a dagger ready to defend or attack.

Taking that as an invitation to enter, Mari opened the door.

Kira sat right next to the window, which was open wide. Mari paused at the sight. Kira had always favored windows, but these days she seemed to want to sit as close to one as possible whenever inside, and wanted the windows opened. But then Kira had been through a lot in the last year and a half. Wanting to be close to a window was a small quirk for anyone to have after all that.

"What?" Kira demanded again, giving her mother that old stubborn look.

For a moment, Mari saw the little girl who had begun butting heads with her mother as a toddler. The image both tore at her and made her proud of this young woman who Kira had become. "About you and Jason—"

"It doesn't matter what you've decided," Kira insisted, throwing down a challenge.

"Yes, dearest, it does." Mari held up one hand to forestall another outburst. "You're right. You should go with Jason."

Kira's hostility changed to surprise and then wariness. "Why? What changed your mind?"

"You're right," Mari repeated. "He's your man. I wouldn't have let your father go off alone, and the one time I did I nearly lost him. I never would have forgiven myself if he'd died because I wasn't there with him when he needed me. I'm . . . losing you to Jason. But that's right. That's how things should be."

Kira stared at her, a smile growing, then jumped up to hug her mother. "Thank you."

Mari held her tightly, trying to savor an experience she knew would come less and less with coming years. "I'm still worried about your problem. But you're not going to find answers locked in your room. You have to go looking for them. Just like I did. And maybe that search will take you to places as rough as Marandur was for me, but I know you can handle it. I'm so proud of who you are. I *trust* you."

"Why did you have to make me cry?" Kira said, stepping back and wiping her eyes. "Mother, no matter how far I am from you, you're always with me. You always will be. You know that, right?"

"I hope that's always true," she said, trying to fight off her own tears. "But I can't come with you this time." Mari patted the bulge of her belly. "I have to think about someone else, too."

"Yes, you do!" Kira agreed. "I hope . . ." Her voice trailed off, unreadable feelings flickering in her eyes.

"Dearest?" Mari asked, wondering if her daughter's problems might be somehow connected to another condition. But why wouldn't Doctor Sino have mentioned that? "Are you . . . ?"

"Am I what?"

"I can understand why you wouldn't have wanted to tell others yet, but are you also expecting?"

"*Mother!*"

"All right! I'm sorry!" Mari said, holding up her hands in a calming gesture. "Are you sure, though? Sometimes it takes a little while to know and even if you and Jason have been taking precautions—"

"No!" Kira almost yelled, before dropping back into the chair and subsiding into a sulk. "Believe me, it is absolutely impossible for me to be expecting."

"Kira, a lot of people wait. You know that your father and I did, and we've never regretted that. But you're unhappy about it?"

"Yes! Because it's not really a choice if every time Jason and I want to do something someone is watching or someone tries to kill me or the world explodes," Kira muttered, her eyes fixed on the floor.

"Oh," Mari said. "That's a problem. A lot of people were trying to kill your father and me, but we did manage to find some privacy. I'm sorry. This isn't some fling you're talking about. You and Jason are engaged. *Don't* feel pressured. But maybe you'll get some chances on this trip."

"Maybe." Kira looked up at her, smiling again at the reminder she'd be allowed to go. "Thanks. How did you get father to agree that I could go?"

"He hasn't," Mari said. "He wouldn't. Because you're his little girl."

"Then how—?"

"We'll both talk to him. Your father can sometimes hold his ground against me, and sometimes he can hold his ground against you, but if we hit him together he's not going to stand a chance."

Kira jumped up, smiling wider. "I'm honored to ride into battle alongside the daughter of Jules."

"That's my girl." As they left the room, Mari felt a wave of anxiety and touched Kira's arm. "You'll be careful, right? Neither of those Mages who attacked you and Jason can tell us who hired them, so whoever it was is smart enough and has resources enough to use cut outs. Don't underestimate them."

"I won't. But I need to go, Mother."

"No, you don't. I had to go to Dorcastle. You don't have to go to Altis. If it looks wrong, if it feels wrong, you'll have the authority to call off the trip. We'll make another attempt when it's safer."

"I promise," Kira said, all serious again. "Thank you for trusting me."

"You called yourself the daughter of the daughter back there. Have you ever done that before?"

"No. But that's who I am, isn't it?"

Mari felt an old stubbornness, an old resentment, rising inside her. She gripped Kira's wrist. "Who you are is Kira. Daughter of the daughter is . . . a job. That job doesn't define you. You define the job. Don't ever let anybody tell you who you have to be. Not even me."

Kira gazed back at her, her eyes troubled. "What if I'm still having trouble deciding who I am?"

"You have to decide. Others can offer suggestions and help and support. But the decision is yours alone."

"Jason should have a say, shouldn't he?"

Mari shook her head, keeping her eyes locked on Kira's. "Jason needs to love you, whoever you are. If he thinks you need to be someone else, he's not really in love with you. I think he *does* know who you are, perhaps better than you do yourself, and that's why he loves you. Now let's go overwhelm your father. We're heading back to home tomorrow for a few days while we set up the trip north. He needs to accept that he's going to be planning for two people to go to Altis."

Thunder could mean trouble, a storm raging through the skies of Tiae with winds powerful enough to threaten buildings that had not been well built, water falling in torrents that Jason called a monsoon, and lighting striking from above with random cruelty. Out here in the country once again, home while the trip to Altis was being arranged, Kira had heard such storms many times.

But when Kira heard thunder close at hand, from somewhere near the front of the house, and looked out the window of her room to see the night sky clear of clouds, her stomach clenched with sudden fear. She hurriedly strapped on her pistol, chambered a round and let off the safety. Holding the weapon at ready, she eased open the door to her room, checking the hallway with her heart pounding so loudly it hindered her ability to listen for trouble.

Had the lightning Mage that had tried to kill her and Jason in Kelsi finally tracked them here and found his way through the security perimeter? She sniffed cautiously, trying to sense either the smell of wood set afire by lightning or the pungent stench of ozone.

Should she check on Jason? Or head downstairs? What if her parents needed help right now?

Kira saw the erratic flicker of electricity dancing through the air, the light coming from the front room.

Holding her pistol ready, she moved swiftly down the stairs, her fear suddenly a far off thing, her thoughts focused totally on dealing with this danger to her family.

CHAPTER FOUR

She heard low voices from the front room. One was her father's. He was still all right, his voice carrying the emotionless tones of a Mage. Her father was either very upset, or speaking with another Mage.

A Mage who cast lightning.

The other voice came again, low, female. Not her mother's. Rougher. Harsher. Also lacking in all feeling.

Kira came around the doorway into the front room, her pistol lining up on the figure in Mage robes standing near the center of the room. Her finger was on the trigger, ready to squeeze—

"Kira! Don't!"

Aunt Alli had always emphasized *don't shoot unless you're sure you want to*. Kira kept her finger frozen in place, ready to pull the trigger but not firing. She kept her weapon aimed at the female Mage, though. Looking over at her mother, standing to one side, Kira saw her appearing worried but not scared. "What's going on?" The front room was mostly dark, illuminated only by the light filtering in from the kitchen, adding to Kira's worries.

Kira's Mage senses tingled in warning as the female Mage turned her head to look at Kira with the dead expression of a Mage taught in the old ways. Even in the dim light Kira could see the marks of age on the Mage's face and the grey in her lank hair. Her eyes held a dismissive disregard for any other person, along with a sense of power and menace.

Kira's father gestured to her to lower her pistol. "You will not need that Mechanic weapon," Alain said. He turned back to the female Mage.. "This one?" Alain asked, pointing toward Kira.

The female Mage turned her head back to face Kira's father. "That one," she said in the manner of someone confirming something said earlier.

Alain nodded, keeping his attention centered on the other Mage. "Kira, this is Mage Nika."

Kira looked around at the others, sensing an undercurrent in the room that she didn't understand, but she lowered her weapon as her father had directed, laying her trigger finger alongside the trigger guard to ensure she didn't accidentally fire. She did keep the pistol ready for use, though, even if it was now pointed at the floor. "Is she a friend?"

"Mage Nika does not have friends," Alain said. "She sees only shadows about her."

Shadows. The former Mage Guild's term for everyone besides a Mage. The world was an illusion, and the other people in it only shadows. Not real. Something to ignore, or treat as a plaything, or kill in the same manner as stepping on an ant that was in the way. Her father had proven that wrong, that people were real, but many Mages still struggled with the idea. "Why is she here?"

Mage Nika ignored her, of course, but Mari answered. "She said she had information that we needed to know."

"I thought she wasn't a friend."

"She's not. Mage Nika has been . . . an opponent of myself and your father more than once since the Great Guilds fell."

"She's an enemy?" Kira fought the urge to raise her pistol again.

Mage Nika, still pretending to be unaware of everything Kira was saying, turned one hand upward and ran her thumb across the tips of her fingers. Kira felt a slight drain on the power available here, and saw sparks appear on the female Mage's fingertips, leaping away like fireflies in the darkened room before vanishing. It was only an illusion of electrical power, Kira knew, yet an illusion powerful enough to shock and burn and kill if Nika had felt like doing that. "This one was offered much money for one task," Nika said, her voice still carrying no feeling.

"What task?" Alain asked.

"A simple task, Master of Mages. To find that one," with a flick of a finger toward Kira, "near this place, and when she boarded a Roc to destroy the Roc and its riders in flight using the lightning that this one can cast on the illusion of the world."

Kira's breath caught. She barely refrained from aiming her pistol at Mage Nika again.

Her father nodded slowly, his face still expressionless. "Has that one met Mage Nika before? At the illusion named Kelsi?"

"That one has not," Nika said, still not bothering to look at Kira again. "That one met Mage Ivor in the illusion named Kelsi."

"Mage Ivor," Mari repeated in tones that carried a wealth of feeling which seemed all the stronger after the dispassionate voices of the Mages.

"Who is Mage Ivor?" Kira demanded.

To her surprise, Mage Nika looked her way again, one corner of her mouth twitching slightly in what passed for a wide smile among Mages. "That one does not know Mage Ivor? The shadow of that one would never have been cast by Master of Mages Alain and the Elder Mari if Mage Ivor had carried out his assigned tasks near Umburan and in Palandur long ago."

Kira's father nodded. "Mage Ivor is the one who sought to kill me twenty years ago on the plains of Umburan, and to slay both me and your mother in Palandur after we had escaped from Marandur. He has struck at us more than once since that time."

"He's the one who attacked me in Kelsi?" Kira said. "You knew his name? Didn't you think that was worth mentioning to me?"

"We didn't know until now that Ivor was the one who attacked you in Kelsi," Mari said. "I wondered if it had been Mage Nika."

"No. I told you it was a male Mage."

Kira realized that Nika was looking at her again, her eyes still holding no feeling, but studying Kira. "That one could tell the nature of the Mage?" Nika asked.

Oh, blazes. She'd revealed knowing something that only another Mage would have been able to sense. Kira, thinking quickly, shrugged as if the matter was unimportant. "I saw his face. When he attacked me on the street. It was well lit."

The interest in Nika's eyes disappeared as she turned away from Kira, once again discounting her presence. "Mage Ivor has failed many times. This one was told that Mage Ivor would also be in wait to strike at the Roc carrying that one. As a precaution, if this one's attack failed."

Most people wouldn't have caught the trace of emotion on Nika's voice as she said that, but Kira had received enough training from her father to hear it. Anger. Whoever had wanted to hire Nika had hurt her pride by hiring backup that Nika thought a lesser Mage than herself. As a Mage following the old ways, Nika would never admit to pride, or jealousy, but Kira heard the traces of it.

"Was that one told if Mage Ivor had accepted the task?" Alain asked.

"This one knows Mage Ivor did. Mage Ivor does not *like* you," Nika said. This time the trace of contempt entering her voice, for Ivor's yielding to emotion, was even clearer for Kira to hear.

Mari spoke up again, her voice low. "Why did that one not accept the task?"

Mage Nika glanced at Mari. "Elder, this one once sought wisdom. Since the Guild ended, this one has learned nothing. This one tires of those she has accepted tasks from. There is no wisdom to be learned from such or the tasks they desire." She ran her thumb over her fingertips again, producing another shower of sparks. "The Master of Mages speaks a wisdom this one cannot accept. However, this one has been told that the Master of Mages also speaks of other paths."

"This is so," Alain said. "There are many paths to wisdom."

"This one cares not for shadows," Nika said. "They . . . distract. Making them cease by use of my spells distracts. This one tires of distractions. This one is told of a place to the west where few shadows have been."

"The Western Continent," Mari said. "Only a few expeditions have visited it so far. The Western Alliance and the Empire are both planning to establish colonies there within a few years."

"One city?" Nika asked. "Two?"

"Small ones," Mari said. "Towns, really. It will be many years before cities grow large on the Western Continent. That continent is larger than the one we now live on. Most of the land there is unexplored and empty, and will stay that way for a long time."

"This one asks that the Master of Mages and the Elder find her means of going to this place," Mage Nika said. "As payment for what was told, and for not taking this task."

Alain nodded again. "You seek the silence of an empty illusion. This one will ensure that Mage Nika is given passage there when next ships travel west over the ocean."

"You understand," Mari added, "that we don't know what lies inland on the Western Continent. There may not be many animals, there may not be plants known to us, plants you can eat."

Kira had the odd sensation the Mage Nika had shrugged without actually moving. The female Mage spoke in the same emotionless tones, though. "This one has walked a long road since becoming an acolyte of the Guild. This one tires of this dream. This one tires of distractions. When the next dream comes, it comes."

"I understand," Kira's mother said, sounding sad. "Can you tell us two things more? Who tried to hire you for this task? And how did they learn that Kira would be flying on a Roc to Altis?"

Mage Nika shook her head. "This one knows only that one once an elder of the old Guild tried to task her with this. The once-an-elder claimed not to know the one who desired it. This one could see he lied. He spoke of the Mage Guild returning, and believed his words. He claimed strong allies among the shadows, which did not impress this one because it showed the once-an-elder's lack of wisdom. How can shadows matter? This one knows nothing else, Elder Mari."

Nika paused, thinking. "The Master of Mages and the Elder Mari are known to be wise. What lies in the next dream? It is said you have been there."

"This one does not know," Alain said. "This one once had visions of something beyond, but saw only the illusion of that dream. It was the same for Elder Mari. The form of the next dream could not be grasped by one still tied to this dream."

"Perhaps this one will learn those answers before the Master of Mages," Nika said, and this time Kira caught the faintest hint of amusement in Nika's voice. "This one will wait in the illusion of Lar-harbor. When the Master of Mages knows of a ship to the empty lands, this one will be there, waiting."

Mage Nika paused again, her hand now held at waist height with the palm facing downward. Kira tensed as she felt a spell forming, her hands tightening again on her pistol.

Sparks fell downward from Nika's hand in a shower of brilliant light, winking out before they reached the floor.

She turned and walked out of the house.

Kira realized that she had been holding her breath for the last several seconds, and finally exhaled. "What was that? That thing she did at the end?"

"Go make sure the security patrols don't stop her or try to fight her," Mari told Alain. "You might also see if they know how she got to us without being spotted. That's happening way too often lately."

Kira's father nodded and left quickly.

Her mother looked at Kira, sighing heavily and running one hand through her hair. Kira realized how tense her mother had been while Nika was here. "What did you say, dearest? Oh. The light show at the end. It was sort of . . . an apology."

"An apology? From an old-school Mage?"

"Yes," Mari said. "Sort of. But also a gesture of regret, even though Mages like Nika don't know that word. And also a sign that her spells would not be turned against us again."

"For people who deny emotions, they sure pack a lot into one ges-

ture," Kira complained. She finally safed her pistol, ejecting the cartridge from the chamber, reloading it in the magazine, and setting the
safety before holstering it. "Do you believe her?"

"Your father would have seen any falsehood in her. And if Mage
Nika had meant us harm, this house would have been hit by lightning
powerful enough that I don't think the lightning rods would have
grounded it all."

"You guys know her? But she's a bad guy? A dark Mage?"

"Not a dark Mage," Mari said. "I'm glad you didn't say that while
Nika was here. She's not one of those who accepted your father's wisdom, but she's not a mercenary dark Mage with no interest in wisdom. She's been a tough opponent on more than one occasion since
the war with the Great Guilds."

Kira's mother sat down heavily, running both hands through her
hair this time. "Our enemies must have some well-placed spies to
already know that you and Jason are going to Altis, and were planning to travel by Roc. I need to tell Sien. One of her trusted aides is
either playing for the other side or is talking too much to the wrong
people."

Kira dropped into a nearby chair, staring at the spot where Mage
Nika had been standing. "If she hadn't warned us . . ."

"You and Jason might both have died," Mari finished, her mouth
tight with distress. "She's very powerful, and very skilled. As your
father and I learned more than once in the past."

"Maybe you guys ought to share some of those stories with me?"
Kira said, exasperated. "You know, stuff about deadly enemies you've
fought in the past who might try to kill me now?"

"You've been warned your whole life about that."

"Not with specifics! Like, Mage Nika. Lightning. Mage Ivor, also
lightning. Why do lightning Mages hate this family so much?"

"They don't," Mari said, looking at Kira again. "Only Ivor. Now,
dragon Mages, they do all hate us. So do troll Mages. But to Nika,
her tangles with us were always part of a job. Ivor really wants us all
dead, though."

"If I'd known about him before I went to Kelsi, he might not have been able to almost kill me there!"

"You weren't supposed to be running around Kelsi on your own!" her mother shot back. "Wasn't there something in there about running away?"

"I did not run away! I was on a mission to help Jason stop that plot by his mother and save millions of lives!"

Her mother paused, then nodded. "That's true. All right. You know about lightning Mages. Their spells work like real lightning. If she'd thrown some at you while you had your pistol up, the pistol would've attracted the bolt, which would've run down your arm and through your body if you were grounded. But you probably wouldn't have noticed because the bolt would've caused every round in your pistol to go off at once and done a serious number on your hands and your face and chest and other important parts."

Kira flinched. "You see, this is the sort of motherly wisdom your daughter needs. Like, don't overcook chicken. Make sure you're wearing underwear that won't embarrass you if you end up being seen by healers at a hospital. And don't let the pistol you're holding get hit by lightning cast by a Mage."

"The underwear thing is really important," Mari said.

"I know. The Northern Ramparts, remember? I'd had to wear the same pair for weeks. I'm glad I was unconscious by the time the healers were pulling them off me, because I do not want to know how they reacted."

"What happened to that pair?"

"I think they burned them. I hope they did."

Her mother smiled slightly. "The last few days at Dorcastle we were on the walls continuously. We fought and sweated and everything but I couldn't change clothes. Then I got shot. But it was in my chest and I was doing the dying thing and then your father brought me back and I don't think anyone noticed the state of my underwear."

"You were lucky," Kira said.

"Uh huh. If I'd been lucky I wouldn't have been shot."

"Mother, we're sharing stories. When did you become someone I could talk to?"

Mari smiled at her. "I didn't change."

"I think you did," Kira said. "I couldn't have changed that much. Um, back on topic. So, what are we going to do now that we know what Mage Nika told us?"

Her mother frowned at the map of the world on one wall near her desk. "You're not going to fly a Roc to Altis. Mage Ivor could be waiting anywhere along the route. And lightning Mages may be fairly rare, but he and Nika aren't the only ones who might have been hired to kill you."

"Mother?" Kira felt a thought forming. "Is this just about killing me? Or is it also about keeping me and Jason from getting to Altis and speaking to Urth?"

Mari raised her eyebrows at the idea. "That's an important thing to consider, isn't it? But if our foes know about those weapons and want them, they might know that we want to disarm them. They wouldn't want Jason talking to Urth."

"Which would mean it's important that we go," Kira said. "And get the answers we need."

Her father returned, troubled enough that Kira could see it in him. "Get Jason," Mari said. "I'll fill your father in on what we've been talking about."

Kira rushed up the stairs, expecting Jason to be alert. Instead, she found him sound asleep. "Wake up! You would've slept through the Siege of Dorcastle, wouldn't you?"

"I'm just conforming to the biological norm for someone my age," Jason protested as he pulled on his clothes. "What's happened? What's the big deal?"

"A lightning Mage who's fought Mother and Father in the past snuck up to the house and warned us that someone tried to hire her to kill us when we flew off on Rocs and has hired other Mages to make sure we die if she failed."

"Oh." Jason didn't ask any more questions before she hauled him downstairs.

Kira's mother and father were looking at the map as Kira brought Jason into the front room, its lights now on.

"At this time of year some nasty storms can brew up suddenly between Tiaesun and Edinton," Mari told them. "And those pirates operating out of Syndar might go after a ship with you on it even if it's one of Queen Sien's warships. Pirate ships carrying Mages can be a serious threat to even the newest warships. Your father and I have jousted with pirates. It's not fun. You'd be better off traveling by land."

"Riding?" Kira said.

"No. You and Jason will take a train north. We'll arrange an armored train with a large escort as far as Gullhaven, and then a Confederation warship to take you to Altis. You'll be safely past the threat of pirates by then."

"Armored train?" Kira asked. "Large escort? Warship?"

Her mother nodded. "I know you prefer not to make a big deal when you travel, Kira, but this will have to be an exception. Someone is gunning for you. If they tried to get Mage Nika, they're hiring the best. We need the best defenses we can arrange against them."

"All right," Kira mumbled.

"Wait. A train?" Jason asked worriedly, having apparently just absorbed that information.

"It's the safest way to travel," Mari emphasized.

"Um . . . have you ever ridden on a train with Kira?"

"I have ridden on trains with her mother," Alain said, his impassive voice somehow still conveying a wealth of concern.

"Our big, strong men," Mari said. "What are you worried about?"

"I have thrown Jason off of moving trains a few times," Kira admitted.

"Well, I never threw your father off a train. He always jumped on his own. When I told him he had to."

"Yeah," Kira said. "Jason, why can't you just jump off a train when I tell you to? Then I wouldn't ever have to throw you off."

"You see?" Jason said. "This is why I'm worried. Why can't we fly on the Rocs?"

"I told you! Because a lightning Mage is waiting to fry us somewhere along the way."

Jason hesitated. "Getting shot down by a lightning Mage might be worse than a train."

"Gee, ya think?" Kira demanded. "Hitting the ground after jumping from a train is bound to hurt a lot less than hitting the ground after falling from a Roc!"

"Um . . ." Jason frowned. "Terminal velocity of a human falling through air is limited by drag, so if you stay face down that's about, um, sixty meters per second which is about, uh, two hundred kilometers per hour. On Earth, and your gravity and atmospheric pressure aren't that far off from Earth. So if you fell off a Roc you'd hit the ground at one hundred thousand lances per hour the way you guys measure stuff."

Kira stared at him. "How do you even know that? How fast somebody falls?"

"I looked it up back on Earth. Your trains travel at, what, about eighty to one hundred kilometers per hour? So that'd be forty to fifty thousand lances per hour. Yeah, it would hurt a lot more to hit the ground after falling from a Roc. You're right."

"Jason," Kira said, "how many times have we gone over this? You argue and calculate and consider and finally tell me I'm right. Think how much time you'd save if you just started assuming I'm right."

"I'm still trying to teach your father that," Mari said.

"Did Father find out how Nika got to the house?"

Alain nodded. "She showed me the path. With perfect timing as patrols passed, she was able to move in the dark from partly shielded place to place, and thus avoid detection. It would take someone as skilled and experienced as Mage Nika to repeat. I showed the commander of the guards the route. He was not happy to learn of it, but now the patrols will know where to look."

"So she did us another favor by spotting a hole in our security," Mari said.

"Yes." Kira's father brought out an envelope. "The commander of the guard had just received this and was about to deliver it."

Kira's mother took the envelope and opened it, drawing out the paper inside. "Hmmm. It's actually about Kira. Her presence is requested by the Queen's Own tomorrow. An escort will arrive early tomorrow to accompany her there."

"The Queen's Own?" Kira asked. "Why?" She knew her alarm and reluctance at the news must be obvious from the way the others looked at her.

"It's a surprise," Mari said. "What's the matter? You were always proud and happy to be part of the Queen's Own Lancers."

"I was never really part of them" Kira said. "I was an honorary officer. That's all. And when I was told my real name, that I was Kira of Dematr instead of being Kira of Pacta Servanda, I couldn't even be that."

"You have not been back since then?" Alain asked.

"No. It's just . . . too weird."

Her mother smiled at Kira. "Dearest, the first time you went to the Queen's Own for training we had to drag you kicking and screaming. But after that it became the one thing in the world that your father and I knew you loved doing. Every time you wore that uniform you looked proud and happy."

Kira ducked her head to avoid her mother's gaze. "Things have changed."

"Yes, and no. You'll go tomorrow, won't you?"

She looked up, surprised. "You're not telling me I have to go?"

"It's time you made decisions like that on your own," Mari said. "But I hope you'll go. Colonel Anders wouldn't have asked for your presence unless it was important. And you know the place that the Queen's Own holds in my heart."

"Yes," Kira said, her voice gone soft. "All right. I'll go. For Major Danel's memory."

"Thank you, dearest."

"Jason can come, can't he?"

"I don't see why not." Mari looked at the deep night outside the house. "You two had better get back to bed and try to get some sleep.

A ride out to the Queen's Own and back tomorrow will make for a long day."

Mari wished that she was able to take her own advice, but after the events of the evening she could only lie awake, hoping that sleep would come. Her nerves on edge after Mage Nika's surprise visit, the baby restless inside her, Mari kept hearing faint noises that normally would have meant nothing but tonight conjured up visions of more enemies sneaking close.

She felt relieved when Alain finally came to bed. "Are you all right?" she whispered.

He nodded, the movement shadowy in the dimness. Sitting down on the bed, Alain reached out one hand to her. "I was thinking," he said, "that perhaps I should accompany Kira and Jason. To ensure they were safe."

"Alain—"

"But I cannot." He turned his head to look at her, his words carrying unusual emotion. "I saw something a short time ago. Foresight." He paused. "I saw myself riding a Roc, approaching the city of Pacta Servanda. It was late at night. But suddenly a great flare of light filled my vision, and when it faded much of the city was gone."

She struggled into a sitting position in the bed and stared at him. "Someone will set off that bomb?"

"Someone might. If I am not here."

"Alain, I know you want to protect Kira, but she's a young woman now. We have to let her go."

He didn't answer for a long moment. "I have seen visions of Kira as well. Like shards of mirrors all looking upon different scenes. Her possible futures are growing in number, yet in pieces, as if something of Kira herself was not whole. Look into her eyes and you see a struggle being fought, though I cannot tell what is fighting inside her or why."

"You're saying that you think we have to keep her here?"

Alain shook his head. "No. What I have felt from those visions was that Kira must find the means to heal herself. I cannot do it. No one else can. She must confront what troubles her. If she stays here . . . I do not foresee her finding that answer."

"She thinks that Jason will help her find that answer," Mari said, trying to make herself believe that as much as her daughter did.

"Yes. He is important," Alain said. "The visions in which he is with her have hope. When Jason is not with her . . . the visions are not pleasant ones."

"He won't leave her," Mari said, and this time didn't have to work to convince herself of the truth of that. "Not as long as he's alive."

"That is so," Alain said. "He is perhaps a bit too much like me in that respect, just as Kira is perhaps a bit too much like you. But both Kira and Jason are not either of us. They have their own strengths, and their own knowledge. We must trust in that. I wish she had not developed Mage powers."

"They did save her life," Mari said.

"I fear now they may cost Kira her life," Alain said. "Jason does hold some key in this, but he may face terrible trials."

"Along with our daughter."

"Yes. But I must also think of you, and the young one you carry."

"Remember when all we had to worry about was the fate of the world?" Mari asked. "Who knew that would be easier than worrying about our daughter and the young man she wants to marry." She reached out to hold Alain, and they lay that way together for a long time.

Woken up early, Kira grumpily wolfed down breakfast, going light on the coffee since she had a long ride ahead. Jason looked as weary as she did and ate only a little before going back up to his room. Her mother and father had the appearance of people who'd stayed up worrying all night. That left her feeling guilty as well as cranky.

As she got up from the breakfast table, her mother spoke firmly. "This is a formal occasion," Mari told Kira. "Dress appropriately."

"Formal? What's going on? Why does the Queen's Own want me there? Is this going to be embarrassing?"

"Yes. I can't tell you. I can't tell you. Probably," Mari replied. "But you will smile and be polite and be a good representative of this family."

Kira glowered at her mother. "Life was lot easier for me when I could throw a tantrum and get out of stuff like this."

"It's been more than a year since you could get away with that, dearest."

"Oh, ha, ha, ha," Kira said before heading up the stairs.

"Jason should wear his suit!" Mari called after her. "Make sure he's ready soon, too!"

"Why is that *my* responsibility?"

"He's going to be your husband someday! You might as well get used to what that means!"

Grumbling under her breath, Kira rapped hard on the door to the guest bedroom. "Jason! Are you getting dressed?"

"Yeah. What exactly are we doing?" Jason called back through the door.

"I don't know. Something embarrassing."

Kira pulled off her usual shirt and trousers, looking over her clothes. Her nicest pants were easy to pick out, but her nicest shirt had been reduced to a tattered, bloodstained rag a few months earlier. She settled on a replacement that had been bought in Danalee on the way home.

She pulled on her cavalry boots, fastened on her shoulder holster and made sure the pistol was firmly set and safe, then pulled on her fitted coat that came down past her hips.

Kira brushed her hair, short and raven black like her mother's. She paused to look in the mirror, her eyes going again to the scar running under one jaw where an imperial bullet had come close, but not quite close enough, to killing her. The scars from the dragon were all concealed under her shirt and jacket, as were those from legionary swords. But that furrow dug under her jaw seemed to dominate her image in the mirror, Kira thought with despair.

"What's the matter?" her mother asked, coming in to stand by Kira. "Oh." Mari ran a fingertip along one side of her own face, tracing the long scar on her cheek. "Try to pretend it's not there, dearest. And, if you do think about it, see it as a mark of pride."

"Does that work?" Kira asked.

"Not always," her mother admitted. "Honestly, it seems the biggest thing when you look at yourself in the mirror, but it's not really that big to others who look at you."

"You learned to live with your scars," Kira said.

"They're not as bad as this thing," her mother said, running her fingers through the shock of pure white amid her black hair. "I keep wondering if those hairs will ever start growing in black again, but they've stayed white ever since your father saved my life at Dorcastle. I try to see it as a mark of your father's love for me. Kira, every scar means an injury that didn't kill you. Your fellow Lancers will see any mark on you as a badge of honor."

Kira felt her mind flooded with memories: legionaries attacking, her own fear, the desperate fight. The fight she had thought would end with her death. "Mother, did it hurt when you died at Dorcastle?"

"I didn't—" Her mother stopped her reflexive answer and sighed. "I don't remember hurting after I was shot, at least not after I passed out. I . . . thought someone was urging me to go somewhere. There was a locomotive waiting for me. But your father wasn't there, so I wouldn't get on it. I went back to look for him, and then after I don't know how long, I woke up. That's when it hurt again."

"I was so scared. Everybody keeps saying how fearless I was, fighting that legion, and I was so scared."

"I know exactly how that feels," Mari said. "For so long you and I couldn't understand each other. Now, we do. I wish we still didn't. Understanding means you went through things that I wish you'd never had to experience."

Kira nodded at her mother's reflection. "I used to think you were more than human. That you were just putting on an act with me, pretending to be someone who could be scared and worried and uncertain sometimes. I'm sorry, Mother."

Mari smiled. "Oh, you've been a little difficult, but my mother always said I deserved a daughter just like me."

"I will never be just like you."

"No," her mother said. "Our scars don't match."

Kira laughed and went to collect Jason as the sound of many hooves outside heralded the arrival of their escort.

The horse-drawn armored coach hadn't been the most comfortable ride, and Kira had felt guilty knowing that Suka was watching her leave, but at least she and Jason had been able to catch up on sleep a little during the hours it took to reach the open fort outside the city, where the Queen's Own Lancers were based.

The carriage rolled to a stop and Kira got out, feeling odd to be coming here in regular clothes rather than a uniform, and in a carriage rather than riding.

But a familiar presence waiting for her brought a smile to Kira. "Sergeant Bete."

"Captain Kira." Bete rendered a salute which Kira returned. "Colonel Anders is waiting for you."

Jason and Kira followed Bete, passing the sentry at the front entry and once again exchanging salutes. Inside, the corporal at the front desk rose hastily to escort them into Colonel Anders's office.

"Thank you for coming today, Captain," Anders said to Kira as he rose to return her salute. Sergeant Bete stood off to one side as Kira and Jason stood before the colonel's desk.

Kira shook her head, feeling awkward. "Sir, that rank was a field promotion in the Northern Ramparts. I appreciate the honor you're all doing me by using it, but I'm not sure it's appropriate."

"Oh?" Anders sat down and picked up a document. "Only a field promotion, you say? I needed to deliver a copy of this to you. It's your official confirmation of rank as a Captain of Lancers."

Dumbfounded, Kira took the paper, running her eyes hastily over the formal verbiage to the signature and seal at the bottom. "Queen Sien confirmed it?"

"That's right. And as subjects of the queen, Sergeant Bete and I and the others of the Queen's Own are bound to follow her instructions, Captain." Anders smiled. "In case you haven't been told, I understand that the Bakre Confederation and the Western Alliance have also confirmed that rank for you."

"Why doesn't anybody ever tell me things?" Kira licked her lips nervously. "Thank you, sir. But you didn't have to go to the trouble of bringing me here to give me this."

"That's not why you're here," Anders said. "You weren't told?"

"No one tells me anything, sir."

"You're not a lieutenant anymore. We need to start keeping you in the loop," the colonel said. "Captain, you're here to participate in a solemn ceremony. A new battle ribbon will be added to the standard of the Queen's Own."

"A new battle ribbon?" Kira asked, confused. "I didn't know the Queen's Own had been in any recent engagements."

"Elements of the Queen's Own participated in a battle in which they achieved a victory in the face of overwhelming odds." Anders unrolled a wide emerald green ribbon onto the surface of his desk so that Kira could read the words NORTHERN RAMPARTS embroidered on it in gold thread.

Kira stared at the words in shock. "I don't . . . I didn't . . . I . . ."

"You were present at that battle, weren't you?" Colonel Anders asked.

Her thoughts managed to settle enough for Kira to speak. "I'm not a member of the Queen's Own, sir! I don't have any right to this honor!"

Anders picked up another document in front of him. "This is a copy of the report sent by General Flyn to Queen Sien. General Flyn, as you may be aware, Captain, is an old companion of Queen Sien's from the days when he commanded the Army of the Daughter. He says that when the Fourth Lancers of Alexdria made contact with Captain Kira, fighting their way through the legionaries besieging her and Jason of Urth, she attributed her survival and success to being a Lancer, and specifically identified herself as a member of the Queen's Own Lancers of Tiae." The colonel bent a sharp look at Kira. "You're not disputing the word of General Flyn, are you? You did say that, didn't you?"

"I . . ." Kira faltered before collecting herself again. "If he said I said that, then I must have. I don't . . . it's hard for me to remember details of what was happening at that point, sir. I was . . . very tired."

"And suffering from multiple wounds inflicted by the legionaries and associated blood loss," Colonel Anders said, smiling at her. "Do you have any idea how proud the men and women of this unit were when we heard that you'd declared yourself to be one of them after such a fight?"

"But, sir, this ribbon . . . I don't deserve—"

"Is not for you. Your name is nowhere on it. It honors the Queen's Own for a victory won by members of this unit. By tradition, veterans of the battle named on the ribbon are supposed to affix the ribbon to the unit banner. That is you."

Kira ran one hand through her hair, trying to order her thoughts. "But how can you say I'm one of you? I can't be. Not when I'm not a subject of the queen."

Anders pointed toward the large board on one wall of his office, where the unit organization chart was rendered in chalk, the names of officers assigned to the regiment also chalked in to mark their assignments, each name in the proper box. "You're familiar with that. Do you see any changes?"

Kira studied the chart, frowning. "What's that empty box? It's shown as part of the unit but there's no command assignment with it."

"That's you," Colonel Anders said. "Queen Sien approved this modification to the organization of the Queen's Own. You're right that legally and officially as the daughter of Lady Mari you can't be part of this unit. However," the colonel added, pointing to the empty box, "unofficially and not written down anywhere, that's you. Your name will never go in there, Kira. But that's your spot. That space will always exist, and always remain open, because it's yours. You earned it. Unofficially, you'll always be part of the Queen's Own as far as your fellow Lancers are concerned."

Kira felt tears coming and wiped at her eyes angrily. "Somebody should have warned me. Sergeant Bete, why didn't you warn me? Sergeants are supposed to keep officers out of trouble."

"I apologize to the captain," Bete said, grinning.

"And now you've made me cry, and captains shouldn't cry." Kira got herself under control again and looked at Jason, who had that goofy, proud smile on his face as he looked at her. "Colonel, Jason of Urth is also a veteran of that battle. Is it all right if he assists me in attaching the battle ribbon?"

"I think that would be highly appropriate," Anders replied. "If he wasn't going to marry you . . . congratulations by the way to you both . . . we'd be trying to get him to join the Queen's Own. Oh, that reminds me. Congratulations as well on your achievement, Lady Mechanic Kira."

"Also dragon slayer," Sergeant Bete interjected.

"Yes," Colonel Anders said. "If your titles keep multiplying, Kira, you just might surpass your mother."

"There's no chance of that," Kira said.

"The Queen's Own is waiting, Captain. Let's get this done."

Hoping that the ceremony would be a small thing indoors, Kira was horrified to find the entire regiment drawn up on the parade ground, each Lancer in full uniform standing next to his or her mount. "Attention to arms!" Sergeant Bete bellowed, the sound echoing across the field. "Present arms!"

The officers drew their sabers and the soldiers canted their lances forward, the butts still grounded and the points inclined toward

Kira as she walked slowly across the front of the regiment, Jason just behind her. The horses, well trained, shifted slightly but otherwise waited patiently beside their riders.

Kira, desperately hoping that she wouldn't trip and fall or do something else stupid, reached the color guard, two Lancers, one holding the staff from which flew the green and gold banner of the Kingdom of Tiae and the other the staff to which was affixed the banner of the Queen's Own. The Lancer holding the Queen's Own banner dipped it toward her. Her hand shaking slightly, Kira fastened the new battle ribbon to the top alongside the others, grateful for Jason's help in steadying her as she got the ribbon attached.

She froze for a moment, staring, as she saw the word on the ribbon labeled *DORCASTLE* that had been added twenty years before. Somehow, she was part of that, continuing a story begun before she was born. And she knew again in that moment how much that had meant to her, how much she had liked having these men and women as comrades, how much they mattered to her.

Kira finally fully understood how her mother felt about the veterans of Dorcastle.

"Do you wish to say anything, Captain Kira?" Colonel Anders asked her.

She raised her voice so it carried across the parade ground. "I wish to say that I am incredibly proud to be one of you! Anything I did, I was able to do because of your example and your support. You were beside me that day, and you will always be beside me, and I will always be beside you."

They cheered then, and that was embarrassing.

The elation from the ceremony wore off on the long ride back home. By the time the carriage stopped at her house Kira felt hungry and exhausted. The effort of keeping her Mage powers suppressed all day had only added to her tiredness, and as the day went on the carriage itself had felt increasingly confining.

She ate dinner quickly, not really tasting it, then went into the front room, slumping in a chair and staring at the fireplace.

"Kira."

She looked up to see her mother standing in the doorway. "Are you going somewhere?"

"Yes," Mari said. "Your father and I are going into Pacta to make the rest of the trip arrangements with Queen Sien, and to see if we can help her figure out which of her closest advisers is telling our enemies what we're going to do as quickly as we decide to do it. We're planning on staying the night at Pacta, and shouldn't be back tomorrow until late morning at the earliest."

"All right."

Her mother paused. "So there's not going to be anyone in the house but you and Jason."

"All right," Kira repeated, wondering why her mother was belaboring that.

"The two of you. Alone. All night."

"All ri—" Kira suddenly got it, feeling outraged. "*Seriously?* My mother is trying to set things up so I can sleep with my boyfriend?"

Mari sighed in exasperation. "As *you* complained, you and Jason haven't had the privacy that any couple needs. And, as you take pains to tell everyone who calls Jason your boyfriend, he's actually your man. The promises you two will someday speak to each other will only formalize the commitments you've already made in your hearts."

"It's still gross!" Kira said, feeling pressured for some reason she couldn't identify. She did want Jason, she did want an opportunity like this, but not if her mother was setting it up.

"Fine." Mari waved one hand in a dismissive gesture, turning to go. "Your father and I are leaving. You and Jason have fun while we're gone."

"We're *not* going to have fun!"

Her mother glanced back briefly. "Dearest, if it's work, you're not doing it right. See you tomorrow."

Kira slumped deeper in the chair as the sky outside darkened into night. She was tired, and frustrated emotionally and physically, and her Mage powers were pushing against the barriers she was holding on them, and she really wanted to but not like this, not if she was being pushed into it, and if she was really honest with herself it was a little unnerving to think about doing that even with Jason.

Jason came downstairs, looking around. "Your parents left?"

"Yes," Kira snapped in reply. "They'll be gone all night."

"Really?"

She heard a hopeful tone in his voice. Her contrariness spiked, turning into stubborn anger mixed with her worries. Slumping even further into the chair, Kira tried to submerge her desire for Jason. "That's right. And—"

They were in bed still mostly clothed her mouth locked onto Jason's her body straining against his body her hands his hands—

"Ahhhh!" Kira shoved him away as hard as she could, shaking with shock and fear.

CHAPTER FIVE

Jason stared at her in momentary confusion before lunging for the knife he'd already discarded along with some of his clothes. "Danger? Your foresight again?"

"No." Badly rattled, Kira stared at him, backing farther away.

"No? Then what—? Did I do something wrong? Did I hurt you?"

Kira drew in a shaky breath, gathering the sheet around her to cover herself, trying to understand what had happened. "What were you doing?"

Jason responded with a bewildered look. "Huh? We were—"

"No, I wasn't!" she yelled at him.

His gaze went from puzzled to horrified. "You were blacked out?"

"Don't pretend that you didn't know! And that you tried to do it anyway!" Kira felt herself trembling from both anger and reaction to the shock.

Jason sat back, shaking his head. "You brought me up here, you said 'I love you' when you closed the door, and when I asked if it was okay you said 'yes' and then a little later you said 'yes' again and—"

"I talked?" Kira felt renewed fear rising in her. "I talked?"

"Yes. You didn't sound any different! If you had I never would've . . . oh, no." Jason drew himself into a huddled ball, sitting on the other side of the bed, avoiding her gaze. "What if you hadn't woken up for a few more minutes? What if you'd woken up while we were—"

"That didn't happen," Kira said, trying get her breathing under control.

"What if it had? What would you have thought?"

She gazed at him, knowing the answer, not wanting to say it, but feeling she owed it to him. "I would have felt that you'd taken something, and not that I'd given you something for us to share."

"Yeah," Jason said in the tones of someone having his fears confirmed. "Why were you trying to do a spell, anyway?"

"What?"

"Why were you trying to do a spell? That's why you blacked out, right?"

Kira felt fear rising into her throat and clenching it like a choking hand. She forced out a single word. "No."

"No?" Jason finally looked at her again, his anguish replaced by concern.

She managed to relax enough to say more. "No. I wasn't trying any spell. Why would I have been? I wasn't trying any spell, and I blacked out, and I talked and acted normal, but I have no idea what happened between the time I was sitting in that chair downstairs and when I yelled at you."

"Kira, this is scary."

"Really? Really? Do you think I don't know that?"

"Sorry," Jason muttered, looking away again. "That was a stupid thing to say."

"No, I'm sorry," Kira said, getting a grip on her temper. "I'm not really angry. I'm scared. Why did I black out?"

"Maybe because . . . you didn't really want to," Jason mumbled, looking away.

She tried to focus on him, on how Jason must be feeling. Somehow that made it easier to handle her own fears. "I do want you."

"Then why did you freak when you woke up?"

"Because . . . blazes, Jason, one moment I was sitting in a chair talking to you and the next moment I was in bed with you going at it hot and heavy! How would you react?"

He glowered at the bed. "I guess I'd be pretty shaken up."

"I wasn't afraid of you, Jason. I was afraid of what had happened." Kira over came a reluctance she knew wasn't fair to him, moving closer and reaching out to him. "Just hold me, okay?"

"Okay," he said, a small smile appearing. "You said that on purpose, didn't you?"

"Yes." She leaned against him, grateful for the comfort of Jason's arms about her. "What are we going to do?"

"Maybe your parents—"

"We can't tell them, Jason. Not Mother and not Father. If they know, they won't let me go to Altis with you. And I *need* to go to Altis with you." Here, now, his arms about her, she felt that stronger then ever. "Somehow you're part of the answer, and going on that trip with you is part of the answer."

"Kira . . ." Jason's voice grew strained. "What if you black out during that trip when it's really dangerous?"

What if she did? What if she awoke to discover herself in a far worse situation than tonight? She had no idea what had triggered this blackout. She had no idea what was going on in her head to cause this.

Kira stared into space, thinking, imagining the worst, and slowly coming to realize that if she stayed here that was all she'd be doing. Imagining the worst, trapped here, waiting for the next black out. There weren't any answers here.

Perhaps the worst she could imagine was sitting here, waiting for it to happen again, unable to learn what was wrong and what might help. Her parents needed to keep an eye on things at Pacta. Jason needed to go to Altis. And she needed to go with Jason. That sureity slowly emerged and gave her some sense of security.

"What if I'm here without you and black out again when it's really dangerous?" Kira finally said as she leaned her head on his shoulder. "I'm safer with you around. I know that."

"Thanks." His arm on her tightened a bit. "We'll beat this, Kira. It'll be okay."

"Not a word to my parents."

"Kira, we have to tell them. You can't keep this a secret."

She started to utter another objection, but realized that Jason was right. "All right. I'll tell Mother."

"Tomorrow?"

"Yes. I promise." Kira got up, feeling uncertain. "We could try again. Right now."

"Who's asking me that?" Jason said.

"You have no way of knowing, do you?"

"And unless I do, I'm not going to run the risk of hurting you."

Feeling a mix of affection and remorse, she leaned over to kiss him. "I made a really good choice of a man."

She put if off, of course. Mari and Alain finally got back close to noon, and then there were details to share of the now-much-more-complicated trip to Altis. At dinner Jason gave a questioning look but Kira shook her head.

But as night fell she went to the front room, where her mother was sitting at her desk. As Kira came in, she saw Mari gazing fixedly at a small fire in the fireplace. "Mother?"

Mari looked at her with a distant gaze that took a moment to resolve into recognition. "Oh, hi, Kira. Sorry. I was . . ."

"There again?" Kira asked as she sat down in the chair beside the desk.

"Yeah," her mother admitted. "Fires . . . for a while after Dorcastle I had trouble with fires." She paused, looking back at the flames. "Retreating from one wall to the next. The Imperials had launched fireballs into the buildings behind us. As we fell back, everything was burning, bright flames all around . . ." Another pause, Mari staring at the fire. "Blood stays dark. No matter how strong the flames, their light couldn't penetrate the blood in the streets. The pools of blood were always dark. But when blood gets on you, on your hands, your clothes, it's bright red."

"I know," Kira murmured, remembering her own battles.

Her mother looked over at Kira, the light of the fire reflected in her eyes. "Yes, you do. I guess that's why I can talk about it with you now."

"I used to like wearing something red occasionally. I don't anymore. I can't wear red," Kira admitted. "It reminds me of Jason's blood on my hands."

"You might have noticed there's not a lot of red in this house," Mari said. "I still like the scarlet uniforms of the Confederation. Those speak to me of friends and defenders. But any other time I see red it bothers me."

"Why do people do it, Mother? I understand defending yourself. Defending your home and your family. But why do other people attack?"

"I don't know. Why did the legions attack? They had orders, but why did those men and women charge the walls again and again? Pride? Loyalty to their friends? Loyalty to their ruler? I don't understand it. I never have." Mari's gaze returned to the fire. "There's one . . . he was coming up a ladder, so close to me, and I was mad with grief at the death of your namesake a few moments before and I put my pistol in his face and he had time to know he was doomed before I pulled the trigger. I could see it. I didn't feel it, then. I couldn't feel anything in that moment. But that face . . ."

"I know," Kira said once more, feeling the pain her mother usually kept hidden, and seeing images of brief glimpses of faces in her own memories. "They don't go away, do they?"

"No, the faces don't go away. They stay with you, always." Mari sighed. "I'm sure you didn't come in here to talk about that." Mari rubbed her eyes, then focused on Kira. "What is it? Questions about the trip?"

"Um . . ." Kira hesitated. "What did Father mean when he said you two *couldn't* come with us? I thought you both had decided you shouldn't, because of the baby."

Mari made a face. "If things were normal, we'd be doing this differently. But normal isn't exactly a good word for this family, is it?

Yes, we don't want to risk harm to the child. But your father also had a vision. His foresight warned that if he was not in Pacta, that bomb might be set off."

Kira felt a chill inside as she remembered the bright flash of light in her own vision. "Might be? It's not certain?"

"He was in the vision. It's a might-be. But he and I are going to stay here and make sure no one gets close enough to that buried whatever-it-is to set off that bomb."

"But if you fail—" Kira began.

"We know what might happen if your father does leave. We're going to guard that buried place, and Pacta. Hopefully you'll get answers from Urth and we can neutralize the threat of that facility for good, while also ensuring our little guy doesn't get hurt."

"So, this way if you have a gun fight or a running battle or something you'll be doing it close to home," Kira said.

Her mother smiled. "Right. And I have to admit I could do without an ocean voyage at the moment. I'm having enough trouble as it is some mornings, keeping food down." The smile was replaced by a serious expression. "I need to tell you something else I've decided. You've called yourself the daughter of the daughter. I'm taking you at your word. On this trip, you'll officially be my representative, Kira. With the authority to act on behalf of the daughter of Jules. Messages have already gone out advising other countries of that. I need to give you that authority, that power, in case you need it. And after all that's happened, I'm sure I can trust you not to misuse it."

"Of course you can." Kira frowned at Mari, rattled by the thought of the responsibility. "Why do you think I'll need that power? Altis and the Confederation should do what we need as long as I'm reasonable, right? And the librarians are old friends of yours."

Her mother didn't answer for a little while, her eyes on the desk before her. Finally, Mari looked at Kira. "Old friends can sometimes change, Kira."

"Change? Are the librarians doing something bad?" The idea seemed preposterous.

Her mother rubbed her forehead unhappily. "Kira, I haven't been able to get to Altis personally for a long time. I'm hearing reports that the librarians are being more and more restrictive about access to their materials. There's growing unhappiness, and a growing sentiment that the librarians have no right to monopolize what they have. Keep an eye out while you're there and let me know what you see."

"Why haven't you gone to check on it in person?" Kira asked.

"There have been a few incidents occupying my time. Including a few involving my own daughter. That's one reason. The other is because I'm the daughter of Jules. The moment I show up, everything revolves around making sure I only see what those in charge want me to see. I want to find out how they treat you. Yes, you're my daughter, but they know you. Or, they know the you from years ago. That's who the librarians will expect to show up."

"Just a kid, huh? Self-absorbed, sorry-for-herself Kira? Not someone to put on a special show for?" Kira nodded, eyeing her mother. "What else is there? There's something else about the librarians you're not saying."

"I never should have let your father teach you how to read people so well," Mari mock-complained. "Coleen lied to me about what's under Pacta Servanda. She's still holding back. I understand her reasons. I know that the librarians survived for centuries only by keeping themselves and what they knew secret. That hasn't been necessary since the fall of the Great Guilds. But I'm getting a growing feeling that the librarians are reverting back to that, becoming secretive."

"Secretive? They love showing off their stuff." Kira paused and thought. "Well, they used to. Do you remember the last time I was there I complained that they stopped letting me have free run of the tower? And it wasn't just me."

"I didn't pay as much attention to that as I should have," Mari said. "Thinking it was just my girl being her unhappy, difficult, teenage self."

"Yeah, that was me," Kira admitted.

"But now there's this problem in Pacta. Kira, everything I know about what Urth is saying in its messages comes through the librarians. Other people are supposedly being allowed to talk to Urth, but I'm having an increasingly hard time finding those people. And Urth . . ."

"I know you're angry at Urth. You have every right to be."

"Yeah." Mari glared at the night sky visible through the nearest window. "Our brothers and sisters. And they tell us nothing. We got a little at first, but then even that stopped. Just meaningless assurances that they're considering our requests. We used to be able to hear Urth talking to the other colonies, but that ceased, as if they shifted everyone else to another frequency, or whatever it is the Feynman unit uses."

"Are they all like Jason's mother and father?" Kira wondered.

"Jason says they're not. He thinks a lot of it is misguided attempts to 'protect' us. Good intentions. Kira, you'd be amazed how many people think good intentions are an all-purpose excuse for anything they do."

"Jason will talk to Urth," Kira said. "Maybe they'll listen to him."

"Let's hope. I'm counting on you two to get this done. And it might do you both some good to get away for a little while on a trip that isn't about you two being chased all over the place." Mari gave her an appraising look. "How are things? You and Jason have seemed awkward today. Did anything go wrong?"

Kira looked her mother in the eyes. "Yes."

"Oh. Inexperience or . . . ?"

"I blacked out. No spell. I just blacked out. I said yes to Jason and everything while blacked out and came to myself in bed with him. We knew we had to tell you. That's why I came in here."

Mari didn't say anything for perhaps a minute. "You still think that you should go with him?"

"Yes."

"To protect him?" Her mother paused again for a long moment. "Your father has had more visions of you."

"What has he seen?" Kira asked, feeling her insides knot with tension.

"The usual. Because of your dual nature as a Mechanic and a Mage, there are too many possible outcomes to figure out which will occur. But he says the visions with Jason in them along with you offer hope. The visions where you're alone . . . are in some cases so bad he wouldn't describe them to me."

"Oh." She couldn't think of anything else to say, couldn't think of how she was supposed to feel at hearing it.

"Kira, the point here is that staying with Jason may be the only thing that protects *you*," Mari said. "Somehow he makes a difference in the outcomes if he's with you. Just as having your father with me saved me more times than I can count."

Having expected a knock-down, drag-out fight over the trip, Kira found herself staring at her mother. "So you're still fine with me going with Jason? You're not going to lock me in my room?"

"We're not going to try," Mari said. "The last person who tried locking you in a room didn't come out of it very well, did he? Yes, you're still going with Jason."

"Thank you." Kira felt like laughing as relief flooded her.

Her mother paused again, watching Kira. "You know what I want to do? Hold you in my arms, safe, and never let you go. Someday, if you have children of your own, you'll know what I mean. You'll see them go off to school for the first time, ride a horse for the first time, grow, fall in love, and grow away from you. And you have to let them do it. There's no joy like the joy of holding your child, and no pain like the pain of letting them go, and no pride like the pride of seeing them do well on their own."

"You really think I can handle it?" Kira said. "Because I'm having some doubts about myself."

"That's because you're smart. You have to be smart enough to second-guess yourself, and brave enough to follow through once you're sure what has to be done. Kira, when I was your age, and for some years after that, there were always plenty of people telling me that I should not be making the decisions I was making, that I should listen to my elders and do exactly what they said and not rock the boat by trying to decide things for myself. And I did make mistakes, some of which nearly ended up killing your father and I. But on the whole I think I made good decisions by using my head but also by following my gut instinct and my heart."

Mari paused, smiling at Kira. "And the decision I made that was most important, that literally changed the world, was to ignore every common-sense argument that told me not to talk to your father, not to get to know him, and to sever all ties with him. I followed my gut. I listened to that something inside, I went to your father, and I've never regretted that. Your gut tells you that Jason needs you, and that you need Jason to solve the problem of the blackouts. I trust that. You should, too. Just come back safely to us."

Kira did laugh this time. "Oh, all right! I guess I can come back safe if you insist on it. You're always pressuring me!"

"That's because I'm such an awful mother," Mari said.

"You're a wonderful mother."

"Yeah. That's not what you thought during all those years when you'd scream at me that you must be adopted since I was too terrible to ever have had a daughter of my own."

Kira covered her face, laughing again. "I'm so sorry! I hereby admit that you are my mother, and that you're actually not really terrible."

"That's my girl." Her mother sighed, looking at the map. "I'll let your father know what you told me. Not the part about waking up in bed with Jason. I don't think he's ready for his little girl to be doing that kind of thing."

"Mother, we didn't actually . . . I woke up before we . . ."

"Really?" Mari eyed her, curious. "Why do you suppose that happened?"

"I don't understand. What do you mean?"

"The blackout got you into that situation, but then lifted in time for you to decide whether or not to go through with it. Was that just a coincidence?"

Kira started to reply, hesitating as she realized her mother had asked a good question. "I don't know. I mean, I don't know why I'm blacking out, so I don't know why it lifted when it did."

"When you blacked out on Maxim's ship, it didn't lift until you'd knocked out the guards, right? And when you blacked out while hiding from the legionaries, it didn't lift until you were well away from them and the situation was past," her mother said. "But this time it got you partway into something and then lifted?"

"Mother, I'm not unhappy about when it lifted! Neither is Jason!"

"Good. But do you see my point?"

"Yes," Kira said. "I just have no idea what it means."

"Maybe the meaning will come clear in time. There has to be a pattern," Mari said. She leaned closer, her expression intent. "Remember what Doctor Sino said. If it comes down to dying, or surviving because you used your Mage powers, your father and I would really rather you survived. As long as you're alive we can sort out the problems with the powers someday."

"I'll remember that," Kira promised.

"Pack everything you need before you go to bed. You'll be leaving before dawn. And make sure Jason has his stuff packed and ready."

"Why . . . ?" Kira sighed. "Because he'll be my husband someday."

"You got it. Husbands are really great to have around, but they need looking after."

"Like horses," Kira said.

"Yeah, actually . . ." Her mother started laughing.

No matter how well you knew a place, it felt strange and different in the dark a couple of hours before dawn, when a special silence fell upon the world and the stars shone in a sky that never seemed to have known the warmth of a sun's light. Kira shivered even though her new Mechanics jacket offered plenty of warmth. Her pistol rested snugly in its holster under the jacket, she had plenty of extra ammunition with her as well as some emergency food supplies, but a curious menace seemed to lurk about the place where she'd lived all her life.

"They're ready," her mother said in a hushed voice.

Kira slung her backpack on and reached out to Jason with one hand so that they walked together to where vague shapes loomed in the dark. As they got closer, the shapes resolved into those of three Mages and two gigantic birds.

Alain reached out to her as Kira reached him. "Be careful," he said in her ear, his voice loaded with emotions her father usually kept suppressed. "Be careful and be wise."

"I will," Kira promised, thinking that if Mage Nika had taken the offered job all of Kira's care and wisdom probably wouldn't have saved her this morning.

She saw her mother giving Jason a farewell hug. "Make sure she gets back to us, Jason," Mari said.

"I promise," Jason replied. "And if there's any way to convince Earth to help, I'll do that, too. You guys . . . I owe you so much."

"You've earned anything you've gotten," Kira's mother said. "Kira, be polite to Sien when you see her."

"You don't have to tell me that!"

"And take care of yourself."

Kira walked to where Mage Alera waited as Jason walked over to Mage Saburo. Despite her tension, Kira felt a rush of affection as she climbed up on the back of Swift, Alera's Roc. "Hi, Swift."

Alera took her place just behind Swift's neck. A moment later Swift leaped skyward, his vast wings spreading out to either side to cup the air and propel the Roc higher.

Kira leaned over, looking to catch a last glimpse of her mother and father on the ground below, their shapes rapidly dwindling and fading into the darkness as Swift climbed. She held her view of her parents as long as she could.

Mage Saburo's Roc Hunter paced them as the mighty birds spiraled into the sky. Anyone spying from a distance would have seen Kira and Jason leave on Rocs, and hopefully believe they were following their original plan to fly north all the way to Altis. But when the birds were so high that they should be lost in the night sky, both Rocs swung south toward Pacta Servanda.

Kira didn't have long to brood in the silence and chill of the night sky before Swift began circling downward toward a large courtyard in one of the newer parts of Pacta Servanda. The lights that normally illuminated the courtyard at night had dimmed, offering some concealment as Swift landed, Hunter coming in nearby.

"Thank you, Mage Alera. Thank you, Swift." Kira unstrapped herself and slid off the giant feathers on Swift's back. No sooner had she reached the ground than soldiers appeared.

"Good morning, Captain," Sergeant Bete whispered.

Kira and Jason, surrounded by Lancers of the Queen's Own, hastened out of the courtyard and down a silent, darkened street to where the lights of Pacta Servanda's train station blazed against the predawn night.

Inside the station, Kira blinked against the sudden glare. After the silence so far, the sounds of the station seemed painfully loud. The rattle and clank of tools, the hiss of steam, the rumble of a boiler building pressure, the occasional snort or whicker of a horse being led into a livestock railcar, the conversations as soldiers and Mechanics prepared for departure.

Kira took a deep breath of air tinged with the scents of lubricating oil and fire, drawing comfort from the familiar sounds and smells. They spoke to her of home as much as her bedroom did. Up ahead she could see the train preparing to depart. One engine up front, a passenger car, a mixed baggage/meal car, another passenger car, the car intended for her and Jason, then another passenger car, baggage/meal car, and finally a passenger car. "I want to go by the engine," she told Sergeant Bete.

As she drew closer to the locomotive at the front of the train, Kira felt a dawning sense of recognition. "I think that's Betsy," she said to Jason.

"Betsy?" he asked, looking at the women around them.

"The locomotive! Betsy's a legend. She's been training Apprentices and hauling trains for I don't know how long." Kira grinned at a memory. "I learned some steam skills driving her. And Mother almost blew her up at Dorcastle."

"Say what?"

"Mother was trying to slow down the Imperial advance, so she rigged some locomotives to blow. She could have rigged Betsy, too, but she didn't have the heart. So Betsy survived and here she is!"

Jason shook his head as he looked at the locomotive. "Is anything safe around you or your mother?"

"You are," Kira said. "Mostly. Why are you so tense?"

"We're going on a train."

"Relax. I have no intention of jumping off this train."

"I've never had any intention of jumping off any train," Jason grumbled as they reached the locomotive. "And yet somehow it ends up happening. Hey, Gari!"

The Mechanic in the cab of the locomotive leaned out, grinning at them. "Hey, Jason. And who's this Mechanic with you?"

"Lady Mechanic Kira," she said with mock severity, then laughed and gave Gari a hug as he came down out of the cab. "Hi, honorary big brother. You're driving Betsy?"

"Yup," Gari said, wiping his hands on a rag. "Me and Apprentices Silene and Yuri."

A young woman and a slightly younger boy came around the side of the locomotive, both smiling bashfully. "Good morning, Lady Mechanic."

"Good morning," Kira said. "I helped run Betsy when I was an Apprentice, too. Is this Mechanic treating you all right?"

Apprentice Silene nodded. "He works us twelve hours straight, gives us a couple of hours off to eat and sleep, and then another twelve hours."

"Twelve hours straight?" Kira asked. "He's going easy on you. When I was an Apprentice they worked us for fourteen hours straight."

"Yeah," Gari said. "Things aren't as hard as they used to be, are they? You two go check the rods again. Make sure none are loose and they're all lubricated." As Silene and Yuri bent to check the rods on the drive wheels, Gari smiled at Kira again. "Congratulations, by the way, Lady Mechanic. Yeah, they asked me to drive this run.

Something about me being reliable. They must not have talked to my parents."

"Alli and Calu would've told them what a great guy you are," Kira said with another laugh. "What's the matter, Jason?"

He shrugged apologetically. "This is a really old piece of equipment? Is it safe?"

Gari nodded, smiling. "Really old, and really well maintained and repaired. Betsy is as reliable as they come. This isn't like that Urth junk you were always boasting about."

"I never boasted about it! Except to Kira a couple of times and after she shut me down for it I figured out that was a bad idea."

"So how dangerous is this?" Gari asked Kira.

"Hopefully not dangerous," she said.

"We're hauling an armored railcar normally reserved for use by the Queen of Tiae, and loading two troops of cavalry," Gari said.

"That's just . . . preventive maintenance. To make sure nothing dangerous happens. And we've got you driving, so no worries there."

Sergeant Bete approached again. "Captain, your presence is requested in the main car."

"All right," Kira said. "Gari, I'd better go. I'll talk to you again!"

"Sure, sure," Gari said with a skeptical waveoff. "Lady Mechanic Captain Dragon Slayer Daughter of the Daughter. Like you have time for guys like me."

"Gari, if I ever put on airs around you, I expect you to slap me down. I mean that literally. Give me a good one, hard enough to knock me on my butt and remind me who I am. Jason, if he does that, don't you dare get mad at Gari."

She and Jason followed Sergeant Bete to the car they'd be riding in. The queen's car, Kira realized. After assuring Gari that she didn't think she was special, she'd be riding in a car normally used only by Queen Sien.

The polished wood on the outside of the car offered no hint of the plates of armor beneath. There were fewer and smaller windows than most train cars had, but with the armored shutters drawn back on the inside they didn't appear designed for protection. An illusion, Kira thought. The car looked like something other than what it was. Her world was filled with illusions, just as the Mages said.

Except for the people. They were all real, she hoped. Just as her father the only Master of Mages said.

Sergeant Bete left them at the door to the car. Kira went inside to the lounge, where two comfortable couches and some chairs faced each other. Leather gleamed and brass fixtures shone around them because, after all, this car was used to greet special guests when the queen was traveling.

Queen Sien herself stood in the center of the lounge, speaking with Colonel Anders. Though she usually wore suits for everyday attire, this morning the queen was in a uniform similar to that of the colonel. "Ah, Kira. Colonel, you have your orders. I'd like to speak with Kira alone."

"Of course, your Majesty," Colonel Anders said, saluting. He nodded to Kira and Jason as he left, all business. Kira noticed he was wearing combat-ready armor and weapons, not the showy gear intended for parades.

"Colonel Anders is personally commanding your escort to Gullhaven," Sien told Kira. "Jason, you don't have to leave. Anything I have to say to Kira you should hear, too. Please sit down."

The queen paused for a moment, waiting, then sat down as well next to Kira. "How are you doing, Kira?"

Feeling awkward, she kept her reply formal. "I'm fine, Your Majesty."

"Kira, you know I'm Sien to you in private," the queen chided her. "You called me Sien as a toddler for years before realizing I was the queen of Tiae."

Kira couldn't help smiling at the reminder. "I'm sorry, Sien. There've been so many things happening the last few years, sometimes I have trouble keeping everything in perspective."

"You're doing a very good job," Sien said, and Kira could see she meant it, which made Kira's face warm with embarrassment. "Kira, in less than a month you'll be eighteen. Legally an adult. There's something you were never told, something that will soon be overtaken by events and never happen. But you should know of it. Especially since you've felt betrayed to learn I was never really your queen."

"Another secret?" Kira asked, dreading what might come next.

"Yes," Sien admitted, her eyes serious as they studied her. "You know that your parents were worried about what might happen to them. Worried that they might be killed, and you be left an orphan. Soon after you were born they made arrangements to ensure that you'd be safe if that happened."

"I guessed that," Kira said. "The only thing I couldn't figure out was who I'd end up with. I thought it'd most likely be Alli and Calu."

"No," Sien said with a shake of her head.

"Dav and Asha?"

"No. None of them could have provided the protection you'd have needed. It would have been me, Kira. I signed the papers some time ago. If the worst had happened, I would have taken you in."

"Oh." That was a major surprise. And not a bad one. "Um, thank you. I'm glad it wasn't necessary. I'm sure you would've made a wonderful guardian for me."

Sien shook her head again. "I didn't agree to be your guardian. I agreed to adopt you."

"You . . ." Kira stared at the queen.

"You would have become Kira of Tiae, my daughter."

"But—"

"And my chosen heir," Sien continued. "Under the laws I've championed, the people of Tiae would have had to accept you as their queen someday, but I think they would have done so. Kira, if your parents had died, if Mari had not been there to deal with so many things and maintain the peace, I thought it likely that I would also die, in defense of Tiae. If that happened, Tiae would need a fighter, someone who could defend this land. I knew you would be such a fighter." She smiled at Jason. "Though I admit to hoping that you would find a partner who would help moderate your wilder behaviors.

Kira, I wanted you to know that I would have made you my daughter. I'm not your queen, I never was, but I'd agreed to become your mother if you needed one."

Kira tried desperately not to cry. "Can I . . . can I pretend that you're still my queen?"

"That can be our secret," Sien said.

She reached out and Kira embraced her. "If Tiae ever needs me," Kira whispered, "I'll fight for Tiae. That can be our secret."

As she drew back, Kira saw Sien smiling. "I think Tiae has plenty of fighters now, Kira. Any number of people could step into the job of defending this kingdom, and I think do well at it. Tiae needs something else in its next queen or king."

"What are you looking for?" Kira asked as she leaned back, wiping her eyes.

"A heart, Kira." Sien glanced toward the windows of the rail car. "My people know how to fight. That was the curse that led to the breaking of the kingdom, and the strength that enabled us to rebuild it, with the invaluable help of your mother and father. Since the reforging of the kingdom, many new citizens have come here and become part of Tiae. There are those who have trouble accepting the newer arrivals. And the newer arrivals need to become one with us while also being themselves. What we will need is understanding matched to that fighting spirit. I still haven't found someone whose heart is large enough and wise enough to embrace all of Tiae. That's why I have yet to name a preferred heir for the people to vote on when the time comes. Jason, you look puzzled."

Jason, sitting next to Kira, nodded. "I'm a little confused. You're the queen. But you said the people get to vote on who comes after you."

"That's my choice, Jason," Sien explained. "I saw, all too clearly, the dangers of leaving the leadership of a kingdom, or any country, as an inheritance to one family. It's far too important a task to be left to the hope that the son or daughter of a worthy person would be up to it, and that their daughter or son would also be. By the laws I've seen passed, even if I have a dozen children, none of them would have a right to the throne. I can name who I wish to succeed me, but who-ever that is must be approved by the people of Tiae. And whoever that is can be removed at a future date if the people decide."

Kira glanced at Jason. "What Queen Sien isn't saying is that her people think the world of her and will vote for whoever she recom-mends as heir."

Sien nodded. "Which makes the matter of choosing an heir all the more important. I don't want Tiae to descend again into the struggles that once broke it, or into the ruthless debauchery of the Imperial court."

"Sabrin will change the Imperial court," Kira said. "She told me that and she meant it."

"I hope she succeeds," Sien said. "So, now you know. The day you turn eighteen the legal agreement for me to adopt you loses all force. But you deserved to know of it."

"Thank you," Kira said. She gave a half sigh, half laugh. "I'm glad it never happened. I mean, obviously, because I wouldn't have wanted Mother and Father to die. But also . . . I grew up feeling so different. So separated from others. Being a sort-of princess too might have been the last straw."

"You wouldn't have been a sort-of princess," Sien said. "Just an actual princess."

"No! Too weird. Though Jason might have been thrilled if he'd ended up engaged to a princess."

Jason shook his head, smiling. "I love the Kira I found here. I wouldn't want her to be any different."

"Yeah. You say that now. Wait'll I'm having a bad day again. Queen Sien," Kira added, becoming formal in her speech and posture, "thank you. For so many things."

Sien inclined her head toward Kira. "You're welcome. Find the means of dealing with the threat that exists under Pacta Servanda and I'll be more than repaid for anything I've done."

"We will," Kira vowed.

Kira sat for a while after Queen Sien left, her thoughts swirling inside her, only vaguely aware of the sounds from outside of the continuing preparations to leave. Finally she looked at Jason again. "Are you sure you wouldn't have preferred a princess?"

Jason smiled. "Would that have made me a prince when we got married?"

"Sort of. You'd have been a prince consort. Royal eye candy on my arm for public events, and assistant in producing royal heirs in private."

"Sounds like a great job."

Colonel Anders entered, all business as Kira and Jason jumped to their feet. "We'll be leaving in a couple of minutes, Lady Mechanic Kira. There are two cars full of Lancers ahead of this one, and another two cars of Lancers behind you. I'll be in the next car ahead of this one. Contact me if you need anything."

"Thank you, Colonel," Kira said. "Are there any stops on the way?"

"Only at Debran, to take on more fuel and water for the locomotive. The Mechanics say the speed of the train will have to be limited because of the weight of this car. Moving too fast might cause a derailment. We won't be able to travel nearly as fast as an express normally would." Anders paused. "Lady, I have orders from the queen to defer to you on most matters. But if an emergency arises, the queen ordered me to take command. If I call you Captain Kira, I will be in command and expect my orders to be followed."

"I understand," Kira said. "I saw horses being loaded into cars. Where will those cars be?"

"Part of another train following us, to reduce the load on the locomotive pulling these cars and also reduce the danger to the horses if something happens to this train."

As Anders left, Kira shot a stern look at Jason. "Why are you gloomy again?"

"He's worried about something happening to this train," Jason pointed out.

"Nothing is going to happen! We're going to have a long, safe trip to Gullhaven, and the only enemy we'll have to deal with is boredom!"

The train lurched into motion as two soldiers entered the car with apologies and sealed shut the armored blinds over the windows before departing.

Kira flopped back onto a couch once they were alone again. "So much for watching passing scenery. What are we going to do for the next two days?"

Jason gave a hopeful glance forward at the bed area, separated from the lounge area by a closed door. "I can think of something."

"No," Kira said. "There are a couple of hundred Lancers sitting in seats in cars in front of us and behind us, wearing their combat armor and carrying their weapons. I would not be happy or comfortable having fun while the soldiers guarding us are sitting up all through the night. That's one reason. The other is that I'm not the queen. I can't lock any doors on this car. Everything has to remain open so the guards can check or get to any spot if necessary. I will not engage in any activity with you if there's a reasonable chance some Lancers might stroll by and start offering suggestions on ways to do it better."

Um, yeah," Jason agreed. "Maybe I can practice throwing my knife. I'm getting pretty good at that."

"I don't think we should throw knives at the queen's fine wood-work," Kira said.

"So what do we do instead?"

"Sien has a small library in this car. See? Hopefully there's stuff we haven't read."

Jason checked out the titles. "Hey, there're copies of some of the tech manuals from the *Demeter* in here."

"*Dematr*," Kira corrected him. "Which ones? And don't make any of those comments about how archaic the junk in them is when that junk is still state of the art for this world."

The day passed as slowly as she had feared, the train rumbling along at an annoyingly sedate pace. More than once Kira felt like complaining to the Mechanic driving the locomotive that surely it would be safe to go a little faster, but that Mechanic was Gari and she knew he'd stand his ground against her.

As wearying as the long day in the train car was, it worsened because her Mage powers kept trying to slip out of their bonds and search the countryside. Kira had to repeatedly clamp down on her powers, and then deal with an unusually powerful sense of confinement in the car afterwards. By the time dinner was done, simple rations like those the Lancers were eating, Kira was fed up with the day. Jason, wisely judging her mood, had stayed mostly silent for the past few hours.

It must be full night outside by now. Kira yawned, wondering how far from Debran they were and whether she should give up and go to bed.

She heard the boom of an explosion, followed by the high-pitched screech of locomotive wheels sliding on the rails after the brake had been pulled. The furniture in the car was all fastened down securely, but momentum shoved Kira against the side of the couch for a few moments before a sickening crash and lurch told of the locomotive leaving the tracks, twisting and yanking at the cars it was pulling. The lights went out, pitching them into darkness, just before Kira's car left the rails, too, tilting and sliding and shuddering until it came to a halt, canted at an angle, the front end pointing downward along the shoulder of the track.

Kira staggered to her feet, trying to balance on the slanting floor. She barely had time to do that, hearing the pop of rifle fire erupting outside, before someone grabbed her and pulled her down to the floor of the car.

CHAPTER SIX

Kira managed to check her attack just in time as she realized that it was Jason who had pulled her to the floor. Before she could demand to know what he was doing, twin crashes came from the front of the car as a pair of projectiles slammed into the armor, followed by the explosion of shaped-charge warheads tearing into the bed compartment. Kira saw light flash around the door to the bed area as it was blown out by the force of the explosions, shrapnel flying past over her, fire bursting to life amid the ruin of the beds and providing flickering light.

"How did you know?" Kira demanded of Jason.

"Ambush. Night. It made sense," he gasped, helping her stand.

"They may have more dragon-killers," Kira said, looking around and holding onto a table to keep her balance on the slanting floor. "We have to get out of here."

"We're not going out the front," Jason said, pointing at the wreckage and growing flames in the bed compartment.

Kira drew her pistol, chambering a round and letting off the safety as she ran up the sloping floor to the back door of the car. But when she tugged at the door it didn't move, jammed in place by the way its frame had twisted when the car derailed. "Emergency exit," Kira gasped, half-sliding/half-running back down the slope and checking her progress by grabbing one of the chairs when she reached the exit located low on one side of the car. She knelt, the erratic light from the fires in the bed area allowing her to spot the levers holding the exit closed.

Jason helped her twist free the levers. Only a few seconds must have passed since the first dragon-killers hit the car, but to Kira it felt like it was taking far too long to get out of what had become an armored death trap.

She braced herself with her hands, kicked at the emergency exit and saw it pop free. Kira went through feet first, grabbing her pack as she fell to pull it out with her, dropping down to the ground, Jason right behind her. Outside, the night was illuminated only by the stars and the flash of rifle fire, the sounds of the battle suddenly much louder.

Kira had barely regained her balance when she heard a whooshing sound and pulled Jason to the ground with her. Another dragon-killer slammed into the car above them, its blast penetrating into the seating area where they'd been moments before.

Kira crouched low, staring about her, trying to figure out who was where. From the look of the rifle flashes, the ambushers were spread out to the west of the train tracks.

"Lancers to me!" a familiar voice called over the sound of the rifles.

"Come on, Jason." Kira ran in that direction, toward the back of the train, finding a confused group of Lancers being formed by Sergeant Bete into a defensive line backed against the derailed cars behind them.

"I need a gun," Jason said, sounding breathless. "This isn't a knife fight."

Kira knelt and picked up a carbine lying next to a fallen Lancer, shoving it into Jason's hands. But to her surprise instead of joining the Lancers lying down to fire back at the ambushers, Jason lay down and rolled onto his back, watching the tilted tops of the train cars.

She tried to catch her breath and figure out what was going on, flinching as the impact of a fourth dragon-killer rocked the armored train car she and Jason had occupied. "Where's Colonel Anders?" she yelled at Sergeant Bete over the crash of Lancer carbines and attackers' rifles.

"Up front somewhere!"

Up front. Where Gari was. Had he been hurt? What would the ambushers do to him? "I need to go up front to check on the locomotive!" Kira shouted.

"No, Captain!" Sergeant Bete yelled back. "You *need* to stay here. Running around in the dark in the middle of this fight is a good way to get yourself killed."

"I'll be fine!" Kira started to rise to her feet, only to halt and stare at Bete as the sergeant pointed her pistol at Kira.

"You'll stay here, Captain, even if I have to shoot you in the leg to keep you here! And don't think your mother wouldn't thank me for doing it!"

"You wouldn't dare, Sergeant!" Kira cried, starting to get her feet under her again.

"Try me, Captain!" Bete shouted, aiming at Kira's leg.

Kira glared at Bete, knowing the sergeant would do exactly what she was threatening to do. Snarling with frustration, Kira dropped to her stomach again as a fifth dragon-killer hit the armored train car. "What the blazes are you doing?" she demanded of Jason, who was still looking up at the derailed cars behind them.

Instead of answering, Jason suddenly tensed and aimed upwards, firing. Startled, Kira saw a shadowy shape on top of one of the cars reel backwards and out of sight.

"I hope that was a bad guy," Jason yelled. "They definitely weren't one of the Lancers."

"Sergeant Bete!" Kira called, gesturing upwards. "Behind us!"

Bete turned, looked, understood, and directed some of the Lancers to mimic Jason to cover the tops of the cars. Moments later two of them fired.

A figure in a Mechanics jacket fell to the ground not far from Kira. She had only an instant of icy fear that it might be Gari before a grenade rolled from the figure's now-limp hand, the primed fuse sputtering.

Jason rolled to his knees and swung the butt of his carbine, connecting with the grenade and knocking it out into the night before it exploded too far off to harm any of the Lancers. "That was either golf or baseball," he called to Kira. "Maybe cricket."

"Teach me!" she called, scrambling over to the fallen enemy in a Mechanics jacket. Rolling the body face up, she saw sharp features that felt oddly familiar. Where had she seen this man before? And why did a train seem part of that memory as well?

On the train north out of Tiae, the day she fled with Jason. The man who had claimed to have been a Mechanics Guild assassin.

"Sergeant! At least some of the attackers are Mechanics!"

Bete passed the word. The rifle fire from the west had faltered for a few moments, but now redoubled, most of the shots passing over the prone Lancers to slam into the railcars. Absurdly, Kira could smell the scent of churned-up soil and cut grass mingled with that of burned propellant from the carbine shots and the wood smoke from the burning armored railcar.

More figures came over the top of the cars behind them, Jason and some of the Lancers firing to drive off that attack.

"Are you all right?" Kira called to Jason, feeling helpless and impotent as she lay next to him.

"I didn't want to take the train!" Jason yelled over the noise of the gunshots. "And, yes, we did have to jump off again!"

"At least it wasn't moving this time!" Kira yelled back. "And I didn't have to throw you off!"

"That's so much better! Thank you!" Jason aimed upward and fired again.

Kira sensed something out there in the night in the direction of the ambushers, a spell from a Mage unknown to her. She concentrated on it, trying to keep her own Mage presence completely masked. Moments later, Kira saw a glowing pillar appear in the darkness, coming toward where she and the Lancers were pinned against the wrecked railcars.

A Mage, using an invisibility spell to get close, perhaps even inside the Lancer perimeter, before lashing out with the long knives that Mages carried.

Another glowing pillar appeared as a second Mage used the same spell, coming from a different angle toward Kira and the Lancers. But invisible to the Lancers, and coming closer every moment.

"Blazes," Kira muttered, hoping that a stray shot would accidentally strike at least one of the Mages, but they were coming from far enough to the left and right that fire aimed at the attackers in front wasn't much of a threat to them.

"Blazes!" Kira whispered again. She had to protect knowledge of her Mage powers. But not at the expense of the lives of others. She wouldn't let a single Lancer die because she wouldn't take a risk on their behalf.

Kira came to one knee and aimed carefully with her pistol. Sergeant Bete noticed, turning to tell Kira to get down again, but instead gazing with a baffled expression toward where Kira's target must be.

Kira fired.

A Mage appeared, stumbling backwards from the impact of her bullet. Kira had already swung to face the other way, aiming at the second Mage, firing, seeing no result, and firing again. The last shot scored, another Mage appearing to stagger to one side.

The Lancers saw the Mages appear and fired in a ragged volley that scored enough hits to knock both Mages down for good.

Kira dropped down to her stomach again, seeing Sergeant Bete staring at her. Kira shook her head in a clear warning to Bete.

It couldn't have been much later that the rifle fire from the ambushers began to falter. Sergeant Bete called out to Kira. "They know they can't get to you, and they have to get well away from here before dawn comes. They're probably breaking contact."

Kira nodded, her eyes toward the less and less frequent flashes of enemy fire. "Do you think we should pursue?"

"No, Captain, I do not. They prepared this attack. There may be traps set out there, and we have wounded we need to leave some Lancers to protect. Any force we sent out in pursuit would be too small and too slow to succeed. More likely they'd be ambushed again and take heavy losses."

Of the things Kira was certain of in life, Sergeant Bete's personal bravery ranked high on the list. So did Kira's assessment of Sergeant Bete's military judgment. If she said don't go, Kira wasn't going to argue. "I agree."

"Why do you think they used only two Mages against us?" Bete asked.

"I'm guessing when we shifted plans they didn't have time to get more Mages they trusted here," Kira said.

The enemy fire stopped completely at least an hour before dawn. But the Lancers waited until growing light made it safe to move before the groups from the front of the train and the rear of the train linked up.

As they waited for Colonel Anders, Sergeant Bete came close to Kira, speaking in a low voice. "Something odd happened during the attack, Captain. Something odd involving those two Mages."

Kira exhaled heavily before replying in the same low tones so they wouldn't be overheard. "Nothing happened, Sergeant. Nothing that should be reported."

"I have a duty, Captain."

"I understand," Kira said. "If you have concerns, if you feel your duty requires, report directly to Queen Sien or to my mother. Tell them."

Bete paused, thinking. "The queen or Lady Mari? Either one?"

"Directly. In person," Kira said. "What you tell them will not surprise them, and I'm certain they will ask you not to place it in any written report or speak of it to others."

Sergeant Bete nodded. "Very well, Captain. Not even the colonel?"

"Not even the colonel."

"Then I will take you at your word, Captain. I know that you, and Lady Mari your mother, would not ask me to do anything that would violate my oath to Queen Sien."

"Thank you, Sergeant. My mother always enjoys talking with you. She often says how lucky she was in the men and women who came to fight alongside her against the Great Guilds."

"It was our luck to have her to fight for," Bete said, smiling.

"But if you had shot me, I think Mother would have been a little unhappy with you."

"Maybe," Sergeant Bete said, getting to her feet. "Or she might have commended me."

Kira watched Bete walk over to where one of the other Lancers was looking down at the body of one of the Mages.

"How do you suppose that happened?" the private asked. "Did we just get lucky?"

"Must have," Bete said. "There were a lot of bullets flying around. A few went through the right spots."

Kira saw the dead being laid out and went to help despite the protests of the work detail that they could handle it. Jason came to help her as well, raising up one of the fallen and carrying him to where he could be laid down side by side with the others in a neat row. It took all of her and Jason's strength to carry one. Kira remembered her mother once wondering why the dead were so heavy, why they seemed so much heavier than when they were alive.

Fortunately there were only three dead here at the rear of the train. "Only" three dead, Kira thought bleakly as she looked at them. She knew their faces. She'd known them. Not well. But Kira had known those who now lay silent and unmoving.

Her mother had done this. She could do it. But blazes, it was hard.

Her brooding was interrupted by the approach of Colonel Anders. She saluted him. "We lost three killed and twelve wounded back here, sir. Some of the wounded were injured when the train derailed."

Anders returned the salute, his expression grim. "It's fortunate the train was moving more slowly than the usual express. I hate to think how many injuries we would've sustained if we'd derailed at twice the speed."

Kira looked around in the growing light, depression weighing on her. "This is all my fault."

"You're not that important, Captain," Anders said, his voice sharp. "These are enemies of the queen and of Tiae. They hit this train because of the mission you're on. But they would have been a danger to us regardless of whether or not you were within a million lances of here. And those killed or wounded were doing their duty as they had promised to do, as well as to their comrades. Grieve the dead, but if you feel sorry for yourself I'll give you something else to do to take your mind off it."

Kira glared at him, knowing the colonel was right. "No, sir. That won't be necessary. But if something else needs to be done and I can do it, I expect to be tasked with it."

"Understood." Anders looked around. "I made far-talker contact with some Bakre Confederation forces. They're on the way. The train bringing the horses managed to stop in time, and didn't come under attack. Stay alert, Captain. I have no intention of losing you to whoever did this."

"Yes, sir." Kira waited until Anders had moved on. "Jason, I'm going up to where the locomotive is."

"Okay." He looked at the carbine he was still carrying as if uncertain what to do with it, then tightened his grip on the weapon and nodded to her. "Let's go." Kira turned to yell. "Sergeant Bete! I am now going up to the locomotive!"

Bete nodded, saluted, and turned back to her work.

"What was that about?" Jason asked as they walked alongside the wrecked railcars, the smoldering ruin of their own car still burning in places.

"That's between me and Bete." Kira could see the locomotive resting at an angle, both drive and leading wheels off the bent rails just beyond where a bomb set under the tracks had exploded to wreck the line. But even though Betsy had gone off the rails she was still upright, and appeared in fairly good shape. None of the dragon-killers had been aimed at the locomotive. "Gari! Are you all right?"

She sagged momentarily with relief when Gari stuck his head out of the cab. "Hey, Kira. Yeah, I'm fine. A little beat up and some big bruises, but nothing bad."

"What about the Apprentices? Silene and Yuri?"

"Also beat up but fine. Silene looks to have a sprained wrist and Yuri a sprained ankle. I'm letting them sleep for a few hours. Maybe our mothers are right when they complain that Apprentices these days aren't as tough as they used to be."

"Oh, please," Kira scoffed. "I don't want to hear that junk about how great people were in the old days again. I'm amazed that you guys managed to keep everything upright when we derailed."

Gari pointed back down the track. "Whoever set that charge in the track blew it too early, so we were able to slow down a lot before we derailed. They probably thought we'd be going faster. But Yuri was at the controls when it happened and he did everything he should've, which also helped. These Apprentices must actually be listening to me! I guess you're responsible for all this?"

"I just got lectured about that, so not funny. I'm glad you and the Apprentices are all right. How's Betsy?"

"Off the rails, which you've probably noticed, and took a few hits, but nothing that can't be fixed." Gari ran one hand over the side of the locomotive. "Betsy now has the distinction of having survived both you and your mother."

"Maybe we'll manage to destroy her next time. Has anybody told you that you get your sense of humor from your mother? Aunt Alli must be so proud."

"She is," Gari said. "Seriously, I'm glad you and Jason are all right. That's probably why they didn't try to hit Betsy after she left the rails. They seemed totally intent on killing you."

"It happens."

"It happens? That's your reaction?"

"Gari, I can't afford to freak out every time someone blows up a train to try to kill me," Kira said, still feeling depressed and very tired as well.

He slid down out of the cab and looked closely at her. "How often has this kind of thing happened to you?"

"Too often," Kira said.

"You hear about it and you think it sounds bad, but actually being in it is . . . well, it's worse. Now I'm going to worry a lot more about you, Kira." Gari looked at Jason. "I'm glad you're sticking with her."

Jason hefted the carbine in his hands. "Tell your mom thanks from me for teaching me how to shoot. It came in handy."

"She'll be happy to hear that. I don't think I could handle this kind of thing too often. I'm not the hero type."

Kira shook her head at Gari. "I've heard your father say the same thing a hundred times. But Mother says when things got tough, Uncle Calu could always be counted on to stick in there and do what was needed. Aunt Alli, too. At Edinton your father led the rear guard even after he got wounded so everyone could get clear safely. Did he ever tell you that? And you know your mother's a dragon slayer, too, right? Also at Edinton. Both your parents were heroes in the war, and I bet you'd be one if you ever needed to be."

Gari grinned. "Thanks, Kira. But I knew I'd be all right. The daughterness of the daughterness wouldn't let anything happen to her honorary big brother."

"Do not start that daughterness stuff on me," Kira warned. She suddenly grabbed him in a tight hug. "I'm so glad you're all right. I tried to get up here during the fight but . . . couldn't."

"I told you, I was fine. If you had come up here they would've attacked this spot and I'd have been in more danger!" Gari rubbed his neck as he looked down the track at the broken railcars. "The Tiae and Confederation Rail Company is not going to be happy about this."

"Gari, our car was hit by I think five dragon-killers. If your mother looked at the remnants of the warheads could she tell if they'd been manufactured by her workshop or if they were knock-offs made somewhere else?"

"My mother could probably answer that by looking at a single metal splinter," Gari said. "Five? I thought I heard that many hit but didn't believe it. Those things are expensive."

"Not expensive enough, apparently!"

Gari leaned closer to Kira and Jason, lowering his voice. "My mother's working on new armor that she says should be able to stop a dragon-killer. It's not ready yet, though, so don't tell anyone."

"She should tell my mother," Kira said. "I have a feeling the daughter of Jules and Queen Sien will be eager customers for that armor."

"I'll pass that on," Gari promised. "So what are you guys going to do?"

"That's up to Colonel Anders," Kira said. "He's getting more transport arranged."

"Are you going back to Tiae?"

"No. Jason and I have a job to do at Altis. We're going to do it."

The morning was half gone, Kira leaning against a derailed railcar chewing on a jerky ration, when the first Bakre Confederation troops arrived, a column of cavalry on tired horses who had clearly been pushed hard. The Confederation cavalry's scarlet uniforms were dulled by the dust of the road, contrasting with the green of Tiae's Lancers.

She and Jason straightened up as Colonel Anders and the major in command of the Confederation cavalry joined them. The major saluted Kira, his movements stiff with shame. "Lady, my apologies on behalf of the Bakre Confederation."

Kira returned the salute and shook her head. "No apology is necessary. The Confederation can't guard every lance of train track."

"No. But we still bear responsibility for the safety of those in the Confederation. Do you know who carried out the attack?"

That was the sort of question usually directed at her mother, who was somehow expected to know everything. Kira shook her head once more. "I know Mechanics and Mages were involved. Most of the attackers seem to have been common mercenaries, though."

The major studied the holes in the armor of what had been Kira and Jason's railcar. "What did that?"

"Dragon-killers. We've collected some pieces of the warheads. If you get them to Master Mechanic Alli in Danalee she might be able to identify who made them."

The major walked over to where several of the dead attackers were laid out. Crouching, he studied them closely. "From their clothing they look like they could have come from anywhere." Spotting something, he reached down toward one of the bodies, pulling out a necklace with an ornamented disc on it. "I've seen something like this before."

Colonel Anders, Kira, and Jason came closer, looking at the angular design punched into the face of the disc. "I haven't seen that sort of thing," Kira said.

"Ah," the major said, nodding as he straightened up. "Of course you wouldn't have. I remember now. That's the sort of design they use in and around Ringhmon."

"Ringhmon," Jason said. "Haven't I heard Lady Mari talking about that place?"

"Yeah," Kira said. "She and Father have a long and unhappy history with that city. I've never been near there. It's just the sort of place to hire out mercenaries, no questions asked." Rogue Mechanics, Mages, and mercenaries out of Ringhmon. Remembering her mother's current worries, Kira spoke to both Colonel Anders and the Confederation major. "There are very likely similar groups, maybe even those who attacked us here, heading south toward Pacta Servanda."

She saw the skeptical glances the other two officers exchanged. "There are a number of possible targets that could be speculated, but there's no reason to believe more groups like this are in the field," the major began.

"I'm speaking for my mother," Kira said, drawing immediate reactions from the others. "The daughter of Jules is concerned about exactly that threat at this time. So is Queen Sien," Kira added to Colonel Anders. "The Bakre Confederation should—" Kira paused, realizing that she'd been about to say something that could have been construed as an order to the Confederation. Her mother always avoided doing that sort of thing except in the worst crisis. Better to change the wording. "The Bakre Confederation might want to consider increasing security around the border and in coastal waters to try to find and stop such groups. Tiae needs to be told the details of this attack so it can take the defensive measures it feels appropriate." There. That sounded like the sort of thing her mother would say.

Her status had suddenly shifted. Not Captain Kira. Not Lady Mechanic Kira. But the daughter of the daughter, speaking with the authority of her mother. For the first time, Kira felt that power, the thrill of it and the responsibility it held, as she waited for the two officers to respond.

The major gave Colonel Anders a startled look.

Anders nodded in reply to the unspoken question. "I was informed by Queen Sien personally that Lady Kira now has the power to speak for the daughter of Jules. Lady Kira has never before invoked such authority. She wouldn't do it without good cause. Lady, can you tell us why those groups would be heading for Pacta Servanda?"

Kira thought, trying not to appear to be hesitating. But she couldn't tell them the full truth, and she didn't want to lie. "There is something of great value, and great danger, at Pacta Servanda. Queen Sien knows as much as I do about it. Jason's and my mission is to learn information at Altis that could help neutralize the danger. That's probably why we were attacked."

"If that's the word of the daughter, it's good enough for me," the major said.

Colonel Anders nodded in agreement.

As the two officers rushed off to contact their superiors by fartalker, Kira saw Jason staring at her. "What?"

"You just seemed different for a minute," he said. "Like . . . a little like your mom."

"Sometimes I have to be," Kira said, looking again toward the wounded and dead Lancers.

Colonel Anders returned first. "I had to relay my message through the Tiae consulate in Debran. Lady . . . what exactly do I call you when you're acting in your mother's name?"

"I've always thought Kira was fine," she said.

"All right. I'm sure you're aware of this already. The border between Tiae and the Bakre Confederacy has few barriers beyond the Glenca River. Most of the fortifications that existed during the time of the broken kingdom and before have been dismantled. The border posts won't be able to find or stop a body of determined mercenaries trying to reach Pacta Servanda."

Kira nodded, looking south. "Yes. I know. Anyone trying to reach Pacta is probably going to be able to get there. That's why it was important that my mother and Queen Sien be warned."

"There's something I don't understand, though," Anders continued. "If their priority is getting to what is at Pacta Servanda, why did they devote such resources to trying to kill you and Jason of Urth instead of conserving their strength for that fight?"

"I think—" Jason began.

"Jason, don't," Kira said.

"But he might be alive!"

She shook her head at Colonel Anders. "Jason is concerned that . . . a powerful former enemy of mine is still alive even though we were told he died. I think it's more likely that those seeking what's under Pacta are concerned that we'll learn how to neutralize it before they can make use of it."

"That's possible," Anders agreed.

The sun had just passed noon when more Confederation soldiers arrived, accompanied by an armored, fully enclosed coach drawn by a team of eight large draft horses. Kira stared at the coach, wondering why she was feeling a sudden surge of panic at the idea of riding in it. Her breathing sped up, and looking down she saw that her hands were trembling.

Colonel Anders approached once more. "Your ride, Lady."

The panicky sensation redoubled. Kira, baffled by the severity of her reaction, tried to talk but couldn't.

Jason spoke up beside her. "Colonel, can I make a suggestion?"

"Of course," Anders said.

"That coach is what on Earth we'd call a threat magnet. That is, it's something that'll attract danger. If anyone else is planning to attack us, they'll assume that Kira and I are in that coach and that's what they'll hit. If they have any more of those RPGs, I mean, uh, drag-on-killers, that coach won't protect us."

Anders nodded. "What's your point?"

"That it'd actually be a lot safer if Kira and I were in the ranks with the Lancers, wearing the uniforms and helms and all, because the attack wouldn't be aimed at them."

The colonel frowned in surprise, glancing toward Bete. "Sergeant? What do you think of that?"

"I think Jason of Urth has a very good idea, sir," Bete said.

"All right. We'll do that. The coach will serve as a decoy. Get these two into uniforms."

"Yes, sir." Sergeant Bete went off to get the uniforms while Anders headed away to carry out more preparations for the ride north.

"Thank you," Kira whispered to Jason, her inexplicable panic subsiding as fast as it had bloomed. "I don't know what happened to me. Sometimes my reactions seem to go to extremes."

"I could tell you were having trouble," Jason said. "This is something new, isn't it?"

"I think I first noticed it at Pacta, after I told you guys about my vision of that thing going off."

"But during the attack you didn't freeze or panic."

"No. It's weird. Why would I be able to deal with people shooting at me but freeze in panic at the idea of being inside an armored coach?" Kira glared at the coach as if it were to blame. "This fear of confinement is getting out of hand. I'm going to deal with it."

If they'd been riding into Debran, they probably would have made it easily before nightfall. But the Confederation's local authorities, worried about danger to the daughter of the daughter and perhaps also about danger to the city itself, instead routed the cavalry column around the outskirts of Debran and into the countryside to the north. By the time they stopped, full night had fallen some time ago, and horses and humans were all thoroughly worn out.

Kira dismounted painfully, feeling the ache in her thighs and butt from the long ride. Once on the ground she staggered, wincing as she led her mount to where the horses were being unsaddled and groomed. Once there, she insisted on dealing with her mount just as the other Lancers were.

Jason, working beside her on the horse he'd ridden, couldn't help an occasional groan of pain as he moved. Knowing he wasn't as used to long rides as she was, Kira could only imagine how much he hurt.

The Confederation had rushed a field kitchen to the site, which took on the aspect of a sudden military camp with sentries on all sides. Between the surviving Lancers and the Confederation troops, Kira guessed that more than five hundred soldiers were now gathered about her and Jason.

She and Jason were sitting side by side wolfing down blessedly warm food when Colonel Anders and an unfamiliar Confederation officer approached. Kira almost fell as she hastened to her feet to meet them, wishing that whatever this was could have waited for morning.

"Lady Mechanic Kira, this is Colonel Rus of the Bakre Confederation," Anders introduced the new officer.

"It's an honor to meet the daughter of the daughter," Rus said. "My father fought at Dorcastle."

"Then it's my honor to meet you," Kira said. "Please send my mother's respects to your father."

"I would," Colonel Rus said, "but he died two years ago. The daughter of Jules sent a personal note of condolence which my family treasures. Lady, we've received some important news regarding the threat to you. At least one lightning Mage is involved. We had a plan to meet another train northwest of Debran and transfer you to that, but the rail line to Gullhaven would offer a predictable route for another ambush, especially through the mountainous areas south of the city. Even going that way by horse would run through a lot of locations that would be easy sites for more attacks. We think it'd be wiser to head for Larharbor, and meet there the Confederation warship that will take you to Altis. Even if we stay on the roads, there are many alternate routes we can take to Larharbor."

It was up to her. Lady Mechanic Kira or Captain Kira could be told to go to Larharbor instead, but not the daughter of the daughter.

Mage Nika might be there already. Or not. Mages sometimes wandered a lot if they didn't have a pressing reason to be somewhere quickly. But even if Nika was in Larharbor, Kira's parents had both been certain that Nika would no longer pose a threat to Kira. For the moment, at least, Mage Nika shouldn't be an issue.

Kira looked north, trying to remember the route toward Gullhaven. As she did so, she heard some of the horses blowing as they exchanged greetings. The horses, the cavalry. They could fight through another ambush. At a cost in lives both human and animal.

The thought of that cost decided Kira. "If in your judgment going to Larharbor offers a safer route, I agree we should head for that city instead of Gullhaven."

"Thank you, Lady," Colonel Rus said.

Anders glanced toward the armored coach. "There's another issue. I'm not a Mechanic. Could you tell me, what would happen if lightning struck that coach?"

Kira traced with her hand the movements she described. "The armor on the outside would catch the lightning bolt and conduct it through the metal wheels into the ground. Right, Jason?"

"As far as I know, yes," Jason said.

"Would there be danger to those inside?" Anders asked.

"If they were leaning against the side, maybe," Kira said. "The interior is lined with wood, right? And some sort of cushions for the seat? Those should insulate and protect anyone inside."

Anders nodded. "Then Colonel Rus and I both believe that you and Jason of Urth should ride inside that coach until we reach Larharbor. I know what happens to cavalry hit by lightning. We can't risk you being hit that way."

Kira felt panic rising and this time ruthlessly tried to tamp it down. "Sir . . ." She had to wet her mouth and swallow before she could say more. If only that blasted coach was open.

Open.

"Sir, may I . . . request . . . that the doors to the coach remain unlocked? And that I be authorized to open them at any time I feel a need to?"

Anders's expression became curious. He came closer, studying Kira's eyes. "You've got a few demons riding with you, don't you, Captain?" he said in a low voice. "From that kidnapping?"

"I think so, yes, sir."

Colonel Anders stepped back. "The doors to the coach will not be locked. You are authorized to open them at any time for any reason. I request that you don't leave them open for long or in any predictable pattern of time."

"Yes, sir," Kira said, relief flooding her. "No, sir. Thank you, sir."

"If I may," Colonel Rus said hesitantly, "standard procedure in the Confederation is for the coach doors to be locked to keep any attacker from accessing the inside."

"That won't be a concern," Anders said. "For two reasons. One is that my Lancers won't let any attacker get a hand on that coach. And the other is that if those attackers somehow manage to get that door open, they'll regret it. These two," he said, pointing to Kira and Jason, "are the ones who together held off that Imperial legion for hours until relief arrived."

"Ah, yes," Rus said, smiling. "I find your reasons compelling, sir."

Kira finally settled down to sleep, gazing morosely at the coach that would be her almost-a-prison for the next few days of travel. Worries lurked in the shadowed corners of her mind as she thought about that, about those who had fallen last night, and about future dangers and past events.

She didn't want to wake up screaming. Not in camp, with so many soldiers around. "Jason, can I ask a favor?"

He gave her a look that was slightly bleary with fatigue. "As you wish."

"What?"

"I mean, sure, anything."

"Will you sleep with me tonight?"

Jason's head jerked with surprise. "Here? With all these people . . . ?"

"I don't mean that. I mean, I need you close. Not just close by. Under my blanket, close to me tonight while I sleep. I never have those dreams when you're holding me while we sleep."

"Oh." Jason nodded. "Sure. It'll be pretty obvious that we're not doing anything but sleeping."

"Right. Thank you. I know it's asking a lot."

He grinned. "Sleep with my arms around you. Yeah, that's one terrible hardship."

"You know what I mean!" She tried to ignore the soldiers around her as she lay down on one blanket and held the other until Jason lay down beside her. Draping the other blanket over both of them, she settled back, Jason's arms about her, feeling the darkness inside and the traces of panic fleeing from that touch.

"You should be happy," Kira grumbled the next morning as they took seats, he at the front facing back and she in the back facing him. Both had been told to stay away from the sides of the coach. The inside was already stuffy and warm. Once the sun got higher it would turn into a sweatbox even if the armored baffles over the windows were cranked open.

She'd had a troubled night. No scream-inducing dreams, but the female Mage had been there, watching Kira from inside some sort of closed room like a prisoner eyeing her jailer. There hadn't been any coffee with breakfast because it been accidentally left behind when the field kitchen was scrambled to meet them out here, leading to short tempers among almost everyone and muttered threats against the cooks. Stiff and sore from the ride the day before and a night sleeping on the ground, Kira was not in a good mood.

"Why should I be happy?" Jason asked, slumping in his seat.

"We're not taking the train."

"Um . . . yeah. Or riding horses. I wasn't sure I could walk this morning."

"By noon you're going to be wishing you'd spent the entire day in the saddle," she told him.

"This world really needs a comfortable way to travel long distances," Jason grumped.

"Don't you dare complain about my world! We wouldn't be having to do this if those guys from Urth hadn't built those weapons and buried them there and set themselves up as the Mechanics Guild and caused a lot of other problems!"

Jason gave her an angry look, muttered something under his breath, and pretended to go to sleep.

She almost went after him again, but realized she was really angry at everything else that was happening. And that he was as uncomfortable and sore as she was. Rather than vent on Jason, she tried to rest even after the coach lurched into motion and began jolting along the road.

By noon, the inside of the coach felt warm enough to bake bread. Soaked with sweat, Kira tugged at her clothing, tempted to just pull it all off and never mind Jason sitting over there because no one not even a man could think about that under these conditions but no a man probably would and anyway she didn't want to expose her bare skin to the hot furnishings inside the coach. Opening the doors occasionally did little to help, since the heat was radiating from the armor surrounding the coach's interior. But even though little in the way of a breeze came through, the dust from the road managed to find its way inside and add to the misery.

She started trying to calculate how hot it would have to get to cook off the cartridges in her pistol.

Fortunately soon afterwards they entered an area where the path wound through trees whose shade provided welcome relief from the sun. The armor gradually cooled to tolerable levels of heat, and by drinking lots of lukewarm water Kira managed to keep her head clear.

Jason clearly wasn't drinking enough water, though. She shoved a canteen at him. "Drink all of that."

"I'm fine," he mumbled, obviously mimicking Kira's usual response to concerns about her.

"Not funny! Drink!"

Glowering, he complied, then flopped down, pretending to ignore her.

Why had she ever gotten involved with a teenaged boy to begin with?

Maybe they'd get ambushed again. At the moment that felt preferable to thumping along in this sweatbox with a sullen teenager.

Two sullen teenagers, she admitted to herself.

But that made her think about the Tiae Lancers and the Confederation cavalry outside the coach, about the Lancers who had died in the first ambush, about how many might die if they were attacked again. It made her angry, and frustrated, to think that others might be hurt or killed because of her. No matter what Colonel Anders said, the risks those others were running were because of her. And that just didn't feel right, couldn't ever feel right. It made her mood worsen.

The icing on the cake came when her Mage powers started getting restive, pushing at the barriers she'd built around them. Already exhausted, Kira had to devote energy to clamping down on her powers. She focused inward, trying to understand what was happening inside her and finding no answers.

A long, uncomfortable day, and another night sleeping in the open awaiting them. Kira really hoped the Confederation managed to get coffee to them before morning.

Alain of Ihris sat in the common area that provided entry to the rooms where he and Mari were staying in Pacta Servanda, as well as to the rooms housing Mage Asha and her husband, Mechanic Dav. Night had long since filled the world outside this building, leaving the room only dimly lit by the indecisive radiance from a single candle set by Alain's chair.

Not far away, Mage Asha also sat, lost in meditation.

Alain had spent most nights since arriving here sitting up at least for a while after the others had gone to sleep. Sitting up, watching for danger. His first encounter with Mari more than twenty years ago had been while a large group was trying to harm her, and that had set the pattern for their first years together. Anyone not trying to kidnap or kill Mari was probably set on killing Alain. Those sorts of threats had diminished after the defeat of the Great Guilds, but had never gone away. Alain had at one time thought that he had become accustomed to them.

But then Kira had come into their lives, a girl as headstrong as her mother but lacking the experience to understand everything required to stay alive in a world that contained many enemies. Any daughter brought her share of troubles to her parents, others had told him, but Kira had come with special concerns that had only multiplied as she inexplicably developed Mage powers along with her Mechanic skills. She was on her way to Altis. Her train had already been attacked. But she was continuing her journey, confronting problems and fighting through them as her mother's daughter would. Still, Alain knew that sometimes problems and dangers could become too much for any man or woman to triumph over.

And now Alain had others to worry about. Sino, the "Doctor" from Urth, said that all was going as well as possible for Mari and the child growing within her, and the healers of Dematr agreed. But none had warned of trouble before Kira's brother Danel died at birth long years ago. Mari only had about a month left before the child should be born, his concerns growing as the date grew closer. He could do nothing about his worries there but worry some more.

And he thought of the boy Jason, who was taking Kira from Alain as young people had been taking daughters from their fathers for as long as such things had been. But Jason had shown himself to be as worthy of Kira as any man might possibly be, and had shown as well that he understood what a remarkable gift the world had given him in her, and that he would not ever take that gift for granted. Jason already felt much like a son to Alain. He did not want to lose another son.

Kira would risk her life for Jason, and Jason for Kira, but all the devotion in the world would not stop the spell of a Mage, or the metal fired from a Mechanic weapon. Alain, remembering the moment when the bullet struck Mari at Dorcastle, had learned that all too well.

Alain had been told by others that he was wise, the only Master of Mages in the world, a man that many came to speak with to learn wisdom. But in the dark and silent marches of the night he knew the same fears as every other father knew, and felt just as helpless against them.

He glanced at Asha, wearing Mage robes just as Alain was, her eyes closed but her expression and posture speaking of meditation, not sleep. She had been company more than once during the nights, understanding his worries. Mari, and Dav, could not understand how two Mages could sit in the same room, not speaking or apparently interacting in any way, and yet be offering companionship to each other. "We learned to find friendship without showing it, or knowing what it was, in ways that others could not see. Not even other Mages," he had heard Asha explain to Dav. That was probably as good a wisdom as any to describe it.

He should probably go to bed. Sitting awake, worrying, accomplished nothing.

A faint sound came from the hallway outside the locked door to the common room.

That wasn't unusual. The guard posted in that hallway tried to remain quiet, but occasionally made some noise.

But there had been something about that sound . . .

Alain focused his Mage senses, trying to feel anything that might be amiss. Was it there, not far away? That tiny trace of something that wasn't there and should be, as one Mage hid the spell of another?

He reached over to touch Asha's hand.

Her eyes came open, instantly alert.

Alain nodded toward the door.

She looked that way, her expression intent with concentration.

Asha turned back to him, her face Mage-calm as always, and nodded once.

They stood up, making no noise, facing the door.

Using his heat spell here, amidst the wood of this building, might well start fires that would imperil Mari and the child she carried. Alain silently drew his long Mage knife from beneath his robes.

Asha drew her knife as well, the sharp blade gleaming in the weak light of the candle.

The area of the door around the lock vanished, gone as if it had never been.

Swiftly and silently, the door swung open.

CHAPTER SEVEN

Asha moved first, graceful and swift, her beauty eerie in the guttering light of the candle. Her knife swung at the area near the door, meeting something invisible that rang with the sound of metal on metal.

Two Mages became visible, knives in their hands, their concealment spells dropped so they could concentrate on the fight. One, another woman, attacked Asha while the other, a man, went for Alain, the sound of metal blades clashing abruptly filling the room.

He parried the first attack and struck back, only to have his knife turned aside and another thrust come at him which Alain narrowly avoided. Their opponents were skillful, using their knives to weave a deadly net about them.

But Asha had always been exceptionally skilled with her knife as well. She got a strike though, drawing a line of blood across her opponent's knife arm. Knowing she'd soon lose strength in that arm, the female Mage made a desperate attack. Asha deflected the blow before swinging her knife backhanded across and through the front of her opponent's neck.

Now alone, the other Mage redoubled his attacks on Alain before Asha could get to them. Falling back, Alain stumbled against a piece of furniture. The Mage leaped forward, knife poised.

The sound of a shot boomed, filling the room, the flash of light momentarily seeming to freeze the Mage in motion. A moment later he jerked sideways, spinning from the impact of the bullet and hitting the nearest wall. Rolling back to face Alain, the Mage drew back his arm to hurl his blade.

Mari fired again.

The Mage fell, lifeless.

Alain looked at Mari, standing in her bedclothes in the doorway to their bedroom, her weapon in one hand, looking awkward with the bigness of her pregnancy but also implacably deadly.

"Is that all of them?" she demanded.

"We do not know," Asha replied, heading toward the hallway, blood dripping from the knife in her hand, as Dav came out of his room also carrying a weapon.

Guards were already boiling up the stairs, alerted by the sounds of fighting and the gunshots. The guard in the hall lay lifeless, slain without knowing that enemies were near. But no other attackers were found.

"This was just a first move," Dav said as the bodies of the Mages were taken from the common area. "The next time, there'll be more of them."

The ordeal in the coach extended through two more days, finally ending late the fourth afternoon when they arrived at the main military fort inside Larharbor. Instead of a rest, though, Kira found herself trying to keep her temper as they were hustled into another enclosed carriage for an immediate trip through the city to the pier where a Confederation warship waited to sail before the sun set.

She and Jason had barely said a word to each other for at least a day.

As the carriage rattled through the streets of Larharbor, Kira felt herself reach the point at which she'd either blow up or divert the pressure. She knew what her father would tell her to do, to turn aside physical discomfort and pain, focusing on what mattered, what was real.

She finally spoke to Jason again. "I'm sorry."

He gave her a cautious, puzzled look in reply. "Huh?"

"I'm sorry," Kira repeated, speaking louder. "I just . . . this sucks. It's not your fault. I shouldn't be angry at you."

He gazed at her, his own anger visibly changing to remorse. "Yeah. I'm sorry, too. I know you're upset about the heat, and being protected like this, and—"

"What?" She stared at him. "Protected? You saw that?"

"Yeah. I've been talking to your dad, and he said some things about your mom, like during the war. He said she always fought against being protected. She thought she should run the same risks as everybody else. She still thinks that way."

"What's wrong with that way of thinking?" Kira asked.

"Nothing. But you're the same way. I can see every time you look outside at our escort."

"Jason, I'm not more important than any other Lancer out there. I can never start thinking of myself as more important than any of them. Why should they risk dying while I sit behind armor plate?"

"Because that's their job," Jason said. "Just like you have a job that means people are trying to kill you, but you do it anyway. You're not staying safe. You're trying to stay alive until the job gets done."

"That's small comfort, Jason."

"I guess."

"But you're right about me feeling guilty," she added. "I mean, it's not like this is fun. But there are people risking their lives for me, and everybody calls me Lady, and acts like I'm special, and my Mage powers are—" She stopped speaking abruptly.

Jason looked concerned. "The powers are giving you trouble again?"

"Not much. Forget it. I'm—" She cut off the phrase just a little too late.

"You're fine?" Jason asked.

"If it becomes a serious issue, I'll tell you," Kira said, getting angry again. "I promised, didn't I?"

"Yeah. Sorry. Didn't mean to push you."

"That's . . . okay," Kira muttered, knowing her use of that word would tell Jason she was trying not to stay angry.

The tension inside the carriage had mostly dissipated, but Kira was still grateful when they reached the pier and she could step out into the open air. As scuzzy as she felt, the scent of the sea and the breeze off the harbor felt almost as good as stepping into a clean bath.

Colonel Anders saluted. "Our orders are to wait at Larharbor for your return. Good luck."

"Thank you, Colonel. I hope the wait won't be too tedious."

Anders smiled. "Larharbor isn't Dorcastle, but even here Tiae cavalry gets a warm welcome. Don't worry about us."

Jason squinted down the pier. "That's our ride at the end? Nice ship."

"Yes, one of the Confederation's newest warships," Colonel Rus said proudly.

Kira took a look. Sleek lines, all metal, no masts for sails at all, just two stacks for the steam boilers that provided propulsion, and gun mounts holding the latest, deadliest designs out of the workshops of Master Mechanic Alli of Danalee.

She wished it had been a ship of the old designs, with tall masts and tight patterns of rigging and sails ready to unfurl. But the engineer in her knew that sometimes practical considerations had to take precedence over aesthetics.

They started down the pier, Confederation troops ringing them in but keeping enough distance that Kira didn't feel too claustrophobic. She breathed in the smell of the sea, which brought feelings of freedom and limitless space to her. For a moment all worries were forgotten.

"Hey, that's *The Son of Taris!*" Jason said.

Surprised, Kira looked to one side at the sailing ship tied up there. It looked just as it had the last time she'd seen the ship, in the harbor at Kelsi, except for the banner of the daughter flapping high up on one of the masts. "Hold!" she called out to the commander of the Confederation escort. "I need to go aboard this ship for a moment."

Up the gangplank and onto the wooden deck she'd once walked with bare feet. Kira stared about, surprised by how familiar it all felt.

"Hi!" Jason called from beside her, waving to the crew on deck.

Kira saw the captain and first mate coming down from the quarterdeck. "Excuse me for coming aboard unannounced, sir," she said to the captain.

He frowned at her, the same authority figure in greatcoat and boots, his beard flecked with gray adding to his aura of command. "You honor us with a visit, Lady."

"Please. I'm not Lady to you, or you," she added to the first mate.

The first mate snorted. "You owe me, girl. Tasking me with a message to the daughter of Jules herself and not warning me of who it was."

"I'm sorry, but would you have believed me? I just wanted to tell you . . . to thank you both. You helped me learn a lot about myself."

The captain gestured upward to where the daughter's banner flew. "We've been well repaid by your mother's favor. The ship and crew prosper, not that we'd be alive or afloat if not for what you did in that storm."

"How are you?" the first mate asked, eyeing Kira. "We heard some of what happened some months back. The legions, was it?"

"That was part of it," Kira admitted. "Jason and I . . . nearly didn't make it. I'm sorry we can't stay and visit. We're on a mission."

"Are you?" the captain asked. He had been watching Kira closely as well. "May an old seafarer offer advice to a young Lady?"

"Of course," Kira said.

"I had this from my captain, long ago when I was as young as you are now. He told me the best sailors are a trap. They do their jobs well. You can count on them in any situation. So you give them the important jobs. One job, they get it done and done well. Two jobs at the same time, they're still doing their best and their best is very good. Then three jobs at once, because you need those jobs done and that sailor can do it. And because that sailor is who they are, they keep doing it all. Until one day that good sailor cracks like a mast under too much strain."

The captain nodded to Kira, his eyes concerned. "That's the trap. That you reward that good sailor by piling him or her with so many important jobs that they break under the burden. It's all too easy to do."

Kira nodded back. "I'll remember that. I won't do that to anyone."

"It's not you doing it to someone else I worry about. It's others doing it to you, and you doing it to yourself. Because sometimes we make that trap for ourselves." He turned to gesture toward the north. "You've fought a dragon, we hear. Faced down those people from Urth, fought Imperial warships and their legions, and now you're on something else. Because you're the daughter of your mother. Don't kill yourself trying to be her."

She blinked at him, surprised by the warning. "I can't be her. I'm not trying to be her."

"If you say so. Forgive me for speaking freely," the captain said.

"No. That's all right. I won't forget what you said," Kira told him. She turned as a Confederation officer came onto the ship.

"Lady, my apologies, but—"

"That's all right," Kira called back. "We'll be right there." Facing the captain and first mate again, Kira nodded and smiled to them. "If you need anything, contact my mother, or me."

Once off the ship, she tried to shake off an uneasiness raised by the captain's words. "Am I pushing it too hard?" she murmured to Jason.

"Yes," he murmured back.

"I'm serious."

"So am I. You need some rest."

Kira looked ahead at the ship they were approaching. "There shouldn't be anything to do for the next few days but rest."

As tired and distracted as she was, Kira still noticed as she boarded the Confederation warship that a whistle shrilled and a new banner was hauled up a halyard to flap in the breeze. She paused to look up at it, puzzled. "Why did you raise my mother's banner?"

The ship's officer on the quarterdeck shook his head. "That's not your mother's banner, Lady. It's yours."

"It's . . . what?" Kira took another look. The same blue field on the flag, but instead of a large multi-pointed gold star in the center, the banner had a smaller gold star up in the right top corner. "I don't have a banner."

"We were informed that you do," the officer replied.

"Jason!"

"I didn't know anything about this," he replied, gazing up at the banner. "It's kind of cool, though, isn't it?"

"No, it's not cool! It's ridiculous! Why do I need a banner? Why are you flying that?" Kira demanded of the ship's officer.

"Lady, we were ordered to do so."

"How can I have a banner and not even know I have a banner?"

The officer spread his hands helplessly. "I don't know how it works, Lady."

Kira's sense of humor came to her rescue. "I guess that makes two of us who don't know how it works. I'm sorry. It's obviously not something you decided to do. But . . . Jason, we need to find out how this happened."

The ship's captain, a woman with the weathered skin of someone who had formerly spent much time at sea on open ships, greeted them warmly, but politely declined when Kira asked that the banner be hauled down, saying that the orders on that didn't allow any discretion. "I was informed that a council of ministers agreed that your banner should be of that design and it should be flown to indicate your presence."

"A council of ministers." Kira shook her head, too tired to argue further. "Captain, I apologize for asking, but Jason and I are very tired from the trip here. Is there any chance we could get a quick meal and then be allowed to pass out for the night?"

"Lady, I'm at your command," the captain said. "Let's get you to your staterooms."

They were small but decent, accommodations on a ship intended for war, not passengers. Kira's was across the narrow passageway from Jason's. She felt a sudden tension as she walked into hers, the nautical fittings and metal about her pulling up ugly memories of the Imperial ship where she'd been confined by Prince Maxim. Kira spun about to assure herself that the hinges on the door were on the inside, accessible to her. The porthole in one wall was sealed but covered only by a curtain, the metal protective plate swung down and unlocked.

Kira breathed in and out slowly, telling herself that this was different, that she was in no danger here, that this was not a prison.

"Are you okay?" Jason murmured nearby.

"Not entirely," she whispered back. "Stay in here with me while we eat."

"Sure."

"I'm sorry. I'm so tired and this room feels a little—" Kira stared, trying to figure out how she'd gotten to the door, her hand on the latch to open it. "What happened?"

"I don't know," Jason said carefully. "You suddenly stopped talking and lunged for the door, but then you stopped moving."

"How long? How long was it from the time I stopped talking to when I asked you what had happened?"

"Just a few seconds."

Kira slowed her breathing. "Maybe I was just so tired I kind of passed out for a moment. Maybe it wasn't a blackout."

"Maybe," Jason said. "It was real quick. I'm as tired as you are, and I feel like I'm going to pass out on my feet."

"I hope we're right."

The food wasn't fancy, but it was better than the cavalry got. When they were done, Kira asked Jason to wait just outside for a moment while she closed the door.

Deep breaths. Calm. She was among friends. Jason was nearby. *Don't black out. Don't black out. Please.*

Nothing. Maybe getting some food had made the difference. Sighing with relief, she opened the door again and nodded to Jason to show him it was all right. "Thanks."

A guard also stood in the passageway, looking nervous over this unfamiliar responsibility. Not someone to keep her from escaping, but someone to ensure no one hurt her. Kira smiled and nodded to the guard, letting the sailor know his presence was welcome and his work appreciated, then shut the door again.

She fell asleep to the sounds of the ship getting underway.

The next morning, Kira got out her change of clothes and walked down the passageway to the officer's head, where a small shower stall offered a means of getting clean. She scrubbed her hair and body for a long time, reveling in the feeling of cleanliness. As she got out, she found one of the female officers waiting to use the shower. "I'm sorry," Kira said.

"We often have to wait in line," the officer replied cheerfully.

But as Kira got dressed, she saw the officer's eyes lingering on the twin parallel scars on Kira's shoulder, the marks of dragon claws. Even here she couldn't blend in. And once Kira had finished dressing, the bullet scar on her neck was still visible to anyone.

"Four days," the captain told Kira at dinner that evening. "It'll take four days to reach Altis."

Even though Kira felt like hiding in her stateroom, she knew she had to socialize with the crew. It was one of the things her mother had always emphasized, to treat others courteously. "The measure of who you are," Mari had told her, "is how well you treat people you don't have to treat well."

Which was why she and Jason sat in the wardroom, eating dinner with the officers and making polite conversation. She would've felt a little out of place in her Mechanics jacket but for the presence of five other Mechanics assigned to the ship to supervise various pieces of equipment.

The meal was interrupted by the arrival of a sailor. "High priority far-talker message," the captain apologized to Kira before reading it. "Hmmm. I think you should see this."

Kira took the paper, reading. "The old emperor is dead." She heard the shifting of the others in the wardroom as they reacted to the news.

"Do you think it's true?" the captain asked her.

"He's been ailing for some time," Kira said. "And the death was announced by Camber."

"I saw that. Who is Camber?"

"He's . . . he was . . . the emperor's closest, most trusted assistant. Very low profile, but one of the most powerful people in the Empire. I don't think he'd lie about the emperor being dead."

"You know him?"

"I've met him," Kira said, before realizing how casual that had sounded. Sure. The daughter of the daughter, hanging out with the most powerful people in the Empire. "When the ship from Urth came to Tiae, he led the Imperial delegation," she explained, "so I was introduced to Camber, and Mother told me a bit about him."

One of the older male officers made a soft exclamation that caused Kira to look at him. "Your pardon, Lady," he said. "It's just . . . hearing you say Mother and realizing you meant the daughter herself. You must have had a remarkable childhood."

Kira decided the safest way to answer that was by saying as little as possible. "Yes. Remarkable." To avoid saying anything else, she read further. "Oh. Princess Sabrin has proclaimed herself empress. That's good."

"Is it?" the captain asked.

Kira paused, aware of how the captain and the other ships officers were listening, intent on her every word. Whatever Kira said would be repeated, and written down, and surely transmitted by far-talker back to the Bakre Confederation. Because she was the daughter of the daughter. She was supposed to know what her mother knew, and what her mother felt, and what her mother wanted. At the moment, she felt more like an awkward teen than a polished diplomat.

She took a moment to choose the right words. "I think so. I've personally encountered Sabrin. She's strong, but, I think, not eager to resort to war. She prefers . . . other methods of competition."

The captain nodded, her eyes on Kira. "Sabrin is part of the Imperial court, though. There are a lot of lurid stories about the court."

"A lot of those stories are true," Kira said. "But Sabrin said she'll change that. She told me the court was weak because it rewarded betrayal of all kinds."

"She told you?"

Why did everything she said sound either stupid or like a boast? "We've met. As I said."

"When the Urth ship came?" another officer asked.

"No, it was . . . later." Oh no. That sounded like Sabrin had been involved with the kidnapping. "She wasn't part of any . . . ummm . . . actions against me."

"Do you think this will lead to more Imperial aggression? An attempt by Sabrin to solidify power by getting her rivals to back her against an external enemy?"

The captain must have been fed those questions by higher-ups in the Confederation. Kira felt as though she was being interrogated. Politely, but clearly being pumped for information. "I don't think so," Kira said. "Sabrin has already lined up a lot of support. Now as empress she'll deal with internal opponents who don't fall into line. And then I expect her to push Imperial technological advances, and Imperial plans to colonize the Western Continent."

"The Western Alliance will want to know about that," one of the other officers remarked.

"It's a *big* continent," Kira said. "Bigger than the one we're on. The Empire is planning to send their ships east, to colonize the side of the continent opposite where the Western Alliance will be when it sends ships west." She knew her mother was already talking to both the Empire and the Western Alliance, as well as other powers, about how to divide up the Western Continent in ways that didn't result in war. It seemed absurd to imagine fighting over the vast new areas when they couldn't be filled for centuries, but as Mari had told her, people had done stranger and even stupider things. "The Western Alliance already knows that," Kira added. "My mother . . . the daughter . . . is already working with all countries to establish areas on the Western Continent for each power that wants to colonize there."

"Nobody else is there?" one of the Mechanics asked. Not much older than Kira, he must have been trained—like her—in the time since the old Guild had fallen apart, the remnants confined to the Empire.

"Not that we know of."

"We didn't spot any human habitation from orbit," Jason said. "No cities or towns or signs of farms or anything else. I mean, in the initial surveys when my ship got here."

Kira felt attention recenter on Jason. Grateful for the distraction from herself, she also watched to ensure no one ganged up on him. Word had gotten around that the people from Urth on Jason's mother's ship had been arrogant and greedy.

"What's that like?" the captain asked. "Being up that high in a ship? I mean, does it feel like a ship?"

"Not like this," Jason said, using one hand to illustrate a rocking motion. "Or like being on a Roc. It's very stable. Unless we were under high acceleration, we couldn't even feel the ship being moved. It was sort of like floating, I guess, floating above the planet where nothing could move us around."

"Isn't it frightening?" another Mechanic asked. "Being that high up?"

"Not really. You're in a ship designed to do that, so it's no more scary than being out on the ocean in this ship. You know as long as nothing goes wrong you're fine."

"Urth's a lot different, I heard."

Jason paused, his expression troubled. "The technology is different. We didn't have the Mechanics Guild suppressing things like you guys did. And that . . . It can be a challenge . . . I guess . . . to remember what's important. Kira can tell you I didn't understand a lot of things when I got to this world. But I chose to stay. I like it here. You guys . . . you know things that I think Earth is having trouble remembering. Not technology. But the stuff inside us, that tells us who we should be."

They liked hearing that, Kira saw. She liked hearing it whenever

Jason said it. The affirmation that while Urth had technology Dematr did not, Dematr had some things to be proud of nonetheless.

"We knew you'd found something here you liked," another officer commented, with a smile and a glance at Kira.

"My father says that destiny brought us together," Kira said, embarrassed.

The captain smiled. "So there weren't any diplomatic considerations involved?"

Kira gave the captain a puzzled look. "Diplomatic? What could . . . ?" She remembered some things she'd overheard Imperials saying. "Are you talking about my mother and Urth? Like this is some sort of arrangement?" The idea seemed too ridiculous to be serious. Like the Imperial belief that Jason was a demon brought from Urth to partner her as the daughter of darkness.

But no one jumped in to deny the idea, instead watching her and Jason closely.

"No," Kira said as calmly as she could. "No. My mother wouldn't do that. Even if it was some diplomatic thing that could have happened, it wouldn't have happened. *I* wouldn't do that. Why would I do that?"

Some of the officers exchanged looks. "To keep Dematr safe," one suggested in the manner of someone repeating a common belief.

"What, like I'm sacrificing myself to save the world?" Kira asked. "By going to a wedding bed instead of holding the wall like my mother did?" She felt her anger building, barely able to keep it under check, hearing her voice tremble. "Stars above, who could think such a thing? Who could think such a thing of *me?*"

She'd thought it was bad that the Imperials believed her to be an unnatural offspring of her supposedly undead mother, but at the moment that paled before the idea that others thought she'd be traded like a commodity, that her body and self could be currency for a political deal.

Silence had fallen in the wardroom, the officers and Mechanics avoiding her gaze.

The captain stood up, coming to attention, her tones formal. "Lady Mechanic Kira, dragon slayer, and we understand Captain of Lancers for your valor against the Imperial legions, please permit me to apologize in the strongest possible way on behalf of everyone present for the thoughtless words uttered here. No one should question your dignity or purpose. It was ill-considered and impolite to suggest your impending marriage is the product of anything but the love and commitment you feel toward each other."

Kira got her anger under control. She knew what her mother and father would expect her to do. She hoped that wasn't the only reason she was doing it. Kira took a long, deep breath before standing as well. "Captain, I accept your apology on behalf of you and the others here. I do not for one moment believe that there was any ill intent or . . . disrespect intended. Forgive me for having difficulty dealing with something I was unprepared for. I know that being who I am, the daughter of the daughter, makes me a bit different in the eyes of everyone. But I hope you all will understand that in many ways I'm like everyone. My mother and father raised me to be like everyone, no different and certainly no better. Please . . ." She fought for the right words, looking down and over at Jason, who was watching her with a somber expression. "Please do not doubt my love for Jason. It was hard-earned by him, and couldn't be better justified. He is of Urth only by name now. He has no other connection. And when we are married he will be fully of Dematr, and will defend this world as strongly and bravely as any of us born to it."

She sat down, feeling awkward and tongue-tied, wondering if she'd made a fool of herself. But the officers and other Mechanics stood, and with slow, rhythmic claps applauded her words.

And after telling everyone how like everyone else she was, her Mage powers naturally chose that moment to surge outward. Kira hid her inner struggle under the guise of modesty, looking down at her lap, as she fought to confine them again, grateful that there weren't any Mages aboard who might detect her unruly powers.

★

She pulled Jason into her cabin when they got back from dinner. "Stars above, how was I? Did they really think I apologized well?"

He nodded, smiling. "I know I did. Man, I was sitting there listening to you talk about politics and what the Empire was doing and all and thinking what an amazing girl you are."

"Oh, yeah," Kira scoffed. "Amazing. They actually seemed to think it was somehow great of me to give myself away to defend Dematr by becoming your wife! Why didn't they see how insulting that was?"

"It would've been a big sacrifice," Jason said, then laughed to show he meant it as a joke. "I mean, if you didn't like me."

"Jason, how could I ever like someone I was forced to marry as part of a deal?"

"I don't know," Jason said, his laughter dying. "Is that sort of thing common on this world? I haven't heard much about it."

Kira waved an angry hand. "Oh, there are always powerful families that want their kids to marry into other powerful families. Combining fortunes and influence. In the Imperial court, who ends up with who is almost always about politics. That's why they kept trying to get me to marry one of their princes, and why Maxim kidnapped me. And the old Mechanics Guild wanted Mechanics to marry other Mechanics instead of commons but didn't insist on it."

"What about Mages?"

She stared at him. "Mages? Mages didn't marry. Have we never talked about that?"

"I guess not. I know people didn't like them."

"No. They . . . we never talked about that?" Kira sighed. "Mages . . . you know they were taught that other people didn't really exist. Just shadows, who didn't matter. And any sort of feelings or emotions were wrong. So they were never supposed to marry, not even other Mages. And if they wanted sex, they were either supposed to have meaningless physical encounters with other Mages, or else they were supposed to . . . take a common person and use them."

"Rape?" Jason stared at her. "A lot?"

"Yeah. People hated them. They feared them, but they also hated them. Because that's what Mages were taught was all right to do to people. I guess that's why no one talks about it much, except people who still hate all Mages, and there aren't nearly as many of those people as there used to be."

Jason shook his head, bewildered. "I can't believe your father—"

"*I'm not talking about my father! How could you think I'm talking about my father?*"

He flinched back from her. "But you said—"

"Father was taught that but he never did it! Even before he met Mother he still felt it was wrong even though he'd been told it was all right!" Kira calmed herself with some effort. "Jason, if he'd tried to force himself on Mother when they met, she'd have . . . well, maybe she wouldn't have *killed* him. Probably would have. But she never would have fallen in love with him. Never."

"Yeah, that's what I figured," Jason said. "But I can see why you guys don't talk about that."

Kira sat down in the one chair the narrow cabin boasted. "Do you think they believed me? That you and I are marrying for love and nothing else?"

"I believed it!"

"Yeah, well, you'll believe anything I say. What can we do to show them that's how we feel? I mean, that doesn't involve those public-affection displays like we had to put on in Tiaesun that time."

Jason flinched again at the memory. "Just be nice to each other, I guess."

"I have to be nice to you?" Kira pretended to complain.

He grinned. "Only if you want to."

She got up and put her arms about him, managing a smile at Jason. "Maybe I could have fallen for you even if it had been some arranged deal."

Jason shook his head. "No. If it had been arranged, if you thought you were being forced into it, you never would have given me a chance. I'd have been dead to you. Forever."

"Ummm . . . yeah, actually that's true. I wouldn't have given you a chance. You do know me, don't you? Are you sure you want to marry me?"

"Yeah," Jason said. "But I thought you thought I wanted to marry you because I was delusional and wasn't seeing the real you."

"Oh, I'm still certain that you're delusional," Kira said, looking into his eyes. "But your delusion has shifted. Now you know who I really am, but you're delusional enough to think you can live with that."

He smiled at her. "How could I ever live without it?"

There were times when being able to tell with certainty whether or not people were lying or telling the truth, Mage skills her father had taught her, had brought Kira no joy. But this time, being able to see with absolutely surety that Jason meant every word was a very good thing. She hugged him tight, laughing softly.

"What's so funny?" Jason asked, his lips near her ear.

"That's not *something's funny* laughing," she said softly into his ear. "That's *stars above I'm so happy* laughing. I love you."

Kira wished that somehow this moment would never end, that she would always be this happy. But in a few more days they'd be at Altis.

Early on a crisp, sparkling morning, Kira stood with Jason along the portside railing of the warship as it entered the harbor of Altis. Rocky headlands that protected the harbor slid past on either side, new cannon having replaced the ballistae that once fortified the headlands against attack.

She'd been afraid of being bored on the trip, but instead regretted that she wouldn't have more time to visit with the Mechanics aboard and learn about their work. Jason seemed to have enjoyed that as well.

"That's where your mother sank a Mechanics Guild ship," a passing officer told Kira, pointing off to port.

"Thank you," Kira called in reply. "But as my mother would be the first to tell you, it was my father who set that ship afire with his heat spell." She sighed as the officer hurried onward. "You know, Jason, I used to think Mother encouraged people to think she'd done everything. But she always tells people how important Father was and the specific things he did. People don't want to hear it, though. He was the helper, she was the hero. That's what they're comfortable with."

"And your father's comfortable with it, I guess," Jason commented, leaning on the rail. "That takes a big person."

"What about you?" Kira murmured.

He knew what she meant. Except for brief bursts of interest, attention had remained centered on her during the voyage. "I'm okay. As long as you think I'm special."

"It's not fair."

"Life ain't fair. Some big ancient philosopher on Earth said that. Plato, maybe. Or Heinlein. One of those people."

Kira looked out over the harbor, uncomfortable talking about it and deciding to change the subject. "Aunt Alli says, when Father set the Mechanics Guild ship on fire it lit the whole harbor. It was at night. And the high city up there was burning because the Guild assassins had done so much damage. I guess the low port didn't get damaged too much. But Alli says it was quite a sight."

"And Altis was cool with that?" Jason said. "Like, okay, you're the daughter of Jules so no problem if you trash our city and harbor?"

"Pretty much, yeah. They were so desperate for freedom, Jason. Some cities to the south had already suffered bad rioting. People were finally losing all hope." Kira looked up at the high city looming above the harbor on its plateau against the inland mountains. "Mother gave them hope."

"And then she gave them freedom."

"A lot of people did that, as Mother will also be the first to tell you," Kira said. "Without them, the daughter of Jules couldn't have accomplished anything but dying."

"Kira, is everything okay right now?" Jason asked cautiously. "Have there been any more problems since that first time on the ship?"

"No," Kira said. "Once I was rested, that problem seemed to go away."

"That problem?"

Oh, blazes. Why had she said it that way? "My Mage powers keep trying to break out," Kira admitted. "I have to keep tamping them down. I'm trying to make their, um, cage smaller so I can make the barriers around it stronger. That's how I think of it."

He nodded, obviously worried but not pushing it. "That's sort of funny, huh? You're so worried about being confined, but you keep trying to build a stronger cage for your powers."

He was joking. She could tell. But Kira felt a jolt of anger at the statement. "It's not the same thing. Not even close."

He heard the edge in her voice and dropped the subject.

At the pier, what looked like a half-troop of cavalry from Altis's small army waited along with a group of dignitaries. Kira tried not to grimace as she spotted "her banner" being carried by one of the cavalry. After a quick series of farewells, she left the ship, meeting the officials on the pier.

One of them, an officer, jerked in surprise as Kira got close. "Is there anything wrong?" Kira asked.

"No! I'm sorry," the officer apologized. "I'd heard you looked a lot like your mother, but I was startled to see how much you resembled her as she was when I met her on her first trip to Altis. I'm Colonel Patila, commander of the Altis High City garrison. If there's anything you need, ask and you'll get it."

"Patila," Kira repeated. "Mother reminded me about you before I left, and how you'd been among the first to help her. Thank you. She sends her best."

Colonel Patila smiled broadly. "That's just like the daughter, to remember me. Major Char commands this detachment, which will escort you to the tower of the librarians." She indicated a solemn-looking major, who nodded in greeting. "Since we were told your mission is an urgent one, they're ready to leave immediately."

"Maybe we'd be a little less conspicuous if they weren't carrying that," Kira suggested, pointing to her banner.

"I have orders," Colonel Patila said, sounding apologetic once more.

"Everybody has orders," Kira muttered, focusing her attention on a government official who had hurried up. "What's wrong?"

"We have word from Tiae," the official advised breathlessly. "Via a Mage message. There was an assassination attempt on the daughter and her Mage at Pacta Servanda. Both assassins were killed. Your parents are fine."

Kira nodded, relieved. "Thank you. Could you send a reply for me? Just let them know we're here safely at Altis and on our way to the tower."

"Of course. I'm . . . surprised you're taking this news so calmly!"

"Oh, it happens all the time." Kira noticed the official staring at the scar on her neck. "I'm just glad that they're all right."

"We don't know what we'd do without the daughter," the official said. "If anything happened to her . . ."

Kira hesitated, trying to find the right words. "You'd do all right. Mother tells me that all the time. Without others, without good, strong people willing to do what's right, she couldn't do anything." Kira pointed up to the city that looked down on the port. "Mother has told me about Altis, about the fight here. Mother says she never would have survived the attacks of the Mechanics Guild assassins if not for the help of the people of Altis, and friends of hers like Sir Mechanic Dav, Lady Mage Asha, and Master Mechanic Alli. Friends like Colonel Patila!" Kira added, turning back to face the colonel, who smiled again.

"Thank you," Patila said. "The day will come when the daughter leaves us. We all know that. But I'll be the first to admit that it's reassuring to know the daughter of the daughter seems to share many of her mother's gifts."

Did no one ever listen? Kira looked at Jason, who replied with a look that showed he understood her frustration. She returned a polite nod to the colonel and the other officials. "We should get going."

The column of cavalry had to take the winding road that led up from the low port on the harbor to the high city above. As they neared the top, about to enter the city, Kira turned in her saddle to look back at the harbor spread out before her, the sight as spectacular as she remembered from her last visit to Altis years before.

She saw a large sailing ship that had been fitted with steam propulsion as well, the stack rising from the deck between the masts with their sails, a common enough thing in a world still trying to cope with the kind of change that had been banned for centuries. A breeze caught the flag on the ship, revealing enough of the colors for Kira to see that it was an Imperial-flagged vessel, from the look of it a passenger ship carrying many people. There wasn't anything unusual about that, either. The ship bore no visible weapons, no sign of threat, nothing to mark it as unusual.

But Kira stared at it, wondering why her Mage senses had suddenly begun jangling in warning as soon as she laid eyes on it. Anyone who was on that ship was well behind them and couldn't be a danger to her or Jason on their way to Altis.

CHAPTER EIGHT

The once-narrow, hidden road inland to the secluded valley where the tower of the librarians stood had been widened and improved in the decades since the fall of the Great Guilds. Kira remembered the last of that work still underway during her last visit, carving a broader road out of the living rock as the path wove along the flanks of mountains. Off the road, the terrain was extremely rugged and rarely level. Kira glanced to the side as the cavalry column rode, thinking of her mother and father struggling though that rocky maze before they discovered the secret road of the librarians.

This was so much better, riding a mount so well trained she barely had to touch the reins. She saw Jason using his, perhaps employing a bit more force than he had to, and resolved to spend more time teaching him to handle a mount in the gentlest way possible, and primarily with seat and legs rather than bridle.

One of the officers riding near Kira and Jason dropped back slightly. "Is everything well, Lady Mechanic?"

"We're fine," Kira said. "You can call me Captain instead. We're all soldiers here."

"Very well, Captain. I'm Vanza. Also a captain as you see," she said with a smile. "Let us know if you or your man need anything."

Kira noticed Jason smiling as Vanza rode a little ways ahead. "What?"

"It's just cool being your man," Jason said.

"It's only fair since I'm your lady." She looked around at the rough terrain again. "The last time I rode this way, I never expected that the next time I went to see the librarians I'd be engaged. Or that I'd have escort like this."

"You didn't have a big escort?"

"No. It was just me and a half-dozen bodyguards."

"Why'd your parents send you here alone?"

"Officially," Kira said, "I was told that time away from them would do me good and let me establish my independence. At the time, I was sure Mother and Father actually thought some time away from me would do *them* good. But since then I've decided they really needed me someplace safe while they did something else dangerous related to the daughter's business."

"Some secret mission?" Jason asked. "And they didn't tell you?"

"Back then? No!" Kira looked ahead, trying to remember that eternity of a few years before. "Mother didn't talk about it because she was trying to shield me from having to get involved in the daughter's work. And back then I wouldn't ask, because anything related to what my mother did was just a reminder of how pathetic I was compared to her."

"Yeah, but only a half-dozen guards and on your own. Weren't they worried about you running off to find yourself or something?"

"Find myself? What does that mean? How can anyone have to find themselves?"

"It's an expression," Jason said. "It's about understanding yourself, I guess. Figuring out who you really are and what you really want."

"Oh. All right. Anyway, I might have been a terror at home, but I was smart enough to know that running off would be crazy." She smiled at Jason. "That was before this guy from Urth showed up and convinced me to run away with him."

"I don't remember it happening quite like that," Jason said. "Didn't you actually insist on running away with me?"

"Wow. That is both technically accurate and really, really wrong," Kira said.

They had to stop for the night at a place where a broad area had been carved out for camping, roughly midway on the journey from the city to the tower. As they ate, Kira hailed the officer she'd spoken with earlier. "Captain Vanza! Can I ask you something?"

"Certainly," Vanza said.

"Am I right in remembering that there used to be a lot more travelers on this road? I seem to recall that when I was here last we met a lot more other people coming from the tower back to the city, and saw more traveling toward the tower at the same time as we were."

Vanza nodded, taking on the guarded look of someone who thought she had to watch her words. "That is so, Captain. There are much fewer travelers these days."

"Why? Do you know?"

"I only know what's been spoken of," Vanza cautioned. "I . . . understand that the daughter of Jules is a close friend of the librarians. I wouldn't want to offend her daughter."

Kira frowned. "My mother asked me to check on what the librarians were doing. She wants to be sure they're still open to visitors."

"If you want my candid opinion—"

"I do."

"They're not nearly as open as before," Vanza said. "It didn't happen all at once. Just gradually. I remember the fuss when they announced they wanted people to send ahead for approval to visit, but we thought that made sense since the crowds in their valley could get large at times. But it seems fewer and fewer people are getting approval."

"What about talking to Urth? On the Feynman unit?"

"I don't know," Vanza said. "I've never met anyone who has. What's that like, if I can ask?"

"I've never used it myself," Kira admitted. "But Mother says it's like a far-talker. You don't get an immediate reply, though. It takes hours for them to hear our message, and hours for their reply to reach us."

"Why so slow?"

"That's really incredibly fast," Jason said. "Radio, I mean, far-talker, signals travel at the speed of light. A message sent that way would take

years to reach Earth. The Feynman unit uses a form of quantum inter-
action to send a message much, much faster than the speed of light."

Vanza shook her head. "I'm just a simple cavalry trooper. All I
know are far-talkers and carbines and pistols. And horses, which aren't
so simple, I guess."

After Vanza had left, Kira stared out into the night. The mountains
hemmed them in, but above their dark peaks the stars shone down
brilliantly. "Do you think Urth will tell you what we need to know?"
she asked Jason.

"I don't know."

"Jason, what are you not saying?"

"Man, I keep forgetting you can do that!" He shook his head. "I
don't have a warm and fuzzy feeling. That's all. Things just don't feel
right. Maybe I'm just nervous about talking to people on Earth. But
I'm going to do my best."

Late the next day they reached the valley, the road coming out high
on a mountain wall and descending in switchbacks to the valley floor
below. The tower stood out clearly, its gray permacrete gleaming in the
sun. Seeing it, Kira felt a chill, reminded of the permacrete protecting
the facility buried under Pacta Servanda.

When they reached the short bridge spanning a river that coursed
through the valley, the column halted. Kira gestured to Jason and they
rode to the front, seeing Major Char talking to a pair of librarians who
were blocking the road. "Is there a problem?" she asked.

One of the librarians gave her a dismissive glance, saw the Mechanics jacket, and decided to answer. "Visitors, especially such a large
group, require advance approval."

"We have approval," Kira said.

"We received no notice that you were coming," the second librarian
said.

"Yes, you did. I was present when my mother spoke by far-talker
to Coleen, head of the librarians, to tell her we were coming. Coleen
didn't indicate there'd be any problem."

"Your mother?"

Kira felt her temper rising again, and wondered why she seemed to be getting angry faster and easier these days. But she kept her voice civil. "My mother, Lady Master Mechanic Mari of Dematr, the daughter of Jules."

"You're Kira," one of the librarians said in sudden recognition.

Just "Kira." No titles. It seemed her mother was right, that the librarians were seeing her as the young girl she'd been on her last visit. Kira decided to let that ride so she could learn how the librarians treated her. "And this is Jason of Urth, who requires immediate use of the Feynman unit."

"We will notify Coleen. If you will wait—"

"We've been riding for two days," Kira said. "The hour is late. These soldiers still have to make camp. We'll proceed to the visitor camp while you talk to Coleen."

Kira rode forward, Jason staying with her, and the librarians hastened to one side rather than physically block her. The cavalry column followed, along the winding path toward the tower and the outbuildings near it.

Once there, the cavalry rode onto the open grassy area between the buildings and bounded on another side by the stream. "We're informed that the visitor rooms are unsafe at the moment," Major Char told Kira after speaking to some more librarians. "I don't see any point in pressing the issue, since it's temperate enough this time of year in the valley that sleeping outside with our mounts will be no hardship."

"Do you have enough food?" Kira asked, irritated by this latest snub and trying not to show it. Looking around, she could see a few more visitors already camping outside, and off to one side a pair of Mages who were sitting separately, ignoring each other as well as everyone else.

"Our wagons have enough feed for troopers and mounts, and we have all the water we need right there in the stream. We'll be fine, Lady Mechanic Kira."

"Let me know the instant you need something that the librarians won't provide," Kira told him. "Come on, Jason. Let's see how soon you can make that call."

At the entrance to the tower, Kira was surprised to see more librarians standing sentry in their robes. "We need to see Coleen, and use the Feynman unit."

These librarians didn't seem surprised by her arrival. But they shook their heads. "Coleen is tied up in an emergency meeting," one said.

"What about the Feynman unit?"

"That is not accessible at this time." The librarian seemed genuinely unhappy to be telling Kira that. Had there also been some disapproval when Coleen's unavailability was mentioned? "You and Jason of Urth are welcome to stay in our guest rooms and use the dining facility as you wait."

Kira and Jason followed one of the librarians to an outbuilding, constructed at the same time as the tower with a similar, nearly impervious permacrete exterior. New electric lights had been strung in some places to replace the original lighting, which had lasted for centuries but was finally failing. When they reached the two rooms given them, Kira stopped the librarian before he could leave. "Is anything wrong? Are you unhappy about something?"

The librarian hesitated before shaking his head. "No, nothing."

"Are you sure?" Kira pressed, having easily seen the lack of truth in his first response. "I'm here to make sure that everything is all right."

"It's nothing you need to worry about. Some internal debate over policies, that's all," the librarian assured her.

Kira waited until the librarian left before speaking to Jason. "He was a lot more upset about that internal debate than he admitted to. And look at this! The guest rooms are unsafe for the cavalry, but we've got two, no problem. There don't seem to be any other visitors in this building."

"I think I heard someone else," Jason offered. "But, no, it's not anything like crowded. I guess we should get some dinner?"

"We'll eat with the cavalry," Kira said.

"Should we insist they be given some of these rooms?"

"No. Major Char didn't want to make a big deal over it. I'm going to respect his wishes."

The soldiers' meal was basic but filling, beans and rice leavened by peas. Back in the guest area afterwards, Kira looked at the wide bed in her room. "Great. We've got a room. But the librarians told Mother there's old recording equipment in these buildings."

"Surveillance devices," Jason said. "Yeah."

"So even if you could trust me to be aware when I said yes, we couldn't do anything without being overheard."

"You are yourself right now, aren't you?" Jason asked. "Because you seem to be."

Kira shrugged. "Yeah. I think I am. Nothing's happened since maybe that first night on the ship."

Jason shook his head. "You seemed yourself that other time. Kira, I don't want that badly enough to risk hurting you or our future."

She sat down on the bed, trying to smile at him. "I got the kind of man I wanted. But it looks like a pretty cold and lonely future at this point."

"We'll find the answer," Jason said.

Kira could tell he wasn't really as certain of that as he tried to sound, but the fact that he wasn't pressuring her but instead giving her the room and time she needed made his concern all the more meaningful. "Yes. And then we'll make up for lost time."

After Jason went to his own bed, she lay unsleeping for a while in her darkened room despite being tired, fuming over this one more reason to be unhappy with the librarians even though it was the one thing that had happened so far that the librarians couldn't control. She couldn't let her frustration with them affect her tomorrow.

Her Mage senses tried to reach out, tried to sense those two Mages she'd seen earlier.

She shut them down viciously, pouring her disappointment into that effort.

★

The next morning, head librarian Coleen still wasn't available. Neither was the Feynman unit. "Others have been promised use of it," librarian Wil explained to Kira. "There is a precedence order."

"My mother told Coleen how important it was that Jason call Urth," Kira said.

"We appreciate that, Kira," Wil said, somehow sounding simultaneously understanding and condescending.

Determined not to overreact, Kira took Jason to the tower, hoping to encounter Coleen somewhere, but found many routes through the tower blocked, including that leading down to the room where a lot of original equipment from the great ship was kept safe. All of it but the Feynman unit hadn't worked for a long time, but it was protected.

She finally gave up and went to lunch, trying not to let her unhappiness spoil her appetite.

"So," Jason said, trying to cheer her up, "you're birthday is coming up."

"Hurray," Kira muttered.

"Eighteen. An adult. What are we going to do to celebrate?"

"Probably sit in a room unable to risk touching each other," Kira said. "While we still wait to get access to that Feynman unit."

"Mari?"

It took Kira a moment to realize that querulous call had been aimed at her. She turned to see who had spoken, standing up as she saw an elderly woman in the suit of an Imperial scholar. "I'm not Mari," Kira said politely. "I'm her daughter, Kira."

"Oh." The woman laughed lightly. "I should have realized! Mari would be older now, wouldn't she? Just like I am. But you look so much like her, just like she did when she first came to the University."

"The university?" Kira prompted, trying to overcome the wariness she felt around any Imperial.

"The University of Marandur in Marandur," the old woman said proudly. "Mari might have mentioned me to you. I'm Professor Wren."

"Professor Wren? Really?" Kira smiled, genuinely happy to see her, enough to lift her mood for the moment. "Yes, Mother has talked about you! You were such a help to her."

"Your mother returned that help a million times over when she convinced the emperor to lift the ban on Marandur," Wren said, tears appearing in her eyes. "If not for her, we'd still be trapped there. Oh, you look just like her! It brings back memories of those days when we had no hope of things ever getting better, but thanks to your mother and your father they did."

"Thank you," Kira said.

Professor Wren gestured toward a librarian standing nearby. "I have to get back to work," she said, sounding almost embarrassed. "They're writing down my story, as if that was important."

"Everyone's story is important," Kira said.

"Would you be available to talk later?" Wren asked hesitantly.

"How about at dinner?" Kira suggested, hoping she'd have been able to call Urth by then.

"Yes! Oh! I have something for you." Wren reached into her bag and drew out a letter. "I was told that Mari's daughter was expected to be at Altis at the same time I was and that I should give this to her." Wren smiled proudly. "It's from the office of the Empress. You see? It must be one of the first letters from her office after she became Empress! For me to carry! Such an honor."

Kira took the envelope, feeling the heft of the paper and seeing the Imperial seal on the flap. Expecting the missive to be for her mother, Kira was surprised to see her own name. "Thank you."

As Wren was led off by the librarian, Jason came closer. "Who was that?"

"One of my mother's old friends," Kira said, looking over the envelope and feeling a strange sense of foreboding.

"And what's that?"

"A letter for me from the Empress."

"Really?"

"Yeah." Kira looked around. "Are you done eating? Let's find a private place for me to read it."

"A private place outside," Jason suggested.

"All right." They finally located an unoccupied bench under some of the trees growing around the tower. A secluded spot, the only clue to others being nearby the occasional sound of a horse neighing or nickering where the cavalry was camped. Kira broke the seal and drew out the letter, seeing lines written with a firm, confident stroke and realizing that Sabrin must have penned this letter personally.

> *Lady Kira of Dematr,* it began. *I will not waste time, for I have received ill news. I am sending it to you using the sort of courier that no one will suspect of being entrusted with such important information.*
>
> *Maxim is not dead. His death was faked, and sworn to by those who have already paid the price for their falsehoods. You must take whatever precautions you deem necessary in case Maxim seeks revenge on you.*
>
> *What I say now is only for you and your mother. Maxim may still intend to seek the throne of the Empire. Civil war is possible. Your mother's backing for me would be a two-edged sword within the Empire, so I do not ask it. But her words on my behalf to those of the West could ensure that Maxim gains no support or refuge there. I have reason to believe that members of the former Great Guilds have coalesced around Maxim as their opportunity to sow enough chaos to give them a chance of regaining power.*
>
> *Before the arrests of Maxim's associates, they were heard to say that Maxim had boasted of knowing how to acquire weapons so terrible that they would ensure his victory. I do not know what he was speaking of, but perhaps you and your mother do.*
>
> *I hope that you will act with me to ensure the peace and security of the Empire and all other cities and states. I have been informed that you spoke publicly of my quality before Imperial citizens during the late conflict. You have my gratitude for that support. Be assured that if you are in need and I can be of assistance, all you must do is ask.*
>
> *Sabrin, Empress*

Beneath the signature another line had been added.

> *You did an impressive job on Maxim's flagship. I'll try not to get on your bad side.*

"What's the matter?" Jason asked anxiously.

Kira took a deep breath before answering. "Maxim isn't dead."

"What? I was right?"

"You were right. He faked his death."

"I knew it! Nobody believed me. But I was right."

"Yes. You were right." She looked around to ensure no one was close enough to hear. "Sabrin is worried about civil war within the Empire, and Maxim apparently knows about the weapons at Pacta. I need to get this letter to my mother."

"Why not call her? There's a long-distance radio here."

Why did hearing him use the Urth name for a far-talker bother her so much this time? She knew it wasn't deliberate on Jason's part. But her nerves were on edge, probably because of finding out about Maxim. "Because it's secret. Too many people might be listening in on a far-talker call."

"You guys really need to develop encrypted call technology." Jason was gazing around as well, as if worried about Maxim leaping out of concealment and personally attacking them. "He's been behind these attacks on us. That ambush of the train. There was serious muscle behind that."

"You're absolutely right. I admit it. Sabrin says Maxim was heard boasting about getting his hands on weapons that would allow him to win. She also thinks the former leaders of the Mechanics Guild and those Mages who are trying to recreate the Mage Guild are part of it. They've combined efforts. Maxim probably thinks he's using them, but they're using Maxim. Civil war within the Empire! That would be horrible."

"So how can we get that message to your mom?"

"Mages. A message Mage. Maybe one of those Mages we saw can send messages." She jumped to her feet and walked quickly toward the last place she'd seen the Mages, wishing she could risk reaching out with her Mage senses but not daring to free any of her Mage powers with other Mages so close.

The nearest Mage, sitting gazing at the mountains around the valley, ignored them as they approached. "This one has questions," Kira said.

The Mage didn't respond.

Giving him a glare, Kira walked to the other Mage, who was sitting a good distance from the first. He stood up as they approached. "Mage Saburo?" Kira asked, stunned to see him here.

Saburo nodded once. He'd been around non-Mages long enough to have learned a few basic personal-interaction skills. "This one listens."

"I'm so lucky you're here!"

"Elder Mari asked this one to come to this place. There was danger if I was seen to be helping you or traveling with you, but alone it was thought I should be able to reach this place. She said that one Kira might require *help*."

"I do," Kira said. She held up the letter. "Can you get this to my mother? Elder Mari? As quickly as possible? It's very important, and no one else should see it or read it."

"Hunter and this one will do this task." Saburo took the letter without displaying any visible interest in its contents. He placed the letter in an inner pocket of his robes before walking away without another word.

They watched him walk into an open area, then stand still. Kira felt the spell building, drawing on the power available in this area, until a giant bird appeared next to Saburo.

"Hi, Hunter," Jason said, grinning despite obviously still being a bit nervous around the Mage creature. Hunter responded by turning a single huge eye toward Jason and dipping his head slightly.

Saburo mounted the bird, Hunter spread his mighty wings, and with a leap upward the bird took to the air, climbing rapidly with every sweep of his wings.

"Good thing your mom thought ahead," Jason said as they watched the shapes of Saburo and his Roc dwindle with distance. "Now what?"

Kira turned a determined face back toward the tower. "We've been stalled long enough. The librarians need to let you speak to Urth right away. I don't care if Empress Sabrin herself reserved the next session on the Feynman unit, and I know she hasn't. If Maxim is after those weapons, they have to be neutralized or destroyed as soon as possible."

Kira simply bulled her way past the librarian watching the stairs leading up to the level where she knew Coleen's office lay. She didn't exactly remember where the office was, so let the shocked librarian run past her and watched which office the sentry dashed into. "There."

Inside, Coleen looked up, outwardly composed, but Kira could see the irritation in her. "This is improper behavior," Coleen said to Kira.

"My mother told you how important it was to let Jason speak to Urth on the Feynman unit. This is a matter of life and death. We expect immediate access."

Coleen smiled. "Life and death? Really? There are many who wish to speak with Urth. We have to remain neutral and not favor any one over others."

Out of patience, Kira spoke in as close to her mother's tones as she could manage. "If Jason is not allowed to speak to Urth this afternoon, I will be on the long-distance far-talker to Master Mechanic Mari this evening, informing her that the librarians are refusing us access to the Feynman unit. I will tell her that even when reminded of the urgency of our mission the librarians still denied us access."

"Access to the unit is ours to decide," Coleen said, all pretense of politeness vanished.

"You know better than I do that a lot of people think the librarians should no longer have exclusive control of the means to communicate with Urth. The daughter of Jules has so far backed the librarians in that debate. I hope you're not assuming that her backing is unconditional or guaranteed."

Coleen eyed Kira for several seconds. "I wonder what your mother would say if she knew you had said that?"

Kira didn't waver. "You'd be really wise to assume that my mother and I talked over that issue before I came here, so I know what her feelings are. You'd also be wise to remember that my mother told you that on this mission I'm empowered to speak for her."

"Even the daughter of Jules cannot give orders here," Coleen said, speaking calmly but with anger clear in the undertones of her voice.

"I could," Kira said, her temper rising, leaning forward enough to rest her hands on the front edge of Coleen's desk. "I've got a half troop of cavalry out there who will do as I say. I don't have any wish to employ force. But I will if you continue to disregard the clear request of my mother on a matter of great importance."

"You wouldn't dare. The cost of such an action would be far higher than you would want to pay!"

Kira reached up with one hand to tap the bullet scar on her neck. "I've faced far more dangerous opponents. Please don't try to intimidate me. It won't end well."

Coleen looked away, her mouth tight, then back at Kira. "This afternoon, one hour from now."

"One hour," Kira repeated.

After she and Jason were outside again, he gave her a curious look. "You went hardcore on her pretty quick."

"Are you criticizing me?"

"No, just wondering why you didn't try more arguing before you started threatening."

Kira shrugged. "I'm tired of dealing with people who won't let me do what needs to be done. You *are* criticizing me."

"No, I'm not!"

"Just make sure what you tell Urth gets us what we need to know."

Jason didn't say anything else as they waited out the hour. He gave her occasional questioning looks, but Kira ignored them.

She could still sense that other Mage's presence.

She shouldn't be able to do that. Not with her Mage powers locked down.

Kira hid her uneasiness, searching inside herself for any flaw in the barriers about her powers.

★

The large room below ground in the tower held a lot of original equipment from the great ship. But the only thing in that room still working was the Feynman unit.

Kira had been here before. So had Jason. "I think the librarians were upset with me," he confessed to Kira afterwards. "They're used to everybody being amazed by how advanced all the stuff in there is, but I was commenting on how old it all was. I mean, I said they'd kept the stuff in great condition, but it was all old."

No one was in the room except for Kira, Jason, and several librarians who seemed to have no other task but to watch Kira and Jason. If there was a long line of people waiting to use the Feynman unit, it wasn't visible anywhere.

Jason leaned close to the unit, grinning. "Ancient interface!"

"Do you know how to use it?" Kira asked.

"Sure." He tapped the glowing screen, read, tapped, tapped, read, while the librarians watched with growing alarm.

"You should not be doing that!" one of the librarians insisted. "No one should touch anything but the transmit command!"

"He knows what he's doing," Kira replied.

"You guys have never looked at any of these other menus?" Jason asked. "Hey, do you guys know this unit is set for open access?"

"What's that mean?" Kira asked.

"It means Earth can send updates or changes to the operating system without any approval from the people here, and can also send commands remotely."

"Commands?"

"Yeah," Jason said, pointing. "As long as the unit is powered up. Like, here? They've blocked this unit from receipt of messages from other worlds colonized by Earth. That's why you stopped hearing them. Oh, man, look at that! The people back on Earth have this unit set for monitoring. They can listen in to anything in here at any time."

Kira looked over at the librarians. "Even if the transmit command hasn't been used?"

"Yeah." Jason looked at the base of the unit and on the sides. "It's probably hard-wired to the rest of the tower. I'd have to dig in a little more, but if this is connected to the original monitoring systems in the tower, they can probably listen in to anything being said anywhere inside the tower or in the outbuildings at any time. You guys might want to think about changing that," he added to the librarians.

Wil of Altis, the senior librarian present, appeared to be both alarmed and skeptical. "We will consider your words. If you will proceed?"

"Okay." Jason grasped the hand-held microphone.

Kira could see how nervous he was. "I'm right here," she said in a low voice. "Look at me while you're talking, and pretend you're explaining something to me. You say things really well when you do that."

"Thanks." Jason braced himself, then tapped the transmit button on the screen. "Earth Relay and Interstellar Signals, this is Jason . . . Groveen. I haven't communicated with you since I chose to remain on this world because I didn't want to interfere with others who needed to use the Feynman unit, but something really important has happened. I know you've been told about this, but maybe it wasn't explained right. We've found a secret underground facility that was constructed by the original crew of the *Demeter*. We have very good reason to believe that facility holds the beta field generators and possibly other weapons constructed by the crew. I don't know whether the underground facility also includes fission or fusion bombs made by the crew, but I do know that there was no trace on the remains of the ship or anywhere else on the planet of the beta field generators the *Demeter* was known to carry. The secret facility sits under a city, so a lot of lives are in danger, and if the wrong people get their hands on those weapons they might try to use them.

"I know you're concerned about misuse of those weapons. But Master Mechanic Mari and Master of Mages Alain and Queen Sien of Tiae and the others who are trying to eliminate this threat only want to get at those weapons so they can be safely dismantled and the pieces destroyed. Master Mechanic Mari personally told me to tell you that she gives her word that the weapons won't be studied, that all the parts will be destroyed, and even whatever instructions you send also destroyed afterwards. Nothing will be left for anyone to misuse or try to copy."

Jason swallowed, nervous, and Kira gave him an encouraging smile.

"The problem is that I don't know enough about weapons technology to safely guide them in dismantling those weapons. I don't want to know any more than I need to know in order to help them safely disarm and get rid of those weapons. We need to know whatever you can tell us. I can understand and interpret anything that might be too far above the current tech level here, so if you've withheld information until now because you didn't think they could use it, that's not really a problem. I don't even have to understand what I'm doing as long as we have step-by-step instructions for disarming and dismantling the beta field generators and other weapons.

"If there's some means of sending a kill pulse through the permacrete that would disable the beta field generators for good, that would be particularly welcome.

"Please answer. I'm supposed to wait here with the Feynman unit as long as necessary to hear whatever you can send. This isn't about me and it isn't about the culture on this planet. It's about saving a lot of lives. Master Mechanic Mari is everything you've ever heard. If she says the information you send us is only to ensure the safe dismantling and destruction of those weapons, then that's what will happen."

Jason paused again, his eyes on Kira. "Ummm, if anybody is concerned about me, let them know I'm doing great. I wanted to stay here, and I've never regretted staying. Jason . . . Groveen, out."

He put the microphone away, making a face. "I didn't realize how hard it would be to say that name again."

"Why did you?" Kira asked. "Your name is Jason of Urth now."

"I had to be sure they'd know who I was." Jason gave the librarians a quizzical look as they walked up to him and Kira. "Is there anything wrong?"

"We're supposed to escort you out," Librarian Wil said. "Without delay."

"So the next in line can use the Feynman unit?" Kira asked, pretending to look around for the nonexistent line.

"You can return at the expected response time," Wil said.

"We will," Kira said.

"How'd I do?" Jason asked as he and Kira left the librarians at the entrance to the tower. "You seem like you think I screwed up."

Kira shook her head, looking up at the sky and thinking about Urth. "No. It's not you. You did great. As usual. It's the librarians. Jason, they *resented* us using the Feynman unit."

"Even I could tell they weren't happy."

"Who else is supposedly waiting to talk to Urth? It's like the librarians are trying to keep anyone besides themselves from using the Feynman unit. But it's their job to protect things and make them accessible!"

Jason shrugged. "It wouldn't be the first time that people responsible for guarding something forgot what they were supposed to be guarding it for."

The sun, dropping down as the afternoon waned, was nearly below the peaks that surrounded the valley of the librarians. Kira frowned at the fading day. "It'll be hours before we can get a reply. Let's meet Professor Wren for dinner. You can hear all about the ruined city of Marandur."

Professor Wren was waiting, nervous at first, but relaxing as she chatted with Kira. "Some others from the Imperial delegation I came with were going to join us, but discovered they had another commitment."

"That's too bad," Kira said, just as glad that she didn't have to deal with other Imperials during the meal.

"After I told them the dinner would be with you, they remembered the other commitment and were very apologetic," Wren said.

Kira smiled even though she knew exactly why those other Imperials had suddenly remembered a reason not to dine with her. She looked at her glass of red wine, imagining those Imperials watching her drink and wondering among themselves just what the liquid in the glass actually was.

Wren paused as if something had just occurred to her. "I hope it wasn't . . . Lady Mechanic Kira—"

"Please, Professor, just Kira."

"All right, Kira," Wren said, smiling at her. "And I am just Wren to you. I was going to say, there are some ridiculous stories inside the Empire about your mother. I hope none of that has rubbed off on you."

"It might have," Kira said. Would Wren recognize the term *daughter of darkness*, and would she be shocked to know that was what many Imperials had labeled Kira? "But don't worry about it. I think my family has a tendency to surprise people."

Wren laughed. "Oh, yes! When your parents first reached the university, narrowly escaping the barbarians in the ruins, the guards at the gate told us that Mari and Alain, a Mechanic and a Mage, had kissed each other. We couldn't believe it! How could the world have changed that much!"

"It hadn't changed that much yet," Kira said. "And there are still plenty of Mechanics and Mages out there who wouldn't come within a thousand lances of each other if they could help it." Though some of those Mechanics and Mages yearning for what they thought were the good old days of the Great Guilds were apparently cooperating with each other now, and not in a good way.

Wren talked for a while about Marandur while Jason listened, rapt with interest. "And Mari made it out that second time as well, though there was a great deal of anger among many of the Masters of the University at the students who had helped her. But what could the Masters do to them? They were already imprisoned in Marandur! It was about two years later when we heard the sound of horns and saw Imperial legionaries marching toward the walls of the university." The old professor's face lit at the memory. "We watched them approach, not believing what we were seeing. And then their commander stood before our gate and read the Imperial proclamation lifting the ban on Marandur and pardoning all within the city. You can't imagine how it felt. As if we'd been dead in truth, and suddenly life was given to us again. We all knew that Mari had done as she had promised. Do you think . . . would it be all right if someday I was able to visit Mari and tell her in person?"

Kira smiled. "Wren, I can promise you that Mother would be very happy to see you again and hear about your experiences. And I know Queen Sien of Tiae would have no problem with you visiting. The queen would probably be eager to speak to you. Please come visit when you can. Let Empress Sabrin know I asked you to come."

Wren laughed. "Ah, a queen! And I carried a letter from the office of the Empress. Suddenly I'm moving in high circles. Oh, Kira, was that letter good news?"

Kira hesitated. "Not exactly, but I needed to get it. Thank you. Please thank Princess . . . I mean Empress Sabrin for me when you see her again."

Wren looked startled. "I haven't met the Empress in person! I was told to deliver it in her name. That letter was from her? The stories are true and you've actually met the Empress?"

Kira smiled politely. "Yes."

"How did that happen?"

"You don't know?" Kira hesitated, not wanting to make things awkward for the old professor, and not certain how much she could share. "I guess you wouldn't. How much did you hear about when I was kidnapped by the former crown prince. Maxim?" "I'm sorry?"

"What's been talked about inside the Empire about Maxim kidnapping me?" Kira asked again.

Wren shook her head, frowning. "Prince Maxim is dead. How could he have done that?"

Kira stared at her, confused.

Jason had also been watching Wren's reaction. "They didn't talk about that inside the Empire, did they?" he asked. "It wasn't reported in the news or anything, was it?"

"Not that I recall," Wren said cautiously.

"The legions that invaded the Northern Ramparts and got badly beaten. Do people talk about that?"

"No. How could the legions have been badly beaten?"

Without her consciously willing it, Kira's hand went to the scar on her neck.

Wren saw. "Is that the mark of an injury? Are you . . . are you saying that's how you were hurt? I don't understand. I'm sorry. I don't know anything about any of this."

Kira realized with a shock that the old professor was telling the truth. "They told you nothing? Professor Wren, Maxim caused the death of many legionaries."

"Are you sure?"

I killed a lot of them. Kira managed not to say that. "Yes."

The rest of the meal passed a little awkwardly.

Afterwards, as Kira and Jason walked back toward the room holding the Feynman unit, Jason spoke up. "Authoritarian states are the same everywhere, I guess. Control the media, the press, and make sure they only talk about what the government wants them to talk about."

"There was a war, Jason!" Kira said. "How does the Empire explain to its citizens why there was a war? How did they explain to all those families why their sons and daughters and husbands and wives and fathers and mothers never came home?"

"Beats me. But you can bet the new Empress is being portrayed as a hero of that war."

"She was, in a way," Kira conceded.

"How was your, uh, *red wine?*" Jason asked.

"It does look like blood, doesn't it? Tastes a lot better, though." Kira laughed despite her upset. "I can just imagine how the average Imperial would take that statement."

But Kira was frowning again by the time they reached the room holding the Feynman unit and found two librarians guarding the door against them. "Excuse me?"

"We weren't told that you had access," one of the librarians said.

"That again. This room used to be open to the public."

The librarians exchanged glances. "That was changed over a year ago," one explained.

Before Kira could ask any more questions, the group of librarians led by Wil of Altis joined them. "We'll watch them," Wil told the door guards.

Once inside, Kira turned to Wil. "What's going on? As long as I've been alive the public has always been welcome here."

Wil spoke stiffly as he replied. "The objects in this room need to be protected. Public access left them too easily subject to harm."

"Some of the objects here have been harmed?" Kira asked. "Why wasn't my mother told?"

Wil hesitated.

"Has anything actually been damaged?" Kira pressed.

"The potential for damage was too high."

What had happened? Kira remembered her mother's description of her first encounter with the librarians, how they had denied knowing anything and tried to block access to the tower. And her fears that the librarians were increasingly restricting access to their holdings. Why were those tactics resurfacing?

She looked around the room again, full of artifacts but empty of people except for her, Jason, and the librarians watching them. "How many people who weren't librarians have been in this room in the last month?"

"I don't have those numbers with me," Wil said.

"Maybe you can tell me how many people who weren't librarians have spoken on the Feynman unit in the month before I got here. That number should be a lot easier to recall."

"I don't have it."

"Give me a round number," Kira said. "Fifty? Ten? One?" Wil said nothing. "Zero?"

"If you have questions regarding policy," Wil said, "they must be addressed to the heads of the librarians through proper channels."

"I have some questions, all right," Kira said. She stopped speaking as the control screen on the Feynman unit lit up.

"This is Earth Relay and Interstellar Signals responding to the message from Jason Groveen."

CHAPTER NINE

As far as Kira knew, the faceless voices from Urth had always sounded friendly, even when smoothly denying requests for information or simply ignoring such requests. Her mother would occasionally reminisce about the joy in the voice of the person who had responded to her message, the first communication with Urth in centuries.

This reply to Jason, though, held harsh tones, reminding Kira unpleasantly of a stern parent speaking to a wayward child.

"Jason Groveen, you are aware of the laws regarding any interactions with the people of the world of Demeter. Your request cannot be granted, for reasons well known to you. Even if the situation were exactly as you describe, it would still be unthinkable for us to share any aspect of advanced weapons of mass destruction technology with a society in an archaic technological condition. Your request itself violates laws regarding proliferation of advanced weapons technology and protecting the unique culture of Demeter, since it is apparent that you have shared the specific names and capabilities of some weapons of mass destruction with the indigenous protected population of Demeter. Profiles of you made prior to your departure and since your abandonment on Demeter indicate a serious propensity for fantasizing and immature acts of rebellion. The stories you have fed the local authorities regarding your supposed acts of heroism have confirmed that those profiles remain valid. Be advised that you are not beyond the reach of the law. Should your interference with the unique culture of Demeter continue, the next ship to reach Demeter will be ordered to arrest you and return you to Earth for trial as an adult. Consider this your formal warning to cease tampering with the culture of Demeter. Jason Groveen, you are instructed to acknowledge receipt of this warning, and state your agreement to abide by all laws concerning Demeter. Earth Relay and Interstellar Signals, over."

Kira had listened with growing unhappiness, seeing how Jason reacted with embarrassment and resentment to the unforgiving words and the angry tone of the speaker.

She'd had it. With Urth and with everybody. The librarians were hiding information instead of sharing it, Maxim was alive, someone had tried to kill Mother and Father again and even though she'd buried her feelings about that they were still there under it all, and the Empire wasn't even telling its own people why two legions had been cut to ribbons because what were a few lives when the reputation of the Imperial government was on the line?

Kira stepped to the Feynman unit, reaching for the microphone, only to be blocked by one of the librarians.

"You're not authorized to use—"

"Get out of my way," Kira told him.

The librarian hesitated. "You're not—"

"*Get out of my way,*" Kira repeated, her voice dropping in register and growing in volume.

The librarian looked at her as if a dragon had suddenly appeared in front of him. He hurriedly stepped away.

She pulled the microphone from its holder, took a slow breath, thinking, then hit the transmit command and began speaking in her best, clearest, Captain-of-Lancers tone of voice.

"Urth, this is Lady Mechanic Kira of Dematr, Captain of Lancers, dragon slayer. The daughter of the daughter. I have four things to tell you, and you'd be wise to pay close attention. Firstly, this world is named Dematr, *not* Deemeeter. You know that, and your continuing refusal to properly pronounce our name for this world is extremely disrespectful.

"Secondly, nothing that you have heard of Jason of Urth from this world has come from him. He has never boasted or bragged or spoken of his actions. Those accounts have come from people such as myself, who have personally witnessed them. Jason of Urth, and that is his rightful name now, has demonstrated great courage and selflessness in the cause of saving lives not only on this world but on Urth as well. I know you have been told of that. He has faced many dangers and enemies beside me, and when death loomed as we fought the Imperial legions he did not falter despite being badly wounded. His blood covered my hands, Urth! Yet still he fought! He is not a perfect man, but he is not the boy who left your world. Whoever you speak to on Urth about these *profiles* knows nothing of the man who stands with me, the man I am very proud to proclaim being engaged to, the man I will someday exchange promises with."

Kira paused to take a breath, her glare fending off the librarians who had taken tentative steps her way. "Here is the third thing. Dematr is our world. We spent centuries under the control of the Great Guilds, unable to set our own course or make our own decisions. Urth did nothing to change that. My mother, Lady Master Mechanic Mari of Dematr, the daughter of Jules, and my father, Sir Master of Mages Alain of Ihris, led the fight to free us to make of this world what we could. We're free now. Do you understand? We're not your pets or your children. We're not an exhibit for your entertainment or your study. We did not ask for your *protection* of us or our culture and we do not want it. This is our world. Cease acting as if you have any right to control us or what we do."

Another pause to breathe, the librarians looking on aghast, shocked into inaction. "And now the last thing, Urth, and listen well. You have threatened my man. We stand together. A threat against Jason is a threat against me, and a threat against me is a threat against my parents. Do not threaten us again. If you come here seeking to detain Jason, I promise you that we will fight. We will do whatever we must to defend our world and our people. Know this, Urth, that no one will take my man from this world while I have any trace of life left in me to fight. You will not help us. Fine. *We don't need you.* But do not dare threaten us again. Lady Mechanic Kira of Dematr, *out!*"

She took a deep breath, acutely aware of the appalled looks on the librarians present. "Do you have anything else to say?" Kira asked Jason.

He shook his head, watching her wide-eyed.

Kira put back the microphone.

"*Kira!*"

She turned her head with slow deliberation to look at librarian Wil, who was glaring at her and shaking with the depth of his dismay. "Are you speaking to me, Librarian Wil?" Kira demanded, her voice flat but very, very forceful.

Wil hesitated.

"Because," Kira continued, "it sounded like you were talking to somebody who you think you can give orders to. A child, maybe."

She had to admire the fact that Librarian Wil had the guts to still try to chew her out.

"Kira, you will not—"

"*Lady Mechanic* Kira. I treat you with courtesy and you'll treat me the same!"

Wil hesitated again before speaking. "I must inform Coleen of this. Of what you've done."

"What have I done?"

Wil stared at her. "This is our only link to Urth! The entire world depends on it! And you've . . . you've . . ."

"Told them what I think of them! What most of Dematr thinks of them!" Kira pointed an angry finger at the Feynman unit. "What is it we depend on that for? As a means for Urth to refuse to tell us anything?"

"It is important not to risk—"

Something suddenly became clear to her. "You never sent those last two requests for information on how to disarm the weapons at

Pacta Servanda that my mother asked for, did you? You were afraid of offending Urth. You didn't even try. You've forgotten that this is supposed to serve a purpose! Everything down here is supposed to serve a purpose!"

Jason spoke up, his voice sounding calm and composed after Kira's. "You guys think you're under siege, don't you? There's been growing pressure for the librarians to allow more access to their stuff. To give up control of what you kept safe for centuries. You're responding to that by raising the drawbridge. But that's not an answer. You can't go back to what was. Why did you keep it safe? What's the purpose of knowledge that isn't available to anyone who needs it when they need it?"

Wil looked down, struggling for words. "You can't understand the weight of our responsibility. How for centuries we sacrificed to preserve what would otherwise have been lost."

Jason nodded. "You're right. But weight tends to distort what's carrying it, right? Over time it can bend things completely out of shape. Is that what's happening here?"

Librarian Wil eyed Jason, his gaze narrow and intent. "We're not here to answer your questions."

"Then why are you here?"

Kira felt her anger dwindling. Unhappy with having spoken so harshly, she reached for Jason's hand and they began to walk out of the room.

But Jason paused for a moment to look back and speak earnestly. "I meant what I said earlier. The Feynman unit is set so that Earth can listen in to anything in this room, and probably anything in this tower and the outbuildings, at any time. They made that change to the settings after you powered up the unit and Lady Mari made contact. You don't want me messing with those controls, but Earth is messing with them whenever it wants to. Earth has a surveillance society. It's been that way for a long time, justified by the need to stop crime and keep people safe. And now you guys are under surveillance, too. If Earth addresses that, they'll tell you it's for your protection. It's up to you whether you want that."

Kira had listened to Jason as closely as the librarians had. "Librarian Wil, in my disappointment with Urth I spoke harshly. Tell Coleen that my mother has long considered the librarians to be trusted friends. We don't want that to change."

By the time they reached their rooms, it was full dark outside. Kira could sense that Mage again. Why were her Mage senses acting up on top of everything else? She channeled her unhappiness into suppressing her powers as tightly as she could, barely aware of their surroundings.

Jason started to follow her into her room.

"Where are you going?" Kira asked, feeling that sudden sense of threat and confinement again.

He seemed surprised. "I thought we were going to talk like we usually do."

"Talk?" She regarded him, annoyed. "Right. We don't have time for what I'm sure you're thinking about doing."

"Huh?"

"Jason, I'm tired. Now's not a good time."

"Wait," he said, acting baffled. "We agreed we wouldn't."

"Yes," Kira said. "So what's with this?"

"Nothing!"

He meant it. She must have misread his intentions. "Sorry." Kira looked around the room, which suddenly felt small and tight. "We'll sleep outside with the cavalry tonight. We'll be leaving first thing in the morning, so that makes more sense than sleeping in here."

"Okay," Jason said.

"Why do you keep using that word?"

"Sorry." He walked away without saying anything else while she gathered her stuff. He was waiting in the hallway when she came out. They walked silently to the cavalry encampment.

"Major," Kira told Char, "we'll leave in the morning. Returning to Altis."

Char saluted. "What time do you prefer, Lady?"

"You choose the time," she told him, going off to one side to lie in the grass and gaze up at the stars. Jason lay down not far away, but not close, either. "Are you angry with me?" she asked him.

"No. Just not sure what's going on."

"I'm tired, I guess. Irritable. I don't know why. It's not you. Maybe . . . Jason, that one Mage is still sitting there."

Jason turned to look. "Yeah."

"What if he's a spy? One of the ones working with Maxim?"

"Can you tell? If you ask him questions?"

"Only if he answers," Kira said. "Maybe to be safe we should . . ."

Kill him.

Stars above, had she just thought that? Thought of killing a man simply because she suspected he might be working for her enemies? "Never mind."

"Kira, you'll tell me if anything is wrong, right?"

"Wrong right. What sort of question is that?"

"Kira," Jason said, and he sounded really worried, so she relented.

"Yes. If I feel like something is wrong, I'll tell you."

She meant it. But neither one of them realized the potentially deadly way in which that promise was phrased.

They were roused before dawn, riding out of the valley of the librarians as the sun began to peep over the peaks surrounding them. The two wagons carrying supplies were considerably lighter now, rattling on the road as the column of cavalry climbed into the mountains. Kira and Jason rode alongside each other near the center of the column. Kira thought that Jason had seemed oddly cautious talking to her at first, but he relaxed as the morning wore on.

She felt better after sleeping and a good breakfast. The Mage was still sitting, gazing at the mountains, but Kira could no longer sense him as the cavalry left the tower area and the valley, which was surely a good thing. Whatever had been causing that problem seemed to have gone away.

The column maintained a good but not hurried pace, the cavalry dismounting at intervals to walk their horses. The two scouts riding ahead were changed out periodically, but none saw anything of concern. The stop for lunch meant cold rations and water. Then on the move again, along the dusty road with only faint breezes reaching them and the sun beating down.

Even an unhurried ride for so many hours took its toll, wearying both horses and riders. They'd passed under an overhang of living rock a short time before, the shade welcome but brief. Kira, feeling tired and sore, was jerked out of her half-doze in the saddle by a sudden feeling of something barely there. Kira looked ahead, wondering what she was sensing. Her foresight wasn't offering any warning, but that could mean either no danger or that her foresight wasn't working this time.

Spells? Yes. Those were definitely Mage spells she was feeling. But why up ahead of the column?

The scouts.

"Major!"

Major Char paused his horse, turning in the saddle to look back at Kira.

She felt it then, nothing subtle about it, a sudden draw on the power in the land here, a big draw, a big spell, building fast.

She'd felt that spell being cast before.

"Ambush! Everybody down!" Kira yelled as loudly as she could, dropping from her own saddle and reaching out to pull a surprised Jason from his saddle as well. Falling, they'd almost hit the ground when lighting whipped down from above. Not from the skies, but from the top of the slope overlooking the road.

The lightning bolt slammed into horses and still-mounted cavalry troopers near Kira and Jason, bringing with it the tingle of ozone and the sudden stench of scorched hair and flesh. On the heels of the lightning, gunfire erupted, rifles all along the slope above them and on the opposite side of the road firing bullets that tore into human and horse alike.

Horses screamed from lightning burns or as bullets hit them, plunging about wildly. Kira saw a trooper trying to dismount fall as at least two bullets hit.

Another spell, another lightning bolt, slaying or injuring more troopers and horses, part of it setting fire to one of the two supply wagons. The team of horses tied to that wagon bolted, fighting their harnesses and snorting in panic. Kira saw the wagon and its team race over the edge of the road to fall to the rocks below. She looked away, sickened.

This was far worse than the ambush of the train. This time the attackers were above them on each side, and they were trapped on a narrow road, nowhere to hide as soldiers and horses died.

Jason had grabbed a carbine from a fallen cavalry soldier, but he had no targets visible to shoot at.

Someone was shouting. Kira looked that way, seeing a sergeant standing up despite the danger and urging everyone back. "Under the overhang! Come on! It's death to stay here! Follow me!"

Finally, something she could do. Kira jumped up as well, her heart pounding. "Back! Under the overhang!"

She and Jason began running along with those troopers and horses not already dead, some of the soldiers pausing to pick up others too badly wounded to move. Kira saw one trooper stumble from a bullet hit, reached to grab him and help him keep moving, Jason taking the other side, carrying the wounded soldier between them as they ran.

A horse had fallen across the road, screaming in that piercing and horrible way that only horses could, blood on its head and neck and body, a trooper pausing in his retreat, tears streaming down his face as he put his carbine barrel against the horse's head and pulled the trigger, then ran onward as the beast fell silent and motionless.

Kira felt something nearby: not the lightning Mage, who must be recovering his strength after those two bolts, but something closer. Ahead. Under the overhang. She looked through the rushing figures of troopers and barely-under-control horses, seeing a pillar of glowing light at the entrance to the overhang where an invisible Mage stood, already striking with his knife at a passing soldier who reeled away with a slashed arm.

"Take him!" Kira shouted at Jason, letting the full weight of the injured trooper fall on Jason. She aimed, her pistol in both hands, flinching at the crack of a rifle bullet from the ambushers passing close by her head, waiting for a moment when that glowing pillar wasn't masked by any of the retreating cavalry.

She got the moment and she fired.

The Mage appeared, falling to lie on the road as the horses and soldiers trampled him in their retreat.

"Kira!" Jason shouted, pulling at her, somehow holding up the wounded soldier with one hand She joined him again and they ran, bullets plucking at her jacket, until they ducked under the overhang where many of the attackers' rifles couldn't reach.

"Get the horses down! On their sides! Get that last wagon to the entrance to the overhang and overturn it there before its team panics! Wounded to the back under the center of the overhang!" Captain Vanza and the sergeant were shouting orders in a continuous stream, shoving and pushing shocked soldiers into action.

"Take him," Kira told Jason again, handing off the weight of the wounded soldier. She knelt just inside the cover of the overhang, breathing hard, her pistol steadied by both hands again, trying to sense any more Mages.

Again. It was coming again. "Lightning! Everyone take cover! Weapons down so they don't attract the bolt!"

Vanza and the sergeant took up the cry. Kira herself went flat on her stomach, feeling her heart pound against the rough surface of the road beneath, the pistol uncomfortably wedged under her stomach. A moment later, lightning lashed at the overhang, sending dirt and rocks flying, but not finding its way inside to kill or injure anyone else.

Kira felt for the power left in the vicinity, finding little. Not enough for another lightning spell. She edged backwards to where Captain Vanza was issuing orders again. "Captain, that should be the last of the lightning."

Vanza stared at her. "How can you—?"

"I can tell. Leave it at that," Kira said.

A few rifles were still firing, sending bullets blindly into the shade under the overhang where soldiers were lying down behind barriers of horses living and dead. Kira shuddered as another injured horse out on the road screamed. As that awful sound faded, she heard gasps and groans from the wounded under the overhang as their comrades rendered first aid and sought to save their lives. Some of the horses with them struggled, in pain as soldiers tried to calm them and deal with their injuries.

Kira looked out on the road, seeing the bodies, the black pools of blood around them, the metallic stench of it filling the air, and felt ill. *The pools of blood were always dark.* Her mother's memories of Dorcastle. At least all of the wounded had been brought in from the road and were sheltered under the back of the overhang.

She had to do something. "Jason? Are you hurt?"

"No. You?"

Kira checked herself, seeing a couple of holes in the loose flap of her jacket and one sleeve. But there wasn't any blood or pain, except for the blood from the trooper they'd helped to safety. "No. Can you take over watching here? You've still got that carbine?"

"Yeah," Jason said. His eyes were glazed by shock, but Jason knelt where Kira had been, gazing cautiously out.

"I'm going to help with first aid for the wounded back there," Kira told him, holstering her pistol. "I might be able to help with the hurt horses, too. Call out if you see anyone coming down from the heights to charge in here and finish us off. But make sure you don't lean out so much they can hit you."

"Got it."

Kira had barely taken two steps away before she stopped, realizing that she had to say something more. "Jason!" He looked back at her as she stood staring at him. "Jason, please be careful. Stay under cover. I need you with me."

"I'll be careful," Jason promised. "Go help."

The heat of the fading day gave way to the chill of night. Kira gave up her Mechanics jacket to help warm one of the wounded, pausing only to remove the loose cartridge from the jacket and stuff it into one of her pant pockets. Jason gave up his jacket as well when a soldier eventually relieved him on sentry duty. Despite the worries of everyone sheltering under the overhang, no one tried to take advantage of the darkness to attack.

By morning the scent of blood on the road had become sickly sweet. The bodies of humans and animals still lay as they had fallen, motionless except for the stirring of hair or garments in the slight breeze.

Kira still felt almost physically ill at the carnage, but also very tired after a night spent trying to help the wounded and worrying about snipers or Mages.

Jason sat near her, his back against the rising slope behind them.

They didn't say anything, content just to be with each other and know the other hadn't been hurt, their minds numbed by the events of the day before.

What if she hadn't had warning of that first lightning bolt?

Captain Vanza, looking dazed, walked up to Kira, her gait stiff. A small stream of blood had dried along one side of her face. "I've confirmed Major Char is dead. He got hit by the first wave of gunfire. We had scouts ahead of us. They never reported trouble."

"The ambush had Mages with them," Kira said. "Your scouts probably died without knowing there were enemies near. How many are left?"

Vanza looked back at the soldiers huddled near their horses. "Sergeant Henzu tells me we've got sixteen left able to fight. Twelve others too badly wounded to be of help, five of those very badly."

"Out of fifty," Kira said, fighting that sick feeling again.

"Yes. It's possible there're a few more still alive on the road."

Sergeant Henzu walked up. "Captain, we have six horses fit to ride. Two other horses can be ridden, but suffered minor injuries. They'd have to be walked most of the time rather than ridden. The rest of the surviving horses shouldn't be ridden today if we want to save them."

"All right," Vanza said. "When's the last time we heard a shot?"

"It's been a while. Permission to send out scouts."

Vanza looked at Kira. "Yesterday you seemed able to warn of a particular kind of threat."

"I don't think there are any Mages close by," Kira said. "Consider that a hunch."

"All right," Vanza said. "Permission granted to send out scouts, Sergeant. Find out if anyone's still out there."

They weren't. The scouts returned, saying they hadn't found any enemies nearby. "They're waiting somewhere farther down the road," Sergeant Henzu said. "Waiting to hit us again if we try to make Altis. And they probably sent a few to hit anyone who tries to head back to the valley."

Vanza looked at the wounded. "We need help. We can't leave our wounded. But if they don't get care soon they'll die anyway."

"All of our far-talkers got fried by that lightning. I'm no Mechanic, but I can tell when something is melted and burnt."

"Lady Mechanic Kira?" Vanza asked, gesturing for Sergeant Henzu to give her the far-talkers.

Kira gazed at the slagged metal and bent shapes. She couldn't even get the access panels open. "The Sergeant is right. These can't be fixed. Even if they could be we couldn't get signals from hand-held far-talkers out through these mountains."

Vanza nodded wearily. "Then we only have one choice. Listen up, everyone! I need three volunteers!"

Eighteen hands rose, Kira's and Jason's among them. Captain Vanza pretended not to see Kira and Jason. "You three," she said, choosing a corporal and two privates. "We've got six horses for you. Ride as fast as possible for Altis, changing out mounts to maintain the best speed you can. Let them know we're here and need help."

As the three volunteers mounted up, Vanza stood by the stirrup of the corporal leading them. "Ride hard. Some of our wounded might not make it if you take too long."

"Yes, Captain," the corporal said. He looked around and up at the heights, his face shadowed by worry. "They're waiting up ahead, aren't they?"

"Probably. At least one of you has to get through."

"I understand. One of us will, even if the other two have to die making that happen."

Kira watched the soldiers riding off. More sacrifices to the mission of keeping Kira of Dematr alive. Two more men, one more woman, six more horses.

Was it just her imagination that the exhausted soldiers remaining were watching her with dull, accusing eyes?

She was sick of it. Sick of everything.

Kira walked to the two injured horses. "Saddle both of these," Kira ordered the nearest soldiers.

The task took only a few moments. Kira pulled herself up into the saddle, gesturing for Jason to mount the other horse.

All of the other soldiers had noticed and were watching.

Captain Vanza came running up, grabbing at the bridle of Kira's mount. "What are you doing, Lady Kira?"

Kira looked down at the captain. "If anyone who wants to kill me is still watching, they'll see me ride out of here and go after me, or tell anyone in ambush to wait for me to get there. You and the rest will be safe from further attack, and the corporal will be able to reach the city."

"Both of these horses are injured! You won't be able to keep up a fast pace!"

"I know that. So will anyone watching me leave."

The captain set her mouth stubbornly. "Our orders are to keep you safe, Lady Kira!"

Kira yelled in reply, her nerves frayed. "Too many men and women and horses have already died here protecting me!"

"I won't allow you to leave!"

"Yes, you will! I won't have another death on this road in my name! So unless you're willing to shoot me to stop me, let go of that bridle right now."

"Sergeant! Help Lady Kira down from her mount!"

Kira drew her pistol in a flash, pointing it at the sergeant, who stopped moving. "Let go of my bridle," she told Vanza.

Captain Vanza glared up at Kira for another moment, then stepped back and saluted. "Since I can't stop you without killing you, good luck, Captain Kira."

Kira returned the salute. "We'll make sure the road is clear for those coming to help." She put her mount into a walk, urging the mare ahead despite the injured horse's reluctance. The soldiers watched silently as she and Jason rode in the wake of the three volunteers, who were already nearly out of sight.

They had to ride through the site of the ambush, the horses skittish around the dead, stepping daintily through the pools of congealing blood and leaving red horseshoe prints behind for a little while.

She and Jason had ridden for a few minutes at a walking pace before Kira suddenly realized something. "I never asked you about this, did I?"

Jason shook his head. "Nope."

"I just assumed that you'd come with me."

"Yeah."

"I'm sorry."

"That's okay," Jason said as he looked around at the mountains rising on either side of the road and the dropoff on one side that ended in a gulley that turned into the flank of another mountain. "I would have said yes. I'm sure you knew that. So, do we have a plan?"

"Ride along, walk along, until they hit us again."

"Okay." Jason touched the butt of the cavalry carbine in the scabbard attached to his saddle. "I'm kinda looking forward to meeting them again."

"They might kill us this time," Kira said.

"Or we might kill them."

"Yeah."

"What about that lightning Mage? Was that the same guy as at Kelsi? That Mage Ivor guy?"

Kira nodded. "It felt like the same guy. Definitely not Mage Nika."

"What's our plan for handling him?"

"I was thinking of maybe killing him so fast he'd be in the next dream before he knew I was anywhere close to him."

"Good plan," Jason said.

She reached down to pat her mount's neck. "We're going to walk soon, girl. Sorry you had to work today." Her mount had a large abrasion on one hip where the mare had fallen and skidded along the rough road. Jason's mount had a smaller abrasion but also a cut where a bullet had grazed her.

Jason reached up one hand to rub the back of his head. "I think I saw someone high up on our right."

"How far off?"

"Way off. Up high."

"Good," Kira said. "Someone posted to watch. Up there they can get a far-talker signal through to someone else posted up high ahead of us."

"So they know we're coming."

"Yeah," Kira said, her eyes on the road ahead but feeling guilt roil through her again. "Jason? Why did you come with me? Is it just because of me? Everyone was focused on me back there, weren't they?"

"Uh huh," Jason said. "I admit it felt kind of odd to be watching everyone go no, Lady Mari, you can't do this, you'll die, and I'm like hello, I'm sitting right next to her on a horse, too, and I'm going, and is anybody gonna say no Jason please don't?"

"I'm sorry."

"No, it's good. It's fine. Really. It's like you're Wonder Woman and

I'm . . . whoever that guy is who gets to run around with Wonder Woman," Jason said. "And that's cool because I get to run around with Wonder Woman. What's to hate about that?"

"Jason, once again I have no idea what you're talking about. You know we're probably riding to our deaths."

"Yeah, there's that," Jason said. "But we probably ought to start walking to our deaths," he added as his mount stumbled. They dismounted and Jason continued talking as they led the two horses by their reins. "But, no, it's not just you. I feel that same thing. How many people are supposed to die protecting me? I know why they're doing it. I know they do it because if they don't, people like Maxim win. But I don't like it. Not at all. So when you decided enough was enough, and all those men and women who died yesterday were plenty for this trip, I said, yeah, Kira's right again. Let's go."

"You really think I'm right?" Kira said, hearing her boots crunch on the gravel that spotted the road surface.

"Yeah. I do. How are you doing?"

She hesitated, unsure how open to be, but decided she had to be truthful. She'd promised never to lie to him again. "I don't know. Jason, do you feel funny?"

"Funny ha-ha, funny happy, or funny strange?"

"Funny strange."

"Not really. A little light-headed," Jason said, wiping sweat from his forehead. "Man, it's already getting hot."

"Good thing we gave away our jackets," Kira said, looking around at the mountains, wondering how many eyes were watching her and how many weapons might be pointed at her this very moment.

"So do you feel funny strange?" Jason prompted.

"Yeah," Kira admitted. "I guess it's because I'm tired. Sometimes it's like I'm seeing the same thing twice."

He spun about, watching her, concerned. "Double vision? Kira, that's—"

"No, not double vision. It's like I'm seeing the same thing two different ways at once. Or maybe one way and then another way? It's hard to describe."

He kept watching her, eyes intent with worry. "You can think okay?"

"Yeah. That part's fine."

"Kira, are your Mage powers still loose?"

"What?" She shook her head, feeling the warm breath of the mount she was leading gust across the back of her neck. "I haven't let them loose at all."

He frowned at her. "How did you do that stuff yesterday, then? Knowing when lightning was going to come, and spotting that Mage on the road?"

Kira shook her head again. "I don't know. Jason, my Mage powers are locked down. It's not them."

"But you can still sense Mage stuff?"

"Yeah. I guess I need to ask Father about that." Kira inhaled deeply, then coughed when some dust from the road drifted into her throat. "Hey, I just thought of something. If my Mage senses are working even when my powers are locked down, I should be able to sense when we're getting close to Mage Ivor."

Jason nodded, glancing back at the carbine in his saddle. "Tell me where he is and I'll show him how to hit something. So your powers haven't flared up lately?"

"No. Not since a minor thing the first night at the tower. They didn't try to act up at all yesterday."

"Huh. I guess that's good. You're sure they're locked down?"

"Let's stop for a moment and I'll make sure."

They both stopped, the horses gratefully coming to a halt as well once their humans ceased moving. Kira closed her eyes, probing, testing. Everything seemed fine, no flaws in the barriers holding her powers in check.

She suddenly had the strange sensation of being in her house. Home. Standing in the front room, the kitchen off to her left. Something was in the basement, though, something that slammed against the floor in a futile attempt to escape. She looked down at it, feeling something angry and trapped, but despite her own aversion to being confined she wasn't even tempted to yield to its attempts to escape.

The moment and the image vanished. Kira shook her head and opened her eyes, seeing Jason watching her.

"Kira?"

"Yeah," she said. "It's me. My powers are locked down. Definitely. In the basement."

"The basement?"

"Of my home. I know. It doesn't have a basement. The home I just saw inside me does have a basement, though. And that's where the powers are trapped."

"Okay."

"Are you just accepting any weird thing I say now?"

"Yeah, pretty much," Jason said. "This is all outside anything I know."

She ran her free hand through her hair in a vain attempt to order it. "I must look awful."

"You've never looked more exotic," Jason said.

Kira couldn't help laughing as they started walking again, the horses plodding in their wake, the heights to either side of the road eerily silent, nothing else moving that they could see but the occasional sway of scrub brush in a sudden breeze. "Are you all right, Jason? I'm surprised you can joke about stuff today."

He shrugged, a shadow passing over his expression. "I guess it's how I keep from being too scared to think. Make a stupid joke instead of thinking about what could happen, you know?"

"So you are scared?"

"Yeah. You?"

"Oh, yeah," Kira said. "But we're still walking. Are we numb or crazy or brave?"

"Maybe all three," Jason said. "Used to be, when I played those games, I thought real *brave* would be some kind of rush. A really great feeling. But if this is what brave is like, it feels a whole lot like afraid."

"Mother and Father used to tell me that being brave was just being afraid and doing what had to be done anyway. I didn't believe them," Kira added. "I thought they were hiding something. But they were right."

"Kira?"

She glanced over at him as they walked and saw Jason looking not afraid but nervous. "What?"

"Do your mom and dad really like me? I mean, since we're maybe not going to make it through today, you can tell me the truth. I'll be okay. Because I know I'm not a hero and I know I'm not special."

Kira gasped a laugh. "You already know the truth. Yes, they like you. Jason, they didn't want me looking for a hero. Father told me a few weeks ago that he'd always hoped I'd find someone who truly loved me, and respected me, and treated me right. And he was happy that I'd found someone like that. But you know what? I found a special hero, too."

He shook his head, looking down at the rough surface of the road. "I just don't want to ever disappoint you. Or them."

"You haven't. You won't."

It was probably close to another hour before Kira felt something up ahead. "He's there," she murmured to Jason. "I can feel him."

"Where at?" Jason asked, pretending to rub his neck again so he could raise his head and look around.

"Almost directly in front of us. I can't tell how far, but he's not close enough to attack us."

Jason nodded. "It looks like about two kilometers ahead of us the road cuts into the side of another mountain. That's two thousand meters, or, um, a thousand lances."

"That's not too far ahead."

"Yeah. We're facing almost a straight stretch, only slight curves until the road meets that mountain and turns. And at that point there's a steep dropoff to the right and a steep cliff to the left. If they hit us there, we'd be sitting ducks, out in the open with no cover anywhere near. Nothing like that overhang that saved us yesterday."

Kira had kept her gaze lowered to avoid revealing that she'd sensed danger ahead, but now stole a glance ahead as they kept walking. "That drop doesn't look like something we'd survive going down."

"No. Definitely *not* a slope. So what are we going to do?"

"I don't want to tip them off that we know he's there," Kira said. "Hey, do you feel like resting for a few minutes? We've been walking for a while."

"Resting?" Jason gave her a puzzled look, then nodded. "Oh, yeah. Perfectly natural to rest for a little while. How about right here? We can lean against the rise on the left side, and a little way below the road on the right there's a nice huddle of big rocks in case we need someplace to hide."

Kira made herself stumble. "Great. Yeah. Act like you're totally exhausted."

"I know how to do that."

They let the horses stop, reins left loose, the ends resting on the road. The horses, tired as well as injured, didn't take advantage of their freedom to do anything except look around hopefully and vainly for anything to eat or drink.

Kira sat down against the base of the rise on the left side of the road. Jason pulled the carbine from his saddle, pulled out extra cartridges for it that he stuffed in his pockets, and then joined her, moving as if he could barely walk.

They sat together for a moment before Jason spoke again. "At least we haven't heard any shots. We know they let the corporal and the other two soldiers through so that they could nail us when we got here. Achievement unlocked. Now what?"

"We think of another plan," Kira said.

"If we move ahead, even if we try to climb up off the road, they'll see us and be waiting."

"Yeah. But we can't just sit here. If we're still out here when night falls, they'll be able to trap us on this road." Kira felt the warm sun, the heated rock at her back, and her own tiredness after the day and night before. "It sounds crazy, but I might actually fall asleep."

Jason startled her with a small laugh. "You're a genius, Wonder Woman."

"I am? And stop calling me Wonderful Woman."

"Okay. What do they do if they see us fall asleep sitting against this rock?"

Kira thought about it, stealing a glance up the road toward where she could barely sense the lightning Mage's presence. "They won't wait forever. They let the corporal and the others through, so they know help will be coming. Or maybe the sound of the fight yesterday reached someone who sent a warning, and a relief column could already be part way here. They'll see us, asleep, out in the open. Perfect targets, if they come close enough."

"You'll be able to tell if the lightning Mage gets closer, right?"

"Yes." She looked at the two horses, standing with heads drooping. "The mounts screen us from shots from the other side of the road. The ones with rifles will have to come closer along this side. Will they try long shots? No," she answered her own question. "Missed shots would alert us. They'll get close enough to be sure of hits before they fire. And Mage Ivor will want to get in the killing blow. If he has any authority among them, he'll insist on that."

Jason nodded, his head leaning back against the rise of rock. "So the plan is, we lure them out of concealment by pretending to be asleep until we think they're almost close enough to kill us?"

"And then we dive for cover in those rocks."

"That's really crazy," Jason said. "It's a good thing I'm crazy, too."

"We could head back toward the others," Kira said.

"But then the relief column might get ambushed," Jason said. "What about those badly wounded soldiers? They need a clear road."

"I guess that means we have to clear it," Kira said, reaching one hand as if scratching herself but reassuring herself that her pistol was ready and secure in its holster.

"We get the worst jobs," Jason said. "Okay. Do we both fall asleep?"

"No. We're not stupid. We're worn out." Kira breathed slowly, thinking. "If I stay awake they'll be less likely to feel safe coming at us even if they see me apparently fall asleep. I'm the dragon slayer."

"And I'm the sidekick," Jason said. "The bumbling sidekick kid from Earth who's supposed to be on watch but falls asleep because the writers are lazy and want the good guys to get in serious trouble using that easy plot device."

"What the blazes are you talking about now?"

"Stupid characters. Which, as you say, we aren't." Jason put the carbine across his legs. "I'm on watch. Have a nice rest."

"Make sure I don't actually fall asleep." Kira slumped back, letting her head drop.

At first it felt relaxing. Eyes closed, the warmth, no weight on her tired feet. The rock beneath her butt wasn't exactly soft, but then neither was a saddle. She soon realized, though, that pretending to sleep was a lot of work. She kept feeling the urge to move and to open her eyes to watch for trouble.

After several minutes, she felt Jason's body next to hers begin to relax. He pretended to fall asleep by stages, gradually sagging next to her. She felt his head jerk up once, then a little later once more. His breathing deepened. "Jason?" she murmured without moving her lips much.

"Yeah?"

"I was afraid you'd really passed out. Sorry."

"And the Oscar for stupid sidekick goes to Jason of Earth," he barely whispered in reply.

She resisted the urge to demand he tell her what that meant.

Perhaps half an hour dragged slowly by, the sun lulling her but occasional insects making Kira wish she could slap at them. Her powers stayed passive, surprising her, but she had no trouble keeping track of the lightning Mage's faint presence.

Her drowsiness vanished as she felt something. "He's moving," she whispered. "Coming closer."

"Yay," Jason murmured. "They're coming to kill us."

"Hush. It's hard for me to tell how much closer he's getting." Kira tried to guess where the lightning Mage was. She barely cracked one eye, seeing the horses still standing where they'd been left, heads hanging down, reins trailing onto the road. Straining her ears, she heard nothing but the buzz of insects and the faint rush of the wind.

Had that been a clatter of rock? Impossible to say.

"Kira?" Jason breathed.

"Getting closer."

How much longer could she wait? How close did she dare let them come?

Kira felt it then, the sudden rush of power being drawn on nearby, the sense of a powerful spell building. One of her hands pushed her away from the stone at their backs and the other shoved Jason forward. "Move!"

CHAPTER TEN

The sense of a spell being formed peaked as she and Jason leaped to the other side of the road past the startled horses, who shied backwards in alarm.

Lightning tore into the road surface just behind them as she and Jason dove off toward the rocks a little downslope. Kira felt the electrical charge in the air above her as she dropped, saw the brilliant flash of light casting her and Jason's shadows on the ground beneath them.

The horses snorted, panicked, the sound of their hooves rapidly diminishing down the road as they bolted.

She hit the ground painfully, rolling, jumping up, running, and pulling herself into the cover the rocks provided, looking for . . . "*Jason!*"

He'd paused outside the rocks, aiming upwards with the carbine.

Kira yanked out her pistol and snapped off a shot at a figure with a rifle who was aiming at them. Jason fired once before rifle shots from other spots sounded and bullets went cracking past overhead. She rose up far enough to grab Jason and pull him into cover.

They huddled among the rocks as bullets tore past overhead or spanged off the stones. "Don't ever do that again!" Kira yelled at Jason over the sound of rifle fire.

"I thought I could hit him," Jason argued, flinching down as stone chips flew from a nearby hit.

"Don't do it any more! Promise me!"

"All right, I promise I won't do that anymore. I thought I could hit him," Jason repeated defensively.

"Did you?"

"No." He lay next to her, holding the carbine. "Our plan worked. What's the new plan?"

"We don't die," Kira said.

"Great plan." Jason looked around. "If they get way up there on the right they might be able to shoot down at us in here."

"That'd be a hard climb," Kira said. "Let's hope they can't." The rifle fire fell off except for an occasional single shot.

"What do you think they're doing?"

"Wait." She felt it, another spell, and knew what it was. "There's at least one more Mage with them. He's using the invisibility spell. Coming this way."

"It's not the lightning Mage?"

"No. Different guy. He feels different. I can't explain it to someone who's not a Mage." Kira tracked the route of the second Mage. "He's coming around this way, on my side."

"What are we going to do? If you show that you know he is there, they might figure out you have Mage powers."

"Can't be helped," Kira said. "Here he comes." She raised her pistol, aiming.

A glowing pillar appeared around one of the rocks, less than a lance away.

She fired into the center of the pillar, lined up her sights and fired again, the Mage appearing with a jolt after the first shot and just in time for the second shot to knock him back and down.

They huddled down again as the rifles opened fire once more.

"Is he dead?" Jason asked.

"Yeah," Kira said, thinking of the soldiers that Mage had helped kill yesterday. "He sort of . . . went out. That's how it feels."

"Weird." Jason, lying full length on his back, raised his carbine to aim toward and above his feet, resting the barrel on the side of a medium-sized boulder next to him. Kira watched a distant figure appear, struggling up the slope on the right of the road with a rifle.

Jason fired. The figure jerked at the sound of the shot, missed a hold, and went sliding back out of sight. "That should discourage any more of that," Jason said.

"Let's hope," Kira said, just before sensing a powerful spell building again. "Get your barrel down! He's going to try to use that as a light-ning rod to get you!"

Jason rolled onto his stomach, the carbine beneath him, as light-ning flayed the rocks above him and Kira. She had her pistol buried under one shoulder, not breathing until the lightning stopped, leaving after-images dancing in her eyes.

The rifles opened up again: careful, single shots trying to bounce bullets off rocks and into the tiny sheltered area where Kira and Jason lay.

She closed her eyes, trying to get a feeling for what the lightning Mage was doing. He wasn't moving, but Kira could sense the amount of power in this area. The two lightning strikes had drawn it down a lot. There was only enough left for maybe one more. That was encour-aging.

She'd stopped trying to figure out how her Mage senses could be working when her powers were suppressed. Without that inexplicable phenomenon ,she and Jason would be dead.

But the lightning Mage had to be wondering how Kira had known just when to dive for cover, how she had been able to target the Mage using the invisibility spell, how she had been able to warn Jason to get his barrel down just before the second strike hit.

That all made it look very much as if Kira had Mage powers. Would the lightning Mage accept that? It was supposedly impossible, after all. She was carrying and using a pistol, which Mages couldn't do. And even though Mages could do things judged impossible by the science of Mechanics, Mages also clung to their own rigid rules for how their arts worked.

Because of that, was it possible he would assume Jason was the

Mage? Jason was an unknown element, after all. Sure he was using that carbine, but he'd come from Urth. And at least some Imperials believed him to be a demon summoned by Mari to be Kira's partner. If this bunch was working for Maxim, they'd have heard that.

And she knew from her own experience that if one Mage didn't know another particular Mage, if there hadn't been any physical meeting between the two that extended long enough to establish who each was in the mind of the other, then sensing the identity of the other Mage could be difficult.

Kira opened her eyes, seeing the sun above. Late afternoon. It was still a little while until nightfall. "Hey, Jason."

"Yeah?"

"You're a Mage."

He didn't answer for a moment. "I am?"

"Yeah." She looked over at him. "That lightning Mage must be deciding one of us is a Mage. But how could it be me? You, on the other hand, are from Urth."

Jason nodded in understanding. "And I'm a demon."

"Right. If we have to explain anything, we have to make it look like it's you."

"Mage Demon. Or is Demon Mage? That's quite a promotion from stupid sidekick." Jason and Kira flinched as a bullet knocked chips off a stone, the sharp-edged fragments hitting the very narrow strip of dirt between them. "I'm not going to have to go around boasting I'm a Mage, am I?"

"No. We still act like it's a big secret."

"Okay. Do you have any water?"

"Yeah," Kira said. "One canteen. Have you got any food?"

"Some dry rations."

"And we've both got extra ammo. We're all set."

"Yeah." Jason looked up, rolling onto his back once more. "Here's comes another one climbing up. Let me know if lightning boy is going to try again."

A lull came, punctuated by shots at unpredictable intervals. They lay as low as they could on the pebbles and the dirt, the sun beat down on them, and the occasional breezes couldn't reach them. Kira worked the canteen out from her pack and took a drink, not too much since it might have to last a while, and passed the canteen to Jason.

He drank as well, then with a sudden grin leaned over, staying low, and quickly kissed her. "I didn't tell you yet today that I love you."

She smiled back, resting one cheek on the dirt as she gazed at him. "Do you want to get married today?"

"Sure."

Another bullet cracked off one of their sheltering rocks.

Kira cautiously lifted herself up to look toward the heights where the lightning Mage and the men and women with rifles waited. "Maybe we really should. I mean, there may not be a tomorrow."

"Have you got the paperwork?"

"No. That doesn't really matter, though." Kira lowered her head to the dirt again just before two more rifles fired, their bullets passing through the space where her head had been. "But I'm not eighteen yet. That does matter. They're waiting for it to get dark, Jason."

"Hey, we'll make it out of this," Jason said. "Why do you suppose they let us get to the librarians instead of ambushing us on the way there?"

She looked at him, realizing he was trying to distract her from thinking about how short their future might be. But the moment he asked that question the pieces fell into place for her. "Because they were behind us. They came in on that Imperial-flagged passenger ship that was arriving at the port as we were riding up to the city."

His gaze on her grew puzzled. "How do you know that?"

"It just makes sense. They posed as tourists or business people or something. It took them a while to get ashore because they had to look harmless and smuggle their weapons into the port with them. They found out we'd left for the tower, followed us toward the valley of the librarians, and when they realized we were approaching on the way back they set up that ambush. That's why we had the overhang to shelter under not far behind us. If they'd had time to pick the perfect spot, they wouldn't have chosen one where we could find cover if we lived long enough to reach it."

He nodded. "Yeah. That does make sense." Jason's gaze went to the heights. "I wonder if Maxim is out there with them?"

"No."

"No? How can you be sure?"

"If he was close I could tell. I could feel if he was nearby."

Jason's expression once more became questioning. "Maxim is a Mage?"

"No. But I'd still be able to tell. It's complicated. I can't explain it." And she couldn't, not even to herself. Why was she so sure she'd know if Maxim was out there? How would she be able to tell? But Kira felt an inexplicable, cold certainty inside her. When she got close enough to Maxim, she'd know.

The rifle fire continued sporadically as the sun dipped toward the peaks to the west, casting long shadows across the area where Kira and Jason sheltered. Jason fired back whenever anyone came into view, his shots accurate enough to discourage the attackers even if Jason didn't know if he'd scored any hits.

However many shooters there were shifted position through what was left of daylight, trying to find angles that would allow them to bounce bullets off the rocks into Kira or Jason. All of the attempts failed, but Kira felt a chill as one ricochet slammed into the dirt next to her arm. Fortunately, the shooter had no way of knowing how close that shot had come, and moved to another position before trying again.

To her own amazement, Kira fell asleep at intervals, awakening each time to see the shadows had grown longer and darker.

As the blue above faded into black spangled with stars, Kira checked her pistol for at least the hundredth time since they'd hidden among the rocks. "How are you doing, love?"

"Okay," Jason said, lying on his back, his carbine resting across his chest. Like her, he was dirty from hugging the ground, dusty from hits on the rocks around them, and sweaty from the long period lying among the rocks with little breeze as the sun beat down. "How about you?"

"Okay," she replied, earning herself a grin. "Feeling exotic."

"Exotic really is a good thing. I wasn't kidding about that. I'm a little hungry, though. Has your mother done anything about getting taco trucks into mountains like this?"

"Not yet," Kira said, knowing he was trying to raise her spirits. "How are you doing on that shave ice stuff you said you were going to make?"

"I'm still working on it. There's this girl I know I want to share it with."

"Oh? She's special, huh?"

"Yeah," Jason said. "And I think she likes me."

"I bet she wants to marry you."

"You think? Why would a girl like that be interested in a guy like me?"

"Maybe she wants to find out what shave ice tastes like." Kira carefully got her arms under her so she could raise herself up rapidly and took a quick look over the rocks before dropping back down. "It probably won't be much longer before they try to rush us. Keep your ears open. There's enough scree on the ground that we should hear something if anyone tries to get close."

"Which way do you think they'll come at us?"

"If they're smart they'll rush us from all sides at once, just popping up over the rocks," Kira said.

"Why didn't they do that already? This isn't like the position we held against the legionaries. We only had to cover one side and part of another. Here if they rush us from all sides we couldn't possibly stop them."

Kira shook her head. "These aren't legionaries, Jason. They're mercenaries, and Mechanics, and Mages. They won't charge guns in broad daylight. They're waiting until dark to minimize the risk to themselves."

"Maybe we should move."

"I was just thinking that we should, but it's still too light." Kira looked at the sky again. Only a few clouds drifted up there, not enough to darken the night much more. But the moon was sinking fast toward the peaks of the mountains. "They're waiting for it to get darker, too. Once the moon sets they'll probably start moving toward us. We'll have to move then, too." She watched the two dots of light that were the Twins chasing after the moon. Until Jason had arrived, people on Dematr had thought the Twins to be small, natural moons chasing the primary moon. But he'd told them the Twins were actually two parts of the great ship that had come to Dematr from Urth. "You kind of ruined the romance of the night sky for me, you know. The stars are just other suns, the Twins are wrecks of that ship, the moon . . . what's the moon like?"

"Sort of like this," Jason said. "Rocks. Dust. But without the plants or birds or animals or insects or water or air. Or people."

"See? Now why would I want to go there?"

"I'd go there if you were there." Jason looked around them. "Speaking of where to go, they're going to expect if we leave these rocks that we'll either sneak back toward the soldiers at the ambush site, or sneak toward Altis."

"Yeah," Kira agreed.

"So maybe we should sneak down the slope away from the road a little more?"

"Maybe we should. Can you remember what it looks like that way?"

"There are more rocks. That's about all I remember."

"Good enough," Kira said, looking up again. The moon was touching the peaks. "They'll move when the moon sets. We need to move before then."

"Now?"

"Yeah. I'll go first, you cover me."

"Kira, maybe I should—"

"I'll go first. Cover me." She looked back over her shoulder, then squirmed around, reversing direction without exposing her body above the rocks where even now the moonlight might reveal her.

Finally facing down the slope, Kira eased into the narrow gap between two rocks, having to turn sideways to make it through. The sound of her careful, slow movements sounded immensely loud against the quiet backdrop of the mountains.

She reached the narrowest part of the gap. Her chest pinched by the rock before her, Kira pulled her upper body through into a small area mostly clear of stones. A little farther down the slope she could dimly see the rocks Jason had mentioned. They didn't look nearly as good an improvised fort as the ones behind her, but in the dark would hopefully be safe enough.

She paused, trying to breathe slowly and quietly, straining her ears for any sounds. Nothing.

Crawl again, moving each limb carefully, trying to set them down without dragging against the loose pebbles below her. Her butt caught in the same tight spot that had pinched her chest. Muttering an extremely bad word under her breath, Kira wriggled through.

She got to her feet, staying low, her pistol in one hand, looking around and listening. The moon had set more than halfway behind the peaks. "Come on. We don't have much time left," she whispered.

Jason followed, painstakingly dragging himself through the same gap. Kira moved a few steps with infinite care, giving him room.

He pulled clear, not having suffered any apparent hang-ups, and came to his feet in a crouch.

Kira led them to the next cluster of rocks, moving faster and staying low. There wasn't room in the middle for both of them, so Kira gestured Jason into a gap that had one side open but the other three covered by boulders coming up to or above Kira's waist.

They settled carefully into place, sitting right next to each other inside the gap in the rocks, Kira finally breathing easier. She put her lips close to his ear. "I'm glad you made it through that narrow space."

He replied the same way. "It wasn't that tight."

"Not for you, maybe. If I was built like Devi, I never would have made it through."

They sat quietly after that, the faint sounds of insects gradually

rising around them as the moon sank out of sight and the night deepened. Kira found herself getting drowsy again despite her tension. She
was so tired . . .

The scrape of something on rock. Very faint, but audible over the
other noises of the night. Kira's sleepiness fell away. Jason had his
carbine up, ready.

Another soft noise, off in a different direction.

A boot crunching on a pile of scree.

Kira tried to sense where the lightning Mage was. He hadn't moved,
as far as she could tell. She couldn't sense any other Mage nearby. At
least this time they'd only be dealing with rifles and maybe pistols.

She caught a glimpse of a shadowy shape moving past their hiding
place, toward the rocks where Kira and Jason had been throughout
the day. Jason looked a question at her and she shook her head. Not
yet.

One more faint sound, somewhere upslope.

"Now," someone said in a low voice.

As the sound of people scrambling over rocks suddenly sounded
nearby, Kira nudged Jason and they both reared up above the rocks
around them, facing toward their former rock fort. Several figures
were visible standing on those rocks, their weapons pointed downward, illuminated by muzzle flashes as the sound of shots boomed
through the night.

The firing ended as quickly as it had begun. "There's nobody—"
someone began.

Kira fired.

Jason fired a moment later.

At least one shadowy figure fell with a cry of pain before scuttling
away. The others scattered, surprised. Kira fired a couple of more shots
at the figures running away through patches of lighter and deeper
shadow, thinking she hit another. Jason fired only once again after
taking careful aim., She thought she saw a running figure drop and
grabbed Jason's arm. "Come on!"

Kira led them in a rapid dash to the side, spotting another cluster of rocks and veering in that direction so they could drop into it as the echoes of the gunfire were still fading.

She lowered her forehead to the scattered pebbles beneath her for a moment, trying to catch her breath, closing her eyes and calming herself. Raising her head again, she nodded to Jason, who lay on the ground nearby. "Okay?"

He grinned, the expression strained by tension. "Okay."

Kira bent her head up enough to see the stars.

There was still a lot of night left.

"Do you think they'll try again?" Jason whispered.

"What do you think?"

"Yeah. Any water left?"

"Nope," Kira said. "Any food left?"

"Nope. Still got plenty of bullets, though."

"Then we're good."

She wasn't sure how much later it was when more faint sounds warned of people searching for her and Jason. Kira huddled up against a large boulder with jagged edges, the remnant of a larger chunk of mountain that must have fallen and shattered when it hit down here. She held her pistol ready, breathing as quietly as possible through her mouth. Jason did the same a little ways to the side, a gap in the rocks here separating them.

A dark patch moved above her, blocking the stars, the head of someone peering over the rocks, the barrel of a rifle visible pointing over Kira's head. If the attackers had used hand lights, they could have seen her and Jason, but they either lacked those or were afraid to use them since it would make anyone who did so a perfect target.

After long, heart-stopping moments, the dark figure pulled back. Kira heard faint noises as the searchers moved onward.

Staying awake required all of her will power, as waves of fatigue rolled through Kira. She couldn't move, couldn't stand up, walk, do anything to help stay awake except bite the inside of her cheek hard enough to hurt.

Yet as her exhaustion peaked, Kira started to feel a strange sense of confidence. Of being almost indestructible. Maybe she should make some noise. That would bring the ambushers running, and she could shoot them. Shoot them all. It'd be easy.

A scuff sounded as someone stood up on top of the rock Jason was hiding behind. The mercenary gazed around from the elevated position, his rifle canted down toward the ground and Jason where he sat motionless.

Kira saw the searcher's head lower to check his footing. Saw a jerk of startled discovery.

She fired, knocking the mercenary off the rock.

Kira kept low, lunging across the gap to Jason, the pair of them rolling over the rocks facing upslope toward the road, landing on their feet and scuttling away from where Kira had fired. She caught glimmers of movement in the night, shadows there then not there in a moment's time, all around them wherever she looked. Jason kept moving, angling up and to their right, trying to get clear of the search area.

The open slope seemed endless, no cover worth the name anywhere, until Kira saw a cow-sized boulder to her right and yanked Jason that way.

They crouched next to the boulder, trying to blend with the shadows near it, Kira wishing she still had her dark Mechanics jacket. How many more times could they get free? If only she was the monster the Imperials thought, she could take advantage of the night and . . .

That strange confidence filled her again. Blazes, why not?

She saw a searcher creeping cautiously past and leaped out at him, knocking him down and kneeling on his chest, using her hand to tilt back the startled man's head, then brought her own head down, trying not to notice the smell of the man and the roughness of his unshaven face and neck, opening her mouth, her teeth biting hard enough on his neck to break skin, the smell and taste of blood suddenly filling her nose and mouth.

The man screamed in terror, hurling Kira off with fear-driven strength that left her rolling to a stop. A hand closed on her arm and she almost struck out before realizing it was Jason helping her up.

"*She's hunting!*" the man she'd bitten shouted, his voice high-pitched with fright as he ran up the slope toward the road. "Tried to drink my blood! She's hunting *us!*"

Spitting out the blood in her mouth, Kira spotted more rocks down the slope. She and Jason stayed low, moving slowly and quietly, as men and women began shouting through the dark on all sides.

"What happened?"

"She went after Bern! It's true!"

"Let the women finish this! They're safe! I'm done until dawn!"

"The blazes we'll do it alone!" a woman shouted in reply. "She likes girls, too!"

The voices were all heading for the road, accompanied by the sounds of feet sliding on gravel as attempts at silence were abandoned. Kira kept moving the opposite way, pulling Jason along.

She found several boulders in a clump and put them between the two of them and the road before stopping.

Jason's voice was the barest murmur next to her ear. "You like girls, too?"

"Not that way. Just for blood, when I'm thirsty."

"I can't believe you did that."

"It worked," she breathed in reply.

"But it was crazy reckless. What if—"

Kira felt a burst of anger. "Why did you use that word? Crazy?"

"Ummm . . . sorry," Jason said.

He did sound sorry, and she couldn't understand why she'd gotten so angry so fast, so Kira let it go. She also knew he was right. The man she'd jumped might have had a lot of friends close by, might have been able to counter her attack, might have responded by grabbing her instead of tossing her away. There were too many ways that move might have ended in disaster.

However, it had worked. They heard occasional shouts and raised voices after that, almost all from the direction of the road. But the mercenaries, apparently already unhappy with the deadly hunt through the dark, had been thoroughly spooked by Kira's attack. She didn't recognize many of the accents she was hearing, which told her that most of the speakers probably came from Ringhmon or the Waste near it. But there were others speaking in the accents of various parts of the Empire, Syndar, the Western Alliance, and even the Free Cities.

No matter how much whoever was in charge demanded that they go looking for Kira and Jason in the dark again, the mercenaries and Mechanics refused. Kira couldn't tell from the snatches of words she caught whether they were all rattled by the teeth marks on one of their number's neck. But all of them argued that they'd already lost some of their number to gunfire while stumbling around in the dark and that none of them wanted to be the next victim, regardless of whether the weapon was a firearm or Kira's teeth.

Kira and Jason huddled among the rocks, waiting for it to grow light. Kira kept waking suddenly, having passed out from weariness. Jason seemed to be having the same problem.

She jolted awake as a rifle fired, the sound followed moments later by the crash of the bullet into the rock she was leaning against. Rock splinters hit her hand, raising a sudden pattern of bright red blood drops.

It was light enough to see better. Light enough for one of the enemy rifles to see her and try to kill her.

Kira shoved at Jason, who was already moving. They covered about a lance of distance, putting some of the nearby rocks between them and whoever had taken that shot. But as they crouched there, Jason looked around and back. "Kira! Run!"

She didn't ask any questions, bolting up and running while Jason ran beside her. A fusillade of shots roared out behind them, the crack of bullets tearing past their ears lending speed to Kira's flight. "When we moved we were exposed to anyone on the ridge above the road," Jason gasped as they ran.

Kira spotted a familiar-looking cluster of rocks, a body in Mage robes lying just outside it. "There!" Another few lances of frantic running, their sudden change of path throwing off the aim of the rifles for a moment, and then she dove over the rocks into the sheltered spot they'd occupied the day before.

Kira was rolling to her back when Jason came over the rocks in his own headlong dive and landed on her, driving the breath from her.

Gasping, she managed to get out from under Jason and get him low enough to be protected.

"Home sweet home," Jason said, breathing heavily. "Sorry I hit you."

"Uffff," Kira managed to reply, still trying to get her breath back.

A bullet struck a rock next to her and caromed off, leaving a metallic smear on the stone. As she fought for breath, Kira stared at that smear, wondering why it seemed to flicker in and out of existence.

Jason also stared at the smear of metal left on the rock by the bullet. "Is that lead? It looks awfully shiny for lead."

Kira took a few moments to reply as she recovered. "No, that doesn't look like lead. Definitely not a copper-jacketed round. Maybe an alloy?"

"Is it silver?" Jason asked as if not believing he was suggesting that.

"Um, it could be," Kira said, then understood. "Oh, yeah. Silver. I guess some of the Imperials came prepared to deal with me, and after last night they're not taking any more chances."

"Your world believes that vampires can be killed by silver?" Jason demanded.

"If you're talking about Mara, yeah. Although I'm supposedly the unnatural child of what you call a vampire, so the rules might be different there. I don't know," Kira said. "Why does that bother you?"

"I've told you how strange it is that your world, with no reference to the legends and literature of Earth, still came up with a vampire legend. And you've also all on your own come up with silver as a way to kill vampires!"

"I guess that is sort of odd, Jason. But the stories say that Mara could also be killed by wood through her heart, so—"

"Wood through the heart? Like a stake of wood?"

"No. Any wood at all. Mara supposedly doesn't like even touching wood."

"That's so strange," Jason said. "And they're actually shooting silver bullets at you."

"Yeah," Kira said, getting annoyed. "Could you stop sounding like that's some really cool thing? Because they're shooting silver bullets *at me*, Jason!"

"They're shooting them at me, too! I'm a demon, remember?"

"Yeah, great, you're a demon," Kira muttered. "Sorry. I'm kinda on edge, and kinda tired."

"Me, too," Jason said, sounding apologetic. "Sorry."

They lay there, waiting for another attack, as the sun slowly climbed into view. But aside from occasional rifle shots ricocheting off the rocks around them, nothing else happened.

Feeling incredibly tired and stressed, Kira found herself looking at a small rock on the ground before her face. The pebble seemed to take on more and more significance the longer she looked at it.

Finally, she figured out why. The pebble wasn't there.

She moved her hand enough to press down on the pebble, feeling it against her palm, knowing it was really there, and also knowing she was only feeling the illusion of feeling that pebble. Both things were true.

"Kira?"

"Yeah?"

"What are you doing?"

She looked over at him, seeing his puzzled expression and trying to figure out why Jason needed so many things explained to him lately. "I'm looking at this rock."

"Uh, yeah," Jason said. "Why?"

"Because it's an amazing rock, Jason. It's not there."

He stared at her for a long moment before speaking unusually slowly. "Yes, it is there."

"I know, Jason," Kira said patiently. "It's there and it's not there. At the same time. That's amazing, isn't it?"

He took a little while to think, seeming tense as he did so, then smiled slightly and nodded. "Yeah. That is amazing. Maybe . . . maybe it'd be a good idea to suppress your Mage powers now."

"Why would I need to suppress my Mage powers? They're already suppressed." She paused, closing her eyes to focus on those internal barriers before looking at him again. "Yes. One hundred percent suppressed."

"Really?"

Why did he look alarmed? "Jason, I'd know if—" She felt something, the draw on power in this area that meant a major spell was being prepared. "Lightning! Down!"

They huddled together, as low as possible against the dirt, while lightning lashed the boulders sheltering them. As the attack ended, Kira felt something else, concentrating to try to understand it. "Jason, he's moving. The lightning Mage. He's . . . he's running, Jason!"

Jason reared up, his carbine ready, searching for a target.

But before he could raise the weapon, Kira grabbed him and pulled him back down just before the crack of rifles heralded the impacts of bullets nearby. "You promised me you wouldn't do that any more!"

Jason pressed his head against the ground, the muscles in his face tight. "I'm sorry. I thought I could get a shot at him."

"And they nearly got you!" Kira paused as she felt something else. "Someone's coming." She turned her head trying to sense the direction. "There. Up the road toward Altis. A Mage is coming this way. Trying to hide their presence but . . . she. She's not very good at it."

"Whoever she is, she's scared the guys we've been fighting," Jason said, looking around cautiously. "Look. They're keeping under cover, but those guys who've kept us pinned down are running. If they're running, maybe she's with the good guys."

"The relief column," Kira said. "That's who it has to be." She smiled at him. "It looks like we survived another one." Leaning in, she kissed him, holding it. Wow. That felt good. "Hey, Jason," she whispered, barely breaking the kiss, her lips still close to his, and trying to catch her breath, "want to have some fun while we're waiting?"

"You want to make out while we're waiting for the relief column?" he asked, also short of breath.

"Something more," she suggested, smiling wider and wondering if they had time. How much time would it take, anyway?

He surprised her with a laugh. "You had me going there for a moment."

Kira hesitated, suddenly wondering herself whether she'd been serious. Had she been? Under these circumstances? Aside from being incredibly reckless, this wasn't exactly a private spot. Let alone a safe one. "Right. Sorry. I shouldn't have teased you about that." As if to emphasize how foolish the idea would have been, the boom of a rifle shot was followed by the crack of a bullet hitting a nearby rock.

"Was that a parting shot?" Jason wondered, rising up slightly to quickly scan what they could see of the surrounding heights before he dropped low again. "Or did they leave at least one sniper to keep us pinned down? We've got no way of knowing."

It was perhaps half an hour later that Kira heard something and took a cautious look up toward the road. Figures moved there. Dismounted cavalry, scouting ahead of the relief column.

If there had been a sniper waiting, they must have fled by now. Kira started to get up, realized there was something in her hand, and looked at it. Her pistol. She should . . . what? Put it away. That felt right. Kira shoved the weapon into its holster and stood up, her empty hands held out. "On the road! We're friends!"

Two weapons aimed her way while the other scouts continued to watch in different directions. "Who are you?" one of the scouts called down.

"Lady Mechanic Kira of Dematr!" she cried, feeling elated. "And Jason of Urth! It's safe! We kept the ambushers occupied, and they ran when you approached. The road's clear from here to where Captain Vanza is waiting with the wounded!"

She saw the scout in charge of the group speaking into a far-talker, then waving to them. "Come on up!"

By the time Kira and Jason made it back up to the road, the main column had arrived, at least two troops of cavalry and several healer wagons. Kira saw a young woman in Mage robes among the riders. She must be the Mage Kira had felt approaching earlier.

She didn't have to worry about a Mage being here, though. Her powers were completely suppressed.

Why was the Mage looking her way, openly perplexed?

Colonel Patila rode forward, her eyes on Kira. "Lady Kira? Why are you out here alone?"

"I'm not alone. Jason's here." The colonel seemed momentarily lost for words as Kira continued. "We came out to make sure the ambushers would let the message get through to you that Captain Vanza needed help. That worked, right? There shouldn't be any ambushers left between here and Captain Vanza's force. They fled inland, though I guess they'll circle back to the road. Oh, Captain Vanza tried to stop us and I threatened to shoot her, so it's not her fault we're out here. You need to keep going fast. Those wounded soldiers need help."

Colonel Patila stared at Kira. "I guess we can sort everything out later. Go ahead and get into one of the healer wagons."

Just like that, Kira knew what she had to do. She shook her head as she felt everything click into place again. "My apologies, but Jason and I are going to head for Altis. Anyone left watching will follow us. Actually, I need them to follow us."

"You both look ready to drop," Colonel Patila protested.

"Oh, we've been through worse. Right, Jason?" She looked over at Jason and he did look awfully ragged. Why was he so worn out when she felt fine? "I need a couple of mounts. And some water."

"And some food," Jason added after a moment.

"Lady Kira—" Colonel Patila began, everything about her signaling reluctance.

"This is the daughter's business," Kira said. "My mother's business. I'm speaking for my mother, with her authority. Two horses. Please."

The colonel stared at Kira, shook her head, then called back along the column. "Bring up two of the spare mounts! Make sure they have canteens and field rations in the saddlebags!" Leaning down, Colonel Patila eyed her again. "Lady, are you certain?"

"Yes. Thank you." Remembering something, Kira turned to Jason. "You're all right with that, right?"

"Um, okay," Jason said. "Thanks for asking this time." He leaned close. "Kira, what's going on?"

"Trust me. I'll explain." As Kira thought about her idea, she felt a growing sense of excitement that she had trouble controlling.

"Lady." Kira looked to see Colonel Patila watching her. "Our Mage says there is another Mage nearby."

"That's right," Kira said. "The lightning Mage. Mage Ivor. But you don't have to worry about him. He's going to come after me."

"Our Mage says the other Mage is female."

"She's mistaken. I know something about this. My father is the Master of Mages. Are the horses ready?"

Two mounts were led up. Kira swung into the saddle of one of them, feeling a new burst of energy and waiting impatiently as Jason wearily pulled himself up onto his mount. "Let's go." She snapped the reins, kicking the horse into a trot down the road toward Altis.

Jason caught up on his horse, staying silent until they rode past the end of the column. "Kira? Isn't this kind of . . . what's the word . . . incredibly reckless? Two words."

Kira shook her head, wondering what was bothering him. "No. Jason, this is brilliant."

"Brilliant?" He shook his head in turn, as if trying to order his thoughts. "Because?"

"They won't expect it. That's one."

"I'll give you that."

"The other thing is . . . Maxim." Kira smiled at Jason. "He's alive, and if he stays hidden they'll never find him. Even Sabrin can't find him. You saw the letter! But Jason, if he knows I'm out there, that I'm out on my own, he won't be able to resist coming for me. I ruined everything for him. He's not going to leave killing me to someone else. No, Maxim is going to want to watch me being killed bit by bit, piece by piece. He's going to want to watch every single moment as they slowly torture me to death. And when I'm almost gone, Jason, when I can't hold on any longer, Maxim is going to want to be the one who deals the final blow and ends my life! Why are you looking at me like that, Jason?"

His expression combined bafflement and distress. "Why am I looking at you like that? Maybe because you just said what you just said as if it was the greatest thing ever."

"It is the greatest thing ever!" Kira insisted, wondering why Jason had to have that explained to him. "It's what will make my plan work."

"Your plan?"

"Yes! He's going to come after me. Oh, and after you, too! He wants you dead also. Maybe he'll keep you alive, though, to help him use those weapons under Pacta, and make you watch me die and stuff before he finally kills you. But that's all good! He won't be able to resist it, Jason! And when he comes for us, we'll have him. We just have to leave ourselves open. As vulnerable as possible. Away from guards and soldiers and stuff that might scare him off." She smiled triumphantly at Jason.

He gazed back, seemingly even more confused. "You think that's a plan?"

"Jason, this is the greatest plan ever." She waited for him to agree, to smile and congratulate her.

Instead, Jason got inexplicably angry. "No, it's not! You want to know a great plan? Yesterday's plan! The one where we weren't going to die! *That* was a great plan!"

She stared at him, confused by his reaction. "You don't like my plan?"

"Kira, do you feel all right?"

"I feel great! I have never been able to think this clearly before! It's all there! Why aren't you happy for me?"

"You promised to tell me if anything was wrong!"

"Yeah. So? Nothing's wrong. Everything's perfect. *I'm* perfect! I never realized that before!"

Jason shook his head once more, his gaze on her growing more and more troubled. "Kira, ummm, are you there? You're not blacked out, are you?"

She glared at Jason, sudden anger rising inside her to instantly burn away the euphoria of a moment before. "Why would you ask me that?"

He hesitated at the sudden shift in her tone. "We haven't really slept for almost two days and nights, and—"

"You think I'm acting crazy?" Kira hauled back hard on the reins, stopping her mount abruptly, the gelding jerking his head in protest. "Like you said last night? Is that what you're saying?"

Jason hastily stopped his own mount, looking back at her anxiously. "I'm just saying that maybe we both need a chance to rest before we make any plans."

"Why? What's wrong with my plan?"

"It'll get us killed."

"No! You're the one who's not thinking clearly!" Kira tugged her horse to one side to ride around Jason. "Fine. I'll go it alone. You go . . . wherever you want to."

"I'm not leaving you," he insisted, riding alongside her again.

"Why?" Kira snapped, still furious. "Because you think I'm blacked out and I'll haul you into bed again? That's what you've been hoping for, isn't it?"

"Kira—"

"Try it, Jason! Make a move! I'll kick your teeth in!"

He jerked back as if she had actually struck at him. "Kira, can't you see you're not acting right?" Jason pointed at the head of her mount. "Look how you're handling that horse! You're hurting him!"

Kira stared at the horse, realizing how tightly she was pulling on the reins, the bridle and bit forcing the animal's head back and up. Horrified, she loosened the reins, taking the pressure off.

Was it the realization that she'd been harming the horse or an abrupt understanding of what she'd said to Jason that triggered an overwhelming wave of remorse? "Oh, Jason, I didn't mean to do that. Or to say that to you. I'm sorry."

"Why were you treating a horse like that? Why did you say that to me?" Jason asked, his voice low.

"I don't know. I . . ." Old doubts assailed her, much, much stronger than she could ever remember. "This is a mistake."

"Your plan?" Jason asked, trying to sound only questioning, but Kira could hear the hope in his voice.

She shook her head, feeling miserable. "Us. You and me. Jason, we're literally from different worlds. Why did we think we could make it work?"

"Wait . . . what?"

"I'm releasing you from your agreement. You don't have to marry me. You don't have to give me your promise. Just go." She choked back tears, her eyes fixed on the head of her horse.

After a long moment Jason finally spoke again, his voice torn by strain. "Kira, I don't want to be released. I want to marry you. And I'm not going."

"Why not?" she demanded, not looking at him.

"Because I think right now you need me more than you ever have before."

Kira saw something out of the corner of her eye and looked, seeing Jason's hand extended toward her.

Just as it had looked when she was falling from the ship in the storm. Jason's hand, coming to save her from certain death.

She inhaled convulsively, reaching out to grasp his hand. "You're still free of any commitment to me. But I'm glad you're here."

He didn't say anything else as they rode through the mountains toward Altis.

But as she stole glances at him, Kira couldn't help wondering why Jason looked like someone who was afraid and trying to hide it.

Maybe once she explained her plan again he'd understand. Kira felt her energy and confidence rising once more.

CHAPTER ELEVEN

Kira woke to sun in her eyes and the muffled sounds of a city street outside a closed window.

She blinked against the glare, sitting up in bed, trying to put together a confusing welter of memories from the last few days. Things were fairly clear until the night before the relief column arrived. After that, her memories seemed to bounce around, sometimes bright, sometimes dulled, pieces of them flashing into place and then away, like trying to remember the details of a dream.

They'd reached the military outpost on the road outside the city of Altis. She could see that clearly enough, the images almost feverishly bright. Leaving the horses there, going into the city as night fell, refusing help from the soldiers at the outpost. Why had she done that? Getting new clothes. All right. Arguing about something. Then sudden lethargy. Jason helping her along until they reached a hostel.

Jason.

Kira looked around frantically, first seeing the thread that led toward him and with its help finally spotting Jason slumped in a chair, fully clothed and dead asleep.

Why did the sight bring relief along with memories of anger, resentment, and anguish?

She crawled out of bed, wondering how long she had slept and surprised to realize that while sharing a room with Jason she was wearing only a shirt just long enough to barely cover her hips. Kira went to the window and looked out, seeing a busy street. This room must be on the third floor of the building. From the angle of the sun and the activity visible it was late afternoon.

Her Mage senses looked, too, stretching out to feel the city.

Kira jerked away from the window, frightened. Why were her powers free of her control? She closed her eyes, focusing inward, seeing that inner house again, shoving her powers back into the basement, trying to make the basement as small as possible and lined with impossible-to-break barriers.

All right. Her powers were suppressed again. But they'd been suppressed yesterday, and . . .

Jason should have clearer memories. Maybe he could explain things.

Worried about what might be happening, she walked over to Jason and spoke softly. "Jason?"

His eyes opened, focused on her, and he bolted backwards away from her.

Kira stared, her mouth fallen open in shock. "Jason?"

He stood still, watching her warily. "Kira?"

"Why—? What's wrong?"

Jason licked his lips nervously. "You're okay?"

"Why wouldn't I be okay?"

"Is everything . . . perfect? Are you perfect?"

"Perfect?" Kira asked. "Me? You know better."

Jason relaxed, running his hands though his hair and then gazing at her. "What's the last thing you remember?"

"Last night? Uh, we got in here, and . . . I was getting undressed to take a bath, and . . ." She shook her head. "Something about you. I was kissing you."

"You were . . . really interested in dragging me into bed," Jason said.

Kira looked down at herself, wearing only a shirt, sudden distress making her gut clench. "Did we . . . ?"

"No. Because I had no idea whether you knew what you were

doing." He shrugged, looking away. "I guess I was right. And you got kind of mad."

"Kind of mad?" Why was Jason averting his face from her? She took a step closer, grabbing his chin and looking at the side of Jason's face that had been turned away from her. "What's that mark?"

"You hit me."

"*I hit you?*" Kira staggered back until her legs struck the bed and she sat down abruptly. "I don't . . . oh, no. I do remember. I wasn't blacked out, Jason. But I hit you. Oh, I'm so sorry. Why was I so angry?"

He came closer, obviously worried for her. "It's okay."

"How can it be okay? Don't justify it! That will never be okay! Why would I do that?"

Moving slowly as if afraid of startling her, Jason sat down next to her. "You were . . . kind of out of it and not yourself before the relief column arrived, but got really volatile after that."

Kira nodded, feeling sick. "I remember, but it's sort of confused. Did I . . . Jason, what did I tell you? About us?"

"You, um, released me."

"I did that?" She stared at him, trying not to break down, her voice wavering. "I really released you from our engagement? Why? Did you ask?"

"No. And it doesn't matter, because I consider myself still engaged to you."

"Thank you. Because I know I didn't mean it. I . . . what was I thinking?"

"Do you remember anything about your plan?"

"My plan?" Kira controlled her breathing, attempting to focus. "Maxim. I was going to . . . Stars above. What was going on in my head?"

Jason shrugged. "I was hoping you might be able to tell me. As it turned out, one part of the plan actually worked. I guess no one expected us to ride alone back to the city that afternoon, because no one tried to take shots at us along the way or anywhere in the city. We made it safely because . . ."

"Because what?"

He gave her a helpless look. "Because no one in their right mind would have done what we did."

"You're right," Kira said. "No one in their right mind."

"It wasn't all bad, I guess. I mean, we probably wouldn't have survived that night alongside the road if you hadn't bitten that guy's neck—"

"I really did that? That wasn't a nightmare? *I really did that?*"

"Yeah."

She lowered her face into her hands. "Stars above. What did you do to get me back to normal?" The question suddenly struck her as darkly funny. "Normal. Right."

"I didn't do anything except let you sleep. I had no idea what to do and I was a little afraid to get close to you. Truth is, I was pretty scared that you'd wake up the same way you were yesterday."

"Why'd you stay?"

"Do you really not know?"

She looked at him, feeling herself calming. "I know why. The same reason I would have stayed with you: because I'd have known that wasn't really you, and you needed help." Kira suddenly realized how high her shirt was riding and tugged it down, embarrassed. "I need to get dressed before we talk more." In response to the thought, a series of memories from the night before cascaded through her mind, mortifying her. "Though . . . I guess you got a good look at everything last night before I put this shirt on, didn't you?"

"Not really," Jason said. "It felt wrong. I tried not to look, because I knew you weren't yourself."

She leaned in close to kiss him gently. "Thank you."

Dressing in the bath area helped calm her even more. Pulling on new trousers and a new shirt, brushing her hair, were all normal things. They helped put the world back into balance. At least whatever had been going on in her head yesterday hadn't caused her to buy different types of clothing than she usually favored. Her new jacket wasn't a Mechanics jacket, probably because you couldn't just pop into a store and buy one. But it was dark and rugged and that was plenty good enough.

Kira was surprised to see her pistol and holster left jumbled on a shelf in the bath area, and more surprised to discover that she had left a round chambered in the weapon and the safety not set. What could have made her that inexcusably careless? Kira cleared the chamber and set the safety before she strapped on the holster over her shirt.

Coming out, Kira looked at Jason. "You didn't get a bath last night like I did, did you?"

"It didn't work out," Jason said.

"Thanks for not elaborating on that. I can remember enough that I don't want to hear more details." She gazed around her. "One room. How did we convince them to rent us one room?"

He shrugged again. "We paid for the room in advance, and you told the desk clerk that we were married."

"I did? And the clerk bought that, as young as we are? I'm still almost a couple of weeks from being eighteen."

Jason finally smiled. "Kira, after the last three or four days, I forget how many, last night you and I probably both looked about ten years older than we are. Maybe twenty years older."

"You're probably right." She sat down on the bed, facing Jason, trying to recover more memories. "How we looked. How things looked. Yesterday, it was like my powers weren't suppressed at all. But I checked. I checked and the barriers were tight. I made them stronger! But . . . was there something about a rock? A rock that was somehow special?"

"Oh, yeah," Jason said. "The amazing rock that was there and not there at the same time."

"There and not there? That sounds like I was simultaneously seeing the world as both a Mechanic and a Mage. That's impossible. Anyone who tried to really believe both of those perspectives at the same time would be driven . . ." She swallowed, suddenly unable to say the word.

"Crazy?" Jason prompted.

She inhaled sharply. "Yeah."

"Can you remember how that was? Seeing things that way?"

"I think so. Looking at that rock . . ." Kira tried harder to remember how it had felt. Her breath froze in shock. "How did I get in front of the window?" Kira asked, feeling the edge of fear in her voice.

Jason spoke from behind her. "You stopped talking. You just sat there for a little while looking at me, then you went to the window. You were only out about a minute, I think."

"Why did I black out just now? I wasn't trying a spell. I wasn't letting my powers free at all."

"You were trying to remember something about yesterday."

"What's going on, Jason? Every time I think I start to understand the pattern, it changes. What if this stuff is as unpredictable and crazy as . . . as . . ."

He came up behind her, touching her shoulder lightly in reassurance. "There's a pattern. We just can't see it yet. But we will."

"Don't leave me, Jason. No matter what I say. Stay with me. Please."

"I already promised you I would. I also promised your mom. I won't leave."

She turned to look at him. "That's the only thing this morning that's giving me any comfort. Right now you can leave me long enough to take a bath. Then we need to get out of here. If anyone was trailing us through the city, if they saw us check in here . . ."

"Right. Quick bath."

She waited impatiently for Jason, trying to order her memories from the day before without delving too deeply into them. When he came out, the mark on one side of his face seemed to stand out more clearly. She had to look away. "I really can't apologize enough for that, Jason." Kira forced herself to look at him again. "What I said and did yesterday. Was it me?"

He scowled, then nodded. "Yeah. But, you magnified. Or amplified. Like the good things and the bad things in you were all hugely exaggerated."

"So I really was angry at you. I really did want to release you from our engagement. I really did want to hit you."

"Yes and no," Jason said, watching her, his expression both earnest and worried again. "Like, we get upset with each other sometimes. And we think we've addressed that. But there's still stuff left behind, right? Like, how could he have said that even if he didn't mean what I thought he did? Or we have doubts, worries, about each other. I think that's normal. It's a huge step, right? Getting married. And we both have tempers. Yours really isn't that bad. Not compared to someone like my mom on Earth, who you hardly ever mention and that's just one reason why I love you. But if you blow any of those things up, multiply them, they seem bigger than they are. I think that's what was happening. It was like everything in you was happening at some exponentially boosted level. Still you, but so much so that it was distorted and not you."

She thought that over. "So much me that it wasn't me anymore. That's kind of scary, isn't it? Jason, if I ever hit you again—"

"You won't."

The certainty in his voice made her smile. "I hope you're not being delusional this time. Let's go before Maxim and his army of mercenaries hit this hostel."

But when they opened the door into the hallway, both Kira and Jason paused, looking and listening. "It's really quiet," Jason whispered.

"Yeah. Spooky quiet. Shouldn't the cleaning staff be working right now?" Kira backed into the room again, closing and locking the door. "You said we already paid for the room? Good. Fire escape?"

"I'll go first."

"I'll cover you." Kira drew her weapon as Jason opened the side window giving access to the fire escape ladder. On the landing outside their window, she studied the alley beneath her. A few large receptacles for trash, a smaller, sealed one for garbage, and a few small pieces of junk. Nothing unusual there at all.

She didn't like it. As Jason went down the stepped ladders to the ground below, Kira chambered a round and let off the safety.

At least she didn't have to worry about a Mage suddenly hitting them with a spell. The closest Mage was a few streets over.

How did she know that? Her Mage powers were supposed to be completely suppressed. Kira swallowed nervously. Jason reached ground level, looked around the alley, and waved her down. She started down the ladders, a little awkward with the pistol still held in one hand, the pack on her back not helping her balance any.

She had reached the last section of stairs, a straight drop down about two lances, when three people suddenly ran out of the side door of the hostel. One leaped toward Jason while the other two raised weapons to target her.

Aunt Bev had always emphasized the importance of reacting quickly. Don't freeze. Do something.

Kira pushed away from the ladder.

She fell, aiming her boots to hit the head of one of their attackers.

Her boots hit with a jolt, the man collapsing under the blow, Kira trying to fall free of him and turn her drop into a roll.

As she came up, one of the attackers jumped her from behind, slamming her against the wall of the alley. Kira twisted, shedding her pack and jacket into the attacker's grasp, and tried to slam her pistol into the woman's face. But she countered, blocking Kira's blow, and landing a hit that rocked Kira back against the wall again.

Kira had a confused glimpse of Jason with his knife out, barely holding off the woman attacking him. The man Kira had landed on was out cold. She brought up one arm in time to stop another blow aimed at her head, realizing that the two attackers who were still conscious weren't using their weapons, instead trying to capture Kira and Jason unharmed, and without making any noise that would summon bystanders or police.

She didn't want to attract attention either, but there didn't seem to be any good options other than that. Both of these attackers were very good fighters. Kira barely blocked another blow, but at the cost of taking a painful kick in her side. She twisted, getting her pistol around just enough to point at her foe and fire.

Another kick knocked Kira's gun hand hard enough that she nearly lost her grip on the weapon, but her attacker stumbled backwards, holding the side of her torso where red blood was spreading. Kira lined up a shot to the side and took out the woman facing Jason. "Come on!"

She grabbed her jacket and backpack with her free hand as they ran from the alley, Kira immediately holstering her weapon and pulling on her jacket again. The sound of the two shots was already drawing curious onlookers. "Somebody was hurt!" Kira called to them. "In there! She needs a healer!"

As the well-intentioned bystanders blocked the exit from the alley in their search for the woman Kira had wounded, she and Jason walked quickly away. "Are you okay?" Jason asked her.

"Yeah. A little banged up."

"We should probably slow down and start walking like a couple of teens on a stroll," Jason suggested.

Kira slowed her pace, trying to relax her expression. "They were trying to take us unharmed."

"Yeah," Jason said. "Maybe your theory about Maxim yesterday wasn't that far off."

That memory shoved itself forward in her mind. "He wants me alive to torture."

"And me alive to help him use those weapons."

"How could I be so crazy and so right?" Kira asked as they turned a corner. She heard the rapping of hardwood batons on cobblestones as the police in the area sent coded messages to alert their comrades. Absurdly, for a moment her mind centered on that, and on her mother's sad comment that the spreading use of far-talkers was threatening to make that old police trick a dying art.

They went around another corner. "Do you know where you're going?" she asked Jason.

"We should be headed toward the road leading down to the port," he said.

"If we get stopped or recognized, it could be dangerous," Kira said.

"But we need to get to the port, right? The Confederation warship should still be there, waiting for us."

"Right." Kira glanced back and saw a team of police running in the opposite direction. "There's a Mage over that way. Two Mages. Coming toward us."

"Kira, suppress your powers. Please."

"*They are suppressed!*" She saw his surprise at the vehemence of her reply and tried to control her voice. "I don't know what's going on. My powers should be completely suppressed. I didn't sense any trace of them between the time I suppressed them after waking up and just before we got jumped in the alley."

"Like they're responding to danger?" Jason suggested.

"Oh, blazes, those Mages are getting close. Jason, they might be able to tell I'm a Mage if they get close enough. I have no idea if I'm hiding my Mage presence anymore."

Instead of answering, Jason grabbed her wrist and abruptly turned into a doorway as they reached it. Kira saw that they'd entered some sort of clothing store. Jason slowed his pace to a casual, unhurried stroll, she matching it, as they pretended to browse down the aisles toward the back of the store.

Kira saw the two salespeople in the store watching her and Jason, suspicion clear on their faces. "Jason, they know who we are."

"Just keep walking," Jason muttered.

She felt something else. "Those Mages. They stopped outside the door to this place."

"That's not good."

"There has to be a back exit."

"Will they let us use it?" Jason asked, looking around for signs.

One of the salespeople was approaching, a no-nonsense look on his face. "Hold it, you two."

"Is something wrong?" Kira asked.

"Another tourist from Tiae? What's in your backpack?"

She stared at him. "None of your business."

"I know shoplifters when I see them! We deal with your kind all the time, young people who think they can get away with theft on holiday! Give me—"

Kira, momentarily stunned into inaction at being confused with a teen trying to shoplift, brought out her pistol as she heard the door to the shop opening. The salesperson stopped talking, his mouth freezing open, as Kira held up the weapon. "Take us to the back way out. Right now." He didn't move. "Now!" Kira growled as her Mage senses told her the two Mages had entered the shop. She canted the barrel of her pistol toward the salesperson's face.

The man almost ran toward the back of the store, Kira and Jason following past the startled other salesperson. The door there opened into a back area with a desk and boxes of unpacked goods, then the salesperson halted at another door. "That's it."

"Thank you," Kira said as she yanked open the door. She took a precious moment to glare at him. "We're not thieves."

She and Jason bolted out into another alley. A fence ahead blocked their way, but Kira holstered her pistol and took it at a run, grabbing the top and pulling herself up, Jason alongside her. They got over the top and raced down the alley on the other side until they reached the street.

Trying to look casual and get their breathing under control, Kira and Jason once again strolled down the street like two people with nothing to worry about. "Can you tell where they are?" Jason said.

"Still back there. I think we lost them for the moment."

"They're tracking you. They know you're a Mage."

"No, Jason, you're the Mage, remember?"

"Oh." Jason glanced back down the street, then around them. "Over that way. Cross the street and then the next left. Kira, you can tell whether a Mage is a woman or a man, right? If those Mages are sensing you, they know it's a woman."

"Yes, but hopefully they won't believe it can be me. I just waved a pistol around in there, Jason. A Mage wouldn't know what to do with a pistol. So it can't be me. It must be you. They'll decide something about being from Urth makes you feel like a female Mage to them."

"I hope none of the male Mages ask me for a date," Jason mumbled as they turned the corner. "Kira, isn't it time to seriously consider going to the military and getting protection and an escort down to the port?"

She shook her head. "No. What's happened to every military escort we've had on this trip?"

"But—"

"The moment we get the escort, Maxim's people know where we are. Am I right? The escort will fly that stupid banner that somebody decided I needed and . . . what did you tell Colonel Anders that armored coach was? Some kind of magnet?"

"A threat magnet," Jason said.

"Yes. Exactly. And that's what my banner is, and that's what you and I are, Jason. Anything, anyone, that's in the way of threats to us gets run over."

Jason looked back again. "Kira, I honestly don't know if what you just said is smart or crazy. All right. Are we still both in agreement that we need to get to the port?"

"Yes. How do we do that without being spotted on the road?"

"You can sense when Mages are getting close? You don't have to see them?"

"Right."

"Follow me." Jason walked faster, Kira keeping up, sensing Mages here and there, none of them apparently coming closer at the moment.

She got a good look at the sun as they came out in the area where streets converged toward the road down to the port. "Look how low the sun is! It's almost sunset. We both slept most of the day away."

"We must have needed it," Jason said, walking toward a wagon with a covered back, drawn by a pair of horses plodding along swiftly enough that they must be expecting a rest once they reached the port at the bottom of the road. "Excuse me!" Jason called. "Can we ride in the back down to the port?"

The driver, a woman old enough to be Kira's grandmother, turned a disapproving eye on them. "It'll cost yah."

Kira dug out a Tiae crown and held it up. "How about this?"

"Sure. Get in. Touch anything and I'll know."

The driver didn't slow down, requiring Jason and Kira to run and jump up onto the back before rolling over the tailgate. Most of the wagon was full of boxes, bags, and barrels, but they wedged themselves together in a narrow space. "We just ride this wagon down to the port?" Kira asked.

"Yeah. It's moving along, but it's not in a big hurry. There's no reason for anyone looking for a couple of people in a rush to get away to be hiding in it," Jason said. "And if some Mages decide to check out this wagon, hopefully you'll sense them coming."

"Hey!" their driver yelled to another driver whose cart was sitting idle alongside the road. "Get these two kids! Too lazy to even walk downhill to the port! Kids these days! It's like they're scared of breaking a sweat!"

The other yelled back, sounding like a man not much younger than their own driver. "It's all those new Mechanic devices. They'd rather sit indoors playing with those than do a hard day's work. If they were my kids I'd be getting work out of them!"

"Bunch of precious flowers, that's what they think they are!" their driver yelled in reply.

"I didn't know our money for the ride down also paid for a show," Jason commented to Kira, grinning.

"You think that was funny?" she complained. As she'd fought and run and worried, her thoughts seemed to be getting both cloudier and clearer at the same time. And nearby objects looked . . . odd. She couldn't explain why even to herself.

"'The morals of children are tenfold worse than formerly,'" Jason said. "Somebody said that hundreds of years ago. Somebody is always saying that. This one guy . . . Horace? Thousands of years ago. He said every generation is worse than the one before it. Just ask the previous generation. Or something like that."

"Must be nice not to worry about that," Kira muttered, feeling resentful.

"Huh?" Jason's expression changed to concern, "What'd I do?"

"Nothing."

"Kira, I said something that bothers you."

She sighed heavily enough to know it sounded theatrical. "The prior generation, with help from the generation before that, freed this world. The daughter of Jules finally came in that generation. That alone makes them special. But they rallied to her and they freed the world. And my generation lives with change and uncertainty and . . . in the shadow of those who came before."

"I knew you felt that way about your mom, but you're saying that a lot of people your age feel that way, too?"

"Yeah." She kept her reply short, still fighting that feeling of resentment.

"What does your dad think about that?"

Another big sigh. "We all have our roles, and the illusion of the world gives us all challenges, and blah, blah, blah."

Jason's shook his head. "I've never heard you talk about your dad that way."

"My *father*. What the blazes does *dad* even mean?" She sat leaning forward, her arms around her knees, staring at the street visible between the cover of the wagon and the top of the tailgate as the horses clip-clopped their way toward the harbor. "You'll never understand, Jason. Just like I hardly ever seem to understand you."

He took a while to reply, then spoke with such great care that she could almost feel each word being formed. "Are we heading toward a bad place again?"

She took a moment to reply, depression settling over her. "We might be."

Jason sat, silent, staring anxiously at the street. Every once in a while his lips started to move as if he were about to say something, but nothing came out.

Kira closed her eyes, trying to find her calm center, and the house was there, the only home she'd ever known. Something dangerous lurked in the basement, pounding at the door.

She'd been chased through Altis. Just like her mother.

Was that some form of the thing that Jason called an omen? Her mother had gotten out of Altis safely, destroying a Mechanics Guild ship on the way.

Get out of Altis.

Kira was still fixating on that when Jason spoke to her again. "We can jump out at any time. We're at the harbor."

She shoved herself forward and over the tailgate, Jason following. The sun had set, night deepening around the harbor, the traffic headed to and from the ships falling off as sailors settled in at the waterfront bars and other businesses closed. Far off to Kira's left was the pier where the warship waited for her. And out in the harbor at anchor rested the Imperial-flagged passenger ship, some boats alongside it to ferry passengers to and from shore.

Kira stood still, oblivious to the remaining foot and wagon traffic veering around her and the yelled insults hurled at her. She stared at that Imperial-flagged ship, feeling something like an icy wind coming from it to wash over her.

Hate. That's what it felt like.

"He's there," Kira said to Jason.

"Maxim? We'd better go, then."

"Yes." Kira turned and began walking to her right.

Jason came running up beside her. "Kira, the Confederation warship is the other way."

She glanced at him. "I know. I'm going this way."

"Why?"

"He's there," she repeated. "Waiting for me. We have to get him off-balance, get him to chase us. And if he thinks we're not protected, he'll come for us. And that's how I'll get him."

Jason was staring at her, his expression rendered strange by the flowing shadows as they walked past widely-spaced lights. "Is this the plan?"

"The plan? Yeah. It's working, isn't it?" Kira nodded to herself. "They're coming out to get us. Just what we want."

"No, that isn't what we want," Jason said. "Why are we going this way?"

"Mother fought her way out of Altis and escaped the harbor in a boat. We have to do the same."

"We do?"

"Yes! It's obvious!" Jason looked like a man in pain. "Did you get hurt earlier and not tell me?"

"No," Jason said. "Kira, what do I have to do to convince you to turn around and go to the Confederation ship?"

"Why would I want to do that? The plan is working, Jason." She looked back for a moment. "And there are Mages back there. And on that ship with Maxim. We need to keep going. We need to stick to the plan."

"Kira! This is crazy!" He ran ahead and planted himself directly in front of her, blocking her path, his arms slightly spread.

"What are you doing?" Kira asked as she stopped walking, hearing the steel appear in her voice.

"Kira, please stop. Let's go the other way, to the warship, get a good night's rest, and then talk about this."

He sounded reasonable. And worried. She should at least think about it. But as Kira considered his words, she felt tension running along her skin like a swarm of ants. And right after that, a surge of fear oddly mingled with confidence. "Back to the warship. To that room on the warship."

"Your cabin. Yeah."

"Where I can be locked in."

"No!"

"You weren't there," she snarled at Jason. "On Maxim's ship, day after day, wondering whether I'd end my life a helpless, mindless slave, drugged and abused and broken into a million tiny pieces. Were you there, Jason?"

He shook his head, looking miserable. "No. I tried to get there."

Her will wavered, remembering the small boat he'd dared the ocean in, how badly off he was when she found him. Kira, one hand clenching into a fist, relaxed it. "I won't hurt you again, Jason. Not ever. But no one is going to lock me up again."

"No one wants to lock you up," Jason said.

Where did the suspicion arise from? That maybe Jason had been working with Maxim all this time? Waiting for the right moment to betray her? Were the officers of the Confederation warship in on it? Suddenly that seemed all too plausible.

She felt the hate rolling from the Imperial-flagged passenger ship in the harbor, shivering with the cold, merciless intent behind it.

There was one way to know if Jason could be trusted.

She moved forward, not attacking, but feinting to one side, then dodging to the other, lowering and rolling her shoulder at the right moment to avoid his futile grab as she slid past him and started walking along the waterfront again.

Her back tight with tension, wondering if Jason would attack.

His feet could be heard, running. Past her and in front and he was standing there again, spreading his arms. "Kira, please."

She feinted twice this time, once again sliding past near him as he lunged off-balance to try to stop her. Kira walked on, at a steady pace.

Running. Again. Standing in front of her, his eyes desperate and despairing. "Kira . . ."

Kira came to a halt, looking at him. "Why didn't you try to stop me?"

"I did. I am."

"You've got a knife."

Jason stared at her, shaking his head. "No. I won't even point a knife at you."

"Take my pistol. Threaten me with that."

"No! It wouldn't mean anything! I can't do that."

Kira leaned closer. "Hit me, then. Knock me out."

Jason shook his head again, looking down at the surface of the pier. "I can't. I can't hit you. Not even to save your life."

She felt relief fill her. "I knew I could trust you. Come on."

Kira walked onward, past a now-passive Jason, following some imperative that led her down a pier lined with smaller craft. Sailboats, all of them. The larger ones were tied up near the end of the pier. She kept going, knowing that Jason was walking alongside her again.

And there it was, a trim sailboat, long and lean, two masts. Even with night fully upon them she could see that it was a boat designed to cross open water with confidence, but small enough for one or two people to handle. "That's it."

"That's what?" Jason asked, his voice dull.

"We're taking that."

"Kira, we can't do that. Why can't we just go back to the Confederation warship? Or Colonel Patila. She knows your mom. You can trust her."

She glowered at him. "I thought we'd resolved this. Jason, stop trying to stop me. If you don't want to come along, you can go back to the Confederation warship and thrill them all with stories about your amazing ship in space."

"You don't really want me to leave," Jason said, gazing at her under lowered brows.

"Yes, I do! Go! It'll be a lot easier on me."

He made a face. "Kira, I've noticed that when you start telling me to go away it's always when you really need me there."

She snapped at him in exasperation. "Is that what your male ego is telling you? That I can't handle life unless you're there to do the heavy lifting? Well, guess what? I handled myself just fine for a long time before you ever came to this world, and I didn't suddenly become helpless when you stepped off that fancy ship of yours! I'm not one of your pathetic little Urth girls waiting to be rescued!"

Jason looked off across the harbor. "Earth girls aren't like that. Okay, maybe some are. But a lot of them are strong. You shouldn't talk about them that way."

"I shouldn't? Why not?"

"Because some of them are . . . *were* my friends. And I don't like anyone saying mean things about my friends. Not even you."

She started to shoot back another angry reply, but stopped herself. "All right. Are you coming or not?"

"Was that an apology? Not to me. To them."

Kira sighed, still aggravated but admiring the way Jason was sticking up for his former friends. "Yes. I apologize to Urth girls. I'm sure they all kick butt and take names and always smell like flowers."

She walked to the edge of the pier, looking at the deck of the sailboat about half a lance below her. A small deckhouse rose amidships, giving access to the interior which on a boat like this would include a bunk or two. "This is just what we need."

"We're stealing a boat? You're really going to do that?"

"We're *borrowing* a boat," Kira said. "Under the authority of the daughter of Jules." She lowered herself off the pier onto the boat, steadying herself as the deck rocked slightly in response to her weight.

He looked down at her. "You never used to do that. Never used to go around saying you have your mother's power."

"I didn't have that power before. Now I do."

"Why are you using it to take this boat?"

"Because it's *important!*" she snapped at him. "What's happened to you, Jason? You used to be smart. You used to understand things. But now every time I try to do anything you're holding us up wanting to know why we're doing this or why we're doing that!"

Instead of replying immediately, he gave her a flat stare. When Jason finally spoke, his voice was as flat as his expression. "I guess I must have changed."

"Change back!" Kira told him. "I need someone who helps me. Not someone who has to have everything explained to him! If you want to stay here, fine. Stay. But please let loose the lines so I can go."

He didn't say anything, walking to the bollards to set free the lines and toss them down to the deck. But when he was done, Jason jumped down on deck to join her before the boat could drift away from the pier.

Kira went to the mast, fumbling with the winch to raise the main sail, while Jason coiled the lines. "Jason, this winch is broken. It's jammed and won't move."

He came over to look. "You didn't release the latch," Jason said, flipping loose something.

"Oh. Uh." She stared at the winch, wondering how she could have missed something that basic. "Thanks."

She cranked the winch, raising the sail, white but looking black and gray against the night sky. Once it was raised all the way, Kira paused, staring at the winch again. "Jason."

"Yeah?"

"Um. The . . . latch."

He came over and flipped it back in place. "Does that bother you?" Jason asked. "That you're having trouble doing simple mechanical tasks?"

"I'm tired. That's all it is."

"Fine." Jason went to the tiller at the stern to steer as the sail caught the breeze, the boat gaining way across the smooth waters of the harbor. "Where are we going?"

"Head for the harbor entrance. We need to leave Altis."

"Should I ask why?"

"So Maxim will follow."

"Sure."

Irritated by Jason's attitude, Kira stood by the mast, facing forward away from him. The boat gained speed, slicing cleanly through the waters of the harbor. All about, lanterns and lights hung from ships, marking their locations at anchor, as if they were sailing amid a field of stars somehow brought down to just above the surface of the water.

She could tell the direction to the Imperial-flagged ship carrying Maxim. As the sailboat coursed over the waters of the harbor, Kira sensed something else. Faint, but it was unmistakable once she'd realized it was there.

Mage Ivor. The lightning Mage was also somewhere in this harbor. Could he sense where Kira was?

She realized something else. "Jason, you're off course! We're heading far to the left of the way out of the harbor."

He didn't answer.

Far to the left. Toward the Confederation warship. "Jason, turn this boat to starboard! Now!"

He sat at the tiller, stubbornly holding course, daring her to strike him, trying to force her to give up.

Her mother said there was always an alternative, if you were willing to take it.

Kira pulled off her jacket and walked to the port side, facing the direction of the Imperial-flagged ship. "Turn toward the entrance to the harbor now or I'm jumping off and swimming to that ship."

He gazed at her in disbelief. "That'd be suicide."

"It'd be a last battle for Maxim or for me," Kira said. "Turn. Or I'll jump on three. One. Two."

With a snarl of frustration Jason jerked the tiller over so the boat veered starboard onto a course leaving the harbor.

She stepped back from the side, holding onto the mast for support. "Jason, why are you making this so hard?"

"I thought we were a team," Jason said. "It looks like you're making all of the decisions."

"I have a plan."

"Something is messing with your head."

She felt a wave of anger threatening to swamp her. Kira fought it, gritting her teeth as she leaned against the mast, refusing to let the rage fill her mind as it wanted to.

"Kira?"

The worry in Jason's voice brought her out of that inner battle. Kira focused her eyes on him, breathing as hard as if she had just run a sprint. "I'm fine."

"But—"

"Get us out of this harbor. If you care about me, get us out of this harbor!"

One of the lights on the water swung around, moving their way. Kira also saw a green light marking the starboard side of the vessel apparently moving to intercept them.

She touched her pistol, reassuring herself that it was ready. "Someone's coming after us already! Get ready for a fight, Jason!"

"What if they're good guys, Kira? What if that's one of the harbor patrol boats?"

"If they're coming to stop us, they're not good guys. Get ready for a fight!"

CHAPTER TWELVE

The boat coming toward them moved swiftly. Kira fumbled out her pistol, wondering why the weapon felt awkward in her grasp.

They were trying to stop her. They had to be enemies.

"This is the harbor patrol!" a voice hailed across the water. "Why are you underway at this hour?"

Kira looked at the weapon in her hand, then toward the approaching boat.

She twitched with surprise as Jason appeared beside her. Glancing back, she saw that he'd tied the tiller in place to hold their course.

"Harbor patrol!" Jason yelled back, cupping his hands around his mouth to project his voice. "This is an emergency! We have to leave the harbor!"

"What's the nature of your emergency?" The patrol boat tacked, swinging about to parallel Jason and Kira's course. "Drop your sails! We're coming aboard!"

"No," Kira said to Jason, gripping her weapon tighter.

He looked at her, read the resolve in her, and looked back at the patrol boat. "This is the daughter's business. Lady Mechanic Kira is aboard. She's on the daughter's business."

A lantern with a reflector to concentrate the light swung over to illuminate the deck of the sailboat. "Holster your pistol," Jason pleaded.

Kira had to force herself to do that, then stepped closer to the side of the boat as the lantern light steadied on her. "I'm Lady Kira. This is the daughter's business."

She saw the patrol boat's officers talking to each other, debating what to do. Finally one called back. "Where are you bound?"

The moment she heard the question, Kira knew the answer. "Cape Astra!"

"Altis can provide a ship—"

"No," Kira called back. "I need to leave now, on this boat."

She saw the officers debate again, but the outcome was foreordained. They didn't dare stop a boat with Kira on it when she was telling them it was the daughter's business.

Something felt very wrong about that, but Kira couldn't remember why.

One of the officers was speaking into a far-talker. Telling her superiors. Getting instructions. Kira tensed again, acutely aware of the weapon in its holster under her arm. Should she draw it again? Be ready to fight her way out of this harbor?

Her mother had been forced to do that. This was all destiny, following the paths her mother had trod decades before. Kira felt that surge of confidence again.

"We'll escort you out of the harbor," the officer finally called back.

Kira smiled and waved and relaxed.

They passed the headlands on either side, the harbor patrol boat turning back as Kira's boat beat through the choppy waters where the sea met the harbor and then onward as the sailboat began rolling through the swells parading across the Sea of Bakre, the lights of the patrol boat fading behind them.

Kira went to the foremast and raised its sail, stubbornly fidgeting with the winch until she got it done. The sailboat leaped forward under the added push, like her horse Suka eagerly breaking into a run as he entered an open meadow.

Suka. Home. Kira wondered why those memories disturbed her thoughts.

"Why are we going to Cape Astra?" Jason called.

"Because . . . it's obvious! Jason, why do you keep asking questions? I need you to help me, or get out of my way."

"Maybe asking you questions is a way of trying to help," Jason said.

"It's not. You're just slowing me down. It's not too late for me to drop you off on the coast of Altis. Why don't I do that?"

His reply sounded stubborn and weary. "You told me not to leave you, no matter what you said. I'm staying."

She felt a need to reassure him. "Jason, this is all working out. See, I told the patrol we're going to Cape Astra. If Maxim has any trouble tracking us, his spies will still be able to find that out before he leaves Altis and he'll know he can catch us at Cape Astra. If that ship gets close enough, though, they'll be able to sense me and follow us that way." Kira looked up at the sails. "If these winds hold we should be able to make as good a speed as they can. And it'll take them a while to get underway. We should be able to stay ahead of them. And I'm doing my best to make my Mage presence feel like you so they won't suspect I'm the Mage."

"Make it feel like I'm really scared, then," Jason said.

So much for trying to cheer up Jason. "If you're so scared, why are you still here?"

"I'm not scared for myself," Jason told her.

Kira looked at the water rushing past the side of the boat, trying to find words. Finally, she looked back at him. "Steer south-southwest. That's a straight shot to the Strait of Gulls. We'll hold that until we can catch the easterly winds that will carry us through the strait."

"Okay."

"Don't say okay! You're always saying that!"

A tiny trace of a smile appeared on his face. "Okay."

Kira recognized the moment he was evoking, knew he was reaching out to her, but found it hard to respond. "That's not funny."

Jason looked up at the sky. "The weather looks fine. No sense in both of us staying up."

As if his words had triggered a spell, Kira felt weariness wash over her. "I'm really tired. Are you good for a while?"

Jason nodded. "I can stay up. Sleep as long as you need to."

Kira gave him a sharp look. "Stay on course for Cape Astra, Jason."

"I am on course for Cape Astra."

"Stay on it!" Why did she have a suspicion that Jason would turn the boat once she was asleep? "Promise me. Promise you will stay on course for Cape Astra."

He looked back at her for a few moments before finally nodding once more in a dejected way. "All right. I promise you I will keep this boat on course for Cape Astra."

"Good. Rest well, Jason." She made her way to the deckhouse and down inside, seeing two bunks, one on either side of the ship, a narrow table between them, and farther forward a door labeled PANTRY. Kira picked one of the bunks, curled up in it, feeling the motion of the waves beneath her, and almost instantly fell asleep.

Kira woke up blinking against sunlight streaming in through a porthole, wondering where she was. This was getting to be a bad habit.

It looked and felt like she was on a sailboat. At sea.

Blazes. What had she done?

At least she still had her pistol and the door to the deckhouse was open, so Kira knew no one had taken her prisoner.

She pulled herself out of the deckhouse into a brisk morning with whitecaps all about the sailboat as it galloped across the waves, the morning sun sparkling on the water..

At the stern, Jason sagged asleep at the tiller. He'd had the foresight to tie it, though, so the ship had stayed on course.

On course for where?

Remembering Jason's reaction yesterday, Kira stayed by the deckhouse as she called his name. "Jason. Hello. Good morning."

He came awake, blinking at her, then all around. "Hi. Which Kira am I talking to?"

"The one who doesn't know what we're doing. Wait. Stars above, did we steal this boat?"

He gave her a sour look. "*We* didn't steal it."

"And we're going to . . . Cape Astra? Jason, why are we going to Cape Astra?"

"I was told that was obvious," he replied. "Kira, I could really use some water."

"I'm sorry!" She ducked back down inside and went to the pantry. The door was locked, but Kira had her lock picks in a pouch on her belt. Mentally thanking her mother for teaching her how to pick locks, Kira got to work. It only took a few minutes to defeat the lock and open the pantry door. Inside were ceramic water bottles sealed with corks and packages of dried food fastened to racks. There seemed to be enough fresh water, but Kira frowned at the food, mentally calculating how long it would last and coming up short.

She took two bottles, drinking one herself as she gave Jason the other. "You tried to stop me. Do I remember that right? At least a couple of times."

"I tried," he said. "But there wasn't any way without hurting you."

She exhaled, exasperated, and took another drink. "Why didn't you turn around when I fell asleep and take us back to Altis?"

His mouth took on an obstinate set. "You made me promise I wouldn't do that. You made me promise to stay on course for Cape Astra."

"Jason, that's not a promise you should have felt obligated to keep."

He shook his head stubbornly. "I don't want to start deciding which promises to you I should keep and which I should break."

"Oh." She lowered her face into her hands. "I put you in an impossible position. I'm sorry."

"Do you have any idea why you did that stuff?" Jason asked. "Why it was so important to go to Cape Astra?"

"No! I just . . . everything made sense. And now I can see it doesn't." She stared at him, fear swelling inside her. "Am I going insane, Jason? Is that what's happening? Maybe it doesn't matter whether my powers are suppressed. They still mess up my mind just by existing. Are my moments of clear thinking going to be less and less? How long do I have before I'm always like that?"

Jason looked at her before letting his head droop. "We have to think it out."

"Think it out? Jason, I'm scared," Kira said as calmly as she could. "Really scared. I can handle any enemy outside of me. But this is inside. And I can't control it. And I can't . . . can't cut it out of me."

His head came up, eyes filling with sudden fear that washed away the weariness. "You're not going to try, are you? You won't hurt yourself?"

She stared at him, realizing that Jason had all too many good reasons to fear that. "No. I won't hurt myself. But what's going to happen to me, Jason?"

He looked down again, avoiding her eyes.

"Jason, this is where you're supposed to smile reassuringly and tell me we'll beat this and everything will be all right." She waited for him to respond, the leaden ache of fear inside her growing heavier and larger until it threatened to fill her.

He finally raised his head to look at her again, his eyes full of pain. "I can't lie to you, Kira."

"Try!" she yelled, abruptly angry and desperate. "Look at me and say it'll be all right!"

"Kira—"

"*Say it'll be all right!*"

His gaze centered on her, firming. "It'll be all right."

"And you won't leave me."

"Kira, the only way you could get me to leave you is by shooting me."

"Don't! Don't even suggest that!" Kira looked out over the water. "I'm fine now. Why am I fine now?"

"You've recovered twice after a good night's sleep," Jason said.

"Yeah. Rest. And . . . it's open here. I don't feel confined. And there's no danger. Stress and tiredness. That opens a door to it." Kira looked at him, trying her best to smile. "You need some rest. Why don't you sleep for a while?"

"Are you sure you'll be okay?"

"Yes. And if I feel any sign of something coming on, I'll call you."

"Okay." He got up, moving like an old man full of aches and pains. Pausing by the mast, Jason looked back at her with a tentative smile. "I can say okay again, right?"

"You say okay all the time. It's sweet. Don't stop. I don't think you could stop, but don't."

"I think maybe sometimes it aggravates you a little," he said, smiled again, and went down into the deckhouse.

Kira looked out at the sea, the wind whipping at her hair, occasional salt spray hitting her with a cold but welcome slap as if the world was telling her to wake up, to be her. On such a morning, it was easy to believe that anything was possible.

For a little while, she'd accept that belief. Until Jason woke up, she'd pretend to herself that no problem was too hard to solve, that he had really meant it when he'd said it would be all right.

Alain stood nearby as Mari spoke and listened at the long-distance fartalker. She wore some sort of hat, like ear muffs, through which Alain could faintly hear the voice of the person Mari was speaking with. Mari had explained to him that this was required on this long-distance conversation because the "signal" was "weak." Alain accepted that the explanation made sense to Mechanics and did not bother with trying to make it fit the universe that Mages knew. He had gotten as far as thinking that the "waves" Mechanics spoke of must be related to water in the air, so perhaps this time there was not enough water in the air.

The room they were in was large enough to contain the Mechanic device, a few chairs, and some standing room. One wall displayed a map of Dematr. The door was closed for privacy, guards outside to ensure no eavesdroppers or interruptions or attacks.

He could tell that Mari wasn't happy.

"What? She did what? When? Nothing else? Are you certain?" Mari paused, her eyes closed as she listened to a long reply. "They were both all right? I can't say. No. Don't do that. Yes. All right. Yes. Thank you. Mari, out."

Taking off the headpiece, Mari leaned back in the chair, resting one hand on her belly. Only a few more weeks before the child should be born. Once again Alain wished that was the only concern he had to deal with.

"Our daughter and Jason made it safely to the librarians," Mari said. "Whatever happened there did not make her happy. I need to send a blast the librarians' way and tell them they'd better inform me what happened. On the way back to Altis, Kira and Jason and their escort were ambushed by a force big enough to kill or wound more than half of them. The attackers included a lightning Mage."

"Mage Ivor," Alain said. "Kira and Jason were not hurt?"

"I'm told neither was wounded. But then they both insisted on haring off to distract the ambushers so a relief column could get through to the survivors." Mari looked at him. "Colonel Patila was extremely apologetic, but said that Kira threatened to shoot anyone who tried to stop her, and that when Patila met her later, Kira invoked my authority to get two horses and head back to Altis with only Jason."

"Kira did not say why?" "No." Mari grimaced, one hand covering her eyes and the other still resting on her stomach. "Then the pair of them apparently wandered through Altis, getting in a variety of clashes that included at least one shooting, before getting down to the harbor undetected and taking a boat."

Alain had to mentally walk through the words again to make sense of them. "Do you mean they rode on a boat or that they took it?"

"They took it. Sailed away with it. There's an unhappy owner demanding answers from the government of Altis. Altis is offering the owner compensation, but wanted to know from me when the boat would be returned."

"Why did they not go to the Confederation warship?"

"Do I look like I know the answer to that? They took a boat on my authority! That girl had better have a good explanation!" Mari waved toward the north. "And she told someone as they were leaving that they were going to Cape Astra."

"Cape Astra? I do not understand."

"Join the club. What the blazes is your daughter up to? And why? I was counting on Jason to be a steadying influence, but apparently that's not working out."

A soft knock sounded on the closed door to the room, followed by the voice of one of the guards. "Your pardon, but there's a Mage who says he has an urgent message."

Alain, his attention formerly focused on Mari, shifted it to the outside and immediately sensed a familiar Mage presence. "It is Mage Saburo." He raised his voice. "Let Mage Saburo enter."

Saburo came in, looking so tired that Alain insisted he sit down before speaking. "You have come from Altis?"

"This one has," Saburo said, producing an envelope from inside his robes. "That one Kira said Elder Mari must see this as quickly as possible."

"You came all the way from Altis that fast?" Mari asked. "That's amazing. No wonder you're worn out."

"Hunter rests," Saburo said.

Alain saw Mari smile at Saburo. The Mages who created dragons and trolls had no emotional involvement in their monsters, not caring when the illusions of the beasts used up the power put into them and ceased to exist. But Mages who created Rocs created always the same Roc, and said that their Rocs were resting during that time when the illusions of them did not exist in the world. Once the Mage Guild had banned both such talk and the attitudes behind it, but Mari had welcomed it, gaining her the early backing of many Roc Mages such as Saburo.

Mari took the envelope. "It's addressed to Kira. From Empress Sabrin." Taking out the letter inside, she read rapidly. "Oh, no. Some pieces of the puzzle just fell into place. Alain, Maxim is still alive. And he's got backing from Mechanics and Mages hoping to create conditions that would allow them to reestablish the Great Guilds. And he knows about the weapons under Pacta. Those Mechanics must have found something in the old files of the Mechanics Guild before the Empire took over."

"A well-organized effort," Alain said, worry growing inside him. "No wonder they struck the train with such force, and were able to nearly wipe out the soldiers protecting Kira and Jason on Altis."

"Is Kira worried about a threat to that Confederation warship?" Mari wondered. "Mage Saburo, did Kira tell you anything else?"

Saburo shook his head. "This one was told only to get that to Elder Mari."

"How did Kira look?"

"That one Kira looked like that one Kira."

Mari clenched her teeth in exasperation.

"Mage Saburo," Alain said. "What did you sense of that one Kira's emotions?"

Saburo paused to think. "That one Kira was . . . concerned. Worried. Un . . . happy. Is that the word to use? Not happy. Also . . . this one does not know how to say."

Alain waited, gesturing an impatient Mari to wait as Saburo thought.

"That one Kira felt not like that one Kira," Mage Saburo finally said. "Not in great amount. Small. But that one Kira was different in small sense. This one felt something . . . unsettled in her."

"That's understandable," Mari said. "She must have been very upset if she'd just learned that Maxim was still alive. Alain, we need to see Sien as soon as possible. She has to know how big this threat is."

"Agreed." A thought came to him. "Is Kira attempting to decoy Maxim?"

"What?"

"Maxim is supposed to be working to get those weapons. But if he knew Kira was within reach, would he divert from that task in an attempt to first get revenge on her?"

"You think she's trying to draw off Maxim to give us more time to prepare?"

"It is what her mother would do."

Mari shook her head. "Don't blame me for this! She gets that from both sides! Stars above, if she's deliberately dangling herself as bait to get Maxim off track, Kira is being very brave and . . . exposing herself to a lot of danger."

"Jason is with her," Alain said.

"Right. He must have agreed with all this. That makes me feel better, but not much. Jason is so in love with Kira that he thinks she can do no wrong."

"I think you misjudge him," Alain said. "Kira would not love a man who always deferred to her. She wants someone who challenges her. This also she gets from her mother."

Mari smiled at him. "That I will take the blame for." The smile went away as Mari pointed to the map. "The Confederation asked if we wanted their warship to go to Cape Astra. I said yes, but the Confederation will have to get approval from the Western Alliance. The warship will probably get to Cape Astra a few days after Kira reaches there."

"Has the Western Alliance been told?"

"The Alliance embassy at Altis has sent messages to the top levels of the Western Alliance. I asked that they also wait until notified by Kira as to what she needs. If she's planning on taking on Maxim and however many mercenaries, Mechanics, and Mages he has with him, she'll need backup."

"Kira must have a plan for doing that."

Mari nodded, rubbing her eyes. "We know Kira has a good head on her shoulders. She's proven that. We have to trust that what she's doing now is part of some well-thought-out plan."

Alain nodded as well. "Kira knows what she is doing."

What am I doing? Every hour took them closer to Cape Astra, and Kira still didn't know why.

She watched the unceasing swells of the Sea of Bakre. Days of travel ahead, at the far end of the Strait of Gulls where the Sea of Bakre met the Umbari Ocean, lay Cape Astra. Long ago, Jules herself had dared that passage, charting the first courses through the ocean and establishing the outpost that became Julesport. In time Julesport became a city and, along with other cities founded by those fleeing Imperial domination, formed the Bakre Confederation.

Kira, not for the first time, felt the huge difference between herself and Jules. She was descended through her mother from the old explorer/pirate/hero, but she wasn't Jules. Surely Jules never felt these sorts of uncertainties.

Cape Astra. Why had her mind seized on that destination?

They only person she even knew in Cape Astra was . . .

Was that why she'd wanted to go there?

Jason got up well after noon, bringing her more water and some of the dried food from the pantry. "Kira, I checked on how much food we have. We'll need to eat sparingly to make sure it lasts all the way to Cape Astra." He paused. "Are we still going to Cape Astra?" He waited for her reply, clearly also waiting to see whether her answer indicated she was having problems again.

"So far," Kira said, trying to sound rational. "Jason, I did think of one reason I might have decided on Cape Astra last night. Kath is there. That's where she lives."

"Kath?"

"Aunt Kath. Mother's little sister."

Jason grinned, relieved. "Your mother's sister is there? Why didn't you say that earlier? She can help us handle anything, right?"

"Ummm . . . not *anything*."

"She's your mother's sister," Jason said. "What is she, some secret agent or special mission type person? Someone high up in the Western Alliance?"

Kira gasped a sad laugh. "She's Kath. Jason, that's all she is."

"I don't get it. Your mother's sister—"

"Stop saying it like that! Like that means Kath is like Mother. She's not!" Kira glanced apologetically at Jason. "Sorry. It's just . . . Kath is a great person. I love her. But she's just Kath. She's not the sister of the daughter of Jules."

"I don't understand," Jason said. "You mean she's like you were when I came to this world? She's never had her skills and abilities come out like you have?"

"She doesn't—!" Kira heard the upset in her voice and paused to control herself. "Kath got lessons. Like I did. When I was old enough, we took some lessons together. And Kath is smart. She learned how to fight and to shoot. She's technically skilled at those things. She knows how to do them right. But she doesn't . . . go beyond that. She doesn't *want* to. It's not *her*."

Jason nodded slowly. "Kath isn't a hero."

Kira shrugged unhappily. "The last time she visited, a few months before you showed up, we went out and shot at targets and blew up a few things, but I realized that Kath was doing that stuff not because she loved it, but because I loved it. Kath was only doing it because of me. Left to herself, she'd do other things. And that's what she does. She's a teacher."

"What does she teach?"

"Several subjects. To what we call low teens."

"Middle school? Teaching in middle school is kind of heroic. Matter of fact," Jason added, "there are a lot of ways to be a hero. So, if Kath doesn't have any super powers like you and your mother, why would going to Cape Astra to see her help?"

"Still not sure what that super-powers thing is, and whatever it is, I'm not," Kira said. "But Kath does know me. We talked a lot when I couldn't talk to anyone else. She's got the biggest heart in the world, Jason. My father doesn't know what to do with all his Mage knowledge. Maybe Kath, knowing what she does about me and being the person she is, might be able to help me."

Jason turned to look over the bow. "Your grandparents live in Farland, right? And Kath is at Cape Astra. This may be a dumb question, but why do Mari's parents and sister live in the Western Alliance? I know they couldn't go back to the Sharr Isles while the Empire was effectively controlling the place, but why not live in Tiae near Mari?"

Instead of answering him directly, Kira bit her lip before asking her own question. "Jason, you know people look at me when we're together, and then they look at you because you're the guy from Urth."

He shrugged. "Or they don't look at me at all, like when we were leaving our escort to draw off the ambushers."

"Yeah, like that. You're all right with that, though, and you've told me why, and it makes me love you all the more that you're that . . . self-confident and self-effacing." Kira looked down at her hands. "My grandparents really love Mother, and even though I'm told my grandfather didn't like Father at first, they get on really well now. One time when they were visiting . . . I was pretty young . . . I asked Grandmother Eirene why she didn't live with us. And she said something like, 'Your mother is so bright she makes it hard for anyone else near her to be seen.' So of course I blamed Mother for my grandparents living far away, but it wasn't her fault. Grandmother and Grandfather want to be . . . noticed. Want to be someone other than the mother and father of the daughter of Jules. If they lived near Mother, that's all they'd be. Even if they lived in the Bakre Confederation, that's *all* they'd be."

"But they are proud of her?"

"Of Mari? Jason, they're so incredibly proud. I mean, Grandfather sometimes seems . . . conflicted? Like, how did his little girl become the daughter of Jules? And then there's Aunt Kath. An absolutely wonderful, smart person. But she's Mari's sister. It kills Mother to know that the world looks at Kath, if they notice her at all, and sees only Mari's sister. And it's hard on Kath. She loves Mari. But no matter how wonderful she is, she'll never be Mari."

Kira felt memories form a frown. "When I was younger, Kath and I bonded over not being Mari. We might not have much going for us, but at least we had each other and could understand how the other felt, lost in the shadow of my mother."

Jason nodded, but then looked concerned. "But now you're . . ."

"What?" Kira gave Jason a questioning look, then his meaning hit her. "Oh, no."

"Yeah. Lady Mechanic Kira of Dematr, Captain of Lancers, dragon slayer, the daughter of the daughter."

"Oh, no! Jason, what am I going to say to her? I know she'll be happy for me, because that's who Kath is. But . . ."

After a moment, Jason spoke again. "Is Kath jealous of Mari?"

"No. Not at all. I could already tell when people were telling the truth or lying, and I saw truth in her when she said things that meant she was just happy for Mari."

"That is seriously cool. You know, if Kath can be truly happy for you, and not be upset that you've sorta become the same thing you two used to not be, then she'll actually, truly, be really amazing. I mean, that takes one huge, amazing person to be able to do that, don't you think? To not be jealous or crushed by expectations or stuff? To be happy with who you are and who other people are? That's a real super power."

"I couldn't do it," Kira said. "But Kath might be able to. She has the biggest heart of anyone on this world. Jason, I so hope you're right."

Jason nodded again, firmly this time. "So that's why we're going to Cape Astra."

"You're good with that?"

"I needed a reason. I thought of another reason, too."

"Really?" Kira couldn't help a laugh. "I'm such a genius when I'm crazy."

"Yeah, let's not go there," Jason said. "Maxim is supposed to be after the weapons at Pacta Servanda. He already went to Altis, to get us, and you in particular. That's off the path to Pacta, and then there's the days he spent at Altis while his goons tried to kill or capture us. If he follows us to Cape Astra to get his hands on you, he'll be delaying again."

"We keep him from going on to Pacta?" Kira nodded as she thought about that. "Because he thinks he can get me? Jason, that's my plan."

"Not exactly," Jason said. "But just maybe your plan turned out to have a side benefit. If Maxim is busy chasing you and maybe me, so he's not there when the others expect him to be at Pacta, that'll hurt the ones trying to get at the weapons. But if everybody Maxim has supporting him hit Pacta all at once, including that lightning Mage, somebody might get close enough to the buried facility to do something that would set off the beta field generator." He stared straight ahead. "While your mom and dad are close by, trying to stop them. Kira, I'm willing to run some serious risks to keep that from happening to your mom and dad. They've been . . . the truth is, they showed me what real parents are like. Not parents like they gave birth to you parents, but parents because they care and love and sacrifice. And I probably sound all mushy, but that's how I feel."

"Why are you embarrassed about that?" Kira asked.

"They're your parents, not mine."

"You are so wrong. They've thought of you as their son ever since the Northern Ramparts. When we're married, they'll legally be your parents. But that's one of the things the marriage will just formalize. It's already true."

He looked at her and smiled. "So we're going to Cape Astra, and hoping Maxim follows."

"Yay, they're coming to kill us," Kira said.

"You stole that from me!"

"What's yours is mine. And vice versa." She nerved herself. "We need to talk about other stuff. Jason, I haven't blacked out again since that brief moment at the hostel, but I also haven't tried any spells. My Mage powers are supposed to be suppressed. I *know* they're suppressed. But they're still coming to the surface, intruding on my thoughts, and . . . unbalancing my mind."

"You see them as locked in a basement in your head?"

"Not in my head," Kira said. "In my center. That's not the brain. That's, um, where the self is strongest."

"Oh, yeah. But the powers are getting out anyway." Jason gazed out at the water again, chewing on a bite of food. "You get a good night's sleep, and you wake up thinking straight. That means at least part of it is due to being tired. The first time I noticed you acting really odd was when we hadn't been able to sleep much for days."

"But yesterday wasn't that bad," Kira objected. "I think . . . Jason, I noticed I could sense a Mage while we were leaving that hotel in Altis. And I was worried at that point."

"We both were. You think that plays a role, too? Being in danger?"

"I think so. At some point, I start seeing things differently. I can't really explain it better than that. The world looks a little strange, like . . . oh. You know that thing Doctor Sino told us about after we got back to Tiae? The thing that was like dobblegonger but different? Cap-something."

"You mean doppleganger? Like but— Oh, yeah. Ummm, Capgras."

"Where someone thinks someone close to them has been replaced by an exact double," Kira said. "Right? They look the same and act the same but the person still thinks they're different somehow? That's how the world looks when I get like that, Jason. It's the world, but it's different." She concentrated on that, trying to conjure up detailed memories of it so she could explain better to Jason.

She was sitting at the bow, looking forward. Kira inhaled slowly, trying to calm herself, before looking back at Jason, who had taken over the tiller. "How long was I out that time?"

He shook his head. "Maybe five minutes."

"All right, so we've got a partial pattern, at least," Kira said, getting up and walking aft. "If I try to remember too clearly how it felt when I was seeing the world simultaneously as a Mage and a Mechanic, I black out. The same thing happened at the hostel in Altis."

Jason nodded. "There's a really old joke on Earth. A guy goes to the doctor and says, doctor, it hurts when I do this. So the doctor says, don't do that."

Kira stared at him as she sat down by Jason again. "You told a joke from Urth that makes sense! Have you ever done that before? I black out when I try to remember how it is when I'm seeing the world wrong, and when I actually use my powers in a spell. So I shouldn't try to do either."

"Maybe in an emergency," Jason began.

"No! You don't know what it's like, Jason!"

"Yeah, I kinda do know what it's like. That's why we're both in a sailboat heading for Cape Astra. Can you remember anything else about how it felt without getting in so deep you black out again?"

"I can remember being so *certain*," Kira said, speaking slowly to try to keep the thought close enough to unravel. "So confident. Like I could solve any problem just by looking at it. But when I try to remember any details of anything, there's nothing there. I know that doesn't make sense, but that's how it feels."

He frowned as he thought about her words. "You're not thinking straight when whatever it is happens. So it makes sense that when you think back on it when you are thinking straight it doesn't make sense."

"Great." She remembered something else. "I told you to go away again last night, didn't I?"

"Yeah, a few times," Jason said, trying to make it sound like no big thing and failing badly.

"Why am I doing that, Jason? I still feel deep inside me that you're a big part of the answer. Somehow you'll help me figure this out. So why would I keep trying to push you away?"

He didn't answer. Kira reached out to hold his chin, gently, and turn his face so that he had to meet her gaze. "Jason, this isn't about me wanting to be free of you. Is that what you're thinking again?"

Jason cast his eyes to the side, avoiding her gaze. "How do you know it's not about that? You realize you love me, and you start having blackouts. You come on this trip with me, and you also start getting crazy. So how do you know it's not about me? How do you know that deep down inside you don't really want to be in love with me? You don't want to be tied to me? How do you know that your feelings for me aren't only surface things, and what you really want is your freedom?"

"Jason—"

He looked back at her. "You keep saying that, you know. How you feel confined. How important being free is to you. And this relationship is about giving up your freedom, isn't it? About being tied to me?"

"Jason!"

"You're not even eighteen years old yet. You could spend another ten or twenty years going out with any guy you wanted to, and not having to worry about them hanging around and tying you down! You could have any guy you like, because any guy on this entire world would give his right arm to be with you! You could be free instead of being locked in with me!"

"*Jason!*" He stopped speaking, staring at her with wide eyes. Kira put one hand on each side of his head, holding him so that he had to keep looking at her. "I know this has been hard on you. I know how badly you've been pushed. But I also know that *I want you!*"

"Then why—"

"*I don't know!*" She felt tears starting and let them flow. "I don't know. Jason, I told you I'm afraid. Don't let me drive you away. Maybe it's my fears trying to do that! But I want you, I need you, I don't want to be free of you. Please believe me. Whatever is talking when I try to make you leave is not what I really want. Together, you and I have learned that surviving, winning, is about finding a way to keep trying even when it seems hopeless. And you're my way! My man. Can't you believe me?"

He lowered his head, his voice low. "Maybe I've never been able to believe that a girl like you could really love me. That you'd really want to marry me. I'm not that big a prize. I'm not a prize at all."

"You're wrong. I'd be dead several times over by now if not for you, and I know I wouldn't have learned how happy I could be if not for you." She raised his head and kissed him, hard, trying to make him feel what was in her heart. When she finally broke the kiss they were both short of breath. "Okay?"

Either the "okay" or the kiss finally got another smile out of him. "Okay."

"It's all right if you don't want to marry a girl who's losing her mind," Kira said. "I can't ask that of you. But I still want to marry you." She started laughing, unable to stop. "You and I are both total emotional disasters, aren't we? I mean, I'm actually going crazy sometimes, but we're both wrecks in every other way."

He started laughing, too. "Yeah, we are. Do you want to get married today?"

"Sure," Kira said. She wiped her eyes again. "I love you."

Jason took over the tiller again for a while so that Kira could trim the sails and search the boat for anything useful. But aside from a couple of marlin spikes that could be used as weapons in a pinch, the boat didn't offer a lot of resources.

She sat down in the deckhouse, hearing the water washing against the side of the boat as it cleaved the waves, trying to think. But nothing came to her.

Nothing.

Was that the answer?

Kira came out on deck again and sat down next to Jason. The sun had fallen a fair ways down the sky as the afternoon wore on, but it was still hours until nightfall. "I have an idea."

Jason's responding look carried ill-concealed worry. "An idea?"

"Not one of my brilliant crazy ideas. I think I'm still fine," Kira said, still not looking over at him. "The problem is my powers. So . . . I need to get rid of them."

"Get rid of them?"

"Destroy them. They'll fight. I know they will. But I have to get rid of them, Jason. That's the only way to save myself." Her voice sounded calm, didn't it? But not too calm?

Jason spent a while thinking before he replied. "I don't know if that's right, but I can't say it's wrong. I mean, we do know the fact the powers exist is at the root of these problems. If the powers weren't there, the problems wouldn't be. I guess."

"Exactly," Kira said. "So, I destroy them. Problem solved."

"Do you know how to do that?"

Kira spread her hands. "Nobody knows how to do that. Not even Father."

"Then how—?"

"I don't know exactly! I'll have to try and see what happens!" She felt a sudden concern and looked around, standing up to scan the horizon. "Somebody's after us. I can feel it. Do you think Maxim's ship is that close?"

"Can you see any masts?" Jason asked, watching her.

"No."

"What exactly are you feeling, Kira?"

"Like we're in danger!" She shook her head, slowly studying the seas all around the ship. "I don't see anything, though. Is my foresight starting to act up? Giving me false warnings of danger?"

"Are you seeing that black haze?" Jason asked.

"No," she said again. "Maybe it's not my foresight. Maybe I'm just spooked because of everything. I don't think I'm losing control again."

"I don't think so, either," Jason said, to her relief. "When you lose it you're really confident of stuff, like you said earlier. You don't say *I think* or *maybe*. You're certain."

Kira stared out to sea, fighting another wave of anxiety. It took her a few moments to identify it. "Why am I feeling confined? I couldn't possibly be less confined. I'm out in the sun and the fresh air. There's nothing around us within sight. We could go anywhere in the world. If we stopped to get more food and water first. How long until we reach Cape Astra, Jason?"

"About three more days, I think."

"I'm going to get as much rest as I can tonight, while spelling you on the tiller because I have no right to expect you to kill yourself doing that while I rest. And then tomorrow, when I'm strong and at peace . . ." Kira looked at him, meeting Jason's anxious gaze. "I'm going to destroy my powers."

She felt another jolt of fear. But even though she scanned the horizon carefully, Kira saw nothing to be afraid of.

The only thing to be afraid of rested inside of her.

CHAPTER THIRTEEN

She sat in the stern, the tiller tucked against her side, watching the dark waters roll past the sailboat. Above, the stars looked down on her. Jason had shown her again which one of those stars was Urth, so far distant that light itself took years to make the journey.

Tomorrow she'd try to destroy something without really knowing how. If she failed . . .

The universe was infinite, Jason said. Too large for the human mind to grasp, the vast emptiness between stars only the tiniest fraction of that immensity. What was a person in all that? What was she? How could she, and whatever happened to her, matter at all?

And yet it did matter.

"Every person matters," Kira's father had told her many times. "It is only they who are real. Nothing else we see is real. It is an illusion we create. But it is our illusion. What we do, how we treat others, is as real as you are. And in all of time, only one *you* has ever existed or ever will exist. Is that not remarkable?"

"If we're so special," ten-year-old Kira had asked Alain, "why are our lives so short?"

"Are they short? Length implies an end, does it not? But when we leave this dream we enter a new dream."

"How do we know that?"

"We do not. I believe it. I may have seen some of it. Perhaps not. But I believe it."

"Will there be horses in the next dream?" young Kira had demanded. "It wouldn't be a very good dream without horses."

"Then surely there will be," her father had said, and given her one of his rare smiles.

Kira, remembering that long-ago conversation, studied the stars for the arrangement that Jason called Pegasus. A horse with wings. It wasn't quite right when seen from Dematr, Jason had told her, but the shape was still there for those who looked.

Sort of an illusion. The winged horse in the sky didn't really exist. People just thought they saw one.

Mages said no horse really existed. All were illusions created by human minds. Even some Mechanics believed that, her Uncle Calu had told her. Something to do with that quantum stuff he liked to talk to Jason about. "Nothing is real," Calu would say to Kira's father, and Alain would answer "Nothing is real," and Kira's mother would yell at them both to stop saying that.

Would she see her mother and father again?

Why did her powers have to be real?

Why did Maxim have to still be alive?

Kira stared at the stars, thinking that she could endure anything except losing herself. Maxim had wanted to enslave her body, but she could have kept her mind free. Her powers, though, threatened even that, to rob her of herself. She reached into her jacket pocket, remembering that there was something there, something she'd kept in her pants pocket until buying this new jacket.

A single, loose cartridge.

Proof that love mattered, that hope should never die, that even the darkest night gave way to morning.

Kira relaxed as her thumb stroked the bullet. The stars above were as cold and distant as ever, but inside she felt a warmth born of the certainty that dawn would come no matter how long the night.

Jason relieved her at the tiller well before dawn so that Kira would be well rested when daylight came. When Kira awoke and came out on deck she felt the seas were rougher. Low clouds scudded by overhead.

"There was a reddish tinge to the horizon when the sun came up," Jason commented. "We might have a storm coming. Hopefully not too bad a storm."

"At least the winds are still right for us to reach Cape Astra quickly," Kira said. She handed Jason his "breakfast"—more dried food—and sat down next to him to chew on hers, finishing well before her hunger was satisfied. "Are you sure you don't want any of mine?" Jason asked, offering the last of his.

"No, I don't need any of yours. Thank you. This is a feast compared to what we had in the Northern Ramparts." Kira inhaled deeply. "I think I'm ready."

"I have no idea what you're going to do."

"Go into deep meditation, go deep into myself, and fight a battle," Kira said.

"What if . . . ?"

Kira gazed at him solemnly. "What if I lose? Tie me up with some of the spare line and deliver me to the Tiae embassy."

"Kira . . ."

"I'm not joking."

"That's not it," Jason said. "Why do you think I could overpower you and tie you up? You're a lot more skillful and practiced at fighting than I am."

"Knock me over the head with a marlin spike," Kira offered.

"No way. I will not hit you."

"You may be forced to decide between that and watching me do something so crazy it'll kill me," Kira warned. "But that's if I lose. I'm going to win, right?"

"Right!"

Kira went past the mainmast and sat down with her back to it, facing forward away from Jason. She wanted as few distractions as possible. For a long moment, she gazed out on the waters, a darker blue today, the whitecaps standing out more strongly, the wind racing across the sea and buffeting the sails above her. It seemed appropriate, the growing storminess of the sea matching the turbulence inside her.

Closing her eyes, Kira tried to place herself in a meditative state, letting her body rock with the motion of the boat, becoming one with the world. As she focused on her center, Kira could feel her powers beating like the waves against the barriers she had created to confine them.

How could she destroy them? Suppress them so thoroughly and completely that they would never manifest again? She had to find a way. Otherwise, she might lose her mind completely and never regain it. Black out, and never awaken.

Someone else would be her. Her body would still be here, still living, still doing things, but she'd be gone. The thought was both strange and terrifying.

But how to do it? Kira knew that Mages could lose their powers gradually by giving up their ability to view the world in the necessary way, but that obviously hadn't worked for her. Apparently no Mage had ever sought to crush his or her powers.

"And you are so powerful now, Kira," her father had said before she left on this trip. "I do not know why your powers grow so quickly."

She would just have to figure out how to do it. All her life she had been taught how to defend herself. This might be the ultimate test of that.

Sinking into the darkness inside her, storm winds blowing through the shadows surrounding her center. But light glowing in that center.

And there it was. The house she'd seen before, the very image of her home outside of Pacta Servanda. Exactly the same, but different. Kira stood before the front door, feeling the powers crouched within, sensing their readiness for her attack.

She went to the front door, not walking so much as being in one place and then another. The door opened and she went inside.

Once again things seemed familiar but different in the front room.

Especially the extra door. A door that led into the basement. A basement that didn't exist in the real world or the real house.

She'd have to go in there. Have to face that part of herself. And take it apart. Somehow.

The door resisted. She pushed, seeing the door become more and more solid, the wood of its initial appearance turning into steel, the small lock growing into massive bolts holding the door closed.

Kira gathered her will and hurled it against that door. The door bent, wavered, and solidified again.

Go around. Kira tried to push through the floor, but it too changed to armor plate. Every blow she tried to strike met an equally powerful barrier.

Despite her lack of success, Kira kept hurling herself against those barriers. But whenever her will peaked to smash through, the force on the other side peaked as well. Kira strained against it, pushing, pushing, and it held and held.

How long had she been trying? Kira had no idea. *Why are you hurting me?* she hurled at the Mage powers behind the door, but the only reply she heard was the echo of her own words. *I will not be beaten!* And again all she heard was the echo coming back at her.

There finally came a point when Kira couldn't strive any longer. She felt the weariness in her spirit and knew the unthinkable had happened. Her Mage powers were still in that basement, still confined, but she hadn't beaten them.

A draw. Which meant a defeat.

Kira withdrew, exhausted, rising back into the world, even more turmoil filling the darkness around her, finally opening her eyes to the growing storminess of a day that seemed calmer than what lay inside her. Her breathing came deep and heavy, her heart pounding as if she'd been fighting a battle in this world, sweat trickling down her face, the tracks chill under the blustery winds.

When she felt recovered enough, Kira stood up, her legs unsteady, holding on to the mast for support. Turning, she saw Jason watching, the question in his eyes. "Hi. It's still me."

"You don't sound happy," Jason said.

"I couldn't destroy them, Jason. Not this time. I have to figure out a way past their defenses. They're . . . really strong. They got stronger as I fought them."

"That sounds like you," he said.

"Yeah. Great." Kira managed to walk back to him without falling as the sailboat plunged through the seas. "Do you think we'll be all right if the weather keeps worsening?"

"You stole a great boat," Jason said.

"Borrowed."

"Okay. Borrowed. I think we'll be okay if the seas don't build much more. We're running with the winds and the waves to the southwest. And, silver lining, this bad weather should make it a lot harder for other ships to spot us and catch us."

"That was part of my plan, too," Kira said, sitting down next to him. "That's a joke, Jason."

"Oh. Good. Um, you're tired now."

"Yeah. Worn out. I feel like I just fought freestyle against three opponents for . . . how long was it?"

"Close to an hour."

"Blazes," Kira said.

"But . . . nothing?" Jason asked. "No feeling of problems?"

"No. Danger must bring them out. Maybe danger is more important than being tired. Or an essential ingredient." She looked at him. "Did I show any external signs of what I was doing?"

"Some," Jason said, trying to look stoic and not quite managing to carry it off. "Groans and low cries sometimes, like you were fighting or striving as hard as you could."

She leaned into him, holding him with one arm. "That must have been hard to just watch."

"Yeah. It was. As long as you brought that up." He sighed. "But after the last few days I'm getting kind of used to feeling helpless."

Kira squeezed his arm reassuringly. "Jason, I know it seems like you haven't been able to do much to stop me, but you've made a big difference. Just being there. Just sticking with me. The first thing I ask myself when I wake up from one of those irrational episodes is, where is Jason? Because if you're there, I know I'm all right."

"You're not just saying that?"

"Of course not. Let me get our lunch, then I'll take over the tiller. I'd like to fight the sea for a while. That's one battle I know how to win."

The stormy seas rose a bit more as the clouds built, and the afternoon light faded into a gray immensity of overcast sky and water with their boat suspended between. By the time night fell the waves pursuing their boat were crashing against the transom at the stern, soaking them at the tiller, because by that time they were both holding onto it to keep the boat on course. Both had tied themselves to the ship so they couldn't be washed overboard, and Kira had reefed both sails to reduce the strain on the masts as the winds grew in intensity.

She and Jason held onto the tiller, the night growing darker until she could barely see even those parts of the boat close by. The sailboat leaped through the waves, the bow rising as each crest came under it, the stern dipping into the trough behind, then the next wave coming on astern, the stern rising and the bow swinging down, like an endless amusement park ride with cold saltwater sprays and battering winds tossed in.

"Stars above, I feel alive!" she shouted to Jason over the wind. "Am I being crazy again? Because I love this!"

"Then I guess I'm crazy, too," he yelled back at her. "There's nowhere else I'd rather be than with you in this storm."

"Hey, do you want to get married today?"

"Sure!"

Another wave crashed over the transom, soaking them. Kira laughed.

By the time the eastern sky paled with dawn, both wind and seas had subsided. The waters remained rough, and the winds brisk, but one person could handle the tiller again.

Kira pulled off her water-soaked clothing in the deckhouse, shivering from the chill, used some of their precious fresh water to rinse out the salt, and hung the clothes up to dry.

And then hesitated before pulling on the spare set of clothing she'd had the sense to buy even when out of it in Altis. Kira looked around the deckhouse, thinking it would be a little cramped in there, but Jason could tie the tiller and . . .

And he knew she'd lost her battle yesterday, and was tired from last night. He wouldn't know if she was blacked out or thinking straight, so Jason would put her off. As he should.

She got into her clothes, ate quickly, then went back to the stern to relieve Jason so he could do the same.

The next couple of days gave them good winds, slowly moderating seas, and increasing sightings of masts and ships as they approached the shipping lanes through the Strait of Gulls. Kira watched every new mast and ship but didn't get any sense of menace from them. Maxim's ship was probably still a distance behind them.

The water grew choppier again as they sailed through the strait on the last night and the early part of the next day, dodging around the larger ships plowing their way along the same course. The last of the food had made up dinner, and their water had given out this morning. As the day grew brighter and Cape Astra came into sight ahead, Kira felt a lift at knowing the trip was almost over, tempered by guilt because the trip was almost over and she hadn't made another try to destroy her powers.

"Thank you for not saying it," Kira told Jason. She was at the tiller while he adjusted the sails.

He knew what she meant, giving her a sidelong glance. "I know when you're ready again to tackle destroying your powers, you'll do it."

"You'd have had every right to ask why I didn't try again yesterday, or the day before," Kira said.

He shrugged in reply, going up to the bow to look ahead. "There's a lot of traffic into and out of the port."

"This boat is a dream to sail," Kira said. "We shouldn't have any trouble. Do you think we could get one like this?"

"You mean steal another one or buy one?"

"Very funny."

They wove between the large ships entering and leaving the harbor at Cape Astra, heading for the piers where smaller boats were tied up. Jason scanned the harbor, calling to her. "That Imperial-flagged ship isn't here yet. We beat them."

"Good." Kira brought them alongside the pier, Jason jumping up to catch the lines and secure the sailboat to the bollards lining the pier.

Getting her pack, Kira patted the deckhouse affectionately. "Thanks. You're a great boat. We'll make sure you get home safely."

Joining Jason on the pier, she saw a man walking their way, a clipboard in one hand. "What boat?" he said in a bored voice.

"What boat?" Kira repeated. "Oh, we never checked. Jason?"

He went back along the pier far enough to see the name on the stern. "Sea Rover!"

"Sea Rover," Kira said.

The dock supervisor gave her a flat look. "Out of?" he asked, wanting to know the port the boat was registered at.

"Jason, out of?"

"Altis," he said, coming back to join her.

"Oh, yeah, duh, Altis. Sea Rover out of Altis," Kira repeated to the dock supervisor.

"You know," the dock supervisor said, looking and sounding not amused at all, "this is my job. There's a port fee and a pier fee. Payable now."

Kira mentally reckoned her remaining cash and pulled out the necessary amount. "You take Tiae crowns?"

"As long as they're real. You came from Tiae?" His gaze on her suddenly sharpened. "A sailboat from Altis? And you're from Tiae? I was told to watch for that."

"Just for the boat?" Kira asked.

"And to make sure whoever was in it reported to the harbormaster when they arrived."

"Sure," Kira said. "Come on, Jason."

"Wait! I'll take you!"

"No need for that!" Kira called back. "You need to stay here and keep track of things!"

They left the pier, Kira angling toward the harbormaster's offices as long as she thought the pier supervisor could see them. As they got among thicker crowds of people on the pier and passing wagons, Kira changed her path, heading out of the harbor and into the city.

"We told him we'd go to the harbormaster," Jason said.

"No, we never said that. He said we should go and I just said 'sure.' That doesn't mean yes. Someone must have told Cape Astra we were coming, but it doesn't sound as if people like that pier supervisor were told who we were. And I don't think I want to check in with the authorities yet."

He studied her closely. "The plan?"

She shook her head. "No. I don't think so. I'm full of uncertainty right now, Jason. But I don't want to risk being politely confined by Western Alliance authorities."

"Why not?"

"I don't know. I'm being honest with you, Jason."

"Okay. When you lose it, you just tell me to stop asking questions, so I guess you're still all right. Where are we going?"

"Kath should be teaching today. She told me she taught at the Jorge School, so we just have to ask directions to there."

The Jorge School proved to be only a few hundred lances inland, a short walk that allowed them to stretch their legs. Kira tried to keep her face averted from the crowds to reduce the chance that she'd be recognized, wondering how long they'd have before Maxim reached Cape Astra.

Reaching the imposing façade of the school, Kira paused and looked at Jason. "I'm too recognizable. You go in and ask for Kath of

Caer Lyn. Say you're an old student of hers. Can you make it sound like you're from somewhere on this world?"

"How about this?" Jason said, his usual Urth accent changing.

She pretended to wince. "You sound like you're from somewhere way south of Awanat. I guess that's good enough."

Kira huddled on a bench outside the school, acting like she was sleeping with her head scrunched down into her jacket collar to lessen the chance anyone would see her face. None of those passing by seemed to pay any extra attention to her.

Jason came back out, smiling. "They said she'll be out in a few minutes."

"Good. I'm nervous being out here in the open."

"How are you feeling?"

"Still like me. So far, so good."

Kira jumped to her feet as she saw her aunt walk out of the front door. "Kath!"

Kath turned to look, startled, paused with another look of surprise, then laughed. "Kira! For a moment I thought you were Mari and couldn't understand how you could look so young! You're looking more like her all the time!"

They ran to each other, Kira hugging her aunt tightly. "It's been way too long," she said to Kath.

"It has been," Kath agreed. "But I was told a young man asked for me."

"Oh, that was Jason. Here he is. This is Jason."

"Jason? Jason! *The* Jason?" Kath clapped her hands together. "You came all this way so I could meet him?"

"Not exactly," Kira said. "Is there someplace safe we can talk?"

"Safe? Oh, yes, Mari's family! Always on guard. Come on to my place. It's not far."

"We don't want to interrupt your work . . ."

"I'm done. This is one of the days I only teach in the morning."

"I've always wondered what teachers did on their time off," Jason said as he followed them along the street.

"Most days we get drunk," Kath said. "Kidding! Have to be a good role model for impressionable minds, you know. That's why Mari wanted me to spend time with Kira."

"Good role model?" Kira scoffed. "More like partner in crime, from what I remember."

"Good role model is actually a pretty ill-defined term," Kath said. "What is good, after all?"

"Good is not an essence, but something to pass on," Jason said.

"Oh, that's an interesting argument!"

"I'm just quoting an ancient philosopher," Jason said, abashedly waving away Kath's impressed look.

"You memorized the quote, didn't you? And thought about it? Anyway, Kira, our days in crime are gone, aren't they? I understand now you're Lady Kira, the dragon slayer."

Kira winced again, this time for real, uncertainty filling her. "Kath—"

"Hey." Kath stopped walking, turning to look at Kira with a smile. "I know what you thought we were doing back then. Because you talked about it to me. But I always knew there was more of Mari in you than you ever wanted to admit. And I knew someday it'd pop to the surface and you'd start slaying dragons and, uh . . ."

"Blowing up ships," Jason said.

"Yeah! You blew up a ship?"

"Sort of," Kira said.

"I have to hear about this."

"You're really all right with it?"

"How could I not be happy to see you doing so well?" Kath asked.

Kira smiled. "Jason was right. You do have a super power."

"I do? What's a super power?"

"It's something some people have on Urth," Kira said as they started walking again. "Like Wonderful Woman."

"What makes her so wonderful?"

"She's a little like Kira," Jason said.

Kira rolled her eyes as Kath grinned. "Don't encourage him, Kath."

Kath's home was one of a row of houses packed together along a street like soldiers standing shoulder to shoulder at attention, all of the houses three stories high with narrow fronts and deep backs. Kira couldn't help checking the size and strength of the door lock as they entered, trying to figure out how long it would hold against a determined attack.

Jason said openly what Kira was thinking. "You're not worried about security?"

"No," Kath said. "I doubt there are a half-dozen people in Cape Astra who know Lady Mari is my sister, and they all know I don't want to make a deal of it, so they don't talk about it, either. I'm just your average schoolteacher."

"No, you're not," Kira said, following her inside. The big room on the ground floor stretched all the way to the back of the building, where stairs led up to the second and third floors. Closest to the door were couches and chairs gathered around a low table whose polished wood surface streaked with different shades betrayed its origin in the forests of Tiae. Farther back was a dining table, beyond that the kitchen, and against the far wall stairs leading upwards. "I love this. You've got this beautifully understated fashion sense, Kath. Subtle and clean."

"Why, thank you, Lady Kira. Do you two want some lunch?"

"Yes! We've been on short rations the last couple of days because there wasn't enough food on the boat."

"Why wasn't there enough food?" Kath asked as she went to the kitchen and got out cuts of ham, a loaf of dark bread, and a block of cheese, as well as a bowl of tomatoes in various hues of green, purple, and orange.

Kira gave Jason a guilty glance. "That's a long story." She took off her jacket as she sat down, exposing her shoulder holster and the pistol in it, but to Kira's relief Kath barely glanced at it.

Kath poured them each a glass of wine, then raised hers. "To the daughter of Jules. May she live long and her peace endure. Kira, don't give me that look. That's a common toast around here, and I do want Mari to live long, and personally I'm in favor of her peace enduring."

"It didn't," Kira said, clinking her glass against Kath's and Jason's before taking a drink. "We had a war."

"Do you think I missed that?" Kath asked as she sat down and they started eating. "But it was short, and it's over, and from what people say, the peace of the daughter is now stronger than ever because the daughter herself told the emperor he'd better behave because he wouldn't get a third chance. Knowing my big sister Mari, I have no doubt she did just that." For the first time, Kath openly looked at the scar on Kira's neck. "Is that where that came from?"

"Yes," Kira admitted after swallowing a hunk of bread that suddenly felt a little dry in her mouth. She tried to change the subject. "The emperor died, you know. Sabrin is empress now."

"Oh? Sabrin? Are you on a name-only basis with the new empress?" Kath teased.

"Well . . . yeah," Kira said. "We've met."

Kath laughed and shook her head. "At some fancy party?"

"No. I'd just escaped and had blood all over my mouth and . . . I think we hit it off."

"Then she blew up the ship," Jason said around a mouthful of food.

"No," Kira said. "I set fire to the ship and that made it blow up."

Kath laughed. "And to think you used to complain you were nothing like Mari! She set fire to ships and buildings all the time."

"I thought Father usually did that," Kira said.

"Not always. Sometimes Mari did it. But always for a good reason. Oh, that reminds me. We were talking about what good meant." Kath turned to Jason, asking about Urth and his studies. Kira watched and listened as Kath drew Jason out until they were discussing good and bad and philosophers or writers no one else but Jason had ever heard of on Dematr.

The lunch took a long time, but Kira didn't mind. She'd forgotten how much she loved just being with Kath. And It was the first really peaceful, relaxing time she could recall in a while. Kath's breezy attitude toward Jason had clearly made him feel at home as well.

"All right," Kath finally announced. "Jason, if I know men, and I think I do, you'd really like to take a bath after that sea voyage. Upstairs. Second door on the left."

"Thank you," Jason said, getting up. He paused, bowing slightly from the waist toward Kath, his hands held together just before him in a formal Urth gesture that Kira had seen directed at her parents a few times. "I really mean that. Thank you."

"Oh, go away with that silver tongue of yours," Kath said with a laugh as she and Kira went to sit down next to each other on a couch.

"Silver is kind of a sore subject at the moment," Kira said as Jason disappeared up the stairs.

"Why?"

"That Mara thing the Imperials believe."

"But they don't think you're Mara."

"Not anymore," Kira said. "Now I'm Mara's unnatural offspring. The daughter of darkness."

"Really? Cool. Can I be your Aunt of Opacity?" Kath grinned at her. "Now that we're alone, we can talk about important things. Like your Jason. He's pretty smart."

"Isn't he? And he's nice, and he's brave. You wouldn't believe how brave."

"And he's all right with being with you? Lady Kira? He doesn't feel ignored by others?"

Kira sighed. "He is fine with it. More than I am! He deserves more attention when we're together. But Jason's parents are both really awful people. I mean awful. As in awful. And they both like to build themselves up by tearing down other people, like look-how-great-I-am stuff? So Jason grew up disliking that. He's actually a lot happier not to be noticed most of the time. As long as he knows he's doing something good, he doesn't want that to be noticed, because then he starts questioning himself whether he's doing it to get credit for it instead of doing it because it's right."

Kath took a quick drink. "Does he have an older brother? Because I'm still looking."

"Whatever happened to that one guy? Don?"

"Oh, yeah, Don. It turned out that Don of Cape Astra and I had differing views on who I should be. Since I insisted on having the final word on who I was, we decided the relationship didn't have a future."

"I hate guys like that," Kira said.

"I doubt you'll have to worry about them now that Jason's here. He really seems to be in love with you."

"He is. He's saved my life like, I don't know, five or six times."

Kath studied Kira. "Is that saved your life literally?"

"Yeah," Kira admitted. "Kath, you need to know that we're in Cape Astra because some bad people are after us."

"Why haven't you gone to the city police? Or the militia, or the military?"

"It's . . . complicated," Kira said. "But we're a little ahead of the bad guys, so I risked stopping to see you because I've missed you so much and . . ."

Kath raised her eyebrows at Kira. "And?"

"I could use some advice."

"Oh." Kath glanced at the stairs. "You and Jason?"

"Ummm . . . yes. That's one thing. Which is tied in to the other thing."

"You're getting along all right?"

"Yeah. Mostly." *When I'm not insane*, Kira thought but didn't add out loud.

"Uh huh." Kath gave her a knowing nod. "Problems in bed?"

"Ummm . . ."

"How many other partners have you had, Kira?"

"Are you asking me how many other guys I've dated?" Kira asked. "Or how many other guys I've . . . Kath, Jason is my first."

"How about Jason? I have no idea how they are on Urth about this."

"He's . . . ummm . . . the same. I'm his first."

"Really? Oh, that's nice. But inexperience can lead to problems," Kath said sympathetically. "Unless it's . . ."

"Unless it's what?" Kira asked.

Kath hesitated. "Is he . . . different?"

"Different?"

"You know. He's from Urth. Is he *different?*"

"Jason can be sort of weird at times and he's always saying things I don't understand and . . . that's not what you're talking about, is it?"

"No," Kath said. "I mean, different, down there."

"Down there." Kira felt her face growing warmer. "I . . . don't . . . think so. I mean, Jason isn't any different! If he was, Doctor Sino would have told me, wouldn't she? She's from Urth! She'd know! I saw her just before we left on this trip, and Doctor Sino is a woman, so she'd think of that, and she would've told me, oh, by the way, there's something you probably ought to know before the wedding, Kira! Right?"

Kath looked confused. "Would Doctor of Sino—"

"Doctor Sino."

"Would she know? If she's from Urth as well?"

"She's a doctor! A healer! She's been seeing men and women since she got to this world. I really think she would have noticed and said something and stars above, Kath, now you've got me worried that Jason is somehow not built right for him and me to—"

"Relax," Kath said. "Breathe."

Kira calmed herself. "All right. Kath, I do know what guys look like, I mean I've been around horses all my life, and Jason seems to be, well, I mean, I don't want to say average. He's . . . oh, blazes, I want him so bad and we haven't. But not because of that."

"What's the problem, then?"

"I . . . I blacked out."

Kira was surprised to see a reassuring smile from her aunt. "Kira, that's all right. Sometimes the physical experience can be so intense—"

"No! That's not what I mean, Aunt Kath! I . . . wait. Really?"

"Kira, what do you think made you black out?"

Kira looked at Kath, overcoming her reluctance to talk about it. "I know what made me black out. It's my powers. I know it's them. They keep causing problems, and making me act strange, and they seem to be making me go insane, and black out, and do things without knowing what I'm doing, and we never told you about the powers, did we?"

Kath's gaze grew troubled. "Powers?"

"Mage powers," Kira said. "I have Mage powers."

"But . . . you're a Mechanic."

"Yes. Don't say it's impossible. I know it is. But it's true."

Kath studied Kira as if she had never seen her before. "What can you do?"

Feeling even more uncomfortable than she had earlier, Kira shrugged. "Um, make myself invisible, sense other Mages, experience foresight—"

"Foresight?" Kath stared at Kira, her mouth agape. "You're a Mage?"

"And a Mechanic."

"And it's causing problems?"

"Yes! I kept pretending it wasn't, but it is. And it's getting worse."

"Why didn't Mari tell us?" Kath demanded, outraged. "Do Mother and Father know?"

"You mean Grandmother and Grandfather? No."

"You didn't tell *family?* You never told *me?*"

"Kath, it developed slowly and then got bigger fast! We didn't even know what was happening for a long time! It didn't really burst out until after I met Jason, and this is the first time I've seen you since then. And Mother and Father are so worried and I've felt like a . . . I'm not allowed to say freak. But, you know."

"You poor thing." Kath leaned in, embracing Kira, and Kira hugged her back, feeling unsettled inside. "What can I do?" Kath asked.

"You can't think of anything?"

"Wow, you expected me to have some answers to that? You've got a pretty high opinion of me, Kira." Kath shook her head, distressed. "Did I hear the word insane in there?"

"Yes. It . . . comes and goes. Jason and I haven't figured out the pattern yet, except that when I'm rested and calm I'm less likely to . . . get crazy. Like now. I'm fine."

"Jason," Kath said. "How is your man taking it?"

"He's . . . trying to help me figure it out. He's sticking with me even when I'm . . . a little hard to be around."

"He's a young man. He's all right with the physical problems?"

"Neither of us is all right with them! But Kath, if I went up there right now and said, let's do it, he'd turn me down, because he wouldn't know if I was aware of what I was doing or was thinking straight. There've been a few times like that."

"He'd turn you down?" Kath asked, smiling. "Eighteen years old and he'd turn down your offer to be sure he wasn't hurting you? You have got yourself quite a man."

"I know. But . . . this is scary."

"What about your father? No one knows more about Mage things than Alain, right?"

"I'm unique," Kira said in a low voice. "No one knows anything."

"Mari should have told me," Kath said. "She's a fantastic daughter of Jules and a great big sister, but the mother thing has always given her trouble."

"That's not true!" Kira objected. "Mother is so great. She's the real Wonderful Woman. I couldn't ask for a better mother."

Kath stared at her as if Kira had suddenly grown a second head. "*You* are saying *that?* The same Kira who once begged me to adopt her and take her away from the horrible woman who claimed to be her mother but couldn't possibly love her?"

"I never said that."

"You were on your knees begging me, Kira! 'Please, Aunt Kath! Save me!'"

"I've never been that overdramatic."

"Oh, stars above! I guess those Mage powers have also caused you to forget most of your childhood."

"Kath, I know I used to have problems sometimes with Mother, but she's not the same as she used to be. I can talk to her now and everything."

Kath managed a smile, but Kira could see the concern it tried to mask. "I'm glad that, uh, *Mari* has changed so much. What are you going to do?"

"Destroy the powers. That's all I can do. I'm going to figure out how to get rid of my Mage powers. I . . . haven't been able to, yet. They're fighting back, they keep getting stronger, but I'm going to beat them." She felt her words resonate inside her, a warning and a promise to the Mage powers that were trying to destroy her.

"All right," Kath said. "You know best when it comes to this. Do you need to stay here a while to work on that?"

"I'm not staying here!" Kira said, wondering why she felt a sudden sense of panic, of being threatened. "It's way too dangerous for you."

"Do you need me to pack any food for you and Jason?"

"Jason?" Kira felt a sudden shock as she realized she had envisioned leaving here alone. Why? "Um, yes, please."

"Kira?"

"I probably shouldn't say any more. I've probably said too much. There are people . . . bad people . . . dangerous . . ." Kira felt a Mage nearby. Maybe one street over. An enemy?

The ceiling felt too low and the walls too close. Kira fought a sense of being locked in.

What if the Mage she sensed was the lightning Mage? What if she had led Maxim and his followers to Aunt Kath's house?

Her plan had worked. But something was wrong. Very wrong. Kath was here. What if they attacked now?

"Kira?" Kath was looking at her intently. Worriedly. "Kira, talk to me."

"I have to go *now*." Kira bolted to her feet, grabbing for her jacket and pack.

Kath jumped up as well. "You can find Jason upstairs, the—"

"There's no time," Kira said, barely able to control an overwhelming urge to flee from the danger stalking her.

"I'll go up and tell Jason, then." Kath stared as Kira ran to the door. "Kira? I'll get Jason down here."

Kira felt words jammed in her throat, unable to get out. She shook her head at Kath and yanked the door open, running outside and down the street.

CHAPTER FOURTEEN

Where was the train station? The train ran north toward . . . Farland. Something in Farland promised security.

Kira realized she was still carrying her jacket, not wearing it, and her shoulder holster was attracting attention. She slowed to a walk to pull on her jacket.

The train station. Don't get noticed. Wait. She wanted to be noticed. Get Maxim following her. Out there in the harbor.

Kira turned and looked, seeing the Imperial-flagged passenger ship dropping anchor. Longboats were already nearby, ready to take the passengers ashore. Passengers. Mercenaries. Mechanics. Mages. All of them wanting to kill her.

And Maxim was here. She could feel the cold hatred flowing from the ship. It had to be him.

She stumbled to a halt, pressing her hands against her head, trying to order her thoughts.

"Kira?"

She jerked about, shocked, one hand going for her pistol.

Jason stood there, breathing heavily from a run, his eyes on her looking accusing and wounded.

"You . . . you caught up," Kira said. "Good."

He looked down the street, then back at her. "You promised never to lie to me again."

"I did promise." Kira tried to steady herself inside. "I . . . I don't know why I ran. I just had to run. And it felt . . . it felt like I was endangering you and Kath and everyone. Jason, I was too scared to think. And if you think it's easy for me to admit that—"

"At least you're being honest with me now, if not with yourself."

"What does that mean?"

Jason kept his eyes on her, ignoring the passing pedestrians. "You were too scared to think, but you didn't hide in a room or under a bed in Kath's house. You ran, so anybody after you would chase you, and not attack me or Kath. Do you think I don't know you by now?"

She struggled for words, surprised. "But I—"

"You're like your mother. You don't think of yourself when you get scared. You think of other people, and how to protect them from what you're scared of."

Why did that settle her emotions even as she rejected what Jason said? Kira breathed out slowly. "I may not be as wonderful as you think I am."

"You're sure working hard to convince me of that. What were you planning on doing after you finished running?"

Planning. Kira looked toward the harbor as her mind seized on that word. "He's waiting for me to be brought to him. He won't come off the ship." Why did she know that? But she did.

"You mean Maxim? Kira, you don't know—"

"Yes, I do. It's so obvious. He's out there on that ship, Jason. Waiting, like a spider." She touched her pistol under her jacket, then looked up at the sky. "It'll be dark in a little while."

"And?" Jason asked, his gaze now wary and worried.

"I'm tired of running."

"Kira, no!"

She fixed her gaze on him, feeling that certainty fill her again. "Two choices, Jason. Come with me, or stay here."

"How about the third choice?" Jason said, his voice trembling. "Stopping you?"

"Do you want to try?" She heard the threat in her voice under the question. That surprised her. This was Jason, after all. But even though Jason seemed to be having trouble thinking, he still must be smart enough to know what would happen if he tried to take down Kira. She'd been taking lessons from Aunt Bev and other experts for more than a decade, while Jason had not much more than a year of such training under his belt. "And don't think about calling for help. If you do that, I'll disappear."

Jason grimaced with frustration.. "I almost wish I had one of those marlin spikes! Almost! Kira, please. Think about this!"

"Are you with me or not? I won't ask again."

He looked down, then back at her, his mouth a thin, stubborn line. "I won't go back to your parents to tell them I left you when you needed me. Okay, daughter of darkness. Let's go get killed together."

Daughter of darkness. She remembered that name. Maybe it wasn't such a bad name. "We need a boat. A small one. So we can get close without being spotted."

"We're going to steal another boat," Jason said.

"Just a little one. Come on."

He followed her, saying nothing.

Kira found a spot with a good view of the harbor that also offered a place where they could lie while concealed from the views of passersby. She and Jason watched as the sun went down and lights were lit around the harbor and on the ships and boats at anchor. A lot of men and women came ashore from the Imperial-flagged passenger ship, some disappearing into the city and others sweeping the waterfront. Kira saw several of them locate the sailboat and go aboard to search it before moving on.

She felt Mages among those searchers, and saw the dark jackets of Mechanics scattered among them as well.

But her sense of Maxim's location remained fixed on that ship. He wasn't going anywhere. Wasn't going to take any personal risks.

"Everything is going according to plan," she whispered to Jason.

"Is it?"

Kira gave him a sharp look, unhappy with the bitterness in his voice. "Is there something I should be doing that would make you happier?"

"I'm just hoping you fall asleep," Jason said.

"Why would I fall asleep? I'm not tired at all." And she wasn't. Despite the long day, Kira felt full of energy.

The only time her confidence and energy faltered was when she saw a figure walking along the waterfront as if searching for someone. It looked a lot like Kath.

Kath was probably very worried.

But that would be all right. Once she'd taken care of Maxim, a lot of things would be all right.

Kira checked her pistol, making sure the magazine was full. "It's almost time."

"What are you going to do with Maxim?"

"Kill him."

Jason stared at her. "You *want* to kill him?"

"Of course I do."

"Kira, you don't want to kill anyone. You never have."

"I . . ." Why did Jason have to keep confusing things that seemed simple? "Maybe you don't know me that well."

"Maybe you're not yourself."

She glared at him. "Maybe I'd be better off doing this alone. Isn't there somewhere else you'd rather be?"

He refused to meet her eyes as he shook his head. "No."

"Don't think you can stop me."

He shook his head again. "I know I can't stop you. My goal is to somehow keep you from being killed while you do this."

She could see that he was telling the truth. "Fine. As long you don't get in my way."

It finally got dark enough for her purposes. Kira had earlier singled out a small rowboat tied up on a short pier attached to a warehouse.

Breaking into the warehouse took little time or effort. "Will you row?" she asked Jason as she untied the boat. "I'll keep watch."

He didn't say anything, but Jason put the oars in their locks and began rowing the boat, moving the blades carefully to avoid making splashing sounds.

Kira knelt in the bow, looking ahead where the lights of the passenger ship gleamed, reflecting on the water. "A little to port. No! My port!" Jason adjusted course, the boat gliding smoothly across the placid waters of the harbor. Faint noises came to Kira. The boom of surf on the breakwater. The rattle of music and loud, raucous crowds at the waterfront bars. A nearby voice above them as someone on a ship they were passing close to spoke to someone else aboard.

It felt unreal. And unreal felt right, though she couldn't say why.

They were getting close. "Over by the stern," Kira whispered to Jason. "About one point to port."

He still didn't say anything, but did as she asked, raising the oars as the rowboat drifted slowly under the back end of the passenger ship. The stern loomed above them, a wide bank of windows across it where the captain's cabin and the adjacent grand suite for wealthy passengers occupied the best spot on the ship. Kira could see light reflected on those windows from the inside, where a few lanterns provided illumination.

Not a modern ship, with electricity. Which meant no fans. Which meant open windows to let air through.

Kira grinned in triumph as she spotted an open window. "Just a little closer. Right under there."

"Kira, please don't do this."

"Right under there, or I'll jump off and swim the rest of the way."

She waited for the right moment, then leaped upward, grabbing at the very narrow shelf offered by a protruding wooden fixture running horizontally across the stern. She felt a brief moment of panic that penetrated the confidence filling her, then her fingertips came to rest, suspending her above the water. Jason was dividing his attention between staring upward at her in dismay and trying to keep the rowboat from bumping against the hull of the ship and giving them away while still keeping it positioned beneath her.

She poised herself, breathing deeply, then pulled herself high enough for one hand to reach up and grasp the bottom of the frame of the open window.

Another pause then, to listen for any sign that she had been heard. But the only nearby sounds were from farther overhead, where a few sailors walked and conversed quietly, complaining about having to be aboard while the rest of the crew enjoyed the waterfront bars.

Kira glanced down once more, momentarily rattled by the look of naked fear on Jason's face.

She shook her head at him and pulled herself higher, feeling a wild exhilaration.

With both hands firmly gripping the window frame, Kira looked cautiously inside the stern cabin.

Two oil lanterns provided flickering light. The furnishings—a table and four chairs, a wide bed/bunk against one wall, a desk with another chair before it—were nice, fairly fancy and luxurious, but surely not as grand as Maxim had been used to as an Imperial prince. Three bottles, brandy by the shape of them, and one of the lanterns sat on the table. One bottle had been opened.

Someone sat at the desk, his back to the windows.

Kira felt her heart racing as she stared into the cabin. The hair, the shape of the shoulders, the fine clothing . . . it had to be him. Visions of her captivity on Maxim's ship raced through her memory. Maxim smiling triumphantly. Maxim gloating. Maxim trying to grope her when she had been drugged.

Kira prepared herself, then with a convulsive effort came up and through the window in a single movement, drawing her pistol as her feet landed on the rug covering the deck inside the cabin.

The man at the desk jumped up from his chair at the noise, turning to look.

It was him.

Kira felt a grin on her face. Not a normal grin. Her upper lip was pulled back and up, curling to expose her canines. "I told you I'd kill you," she whispered.

Maxim stared at her. "What do you want? Name your price."

"I want you, you worthless piece of garbage. How many people have died at your orders? How many have you killed with a careless word?"

"You could be empress," Maxim said, his voice shaky. "I'll give you that. You can sit beside the throne. Just as your mother once did long ago."

"I don't want that. I never have."

"Then name your price! Anything! I'll call off any more attacks on you!"

"Any more attacks?" Kira asked. "So it was you behind those? Even those Mages that attacked us in Tiae?"

"I don't know everything my subordinates were doing!" Maxim insisted, oddly indignant. "Yes, I was trying get you killed or captured. But you have my word that in exchange for my life I'll stop sending killers after you."

"Your word? What's that worth?"

"I'm an Imperial prince!"

"Shut up." Why hadn't she already shot him? Kira didn't know. The longer she spent in here the greater the chance that someone else on the ship would hear her, or check on Maxim. She tried to tighten her finger on the trigger, but it wouldn't. Something was stopping her.

"You don't want to kill anyone. You never have." Jason had said that. And she had denied it, but now, standing with her pistol pointed at Maxim, Kira knew that he was right.

Maxim stood there, watching her immobility with growing curiosity. Not attacking her. Not even running.

She couldn't kill someone in cold blood. Not even when this strange elation filled her. Not even someone like Maxim.

But she couldn't just let him go. "You're coming with me I'm turning you over to the Western Alliance."

Maxim looked momentarily perplexed, then slowly that superior smile appeared. "You can't do it, can you? All words. Go ahead! Shoot me!" He spread his arms. "The great hero. The dragon slayer. And she can't even pull a trigger!"

Kira swallowed, wondering how this had all gone wrong.

She heard footsteps outside the door to the stern cabin. "Is anything wrong, my prince?" a voice asked from the other side.

Maxim, still smiling, turned to answer.

She couldn't let him escape. Kira's free hand swept up one of the brandy bottles and hurled it to the deck in front of the door, glass fragments flying as the bottle shattered and splashed brandy on the wooden door and the deck.

Maxim jerked back, trying to avoid getting hit by the shards of glass.

Kira threw another brandy bottle, and then the third as the door opened.

She shot at the man trying to come through, her free hand grabbing the oil lantern from the table and throwing it to crash where the brandy pooled on the deck.

Flames shot up, filling the doorway, running up the door and along the frame, racing over the top of the pools of brandy to ignite the rug and the deck.

Kira leveled her pistol at Maxim again as cries of alarm erupted on the ship outside the cabin. "Come on. Out the window."

"I'll see you dead first, you creature of the night!" Maxim shouted, his face rendered strange by his own fury and the twisting patterns cast by the flames. He turned to the desk and grabbed a large pen tipped with silvered steel, the fine wood of the pen's body gleaming in the light of the fire. "Silver and wood through the heart! Even you won't survive that!"

He leaped at her.

Kira, surprised by Maxim's sudden action, got her free hand up in time to stiffen her arm and catch his chest as the momentum of his charge shoved her back against a closed window. She felt glass break behind her shoulders as Maxim raised his arm to plunge the pen into her breast.

Her pistol held at waist height, she fired, the sound of the shot muffled by Maxim's clothing as the barrel of her pistol touched his belly.

He froze in shock, staring at her, mouth agape.

Kira fired again.

Maxim lurched back toward the flames now filling the front part of the cabin, blood on the front of his shirt.

Her mind numb, Kira leveled her pistol, but once again her finger trembled above the trigger, unable to shoot.

Maxim had fallen against the desk, his face turned to her, disbelief warring with pain.

He used one arm to force himself up and lunged at her again, the sharp-pointed pen still glinting in one fist.

Kira fired a third time, Maxim's head jerking loosely as the bullet struck.

She stood there, unable to think or move, seeing the fires, Maxim's body sprawled before her, shouts from everywhere. What was she doing? She felt paralyzed, even while the flames spread close to where her boots were planted on the rug.

One shout somehow separated itself from the other noise. "*Kira!*"

Jason.

Kira slammed her pistol into her holster, zipped up her jacket and spun about, diving out through the open window.

She caught a glimpse of Jason in a rowboat, staring at her in the staccato light from the muzzle flashes of rifles and pistols firing at him. Sailors were on the quarterdeck of the ship, leaning over the stern rail to aim at Jason. Spurts of water were bursting upwards and splinters flying from the rowboat as the bullets struck around Jason, but his eyes stayed on her.

Kira hit the water hard, sinking down, dazed.

A hand grasped her arm, pulling her back toward the surface, where the lights of muzzle flashes and the growing fire onboard the ship painted kaleidoscopic patterns on the dancing water.

Her head broke the surface. Kira inhaled desperately. Someone was

holding her head up, swimming, pulling her away from the ship. The
gunfire from the quarterdeck was falling off as the flames leaped up
from the cabin below and made the area a sea of fire.

Bells were ringing frantically. Shouts. Water slapped against her
head. Flame crawled up a mast behind them and made a giant torch
of it. Kira lay passively as she was towed toward the piers, her eyes
gazing up at the stars.

Her body hurt. Kira lay still, trying to think. Her clothes were soaking
wet. She was cold. Someone nearby spoke loudly. "Are you from off
the ship? How many were onboard?"

"I don't know," a familiar voice answered.

"You don't know?"

"A lot were ashore!"

"Get her over to the side there for the healers to look at!"

Someone put their arms under hers and tugged Kira over bumpy
wooden planks. The movement stopped, and a face came into her
field of vision.

"Kira? Kira, please answer me."

"Jason?" She coughed, tasting salt in her mouth. Was that from the
harbor water or from blood?

Blood. Maxim's shirt.

"He's dead," she said to Jason.

"Okay." Jason said the word as if her news didn't matter, staring at
her. "Are you all right? Kira, come back to me!"

The world snapped back into focus.

"Jason?" Kira sat up, staring about her. The once-peaceful harbor was a riot of noise. A towering pillar of fire marked the death-
throes of the ship that had carried Maxim. Small boats were bobbing
around it, looking for survivors who had leaped into the water.
There were not many survivors. Hardly anyone had been aboard.
Kira remembered the men and women who had landed from that

ship and disappeared into the streets of Cape Astra. "We have to get out of here."

"No! We have to wait here for the police and the military so we can get you to a hospital!"

She grabbed the front of his jacket, soggy like her own. The tight wrist cuffs and waist had helped trap air inside the jackets, allowing Jason to get her ashore, but the outer fabric was still soaked. "Listen. The Mechanics and Mages and the others with Maxim are still out there, Jason."

"Which is why we need to contact the police and the army!" Jason insisted, glaring at her. "Haven't you snapped out of it yet? What is it with you and your mom setting fire to ships and buildings and stuff? Normal people don't do that!"

"Jason, the job isn't done!"

"It's not? Wasn't killing Maxim enough for you?"

"He attacked me, Jason! I was going to take him prisoner! I . . . I couldn't shoot him. Not until he came at me and tried to stab me."

"You didn't just shoot him?" Jason said, surprised.

"No. I couldn't." Kira shook her head, trying to sort out the memories. "I had to set the fire. To stop him. I couldn't shoot. I wanted to take him prisoner."

"You couldn't shoot him?"

"No. Not in cold blood. No. Not even him."

He exhaled heavily, sagging with relief. "You're still Kira. Oh, man. You're still Kira. I thought I'd lost you."

"You got me to the pier, Jason."

"That's not what I meant."

She tugged at him, getting to her feet. "Come on." Maybe it was because he was still smiling with relief, but Jason didn't resist, walking with her away from the noise of the waterfront. Crowds were heading toward the harbor, drawn by the spectacle, forcing Kira to fight her way inland. "We need to get to the train station."

"Why?"

"That's where they'll be looking for me."

"Kira!"

She spun to face him, pausing briefly, once more knowing exactly what needed to be done and how to do it. "This head of the snake is dead, but there are other heads. I guarantee you the Mechanics working with Maxim will go ahead with their plans. So will the Mages. They know I'm after them, that I destroyed that ship. Even if they don't have orders from Maxim to kill me, they're going to try to stop me so that I can't take out any more of them or rally the authorities against them. That means we have to get them out of the woodwork, have to get them out in the open, so we can stop this batch of them."

"This batch?"

"The ones who attacked our train in the Confederation weren't on that ship, Jason. They're probably still aiming to hit Pacta Servanda. We have to make sure this group doesn't join up with them. Didn't you tell me that?"

She started walking toward the train station again, and Jason followed. "Kira, I don't think it's a good thing that I'm having more and more trouble distinguishing between you when you're all right and you when you're crazy."

"Why do you think it's all right to call me crazy?" she snapped at him.

"Maybe your Aunt Kath—"

"No! If their Mages can track me, I'd be leading all of them straight to Kath!"

He took a moment to reply. "Yeah. More and more trouble. Because that's absolutely right."

Kira walked down the street, not trying to hide her face, knowing that among the crowds passing by were men and women who were watching for her, who would see her and report to their fellows where she was going.

They'd come to her. And she would end this.

The guard spoke quickly. "Your pardon for disturbing you so late in the evening, Sir Master of Mages Alain, but Queen Sien wishes to inform you that a large group of people have been discovered trying to tunnel down in a southern part of the city. At least one dragon has already appeared. A battle has erupted and the queen is sending reinforcements."

Alain took the news calmly, actually glad that the axe had finally fallen.

But Mari came out her room, tugging on her jacket, which was impossible to close over the bulge of her pregnancy. "Come on, Alain."

"We are not going to the place where they are fighting," Alain protested.

"No, we're not. I'm worried about a diversion. We're going to the building that has the excavation to that triple cipher thing under it."

"I can do this alone—"

"No, you can't." Mari paused on her way to the door. "Kira had it right. We don't let our men face danger alone."

Knowing that further argument would be useless, and that Mari's worry was a legitimate one, Alain followed, pausing only to speak to the commander of the guards. "Inform Queen Sien that Lady Mari fears the site of the door may be attacked while our attention is diverted to the current fighting."

"The site of the door?" the guard commander repeated.

"Yes, Queen Sien knows what that means. She should send reinforcements there as well."

He caught up with Mari as she waited impatiently for a carriage. A nearby street light cast a pool of radiance along the sidewalk, but out of long habit Mari stood away from it, in the shadows where she could not be so easily targeted by a sniper. "This is one time even I'd prefer to be able to ride a horse," she grumbled.

"How are you feeling?" Alain asked.

"I'm all right. The kid is kicking like nobody's business, though."

"Perhaps you should stay—"

"Alain, don't bother finishing that. You know the answer."

The carriage arrived. Mari hauled herself into it, Alain following. "I'm going to be so happy not to feel like a pregnant mare anymore once this kid is safely born," she complained to Alain as the carriage rattled along darkened streets where late-night crowds still lingered "What, no comment? Are you giving me the silent treatment because I'm insisting on checking this out myself?"

"You know my feelings," Alain said, letting his unhappiness sound clearly in his voice.

"And you know everything has been going fine. I'm pregnant, not an invalid. I won't sit home safe while other people risk their lives!"

He sat next to her, resigned to trying to protect her once they reached the building under which the cipher doors lay. Off to the south, he could hear the distant rattle of Mechanic weapons and the boom of explosions. Many of the people of Pacta Servanda that they passed were standing still, staring in the direction of the sounds of battle.

A half-dozen alert guards stood on the street outside the building. They came to attention as Mari and Alain got out of the carriage. "There may be trouble coming this way," Mari warned them. "Stay very alert."

"Why is there no Mage here as part of the guard?" Alain asked the one in charge.

"The one assigned fell severely sick soon after coming on watch and had to be taken to the hospital," the guard commander replied. "We're waiting for a replacement to show up."

"Sick?" Alain looked at Mari. "Or poisoned in food or drink."

"Be ready for anything!" Mari ordered. "Let's get down there and check inside."

The trip down the stairs to the basement took longer than usual, Mari having to go slowly. "It'll be nice to be able to see my feet again, too," she said when they finally reached the floor and went through a reinforced door to the excavation.

Queen Sien's word had been good, but then it always was. Alain could see another wall of masonry facing him, the door in it also reinforced. Beyond that, he knew, other walls stood, preventing any Mage or Mechanic from reaching the cipher area without approval.

"Everything is fine here?" Mari asked the four guards posted at this final checkpoint.

"Yes, Lady. Nothing is happening here."

Multiple explosions sounded outside.

After a single, shocked moment, the guard jumped to the door and hauled it closed, shoving the bolts in place to hold it shut.

He and the other three guards held their rifles at ready, facing the door.

"Alain," Mari said, "check the side walls to make sure they haven't tunneled close to here already and are planning to burst in that way."

He was on one side of the room, testing the wall there, Mari on the other side, when an explosion tore through the doorway, a storm of fragments flaying the guards in its path.

"Dragon killer! How many of those blasted things has Alli made?" Mari struggled back to her feet, her pistol out, and with grim resolve began firing rapidly at the doorway. Alain saw the first mercenary coming through the shattered door fall, then a second, then a older man in a Mechanics jacket, another Mercenary . . .

As Mari had been firing, Alain had been preparing a heat spell, putting into it all of the power he could to increase its strength and use up the power here so the attackers could not make use of it. When Mari paused firing to reload, Alain sent the heat to the doorway.

Screams erupted as those on the other side of the door felt the air nearby suddenly become horrifyingly hot. The doorway burst into flames.

Shaking from the expenditure of his strength in the spell, Alain drew his Mage knife. The fire and smoke in the doorway billowed out as someone came through who couldn't be seen.

Mari, her weapon ready again, fired three times into the center of the doorway. An old Mage appeared, probably an elder of the former Mage Guild, falling to the floor unheeding of the flames that had sprung to life on his robes.

"You set fire to the building we're in, Alain," Mari said, keeping her weapon aimed at the doorway. "Again. Didn't we agree that was a bad idea?"

"I do not recall reaching agreement on that," Alain said. "I had thought it was important to react to events as they occurred."

One shot, then another, came flying through the door, aimed blindly, smashing into the outer wall protecting the cipher locks.

Alain felt a spell draining the last remaining power around here. "Another Mage," he warned Mari.

She was ready when the smoke in the doorway swirled again, firing another three shots in quick succession. A second elderly Mage appeared, staggering backwards out of sight before they heard the thud of him falling to the floor.

But Alain felt another Mage approaching, something with her coming down the stairs with heavy, ponderous footfalls. "Mari, they have a troll."

"A troll."

She lowered herself far enough to pick up the rifle of one of the fallen guards. "How do we stop a troll, Alain?"

"I do not know. There is no power for spells left here."

"It's going to have to pause coming through that door as it breaks its way in, because it'll be too big to get through," Mari said. "Alain, when I toss down this rifle, give me another from the floor. I can't bend down too well these days. Try not to push the trigger."

"The trigger is . . ."

"Just don't push anything."

One of the guards staggered to his feet, rifle in hand, blood dripping down one arm and the side of his face. "What should I do, Lady?"

"Aim for the troll's eyes. He'll be close. He'll have to pause in the doorway."

"Troll?"

"We are beside you," Alain said, his knife in his hand, and the guard steadied.

"I'll take the left eye," Mari told the guard. "You aim at the right."

"What-what if we don't hit the troll's eyes? What if it gets in?"

"Then we're in trouble," she said. "Try to avoid getting hit by the troll and try to shoot anyone following it into this room."

Alain saw a dark bulk appear on the other side of the door. Taller and wider than a human, immensely strong, but with barely enough intellect to destroy things and follow the orders of the Mage who created it, the troll halted just outside the door as it was confronted with an opening too small to get through..

The Mage controlling the troll shouted orders and the troll shambled forward, hands the size of shovels reaching out to grab at the battered, burning doorframe. Oblivious to the pain from the blazing wood, the troll pried and tore at the frame and the wall around it, widening the opening.

"Steady," Mari said to the guard. She looked at Alain as the light of the electric lights flickered. "I love you."

"I love you," he said, raising his knife to guard position.

A large chunk of the top of the doorway fell inward, exposing the face of the troll beyond. Rough, primitive, as if a child had tried to form that face from clay. No emotion except nearly mindless ferocity.

Mari's rifle crashed, followed by that of the guard. Alain saw bullets strike around the eyes of the troll, the Mage creature batting at them like a person waving off flies. This close, some of the bullets managed to penetrate the troll's skin, but even at this range they couldn't pierce its skull. None inflicted enough damage to slow the monster. The noise of the Mechanic weapons filled the room. Alain heard something snap past one of his ears as a bullet bouncing off the tough skin of the troll came a little too close to be comfortable.

The troll flinched, roaring loudly enough to drown for a moment the sound of the rifles. Alain saw dark ichor dripping down the troll's face from one of its eyes, where a bullet had gone home.

"Get the other eye!" Mari yelled to the guard.

Alain saw someone trying to slip past the troll to get into the room, a hand and arm coming around the edge of the door. He stepped forward, swinging his long knife, and the person fell back.

Another tried the same trick on the other side of the troll, but this time the troll, irritated and in pain, noticed and slammed a mighty fist down to crush the skull of the interloper.

The troll punched at the remaining portions of the doorway, knocking a big chunk of wall into the room to rebound off the wall behind Alain and shatter.

The guard, still on his feet, quailed, but then looked at Mari standing and firing without flinching. The guard slammed home another magazine and fired again.

"Alain!" Mari called. "Rifle!"

He bent to pick up one of the Mechanic weapons, trying to grab a part of it that seemed harmless, and passed it to Mari as she dropped the one she'd been firing.

The troll began forcing its way through the enlarged opening, but one massive shoulder caught. Instead of backing out and clearing the way, the troll stubbornly kept slamming the shoulder against the projection of the wall that was holding it. The projection gradually gave way, the troll filling the opening with its bulk.

More explosions sounded outside, followed by an eruption of rifle fire.

The troll shoved itself halfway into the room.

"Mari!" Alain yelled.

But she was moving, angry at being unable to get a good shot, moving to where those massive troll hands could reach her if the creature noticed her. Raising her rifle, her jaw set, and firing. The troll bellowing again in pain and anger, Mari stepping back before a blindly flailing troll paw could strike her.

"I got its other eye. We just have to stay out of its way now," Mari called.

Alain looked around the room they were in, which when the troll made its way inside would be nearly filled with bodies. "Is that all we must do?" he called, letting his anger at her recklessness show.

The rifle fire outside rose to a sustained roar, growing closer.

The troll paused in the door, as if getting new orders.

Alain felt the Mage who had been controlling the creature cease, her presence vanishing as she died under the guns of the soldiers of Tiae. "The Mage who created the troll is dead."

"Nobody's controlling it now?" Mari yelled back. "Blazes!"

"It could be a problem," Alain agreed.

The troll stood, wedged in the opening, making inarticulate noises that somehow evoked confusion and pain. Alain could see blood dripping from the troll where the close-in rifle fire had penetrated the Mage creature's thick skin.

A fusillade of rifle shots sounded on the other side of the wall. The troll jerked under the impacts, roaring again, shoving to get itself out of the doorway and back into the outer room.

"Stop shooting," Mari told the guard with them.

Alain coughed, the fumes from the Mechanic weapons thick in the air, as the blinded troll stumbled out of the doorway and staggered toward where it thought its attackers were in the outer room.

Without the troll blocking the opening, the sound of the rifles firing nearby was once again deafening. The troll shambled about the outer room, the soldiers there dodging and evading as it swung futile blows through the air. Stumbling into the far side of the basement, the troll began hammering at it. It stood there, hitting the basement wall again and again until the stone crumbled and the rock and soil beyond shattered or compressed under the blows.

The soldiers kept shooting, the blood flowing from the troll, until suddenly its long arms dropped, the mighty hands hanging close to the floor. The troll stood like that for a long moment as the rifle fire paused.

It fell to the side with a thud that made the entire structure shiver.

Soldiers rushed in to help the injured guards.

"Mari . . ." Alain said, grateful beyond words that they had once more escaped dying, and that they had stopped this attack before it reached the buried wall and perhaps triggered the terrible weapon that Kira's foresight and his own had warned of.

He looked back at Mari and saw her grimacing, leaning against the wall behind her to stay on her feet. "You are hurt?"

"No," Mari said, getting the word out from between clenched teeth. "It's a little early, but this kid has decided that now is the time to come into the world."

"The baby comes?" Alain turned to the soldiers. "A stretcher and a healer wagon for Lady Mari. Quickly! Doc-tor Sino must be told!"

CHAPTER FIFTEEN

Cape Astra's original train station had been large enough to suit the purposes of the Mechanics Guild, which limited tracks and trains to maximize its own profits and prevent too many common folk from getting a chance to learn anything about the Guild's technology.

The rail networks had expanded everywhere since the fall of the Great Guilds, and so had this station. A new, soaring roof held electric lights that shone down on the busy concourse and the multiple tracks and platforms that ran through the station.

Kira had walked in, ignoring the eyes that had followed her across the station. There were least two Mechanics, one of them fairly old, with the bitter expression of those who regarded the fall of the Great Guilds as a tragedy. The other was a lot younger, but cocky and arrogant.

"Farland," she said loudly enough to be heard. "Two tickets."

"You want the express or the local? The local doesn't leave until morning."

"The local." Paying for the tickets, she turned to see Jason watching her with dejected eyes.

"Kira, please tell me what we're doing."

She let him urge her to one side of the great hall. "It's simple, Jason. Maxim is dead. The ship has been destroyed. But the Mages and Mechanics and hired mercenaries brought here aboard that ship are still in the city."

Jason nodded, watching her closely. "Right. We talked about that."

"If they were coming with Maxim, some of them might have those codes you said were need to open those three locks."

"The triple simul-cipher, yeah."

"If they scatter, it'll be very hard to run them down. The threat to Pacta, to this whole world, will remain for who knows how long. Or they might hold together and make it to Pacta and attack my parents. There is only one thing that could motivate them to remain together right now and come into the open. Someone they fear and hate."

"Kira," Jason said, "this is sounding like another we-need-to-be-bait idea."

"It is," Kira said. "They won't have heard that Maxim is dead. I'm sure they have orders already to kill me. And if they have those codes, they'll still want you to show them how to use the weapons, because they think you know that. If they know where we are—"

"They'll kill you and kidnap me."

"They'll try. Jason, we have to stop them! To stop them, we have to get them out of hiding! What else do you want me to do?"

His gaze caught her eyes and held them. "Please ask for help. We can't do this alone."

There were Mages in the area. Coming this way. After a moment of worry she felt a surge of confidence. "Who else could I trust? And why couldn't we handle them on our own? We did all right on that road in the mountains of Altis. And when we got rid of Maxim. It'll be simple. We get on the train, they attack, we stop them."

Jason hesitated, looking around them, plainly seeking another argument. When he found it, he spoke only a single word. "Bystanders."

"What?"

"Innocent bystanders, Kira. On that train with us. Look at them. All over this station, waiting to get on the same train we'll be riding. Old men and women. Mothers. Fathers. Children. Babies. What's going to happen to them when the train is attacked by people wanting to kill you and kidnap me?"

His words tore through her confidence like a steel rod through paper. "Children. Babies. Stars above. But . . ."

"How are you going to prevent them from being hurt or killed?" Jason pressed. "I know you're still in there, Kira. For some bizarre reason you think you and I can survive anything. But what about others? I know you'd never put babies in the line of fire."

"No." The word warred with her desire to see this through herself, her almost insane level of confidence.

Almost insane. Why had that term come to her?

She took a deep breath. "All right. I'm going to ask for help."

Jason sagged with relief, looking around. "There're a couple of police."

"Police can't handle this. We need Western Alliance army. You know what their uniforms look like, right? Black and green. Mostly green, and darker than the green of Tiae."

"There are two," Jason said, pointing.

She looked. "Officers. The older one looks pretty senior. Let's go."

This time she tried to lose herself in the crowd so no one watching would see her meeting with the Alliance officers. As she wended her way through the crowded station in the wake of the officers, Kira felt an urge to abandon this, to go back to planning to handle the attack on her own along with Jason.

They passed a family, the parents ushering toddlers toward a bench where they could sit down. Kids. Parents. No. She had to make sure no bystanders were hurt.

"They're heading for the bathrooms," Jason said. "I can—"

"They won't listen to you. I need to talk to them."

"Kira, they're going in the bathroom."

"I'm not a child, Jason! I know what men look like! Not that I want to know what these men look like, but I have to risk it."

Kira headed into the short hallway leading to the rest facilities, the door for women to the right, that for the men to the left. "Jason, stand here and make sure no one comes in." Kira shoved open the door to the left and walked in, hoping that she wouldn't see anything she didn't want to.

The two men in Western Alliance uniform were washing their hands. They turned and stared at her entrance. "Wrong door, girl," one said, smiling.

"Right door," Kira said. "I need to talk to you."

"Listen, if you're—"

"My name is Lady Mechanic Kira of Dematr. The daughter of the daughter."

The two officers hesitated, looking at each other. The older one, whom she could now see wore the rank markers of a Western Alliance general, stepped closer to Kira, staring at her. "You look like her. I served in the daughter's army twenty years ago, and I'll never forget her face."

"But General Shun," the more junior officer protested, "that's not proof."

"You want proof?" Kira demanded. She pulled down her jacket collar to expose the bullet wound on her neck, then yanked down one side of her shirt enough to expose the twin scars on her left shoulder that had been made by a dragon's claws. "How about this?"

General Shun nodded, smiling. "I don't think anyone else boasts that particular set of scars of honor."

"I'm glad they were good for something."

"We'd been notified that Lady Kira was coming to Cape Astra for unknown reasons. And that you speak for the daughter herself. Why do you need to speak with us?"

"There're . . ." Kira realized summarizing it all wouldn't be easy. "Some of what I'm going to talk about are state secrets of Tiae, but I know Queen Sien and my mother would want me to tell you about it so you'll understand the urgency. You've heard of the great ship that brought people to this world from Urth? The crew of that ship, who broke the oaths given by their ancestors before leaving Urth, buried terrible weapons under what is now the city of Pacta Servanda. Jason and I were trying to get Urth to tell us how to deactivate them. The problem is that the remnants of the

Mechanics Guild have also learned of those weapons, and want to use them to try to return to power over this world. They have the assistance of some Mages seeking the return of the Mage Guild, and Imperials and mercenaries working for Prince Maxim."

"But Maxim is dead," the junior officer protested.

"He wasn't. He is now," Kira said. "But his followers very likely don't know that yet."

They both looked at her for a long moment, then at each other, before looking back at Kira.

"Terrible weapons?" the general asked. "What does that mean?"

"One of them can make a city disappear. Completely destroyed, as if nothing existed there."

"Tiae has that kind of power?"

"No," Kira said. "Queen Sien does not control those weapons. They are still sealed in their protection. And I give you my word that my mother and I and Queen Sien are determined to deactivate and destroy those weapons so they can never be used by anyone on this world."

"The word of the daughter herself?" General Shun nodded. "Queen Sien is highly respected, but . . . such power would tempt anyone but the daughter of Jules."

"Even she might be tempted," the junior officer said.

"No, no," the general said, waving off the comment. "You were too young, Captain Taras. But I was there, at the meeting where Lady Mari was offered control of every land outside of the Empire. She could have been ruler of all of us, and not by striving but by being given that power. And she rejected it. She's already passed that test."

"Thank you," Kira said. "You're right. Here's the problem. Many of those Mechanics, Mages, and others who followed Maxim are in Cape Astra. The ship they came on . . . is no longer available."

"That burning ship in the harbor? That was your work?"

"Maybe," Kira said. "If those people go to ground, they'll be an ongoing threat. They'll keep trying to get their hands on those weapons. But they know I'm here. Their last orders from Maxim were to find me and kill me, and to kidnap my man, Jason of Urth, who is here with me, just outside. And those people who want to kill me know that I have tickets for the early morning train north to Farland. The local, not the express."

"How do they know that?" General Shun asked, his eyes studying Kira.

"I let them see me buying the tickets."

'And you think these Mechanics and Mages and their mercenaries will attack the train to get at you?"

"Yes. It'll be a chance for the Western Alliance to eliminate a danger to it, as well as other countries in the west. They'll come out to get me, and you can get them."

Captain Taras nodded. "We were informed by the Bakre Confederation that an armored train carrying you was attacked and destroyed a few weeks ago."

"You're willing to serve as bait for a trap?" the general asked.

Kira nodded. "Both Jason and I."

"I see the stories we've heard are not exaggerated," General Shun said. "You are your mother's daughter. What do you think?" he asked Captain Taras. "If they know she's supposed to be on the local to Farland?"

"The trains have to slow down as they pass through the area where those old warehouses are being torn down on the north side of the city," the junior officer replied. "I know every time I go through there, I think that would be the perfect place to stage an ambush."

"The local also stops at that freight station only about a thousand lances north of here, doesn't it?" the general mused. "These people who want to kill Lady Kira will watch to see if you leave on the train and if all is normal. But if when the train makes its stop at that other station, it offloads passengers and loads soldiers . . . Do we have time?"

"Sir." Captain Taras gave Kira an apologetic glance before he spoke to the general. "I feel obligated to point out that Lady Kira has brought a serious threat to the Western Alliance and now expects us to clean it up."

"That's what you think?" General Shun said.

"It's what has happened, sir."

"That's one way of seeing it. But there's another. Again, you don't remember this. When the Great Guilds fell and the peace of the daughter was proclaimed, one of our biggest immediate problems became trying to identify good Mechanics from bad ones. Good Mages from bad ones. Blazes, man, before the daughter began gathering her forces the idea of a good Mage didn't even exist! Sir Master of Mages Alain led the way on that."

The general pointed at Kira. "But one Mechanic looks like another. One Mage looks like another. How do we know which are truly working for the new world of change, and which are working against it? Twenty years on, that's still a problem.

"The daughter of Jules has brought us a partial solution. Through risking her daughter for *us*, which is what the daughter of Jules does. If they go after that train to kill Lady Kira and kidnap her man, we'll know that every Mechanic and Mage taking part in the attack is a bad one. We'll kill some, we'll hopefully capture the rest, and a major internal security problem will be greatly resolved."

Captain Taras stared at General Shun, then suddenly saluted Kira. "Forgive me, Lady. I didn't understand."

"That's all right," Kira said, smiling and returning the salute. Finally, someone else was recognizing the brilliance of her plan.

"Lady, where will you be?" the general asked.

"Inside the station for the few hours left until morning, then on the train," Kira said.

"If you'll forgive us for rushing off, we have a lot to do and a short time to act." General Shun paused, though. "I understand why the people you describe would want the death of the daughter of the daughter. But why do they seek to capture Jason of Urth?"

"They believe he knows things about Urth technology that could help them employ those terrible weapons."

The general's eyes studied her again. "Does he?"

"No. He does know more about such things than anyone else on this world, but he would never consent to helping such people. He's risking his life, along with me, to try to ensure that danger never threatens the people of Dematr."

"I'd expect nothing less of the chosen man of Lady Kira. I'll see you when the train stops at the next station," General Shun said. "Until then, Lady Kira."

She let them leave, waiting a little while before following the officers out.

Jason was still guarding the door, as she had asked. "Well?"

"We're on. The army of the Western Alliance is setting things in motion."

"Thanks, Kira." He meant that, which cheered her up again. "Why did those two guys look at me that way when they went by me?"

"What way did they look at you?"

"Like I was somehow impressive?"

"Oh," Kira said, "they're impressed by your willingness to sacrifice yourself for the people of Dematr."

"Excuse me?"

"They think you're a hero! Why does that bother you?"

"Didn't I hear the word sacrifice in there?"

"Jason!" She threw up her hands in exasperation. "There's no making you happy. And I'll have you know they thought my plan was *great!* Just wait here while I use the women's facilities."

"Am I going to have time to use the bathroom too before we start getting shot at again?"

"Yeah, you should have time for that. But don't take too long."

A few hours later Kira sat in a railcar packed with children on the way to school, workers on their way to their jobs, others returning from work to home, and a variety of others. There were indeed babies. She thought about what might have happened if she hadn't listened to Jason, and felt ill.

During the wait for the train to leave, a period of enforced rest for her with the knowledge that the army of the Western Alliance was preparing to help them, Kira had felt herself calming as well as regaining strength. And as she did so, her worries increased. Why had she been so certain of this plan? There were so many things that could go wrong.

But then she saw some Mages watching her before the train left the station, and her worries spiked again before resolving into renewed confidence. A tiny part of her wondered at such an odd feedback mechanism, but otherwise it all felt right, so Kira relaxed.

Jason wouldn't relax, though. If he wasn't gazing worriedly at the crowds in the station he was stealing worried glances at her.

What was wrong with him these days?

"Jason, calm down. I know you always worry about what's going to happen when we get on a train, but this time we know exactly what it will be."

He nodded, his eyes still watching the crowds. "We're going to be ambushed."

"Yes! There's no uncertainty to worry about."

"You mean except for the uncertainty of whether or not we'll be killed?" Jason asked.

Her sigh held an extra dose of aggravation. "Honestly, Jason, you used to be fun to be around but now you get upset over every little thing."

When the train finally arrived and they pushed their way aboard, they found seats that allowed Kira to look out at the station as they departed, which also allowed those at the station to see her. Was that someone speaking on a far-talker? She thought so. "It's working," she whispered to Jason.

"Yay," he whispered back.

The train rumbled down the track for only about five minutes before stopping at a freight platform.

"Attention," a soldier announced as he entered through the car doors. "This is an emergency situation. Everyone must disembark this train now."

Kira heard startled cries and grumbles of complaint, but as soldiers came down the aisles the people shuffled out of the car with bewildered expressions. "You, too," a soldier told Kira. "Up and out."

She gave him a flat look. "Have a talk with General Shun. I need to be on this train. Him, too," she added, pointing to Jason.

Soon enough the general came by, nodding to Kira. "The stop will be a bit longer than usual, but hopefully not enough to arouse suspicion. Are you sure you want to be on that side of the car? That side will probably face any ambush."

"The ambushers need to see that we're on the train," Kira said. "We'll be fine."

"As you wish, Lady."

Kira watched soldiers rushing into the cars. The ones seated next to the windows wore civilian shirts and coats over their uniforms, their weapons held beneath the windows. "Jason, you look too tense. Like you're expecting trouble. Relax."

"I'll try." He looked about him. "We've got plenty of help. Thanks again for listening to me."

The train lurched back into motion, still moving slowly through the city. Kira heard word being passed down to the soldiers now seated in the railcars. "Ten minutes. We'll pass the probable ambush site in ten minutes."

She'd never realized how long ten minutes could take.

"Warehouses," Jason said as the train slowed even more. "This is the place." He got up and stood next to her window.

"Jason, you're blocking their view of me," Kira said.

"I'm blocking their line of fire."

"Jason!" She sensed something. "There are Mages near. A spell is building. I think it's Mage Ivor again."

A moment later lightning rippled somewhere up near the locomotive, and the brakes on the cars began screeching to halt the train.

Jason pulled her to the floor as gunfire erupted from the partially demolished warehouses facing the tracks.

A command rang through the railcar. "Hold fire!"

Kira lay on the floor, Jason on top of her, sensing Mages getting closer, hearing shots impacting the sides of the car. Her massive confidence abruptly shattered, and her mind was clear again. She was on a train? With soldiers on the floor of the car all around her? "Jason, what are we doing?"

"We're being attacked! Just defend yourself!"

Kira had her pistol out as another command was yelled through the train. "Open fire!"

Soldiers reared up, rifles at ready, and unleashed a devastating fire.

Kira got up as well, staring through the window at the mercenaries who were rushing the railcars, many of them falling and others turning to run as the ambush turned upon them. A pair of men in Mechanics jackets fell together not far from her car. A Mage with a knife jerked from hits and dropped.

A big section of the side of her railcar disappeared as a Mage worked a spell, leaving Kira totally exposed to the ambush.

Knowing she was a sitting duck, Kira dove through the sudden opening, rolling as she hit the ballast along the tracks, the sharp edges of the rock punching her even through her jacket. She came to a halt, Jason rolling to a stop beside her.

Kira started to rise, but felt a major spell building again. "Take cover!" she shouted, grabbing Jason's head and shoving him down with her.

Lightning again, racing along the track, but being attracted to the rails and drained off. A number of the wooden rail ties burst into flame, though, threatening the cars above them.

She looked up again just as a older woman in a Mechanics jacket, her face twisted with hate, leveled a rifle at Kira's face. Before she could fire, a quick succession of holes appeared in her jacket as bullets struck. The Mechanic stumbled backwards several steps and fell.

It was like awakening into a hurricane. Only the presence of Jason beside her offered any guidance, any hope of figuring out what was going on. "We're still in Cape Astra?" she yelled over the gunfire. Someone was aiming at her. Kira aimed and fired her pistol in one motion. Had she scored a hit? It was too hard to say, her target dropping so she could no longer see them.

"Yes!" Jason yelled back. "This is your brilliant plan!"

"Is it working?"

"I sure hope so!"

Kira felt a Mage close by drawing power for a spell. She aimed again and fired, the Mage reeling to one side. "The power here is almost gone."

She spotted another Mage using the invisibility spell and aimed a shot at the pillar of fire marking the Mage's presence. The Mage appeared, falling.

Another Mage flashed into view as the last traces of power in this area drained away. Exhausted from trying to maintain the spell with her own strength, the Mage held out her empty hands in surrender.

Soldiers in the green and black of the Western Alliance sprinted past Kira and Jason where they lay, charging the warehouses to catch fleeing ambushers.

Kira stared at them, sensing Mage Ivor's presence fading. He was running again. The soldiers wouldn't get him.

The world suddenly jolted about her and her uncertainties vanished. She knew exactly what to do.

"Come on," she told Jason.

"What?" Jason hastily got to his feet, following Kira as she ran to the train.

She spotted a dropped Western Alliance far-talker and scooped it up, running on between railcars and away from the fight, onto roads leading between the warehouses on the opposite side.

"What are we doing?" Jason demanded.

"Mage Ivor got away."

"And?"

"We need to get him. We need to end this."

"You're gone again, aren't you?"

"What are you talking about?" Kira kept them moving fast until they cleared the warehouses. "Transport north. We need transport toward Farland. Something slow. So Ivor can come after us."

Jason used his open palm to hit his own head several times, hard.

"Why are you doing that?" Kira said.

"Because I can't hit anybody else and I have to hit somebody! You know, for about thirty seconds there, I thought this was over and we'd go home and everything'd be all right."

"That wasn't very smart. Of course it's not over. Mage Ivor got away, and maybe some others."

Jason didn't answer, walking along quickly beside her as Kira headed for the nearest coach station.

Horse-drawn coaches had fallen on hard times as the number of rail lines increased and more trains rolled along them. But there were still plenty of places without rail service, and still plenty of coaches serving them. Kira bought tickets on a coach heading north.

She and Jason sat outside the coach station waiting for theirs to depart, watching the horses being harnessed.

"I still love watching that," Jason said.

"Are you all right?" Kira asked. "You sound really unhappy."

"I wonder why I'd be unhappy?"

She had to unclench her teeth before replying. "You know what, Jason? You're getting to be a little difficult to be around."

He stared at her. "*I'm* being a little difficult to be around. *I* am."

"Do not start, Jason." She gave him her worst glare. "And don't you dare call me crazy. If you do that one more time I swear that I will rip out your guts with my bare hands and strangle you with your own intestines."

His expression changed, surprising her with a thin smile. "Yeah, okay. Because that's exactly what someone who's sane would say. You're right."

"Jason!"

But he fell silent after that, either too tired to argue any more or too depressed. She wondered what was making him so unhappy.

They'd been able to hear the occasional crash of a distant shot for a while, but that had ceased. The ambushers had been ambushed, and from what Kira had seen, Maxim's force had been nearly annihilated.

Nearly. If Mage Ivor had gotten away, some other powerful or high-ranking members of the group might be with him.

The coach finally ready, they wedged themselves onto hard seats along with others taking the lowest and slowest form of mass transit. The coach rattled off, the fresh horses stepping fine over the streets of Cape Astra.

Kira watched for any checkpoints, worried about being stopped, but none materialized as the coach cleared the northern reaches of the city and headed into the countryside beyond. The road dipped between low, rolling hills that she knew would soon give way to the southernmost stretches of the Great Woods, fewer and fewer structures visible, the fields of crops on either side giving way to pastures dotted with sheep and cattle.

At some point she fell asleep, securely pinned between one side of the coach and Jason. In her dreams, darkness swirled around her like a midnight storm. Kira walked through the turbulent dark, seeking a way out, but no matter which way she went she found a wall blocking her. When she raised her arms to beat at the barriers penning her in, she saw that she wore Mage robes instead of a Mechanics jacket. Had the Mage watching her in her earlier dreams been herself? Or someone else? "Why are you doing this to me?" she shouted into the darkness. "Let me go!"

Instead of an answer, all she heard was her question flung back at her from the walls penning her in.

They stayed on the road north for three days, making slow progress between stops at various way stations serving small towns and even large individual farmsteads.

Kira had awoken the first of those days with a clear head, but as they traveled without getting much sleep, and her worries about Mage Ivor and her own powers gnawed at her, Kira found herself repeatedly slipping into periods of which her memories afterwards were fractured.

She knew when she'd been berating Jason because of the way he glowered sullenly and stubbornly ahead after such times. Their traveling companions changed with each stop, but Kira could tell from the expressions of those who'd ridden with them a while that she'd shown her worst side again and again.

How could she destroy her powers when she couldn't get rest?

Some of the vendors at the stops offered herbal concoctions and brews that would aid sleep even on a coach jolting along rough roads. Kira studied them with worried eyes, remembering Doctor Sino's advice, but also recalling that terrible night when she'd been drugged by the Imperials. In the end she always turned away and spent miserable hours unable to rest.

Where was Mage Ivor? She was giving him a perfect target. Whenever her confidence in the wisdom of that plan wavered, Kira found herself plunging back into that state of perfect confidence, or occasionally blacking out for short periods.

She didn't tell Jason about the blackouts. He didn't ask, so she didn't have to lie about it, and she didn't volunteer the information. Jason had enough problems to worry about. So did she.

As her lucid periods grew briefer, Kira felt fear settling in on her, a constant companion. Every time she woke into clear thinking, Kira wondered if that would be her last, if the next time she'd be forever trapped, until one last blackout stayed for as long as her body remained alive. Someone else. Not her any longer.

Doctor Sino's encouraging words, that when blacked out she was the same person, meant nothing anymore. Because how could she be the same person and not know what she was doing? Kira sat watching the road go by, feeling as she were irreversibly losing her mind and her self, that the battle might be already lost. Jason stayed with her. Jason kept insisting they'd find the answer, but she could read the fear in his eyes and hear the dismay in his voice even as he sought to reassure her.

"Megan's Crossroads," the coach driver called down as they rolled to another stop.

Kira got out, feeling near the end of her rope. She stood in the open air, looking up at an afternoon sun peeking through the trees that soared about them. The Great Woods. They'd reached the southern reaches of that vast forest. She'd always wanted to visit the Great Woods. The irony of being here under these conditions felt coppery and bitter in her mouth.

"Want to see what's inside?" Jason asked her, pointing toward the small wooden station house. It was one of those structures that could have been built centuries ago or last week, sturdy and unadorned. A place to shelter passengers and goods for short periods.

"Sure." Kira walked to the station, where the coolness of the shade inside didn't compensate for the mustiness of the air. She paused for a moment, gazing at a calendar posted there. The picture on the calendar was a common one in the West. Lady Mari stood on the last wall of Dorcastle, defiant as she rallied the defenders, Mage Alain beside her, her banner flying, the Imperial legions falling back in defeat. But it wasn't the familiar picture that held her attention. "Hey, Jason."

"What?"

"It's my birthday."

He looked at the date as well. "Happy birthday."

"I'm eighteen." Kira stared at the numbers on the calendar, a strange darkness filling her. "I'm not going to live to be nineteen."

Jason squeezed her arm just a little too tight to be comforting. "Yes, you are."

"Let go of me. That hurts."

His hand instantly let go. "I'm sorry."

Kira looked at him, her anger evaporating as she took in his haggard face. "What have I been putting you through?"

"You can't help it," Jason muttered.

"That's no excuse. Why don't you leave? You can't do anything that makes any difference. So go. You'd be safe."

He looked at her for a long moment before shaking his head. "No. There must be something I can do. Why do you keep asking me to go?"

"Because I don't want you to die!" She hissed the answer in an angry whisper. "Why is that so hard for you to understand?"

"There are easier ways to protect me," Jason said, not yielding at all. "And you. But you keep rushing off to danger and trying to make me go away. Why?"

"I don't know!"

"Are you sure? Kira, you told me before we left your parents that you were certain finding the answer to your problem involved me. Were you lying?"

"No!"

"But if you make me go away, maybe you won't find the answer." His eyes lit with sudden understanding. "Is that what you're trying to avoid? Are you afraid of learning what the answer is? Don't you want help?"

"That is so stupid! Why would you ask me that?" Kira demanded. "I don't need help. I don't need you here. I can handle this myself."

"I don't think so."

Kira had to look away, feeling trapped. "I don't need help. Back off."

"Why won't you—"

"Back off!" She shoved him out of the way and headed for the door.

Adding to her anger, she could see out of the corner of her eye two older men shaking their heads at Jason behind her. Kira heard one of them as she plunged out the door.

"Whatever it is, a wise man would give her room and time to cool off."

The coach was ahead, the four horses drawing it resting in harness before beginning the next stage of the journey. Kira stared at them as for the first time she realized that an attack on the coach to kill her might also kill or injure those horses.

She was a danger to everyone and everything. Including herself. Mage Ivor would catch up with her eventually, and when that happened she'd have to ensure she was the only one who could be harmed. Maybe she could still take down Mage Ivor, but whether she won or lost no one else should die because of her.

Kira spun on her heel, walking toward one side of the station. Behind it, she could see another road wide enough for wagons heading into the woods. But off to her left was a trail suited only for one or two people walking side by side. Low-hanging branches ensured that riders couldn't use it. Kira walked quickly that way, swiftly finding herself swallowed by the forest. Within twenty steps the sounds of the station had faded and the sight of it was blocked, as the trail wove around the trunks of trees so large and old that they must have begun growing when the great ship seeded Dematr with plants from Urth.

She had no idea what she was doing. All Kira knew was that something was close to breaking, and she had to get away.

But one sound stayed with her, the steady tread of someone following. Not trying to catch up, just staying behind her a short distance.

Kira finally stopped and looked back.

Jason stopped, too, watching her.

She tried to keep her voice calm but heard it crack on the first word. "Will you please stop following me."

"What will happen to you if I do, Kira?" Jason asked.

"I don't care. I just want you to be safe. You said it yourself, Jason. I keep taking you into situations where you might die. I don't know why I'm doing that."

"You could stop me if you really wanted to," Jason said, staying about three lances behind her, not trying to get closer. "Break my leg, knock me out—"

"Stop! I won't hit you again!"

"Kira, you told me you think the answer involves me or needs me or something. So I'm going to keep following you until we find that answer."

"Why?"

"Because I love you, and you need me. And I promised you I would."

"I'm releasing you from that promise. Go!"

He just stood there, saying nothing, until Kira turned away and started walking again. Maybe if she just kept going Jason would eventually give up.

She couldn't see the sun, hidden behind the leaves of the towering trees, but the shade under their limbs grew steadily darker as the sun drew near the western horizon. Her legs ached with fatigue, but Kira kept going, trying to walk away from whatever was out to hurt her and whoever could get hurt because of her. The trail faded out at some point, leaving only the leaf-covered soil pocked with patches of tough grass that managed to survive on the little sunlight that filtered down through the mighty trees. But she kept walking, weaving between tree trunks.

She had no idea where she was, Kira realized.

When she reached a small open area, Kira came to a stop, feeling both very weary and trapped despite the open pathways under the trees all around her. The shadows under those trees mocked her, seeming to conceal hidden foes.

Tired of running from a danger she couldn't seem to find or escape from, Kira walked to a tree and sat down, her back against the broad trunk.

Jason came into the clearing, moving like someone who was relying on willpower alone, and sat down on the opposite side.

Neither of them said anything as the night darkened.

"Why won't you just go?" Kira finally asked in a low voice.

He didn't answer.

Desperate, she sought for something that might drive him off, keep him safe from whatever was happening to her. "Is it because of the wedding? Well . . . forget it. The wedding is off. We're . . . not right for each other. You're not . . ." The words nearly choked her as she fought to say them. "My man. You're *not* my man."

Jason, slumped against the tree behind him, shook his head slowly. "You can tell when people lie, Kira. I'm not all that good at doing that, but even I can tell you don't mean what you're saying."

"Yes, I do! I'll never marry you! Go away! Go back to Urth! I don't care!" Kira heard her voice break again on the last word. "Why are you still sitting there? Aren't you listening to me?"

"I'm listening," Jason said, his voice dull. "You don't have to marry me. Or go out with me ever again. But I'm not leaving you to die."

"You'll die if you stay!"

"Okay," he said, sounding resigned to his fate. "Because I couldn't live knowing I'd bought my life by letting you die. I just can't. I'm not a hero. I never pretended to be. I'm not brave. But this girl I know . . ." Jason struggled to speak, his face working with emotion. "She showed me things. She showed me that when someone needs help, you help them. And when a job needs to be done, you do it."

"I never taught you to sacrifice yourself needlessly!"

"I guess not," Jason said, looking at her as if she was the fading remnant of a dream. "But maybe this is my way of standing between you and what's trying to kill you, just like you stood between me and the legionaries who were trying to kill me. And maybe I'm down to my last three shots and next time it'll all be over. But I'm going down fighting, Kira. Fighting for you. You don't owe me anything for that. You've already given me more than I ever thought life could hold."

He was going to die because of her. Kira stared at Jason, her thoughts churning wildly. She felt her powers straining against the barriers holding them, as if also preparing to attack her. The only thing that stood out, the only thing that was still clear, was that Jason would die because of her. "No. You're going to go."

Jason shook his head wordlessly.

Her powers. They were causing this. If only she could destroy them this instant. Despite her weariness, Kira focused on a desperate attempt at forcing her powers into nothingness. A wave of panic responded, as if the dark woods about them were suddenly full of enemies ready to strike and Jason had only moments left to live. "You need to leave now!"

"No," Jason said.

"Listen to me!" Desperate, panic overwhelming her, Kira reached inside her jacket and drew her pistol, holding it pointed up. "Don't make me use this."

Jason stared at her in shock. "You're threatening me with that?"

"It's the only way to save you!"

He gave a short, sad, tense laugh. "You're going to shoot me to keep me from getting hurt?"

"If I have to." She flipped off the safety. "Get out of here, Jason, or I'll use this!"

He didn't move. "No. Kira, you need me so much right now—"

"Stop it!" Her mind filled with anger and confusion, Kira worked the slide to load a round. "Go!"

"No."

Kira brought the weapon even with her chest, leveling it toward Jason, knowing only that she had to get him away from her. "Jason!" Her hand holding the pistol shook, the barrel close to being aimed at him. "This is your last warning! Go away! I mean it!"

He stayed sitting against the tree, shaking his head. "No. I'm not going away. Not until you're safe. Then I'll go, if that's what you want."

A small part of Kira watched herself, terrified, as she threatened Jason. She was the biggest danger to him. How could she stop herself? "If you don't go, I swear I'll . . ." Kira flinched as her Mage powers suddenly flared inside her again, her inner barriers crumbling. The world wavered about her. "No! I won't—!"

Kira stumbled to a halt, staring around her. She was on her feet. The clearing that she had been sitting in was nowhere to be seen. The woods on all sides were pitch dark except for the eerie glow of moss on the old trees.

She must have blacked out again and started walking. How long had it been? Where was she? It felt late, very late, and her legs quivered with weariness, as if she'd been blacked out and walking for another hour or more. Her powers were quiet, like a dark pool inside her whose depths masked their actions the way shadows hid whatever lay beneath the trees of the forest. Kira slumped against the thick trunk of a nearby tree, concentrating on trying to block her powers again.

Something wasn't here, she realized. Something that should be here. Not something.

Someone.

Kira spun around, looking for Jason. Where was he? "Jason?" she called softly. No answer came.

Her hand hurt. She looked down, seeing her pistol still tightly gripped. She must have been holding it ever since . . .

The last thing she remembered was facing Jason, her pistol out, aimed toward him, ready to—

Where was he? She looked down at herself, panic building inside again. No thread was visible leading into the darkness. Leading to Jason.

Fumbling with fear, Kira ejected the magazine on the pistol and checked the chamber. She counted the cartridges. No, that had to be wrong. Count again. No. That couldn't be right. Unload the magazine. Count every cartridge. No. Count again. No, no, no.

One was missing.

She'd fired her pistol.

The last thing she remembered was pointing it in Jason's direction.

Kira looked around again, the darkness under the trees foiling her search. Why couldn't she see the thread that should lead toward him? "Jason? Jason, please answer me. If you're hiding, please come out. This isn't funny, Jason. Jason?"

Why hadn't he followed her? He'd said he'd stay with her. No matter what. But he wasn't here.

"Kira, the only way you could get me to leave you is by shooting me."

He'd said that. Back on the sailboat.

"What have I done?" Kira whispered. "What have I done? Stars above, what have I done?"

The pistol fell from her limp hand to lie among the discarded leaves. Her other hand relaxed and dropped the loose cartridges and empty magazine beside it.

Kira looked back into the dark, silent woods again.

"Jason?"

The horror of what she'd done overwhelmed her. Kira screamed, the sound tearing her throat as it filled the forest.

CHAPTER SIXTEEN

She walked through the woods, the sky brightening to show it was past dawn. Kira had no idea where she was, had no idea where she was going. She had left her pistol lying on the ground, her throat raw from her scream, and started walking, her mind numb, walking into low-hanging branches rather than moving them aside, leaving a trail of snapped twigs in her wake. Her legs trembled with exhaustion but she kept walking, driven by fear and horror at what she had done.

The light ahead grew stronger as the trees about her thinned. Kira stepped out into a large clearing where patches of herbs and vegetables grew on three sides of a cottage. She kept walking, unable to form a coherent thought, until an older woman stepped in front of her.

"Hello?" the woman asked, peering at Kira with curiosity that changed to concern. "Are you all right?"

Kira wavered on her feet, staring at the woman. "Help," she managed to gasp in a small voice before the world whirled about her and she fell into darkness.

When she awoke, her mind still felt feverish. Kira was on a narrow cot in a very small side room, not much more than a closet with no door, that must be inside the cottage. She guessed from the light visible outside that it must be late afternoon.

The older woman came into Kira's view, studying her. "How are you?"

Kira shook her head.

"Can you speak? What's your name?"

"Kira."

"I'm Vina, Kira. I don't know what the trouble is, but I can tell you are in great need of rest. If you are willing, I will give you something to drink that will let you have a full, restful night's sleep. Is that all right?"

Something that would put her to sleep. A drug. Like the Imperials had used against her. But Kira felt her reflexive rejection fading. Too tired to argue, her mind a confused welter, Kira nodded. Someone else should be here, but her mind shied away from that thought.

The drink that Vina brought in a mug was warm, bitter, and earthy.

Kira drained it. Within moments her eyes began to droop, and she surrendered to the urge to sleep.

The next time she awoke, the light outside spoke of morning again. Kira stared at the rough ceiling above her, where bunches of dried herbs hung from the rafters. Her thoughts were clear enough to terrify her. "Jason?"

Vina came to lean over Kira again, searching her eyes. "That rest did you a lot of good, Kira. I heard you cry out for that Jason quite a few times. Is he a friend of yours?"

"He's my— Oh, no. I— Yes. Yes. He's my man. I love him. He was trying to help me. But . . . I . . . think I . . ."

Vina moved aside, and Jason came into her view, looking down at her with somber eyes. "I'm here, Kira."

She stared at him, wondering if he was really there, or a ghost come to haunt her. "I didn't kill you?"

"No." A bit of his old smile appeared. "Not yet."

And there it was again, the thread connecting them, pale in the sunlight but there. Kira started shaking with relief. "I thought . . . I thought . . . I fired . . . I thought . . ."

"It's okay." Jason sat down beside her and held her, and his arms were real and he was here.

But one thought dominated all others inside Kira. After a few moments she pushed him away. "You have to go. Right now. I'm too dangerous to you. Please, Jason, listen to me this time."

"And break my promise to stay with you?"

"Please don't joke. I thought I'd . . ."

"I know." He pulled back enough for her to see his reassuring smile. "But you didn't. And I think I figured out some things. I think I know what's causing the problems."

"We already know that!" Kira protested, dropping her voice to the barest whisper so that Vina wouldn't hear. "My powers. They're what's causing the problems."

"No. What's causing the problems is you. Which means maybe you can fix the problems." Jason reached into the pocket of his jacket and held out something.

Her pistol.

"I found this. Thought you might need it."

She didn't want to touch it, the memories of what she thought she'd done filling her, but Jason held it out to her with perfect calmness, as if totally unworried about what she might do. Kira reached slowly for the weapon, checking to see that the safety was set. "Is it loaded?"

"No, I cleared the chamber." He smiled at her again. "I wonder what Alli and Bev would say if they knew you'd left it in unsafe condition?"

"How can you be joking? I didn't hurt you, but I could have."

"I think I know what the problem is," Jason repeated.

"Why couldn't I sense the thread connecting us last night, Jason? I tried and it wasn't there. I . . . I . . . Oh. I'd suppressed my powers as much as I could, and I was too tired and confused to think straight," Kira realized. "I should have remembered that suppressing my powers made the thread vanish. But I was so scared, so tired, I couldn't think."

Jason nodded, serious. "I know how hard it is to think when you're scared and tired, believe me. But we're both rested. When you feel up to it, can we go somewhere and talk in private?"

"I'm up to it now," Kira said, realizing that she was strong enough to rise. She sat up on the cot. "Vina? Jason and I need to go somewhere to talk."

The old woman looked carefully at Kira. "You seem well enough. You're sure you'll be all right with this fellow?"

"That's about the only thing I'm sure of," Kira said. "That I'm safe with him."

Outside, she blinked in the sunlight. She shivered as a strange sensation rolled over her, and realized that this place was filled with power. She'd never felt it so strong, as if she was bathing in the energy that allowed Mages to work their spells. Had the pull of that power brought her here as she walked heedlessly through the night? "Do you want to talk here?"

"Can we go in the woods a little ways?" Jason asked. "Vina seems nice enough, but I want to be able to talk without worrying about anyone else hearing."

"All right. How about this way?" She felt it drawing her, like a spring from which the power here was flowing.

They walked for a good fifteen minutes into the woods, Kira achingly aware of the events standing between them, before coming into another small open area, maybe three or four lances across. A tree had fallen recently, opening this spot, and grass had rapidly grown to bask in the light created by the gap in the tree cover, but saplings hadn't yet had time to compete for the sudden access to sunlight. Pausing to feel the power wash over her, Kira turned to Jason. "Can we stop here?"

"Sure."

"Why don't you hate me?"

"I've got reasons. Let me talk, okay? Do you want to sit down?"

"All right." Kira sat cross-legged on the grass.

Jason sat down facing her, close enough to reach out to Kira but far enough off to give her a sense of room. "Okay. I think I finally figured something out."

"I shot at you," Kira blurted out, blinking away tears. "I don't remember doing it, but there's a cartridge missing from my pistol."

"No, you didn't."

"But I fired—"

"Yes, you fired a shot. And it did scare me," Jason said. "But I don't think that you shot at me. It was an accident."

"There are no *accidents* with guns, Jason! I let the safety off, I loaded a round in the chamber, I pointed it toward you, and I pulled the trigger!"

"That's not what I mean. Kira, how far apart were we when you fired?"

"Had I moved?"

"No."

"Um . . . three or four lances, I think."

"Three, at the most," Jason said. "Less than six meters. I was sitting against a tree, not moving. I've seen you shoot. Is it even possible for you to miss a shot at a target like that at that range?"

She inhaled deeply, trying to think. "Not often."

"If you'd shot *at* me, you would have hit me," Jason said. "The bullet didn't even come close, though I went to ground fast anyway. Kira, do you remember talking to me about Mages soon after we met? You said your father still couldn't use a weapon like a pistol. He just couldn't figure it out. But you said he could accidentally fire one if he was holding it, without knowing what he was doing. I think that's what happened with you that night. Because, aside from missing me, when the pistol went off you also looked shocked and frightened."

Kira gazed at the ground between them. "They didn't try to kill you?"

"They?"

"My Mage powers."

"No, I don't think so. I think they . . . you . . . when blacked out were just as scared that you'd hurt me as the you I'm talking to."

"Why . . . why didn't you follow me again after that? I mean, I don't blame you! But—"

"You disappeared," Jason said. "I don't mean you ran off into the dark. I mean you disappeared. Using that Mage spell. I had no idea which way you'd gone. I tried running after you, got totally lost, and when I was about to sit down and give up on everything I heard you scream a long way off. That . . . scared me worse than anything else so far. I ran that way, eventually stumbled across your pistol, and from that I found what I hoped were marks of you walking through the woods, and followed them. I had to sleep once, actually I passed out for a while, and it was a lot slower tracking you because I'm no Davy Crockett—"

"Who's Davi—?"

"—but late last night I finally found Vina's cottage, where she seemed worried that I was some crazy stalker after you. But she let me sleep outside while we waited for you to wake up." Jason paused. "Kira, you call your Mage powers *them*. Have you noticed that?"

"They're not me," Kira said.

"That's not what Doc Sino said. Remember? She said it seemed like you were still you when you blacked out, that you didn't do anything when blacked out that you wouldn't do when aware."

"We've talked about this a hundred times, Jason. I've been doing crazy things. If that's me, then get out of here, now."

He shook his head. "Kira, my point is, the Mage powers you call *them* are part of you. Have you noticed how you talk about them now? You used to talk about confining, suppressing them. But that changed. Now you say destroy, eliminate, things like that."

"I'm trying to get rid of them. Do you blame me?"

"When did they start getting stronger? Wasn't it when you started trying to suppress them? I mean, really confine them and push them down?"

Kira stopped and thought, her eyes on the beams of sunlight coming through the trees but her mind tracing back in time. "Yes. I think so. Why is that important? Do you think they were . . . fighting back?"

Jason nodded. "I had a long time to think while I was trying to find you. Kira, if the Mage powers are part of you, and you're trying to confine them, to kill them, what does that mean? I've been around you when people were trying to kill you. You don't just lie there and wait for the end. You fight. You fight hard."

She eyed him, puzzled. "What do you mean?"

"Maybe the problems are rooted in you trying to confine and destroy part of you, and that part of you is acting the same way the rest of you does when attacked. It's defending itself, it's fighting back, it's not going to give up and let you kill it. Because it's you. Every time you hit it harder, it comes back stronger. Because that's you. Your dad couldn't understand why your powers were getting so strong so fast. Maybe it was because part of you, those powers, were fighting to free themselves and save themselves."

Kira leaned back, her eyes on Jason but her thoughts racing in a hundred different directions. "So what are the blackouts? Why am I doing that to myself, if you're right?"

"I didn't know," Jason admitted, "until I thought about how you were also having those blackouts when you tried to remember seeing things as both a Mechanic and a Mage. Are we in agreement that when you see things both ways it makes you crazy?"

"Yeah."

"So remembering exactly how that was would make you crazy again, wouldn't it?"

She stared at him. "It's a defense? I'm blacking out to protect myself?"

"I think so. Your mind knows what hurts it, and so when it can, when it recognizes what's happening, it's not letting you be aware of that thing that hurts it."

"But then when I do spells . . . oh. Yes! Jason, I have to think like a Mage to do spells. If the Mechanic part of me is fully aware of that, it hurts. I feel like the universe is wrong. That's what happened the first time I did a spell, in Ihris. So my subconscious mind must have said, no, from now on you can't be aware of what you're doing because it would hurt you. Jason, this all makes sense. My powers haven't been attacking me. They've been trying to protect me."

"And when you attack your powers," Jason said, "when you feel the desire to destroy them, part of you thinks it's in danger and under attack. And when Kira is under attack, Kira protects herself."

"Or runs away to protect others from her. But—" She felt a sudden understanding. "To protect you. That's why I blacked out last night. No, it wasn't last night. Whenever it was. I was losing control. I was scared about what I would do, and I blacked out. Because part of me was afraid that I would hurt you."

"Kira," Jason said, leaning a little closer to her and speaking earnestly, "you've also felt confined more and more. Even when we're out in the open, even when we're in a boat on the sea. Is that because you're confining part of yourself? Locking up the part of you involved with your Mage powers?"

Kira buried her face in her hands. "That's why my internal barriers aren't holding. I'm trying to confine my powers, and they're trying to free themselves. Just like I would. So they figured out how to get past those barriers, and intrude on my mind when I wasn't really aware of it. That's how I started being able to use Mage senses all the time, to see things as a Mechanic and a Mage simultaneously. I figured out how to do it because I couldn't stand being confined, and every time I reinforced the confinement it made me want to break out more."

She paused, probing her inner self cautiously, and there it was. Fear. Just as it had been for some time, and growing all the while. Right there, but not what she had thought it was. Not fear of some external thing, but fear of herself. "Father told me that people who are scared stop listening. I've literally been fighting myself, and paying less and less attention to what I was trying to tell myself," Kira said, her eyes on Jason again. *Why are you hurting me?* The question that had echoed back at her. "Every time I resolved to destroy my powers I was resolving to destroy part of myself, and that part got scared and all I knew was that something was after me."

"And since you won't give up, you couldn't win."

"Which meant I was destroying me." Kira breathed in deeply, looking up at the sky. "And fear of something else. I see it now. All this time I was being mean to you, putting you in danger, I was trying to make you leave so you'd be safe. Safe from me. I knew I was in danger,

I felt more danger every time I threatened the part of me that is my Mage powers, and I wanted you away so you'd be safe.

"I'll bet I blacked out when I took you to bed that time because I felt kind of trapped and I was fighting what I wanted to do and I was a bit scared of the whole thing and not admitting it, and the defense mechanism sort of bled through. I ended up trying to defend myself from something I really wanted. Which just made it worse. It fed the fear. Jason, at least I was right about one thing. One very important thing. You've figured it out. You've given me answers by seeing things I wouldn't let myself see. Now what do I do, Jason? How do I fix this?"

"I don't know," Jason admitted, looking crestfallen.

Kira looked at him again, trying to smile. "I couldn't expect you to do all the work. You've already helped a lot. You . . . you stayed with me when I was doing everything I could to drive you away."

"That wasn't easy," Jason admitted. "You were really good at the driving-away stuff."

"I'm so sorry." She remembered something he had said. "You held the line, Jason. Just like I did protecting you from the legionaries, you protected me from . . . myself. And I'm a pretty tough opponent, I think."

"You're a very tough opponent," Jason said. "Can we go back to being on the same side?" The words were half-humorous, but she saw the need and the worry he tried to hide.

"Yes," Kira said. "You're my man. Forever. I'll never forget that again."

"Thanks," he said, smiling at last. "What do we do next?"

"I have to master my fear. And that means . . . I have to stop being afraid of that part of me, stop fighting that part of me. I have to accept it. How do I . . . talk to my powers?" She paused, thinking. "I've never seen them. I mean, not even as a metaphor, unless you count the door they're behind."

"The door?"

"Yeah, it's like I'm in the house, which is my home but not my home, and the powers are behind a door there. In the basement that isn't really there, remember? Does that give you any ideas?"

Jason frowned, thinking. "This probably won't help, but I remember something about houses in peoples' heads. What was that? Oh, yeah. It was something people did on Earth a long time ago. I read about it when I was doing a report on memory storage. They didn't have many books or means to write stuff down, so they organized everything in their heads to help remember things. They imagined there was a house inside them, and each room held a type of thing and all the stuff in each room was something to trigger a memory about a specific thing. Like one room would be about stories and in that room a table would remind them of something and a book on the table would symbolize something else. But that's not what's happening with you, is it?"

"No, but . . ." A house. Divided into rooms. Because each room held . . . "Each room held something different!" Kira laughed, surprising herself as well as Jason. "That's why I'm seeing a house! Not to help me remember things. To organize things! To organize me! To give each part of me a place where it belongs. I get it! Jason, thank you! I was trying to give myself the answer and I couldn't see it!"

"Really?"

"Yes. It's not a real house I'm seeing in my head, of course. The house, and everything in it, is just my mind's way of portraying things in ways I can understand. It's all mental metaphors. Illusions."

"Nothing is real?" Jason asked, smiling in reaction to her enthusiasm.

"Right! Be sure to say that again around my mother when we get back."

He nodded, smiling wider. "When we get back? So you think this can fix things?"

"I think it has a really good chance. I mean, I kept trying to tell myself these things. So it must be important." She paused, carefully examining her thoughts.

"What's the matter?" Jason asked.

"I remember being really sure about things at times in the last few weeks," Kira said. "I want to be sure this isn't that kind of sure."

"It's not," Jason said. "I can tell. If it was, you wouldn't be asking yourself that. You'd be absolutely certain that you were right and this would work, and wondering why I couldn't understand it."

Kira sighed, gazing at him. "You had far too many opportunities to learn about how I am when I'm not thinking straight, didn't you? All right. Let me think. How do I get to the house and . . . try to set things right in there?" She bit her lip as she thought. "I need to do it the same way I tried attacking my powers. Meditate. Go really deep. I don't know how long I might be in there. Can you keep watch?"

"Yeah, I think I can do that." His expression took on a worried cast again. "Can anything go wrong? Can you still end up . . . worse off?"

"I don't think so. I'd have to keep doing the wrong things, and now that I realize what the wrong things are, I won't. Jason, I should have figured this out! I could feel what was happening but instead of realizing why it wasn't working, I just kept trying harder to do the same thing."

"A lot of people do that," Jason said. "And, after all, you're only mostly perfect."

She grinned at him. "So are you. Mostly perfect enough to help me finally see what I wouldn't see. I am so going to marry you."

He shrugged, uncomfortable. "You don't have to. I mean, you said—"

"Those were fears, Jason. Out-of-control fears. And even when I was saying those things I knew they weren't true. Every time I've been centered, every time my mind has been clear, I have wanted to be your wife someday. That's how you'll always know when I'm myself and thinking clearly. When I say I want to marry you. All right? All right. This is a good spot, so I'll stay sitting here. I'm going to go pretty deep inside myself. Don't try to wake me." Kira saw the worry in him as Jason nodded. "I know it's going to be hard for you. We've been fighting battles together for a while, and now like on the boat, I have to fight alone while you can only watch."

"Maybe I'm in there somewhere and can help," Jason suggested.

"Maybe you are." She settled herself, hands resting loosely in her lap.

"Kira? Remember, this isn't a battle. This is making peace."

"You're right. Maybe a symbol of love and survival would help me." Kira dug in her pocket until she found the loose cartridge and folded her hands around it, once more resting them in her lap. Feeling safe with Jason watching for trouble, she began controlling her breathing and relaxing her body. Kira closed her eyes, focusing inward . . . inward . . .

Darkness. Conflict. Somewhere just outside of her awareness a battle was raging. But that battle she had been fighting was both doomed to fail and a distraction. She needed to find the cause. Kira continued on through the tumultuous darkness inside her, seeking her center.

She didn't know how much time had passed when she found herself before the house again. It seemed clearer this time, but though she could see details when she focused on any particular portion, that made the rest of the house blurrier.

Kira imagined walking up the front steps and inside, the front door opening at her touch. Something told her that this time she should explore the house before heading for the basement door.

The kitchen should be there.

She was in it, or something very like it. Hoping that images of her parents might be there to offer comfort and support, Kira was startled to sense two balls of light glowing in the kitchen, blinding in their radiance. Kira flinched back at the same time as she felt a sense of . . . what? Warmth? Belonging? Security? Love? Awe? Frustration? Authority? All of those things. Was this how she "saw" her parents?

She was welcome here. She could feel that. This room was . . . home. The home she carried inside her wherever she went.

What else was here? Kira sought her own room, the place where she had always found refuge from the world, her sense of self drifting up the stairs until she found herself there. Her room did feel welcoming, but oddly bigger and smaller at the same time. Bigger as it had seemed when she was little. Smaller now that her world was so much larger. Her desk, her bed, her mirror, her window open but nothing visible beyond it. It felt good, peaceful, a refuge from everything, from all of the people who didn't understand her and wanted to hurt her or use her.

Kira realized that she could close the door of this room and sink gently into stillness . . . into a place where nothing could reach her . . . a place where she would always be tranquil and at peace.

Into . . .

Some kind of coma? Locked inside herself? She jerked away, frightened. Her old room was both a mental refuge and a possible trap to be escaped. Kira willed herself out of there, finding herself in what felt like the hall outside.

The guest room. There was something in there as well. Kira went to it cautiously, the door dissolving as she reached it.

Inside, another warm, bright globe. She touched it, feeling Jason. He was here. Or was this him? No. It was the sense of him that she carried inside, the Jason that lived in her mind and her heart.

She spotted the thread running from the sphere, disappearing as it ran off toward Jason. That's what was happening with the threads. They were a tie between the real person and the sense of that person held inside the Mage.

Cool.

Her parents were here, in a way. Jason was here, in a way. Kira suspected that if she kept searching she would find others, her many honorary aunts and uncles, Aunt Kath, Uncle Petr, Queen Sien, all those who filled her heart and her world. She felt certain that there would be rooms for them, that this house could hold as many rooms as she needed to hold everything she wanted to hold and had to hold.

Even this deep inside herself, she wasn't alone. She never would be.

Kira paused as she passed another door, one that wasn't in her real home, this one made of wooden timbers, heavy and dark, bound with iron straps. A chill breeze came from that door, and a sense of darkness. She stared at it, somehow knowing that on the other side lay the Northern Ramparts and a night when she had been down to three cartridges, bleeding from wounds, Jason close to dying by her side, and the Imperial legionaries preparing to attack again. She'd left that battlefield behind, but part of it would forever live in her.

Just as somewhere inside her mother the siege of Dorcastle also remained forever. And the death of Kira's brother. And the day she met Kira's father. And . . . some sense of Kira herself. Hopefully a warm, supportive sense, but Kira knew she'd sometimes been more like this dark, forbidding door toward her mother.

But not now. Surely her mother felt Kira's love inside her along with the memories of more difficult times. What lay behind the doors didn't change, but how she saw such things, how she remembered them, could change. Kira felt the loose cartridge in one hand, the one brought from that battlefield in the Northern Ramparts, and the door she now confronted seemed less foreboding. Not a place she wanted to go back to, but also one that held something she wouldn't want to lose.

This was her house, within her. How she saw it, felt it, how she let it affect her, was at least partly within her own power. Reassured, confident, Kira knew it was time.

She found herself in the main room, facing the door to the basement. But, no, not the basement. That was for things she never wanted to confront. This door led somewhere else, to a room that she hadn't known existed even while always being aware of it.

Kira willed herself to the door, fighting fear, feeling the fear reflected back at her and trying to dampen it. It's all right. This is me. It's time to take a look at this part of me. Which hasn't been trying to hurt me, hasn't been trying to take over, but in its own clumsy way is trying to protect me. And protect Jason.

There was a wariness behind the door, a worry about her own intentions. Kira could tell it was waiting for another attack. She tried to center herself on reassurance, on calm, but the door stayed locked. It reminded her of something, and as she saw the dark glimmer of armor on the door Kira realized it was like the door to the armored carriage. The door that had felt intolerable as long as she thought she couldn't open it.

Kira relaxed herself again, and instead of pushing on the door imagined it as having no locks, no latches, no way to seal it, able to swing open or closed without hindrance. You can come out. Anytime you want to. You don't have to let me in. But I'd like to. Is it all right?

How many times did she repeat that plea? How much time passed? But suddenly the door that had fought her, that had felt like an impenetrable barrier, swung open easily.

The door let into a room whose dimensions felt uncertain. Large windows faced her, but were covered by curtains. Kira reached for a curtain and paused, somehow sure that the view out of the windows would be something that she shouldn't see.

A Mage's view? Was that what the curtained windows symbolized? Something part of her could see but the rest shouldn't look upon?

Shelves of books lined the room on either side. Kira bent to look, but the titles were impossible to read. Perhaps that represented knowledge inside her, but not something she should consciously examine.

She suddenly noticed a mirror in the center of the room. Or was it a mirror? An image of herself floated there, looking back at Kira. The other Kira wore Mage robes. She was worried, defiant, ready to fight if necessary. *Why are you hurting me?* It hadn't been an echo. It had been this Kira. This part of her. Trapped in the place where Kira had tried to imprison her, feeling in danger as Kira vowed to destroy her, fighting back when Kira attacked. Kira finally understood her, and why this part of her had done what she had. It's all right. I'm sorry. I accept you. I'm not going to attack again. She reached to that image, but it only gazed back, suspicious.

Kira looked down at her hands, trying to work out how to reach that part of herself, to convince her, and saw the loose cartridge in them. The one that spoke of hope, of perseverance, of love. It wasn't really here, she knew, but even here its image represented those things.

She reached for that other image with the cartridge in her open palm. I'm sorry. I was afraid, and I tried to hurt what I didn't understand. I won't do that again.

The image of herself watched her, the suspicion fading to wariness.

After a time that Kira couldn't measure, that other her reached out in return until their hands touched, their palms coming together, the image of the cartridge and all it represented enclosed within them. And then there was only her, and this room was as much a part of her as the rest of the house.

There was no more need for barriers. She could hide her Mage presence, but the powers themselves, swollen by the need to protect themselves against her, were already subsiding, content to be here as long as they were safe and knew the door was not that of a prison.

I have to know I can open the door whenever I want. Just like in the armored coach. And like at home, when she had tried the invisibility spell and then tried to run, that part of her tied to her Mage powers fearing confinement and seeking freedom.

Kira stepped out of the house, feeling the darkness around it filled with an infinity of other memories and metaphors, the sense of herself. But there was no turmoil now, no pain of clashing selves battling for dominance or survival. There was only her.

She felt herself serenely, quietly, at peace inside as she began rising upwards, through the layers of thought that lay between her and the world.

Kira slowly opened her eyes, startled by how vibrant the world appeared. Every color seemed brighter, every object sharper and more clearly defined. She stared at the blades of grass and the fallen leaves on the ground as if seeing such things for the first time. She was fully herself, yet also felt connected to everything around her in ways she had never experienced.

The shadows under the trees had moved. She must have been inside herself for at least an hour.

Kira felt the sense of power here wash around her, as if her Mage senses were also more sensitive now. Tremendous amounts of power filling the air and the ground. Her skin tingled just as if static electricity were playing along it.

"Kira?"

She turned her head, seeing Jason standing not far away, his anxious gaze on her. Kira smiled at the sight of him, smiling wider as she saw how brightly the thread between them glowed even in the full light of the sun. "Hi."

He smiled back, worry still riding the expression. "Are you okay? Did it work?"

She pondered the question as she looked at him. "Yes." Jason. Standing there. Watching. Listening. Protecting. Caring. The warm, bright presence she had felt inside was still there. He had chosen to be hers, and had stayed with her through the worst crisis she had ever endured. "My hero."

And she knew what she wanted, all fears and doubts gone.

Kira got up, moving carefully as she left her meditation stance. Once on her feet, she put the loose cartridge back in her pocket, then walked to him and without another word kissed him, pressing herself against Jason.

To her surprise, Jason suddenly broke the kiss, grasping her hands to restrain them. She looked at him, still feeling very calm and centered but also perplexed. "You do know what I want to do, right?" Kira asked.

"Yeah," he said, breathing hard, "I know."

"Then why are you stopping me?"

"You know why. Who am I talking to, Kira? Who wants to do this? Can you really say yes?"

She smiled at him. "What a man I have." She kissed him once more, lightly, then met his eyes with her own gaze. "I'm myself, Jason. I'm fully here, and I know what I'm doing."

He looked back at her, still worried. "I wish I could be sure."

She thought about her actions over the last several weeks and understood Jason's hesitation. He was rightly concerned about betraying her trust. Betraying . . . a promise.

There was the answer. Kira looked at the forest around her, then back at Jason, certain that this also was right, that it was time, and that this was a good place. "I told you that there's something I know when fully myself, something I'm sure of, something we've both already agreed to, something lasting. Proof that I am here, and proof that I want to be with you. If you still want that after everything I've put you through, tell me this. Do you want to get married today?"

He studied her eyes with his, nodding. "Yes."

"All right. We will. I, Kira of Dematr, freely and without reservation promise myself to you, Jason of Urth. I promise to always stand beside you, and to never betray my promise to you by word or by deed, as long as our bond shall last."

He stared at her, momentarily wordless.

"You need to say the same thing to me," Kira prodded. "If you still want to."

Jason nodded quickly, his eyes fixed on hers. "Of course I still want to. The same thing? I, uh, Jason of Earth, uh . . ."

"Freely and without reservation . . ."

"Freely and without reservation promise myself to you, Kira of Dematr. I promise to, uh, always stand beside you, and, um . . ."

"To never betray my promise to you . . ." Kira prompted.

"To never betray my promise to you . . . by word or by deed . . ."

"As long as our bond shall last."

"As long as our bond shall last." Jason stared at her as if unable to believe what was happening. "Is that it?"

"Yes," Kira said. "That's it. Now kiss your wife." She brought her lips against his again, and this time neither Kira nor Jason stopped the other.

Afterwards, they lay side by side, Kira resting one hand on his chest where she could feel his heart beating. "If you are different," she murmured, "it's in a good way."

"What?"

"Nothing. Just thinking out loud. You were right. We figured it out together. Both of us just had to be where we needed to be."

"We're really married?" Jason asked.

"Why are you asking?" she teased.

"I'm kind of curious. Not unhappy. Not at all. Just curious."

"Yes, and no. But yes in the way that matters," Kira explained. "Technically, we still have to get an official license, the papers, and repeat our promises in front of witnesses. But just about everybody agrees that what really matters is the speaking of the promises to each other. And we've done that. So, yes, we're married. Not that we can go around telling everybody and wearing promise rings until we do it again officially with the witnesses. Too many of our friends want to be there for that."

"Yeah. Like Alli and Calu. Hey, if that's what it takes to be married, why'd your mother have to rush through that marriage thing with your father in Caer Lyn?"

"She needed that paper," Kira said. "Mother wanted proof in her hands that she and Father were married. Because a Mechanic and a Mage getting married is still unusual, but back then it was so bizarre that no one would believe it unless she and Father were standing there saying it, and if one or both of them had died they couldn't have done that. But the paper would still have proved to everyone that they were really married. She'd decided that if she died, she wanted it to be as the promised partner of Father, and she wanted to be sure everyone knew that. So she ended up marrying him in so much haste that she couldn't explain what was going on until it was over, even though she'd always thought that she was one person who'd never get married in a rush!" Kira laughed.

"We weren't in a rush, either," Jason pointed out.

"And we still wouldn't be," Kira said, running her hand over his chest. "I could have waited a hundred years to marry you, as long as I knew you were there with me. You know, that original paper Mother got is bloodstained because it was in an inside pocket of her jacket that day in Dorcastle, so now it's an artifact. But Mother still carries a copy of it with her everywhere she goes."

"Really? I'm glad we didn't have to wait a hundred years, but . . . yeah. This hallucination of mine just keeps getting better."

"You're making it better. Without you, I wouldn't have found the answer." She looked up at the sky visible between the branches and leaves swaying in the breeze. "Jason, I want to lie here with you like this for the rest of forever, but we need to get back to the cottage and let Vina know we're all right. She'll be worried."

"Always thinking of others," Jason jokingly complained. "Can't we stay like this a little longer? I don't think anybody could have followed us here."

"No, but—" Kira felt a chill inside as she realized something that other events had kept her from thinking about. "Jason, I can't remember everything clearly over the last few days, but I did that invisibility spell for I don't know how long. And before that, and maybe after, I wanted Mage Ivor to find me. I wanted to end the whole thing. I don't think I was hiding my Mage presence, not until this morning. Mage Ivor could have sensed me, maybe from a long way off. He might be very close."

"He might know where you are right now?"

"No. My Mage presence is well hidden again. But he might have tracked me to Vina's cottage."

Jason didn't say anything else, joining her in hastily getting dressed.

She had an oddly easy time finding their way back to the cottage, as if her Mage senses were guiding her without being consciously summoned. That frightened Kira for a few moments, wondering if her problems were going to resurface, but nothing else about the world felt off. And she certainly wasn't feeling irrationally confident.

Jason had drawn his knife. Kira had her pistol out, ready to fire, as they left the cover of the trees and slowly approached Vina's cottage. She swung her pistol from side to side, searching for danger.

"Where's Vina?" Jason whispered.

"Good question."

Kira was still a few lances from the door to the cottage when she felt a sudden draw on the vast reserves of power around them. "Jas—!"

Mage Ivor stepped out from behind the cottage, his hands already glowing and thrust toward her.

She was swinging her pistol around to target him, knowing that his lightning would strike her before she could get her weapon around, feeling like she was trapped in one of those dreams where her strongest efforts were too slow and too late.

Something slammed into her, knocking Kira away and to the ground as lightning flared.

Someone, not something.

Jason, still off balance from having shoved her aside, took the lightning full on, the force of the bolt knocking him back past where Kira lay.

Rage welled inside her as she saw Ivor preparing another spell as quickly as possible.

He was almost ready to release the next spell when Kira finished rolling up onto one knee and put six shots into his chest, firing as fast as she could aim and shoot.

The growing power of the lightning spell vanished.

Mage Ivor's body was still falling lifeless toward the ground when Kira leaped to her feet, spun about, and raced to where Jason lay.

His clothes were smoldering from heat. Severe burns marked one side of his face and one hand.

He wasn't breathing.

Kira frantically searched for Jason's pulse.

There wasn't one.

She heard an inarticulate cry of unbearable pain and realized it had come from her.

CHAPTER SEVENTEEN

Jason's heart had stopped. Kira tried to think through her almost overwhelming despair. Lightning was electricity. She had to treat this as a case of electrical shock.

Kira tilted Jason's head back to make sure his airway was clear, knelt by his chest, placed the heel of one palm directly over his heart, the other palm on top of that, and began rapidly pumping Jason's chest. She kept it up for about half a minute, counting off the seconds, then after taking a deep breath leaned over and breathed into Jason's mouth. His chest rose in response, relaxed as Kira took another breath, then she blew that air into him as well.

Back to the chest, pumping with grim desperation, feeling no response to her efforts.

Another two breaths.

Pumping again, her arms beginning to ache, sweat forming on her face and running down to mingle with the tears that were falling onto Jason's clothing as Kira worked without pause.

Two more breaths, refusing to give up.

She settled into position and pumped again, ignoring the pain in her arms, fighting against despair. It wasn't working. He wasn't responding, and there was nothing else she could do. *I'll do anything. Anything. I don't care what it costs me. All that matters is saving Jason. He's all that matters.*

Something nudged at her inside, a sense of a door opening. Kira let it. She didn't black out, but she experienced a strange sense of double-sight, of being both inside herself and outside, watching her frantic efforts to save Jason.

Kira felt her Mage powers reaching out to the power available around her, the immense reserves of power that the lightning Mage's spell had only slightly reduced. Some sort of veil remained between her and the Mage activity, clouding her ability to grasp what was happening, so Kira didn't have any sense of visualizing a spell as she watched herself. She must be preparing a spell, though. But why? What spell could possibly help?

Her father had saved her mother at Dorcastle.

And almost died doing it.

I don't care, Kira told herself. As long as it saves Jason.

Kira felt herself sending that surge of power down her arms and into Jason's chest, where she realized she could somehow see his heart lying limp beneath her physical efforts.

The power hit and Jason's heart jerked.

Kira watched herself, still not knowing what she was doing, but feeling herself focusing all of her strength into gathering more and more power for something. *Be well.* Was she thinking that or willing it? Her arms stopped pumping, resting on Jason's chest, but before Kira could fight against the halt to her efforts, she felt the power race down her arms once more, a mighty wave, a hammer, seeing Jason's heart and the power flowing into it all at once, filling his body as it had just filled hers.

The heart jolted, and pumped. And pumped again. And again.

Kira sat back, fully herself once more, the odd double-self-vision gone, not understanding what she had done. Her arms trembled with weakness that filled her whole body, and she knew it must be caused by the spell as well as her recent exertions. She stared at Jason, her mouth hanging open in wordless hope, before quickly leaning down and breathing into him again.

Her second attempt to give him breath stopped when Jason inhaled on his own.

Kira felt herself shaking from surprise and exhaustion, unable to believe what had happened. She leaned toward Jason again, to feel his pulse.

"That's enough," a harsh voice called from not far off. "He's dead. You couldn't revive anyone after a shock like that."

She turned slowly, seeing an older man with a stout build standing a few lances away, an old-style Mechanics Guild revolver in one hand pointed steadily at Kira.

Whoever he was, he didn't know that Jason was breathing again, his heart going again. She had to keep him from realizing that. And her own pistol lay a lance to one side where she had dropped it in her haste.

Kira stood up as quickly as she could, wavering on her feet and fighting off dizziness because of how weak she felt, seeing the pistol shift slightly to remain centered on her. She eased a little toward where her pistol lay, hoping that the man hadn't seen it, but he shook his head and gestured in the other direction.

She stepped to that side and a bit toward him, then took another wobbly step, to keep the man's eyes and attention centered on her. He seemed too old to be a mercenary, and had the arrogant tone and attitude of the old-style Mechanics that Kira had occasionally encountered. Mage Ivor had escaped the ambush at Cape Astra. Was this Mechanic his counterpart? "Who are you?"

The man's smile was thin and triumphant. "I am Senior Mechanic Stimon."

"And?"

His gaze on her grew furious. "You must know who I am!"

"Sorry," Kira said, taking another step to the side and a little closer to him. Despite the almost overwhelming weakness still hindering her movements, her only chance would be charging him, hoping not to take a fatal hit from his pistol. She needed to be sure that Jason was out of the line of fire when she made that last-ditch attempt. "I've never heard of you."

"Ringhmon! I was Guild Hall Supervisor at Ringhmon! Before that fraud Mari destroyed everything!"

Kira measured her chances of getting to Stimon before he could fire and didn't like them at all. Keep talking. Give herself time to recover more strength. Maybe make this Stimon mad enough to do something stupid. "Why do I keep running into people who want to blame my mother for the results of their own bad choices?"

His face tightening with anger, Stimon raised the pistol to aim. "You look so much like Mari did when she messed up everything in Ringhmon that this is going to give me extra pleasure, like I'm killing both of you at once. I'll shoot you first in the leg. Then the other leg. Then both arms, one by one. Maybe I'll see how long it takes you to bleed to death, or maybe I'll shoot you in a few more places."

Kira braced herself to leap, knowing she had little chance of success.

Her eyes caught the glint of sunlight on steel as Jason's thrown knife flashed through the air and buried itself in Stimon's stomach.

Stimon staggered, staring down at the handle of Jason's knife, his pistol hand dropping momentarily.

Already readied for action, Kira burst into motion. Stimon belatedly noticed her charge, trying to bring his revolver back up to bear on her. He almost made it, but she was able to knock the barrel aside just before it fired, the bullet flying off barely to one side of her.

Kira locked her grip on the wrist of Stimon's gun hand, but the old Senior Mechanic was strong enough to keep a firm hold on the weapon. His free hand swung at Kira's head. She blocked the blow, grabbing his hand, and for a moment they strove against each other, deadlocked. But he was strong, and she was still far from recovered from the effort of the spell. She would lose this struggle if it went on much longer.

Jason's knife still protruded from Stimon's stomach. Kira raised one knee and slammed it against the knife's handle, producing a grunt of agony from Stimon. His grip on her loosened.

Breaking Stimon's hold on her hand, Kira brought it to the same arm holding Stimon's pistol so she was grasping that arm with both hands. She brought the forearm down on her knee with brutal force.

Stimon screamed as bones cracked. His gun hand relaxed, the pistol falling to the ground.

Free of the threat of the weapon, Kira turned on Stimon with both hands, landing a furious series of blows rendered more powerful by her anger and worries over Jason. Her last strike dropped Stimon senseless to the ground.

Pausing only long enough to stoop and pick up Stimon's revolver, Kira raced back to Jason, barely able to stay on her feet.

He was still lying down, but his eyes were open, watching her anxiously. "Did I hit him?" Jason gasped.

"You hit him," Kira said, dropping to her knees beside Jason, fighting off another wave of tears as she looked at him breathing, watching her, alive. "You didn't need to practice throwing your knife in the queen's railcar after all, did you?" Her vision wavering with exhaustion, Kira wanted nothing more than to collapse next to him, but she knew she couldn't give in to her weariness. "I . . . I need to check on Vina and make sure no one else dangerous is nearby. Are you strong enough to use this?" she asked, placing the revolver in Jason's hand.

"Yeah," he said.

"I'll be right back." Tearing herself away from Jason was one of the hardest things she had ever done. So was getting to her feet again when her legs seemed to be made of gelatin. She staggered over to where her own pistol lay and after managing to pick it up without falling over, stumbled to the door of Vina's cottage. After taking a moment to recover a little strength, holding her pistol at ready, she swung inside, searching for targets.

Aside from Vina, lying bound and gagged on the floor, there was no one else inside.

Kira pulled out her own sailor's knife and dropped down by Vina, cutting loose the gag. "How many are there?"

"Two," Vina gasped, breathing quickly and deeply with the gag off her mouth. "One talked and looked like a Mage. I don't know about the other."

"Just two? You're sure?"

"Yes! They argued. The one who wasn't a Mage said he'd go off looking for you." Kira laboriously sliced through the bonds on Vina's arms and legs, the simple task rendered difficult by the weakness in her arms and hands. "The Mage is dead. The other one came back when he heard me kill the Mage but isn't going to bother anyone else for a while. I need to get back to Jason."

She only got to her feet again by grabbing onto a nearby chair and using it to pull herself up. Kira staggered outside, ignoring the figure of the still-unconscious and bleeding Stimon, once more falling to her knees beside Jason and staring at him. "How do you feel?"

"Kind of weak. Better than you seem, though. What happened?" Jason asked. "You're looking at me . . . sort of strange."

"You were dead."

His gaze grew even more anxious, then to her surprise Jason suddenly grinned. "I must have been only mostly dead."

She looked at him in bewilderment. "Why is that funny?"

"I . . . it's a long story." Jason gasped again, breathing deeply. "Wow. So, my heart stopped?"

"Yeah. No breath, no pulse."

"And you used CPR on me?"

"I have no idea what CPR is," Kira said. "I used HBR. Heart Breath Recovery. Something Mechanics learn. Just as if you'd been shocked by a piece of equipment."

"Okay," Jason said, smiling. "Whatever you call it, I'm glad it worked."

"It didn't work, Jason. You didn't respond. I couldn't get your heart beating again."

His smile vanished, replaced by apprehension. "You . . . it . . . what is this? Am I—?"

Relief and happiness flooded her as Kira tried to explain, words spilling out in a more or less steady stream. "The HBR wasn't working and I was thinking that I'd do anything that would work, no matter what, because you were all that mattered, but I didn't know what else to do, and then I felt my Mage powers trying to help, and I let them,

Jason, I trusted them, and I didn't black out this time, I was, it was really weird, it was like I was there and outside there at the same time, and my Mage powers gathered the power available here, there's an enormous amount of power here, Jason, absolutely enormous, and she sent it down her arms, I mean, I sent it down my arms, and into your heart, because I could *see* your heart, Jason, and that was really weird, too, and it didn't work the first time so she, I mean I, tried again, and this time I really hit your heart and I think maybe I told it to be well, told everything to be well, and your heart started beating again, Jason, just like it should, and then you started breathing, and I couldn't believe it but here you are you're alive and talking and looking at me and you didn't die."

Jason's stare on her stayed fixed. "Um . . . so . . . you used your Mage powers to get my heart going again? I feel a lot better than I should after a heart stoppage."

"Yeah, I don't know exactly what I did but I think I was trying to make it all right again and— Oh, wow. It fixed your burns, too. They're all healed. I didn't notice that. I'm weak, but I'm all right, too, and I don't quite understand that because it almost killed Father when he saved Mother. Maybe it's because she'd been shot and had a lot of injuries and lost a lot of blood and you didn't really have anything broken, you just needed your heart restarted and everything set back in balance. And I had so much power to draw on here so I didn't have to drain myself to save you. I'm sorry I'm talking so much."

His smile reappeared, matched to a wondering look in his eyes that made her feel embarrassed. "Kira, you are the most awesome girlfriend ever."

She laughed. "No, I'm not."

"You're going to be modest about this?"

"No, you can call me awesome," Kira said, smiling at him. "But I'm not your girlfriend."

"Oh. Yeah. That's right." His smile grew even wider. "You are the most awesome wife, ever."

"That I will accept," Kira said. She leaned down to kiss him, marveling at the feel of his breath, understanding now just what a wonder each breath was.

"Kira!" Vina called. "If he is all right, I need your help with this one to keep him from dying."

Kira grimaced. "That wouldn't be any loss," she muttered.

"Kira," Jason said, "go help. He wouldn't have helped. Don't be like him. Don't let people like him make you into someone like him."

She frowned down at Jason. "Is this my reward for saving you? That you'll be my external nagging voice of conscience?"

"Um, yeah. Pretty much. Among other things."

"All right," Kira said, smiling again. "Keep your hand on that revolver," she added as she slowly, carefully stood up, still trying to recover her strength. "Just in case someone else shows up."

Kira joined Vina, working to deal with Stimon's most serious injuries. "Hold this tightly for me. This fellow looks like he was beaten up by a whole gang," Vina commented, looking sidelong at Kira.

"I was kind of upset," Kira said.

"Uh huh. It takes more than mad to hurt someone this badly that quickly. Skills are involved. Are you a soldier or something?"

"I'm a Lancer," Kira admitted.

"Why did these two want to kill you?"

"Because . . . I'm Kira of Dematr."

Vina frowned at Kira. "Of Dematr? How can anyone claim the entire world as their home?"

"It's . . . complicated," Kira said. "I guess you don't pay much attention to news of the rest of the world?"

"Not really."

"Then I guess the best quick explanation is that they wanted to kill me because of my mother."

"Because of your mother?" Vina shook her head, leaning down to work on Stimon. "Everything is always the fault of the mother, isn't it? All right. That's the best we can do. He won't die soon, but we need to get him better care."

"Is there a Forest Warden station nearby?" Kira asked. "I'm afraid I have very little idea where we are."

"You're at Vina's cottage. Everyone around here knows where that is. Forest Wardens. The nearest location is Station Fourteen, but that's about a half-day's ride and a long day's walk."

"Do they have a far-talker?"

Vina shrugged. "Several months back I think one of the wardens told me they had one, but I don't pay much attention to that, either. I was never one for arrogant Mechanics and their gadgets."

"A lot of Mechanics are nice," Kira said, "but if you don't have a far-talker . . ." Remembering something from Cape Astra, she forced herself to her feet once more, finding the pack she'd shed while doing HBR on Jason. Digging inside, Kira found the Western Alliance far-talker she'd picked up at the site of the train ambush. "I hope we're close enough for this to work." Setting the far-talker switch to the emergency frequency and making sure it clicked firmly into place, she spoke clearly and loudly. "Forest Warden Station Fourteen, Forest Warden Station Fourteen, can you hear me? Over."

She repeated the call twice before a reply came, not strong but loud enough to be understandable.

"This is Station Fourteen. Do you have an emergency? Over."

"Yes, we have an emergency. One person is dead, and another badly injured and in need of medical care. The injured man is a criminal who will need to be guarded. Over."

"One dead and a criminal injured? Where are you? Over."

"At Vina's cottage. She has not been harmed," Kira added quickly. "I am also there, along with my—" She had been about to proudly say 'husband,' but remembered in the nick of time that that particular news shouldn't be broadcast. "With my man. Over."

"At Vina's cottage," the warden answering from Station Fourteen repeated. "Who are you? Who is speaking? Over."

She'd have to face things sooner or later, Kira knew. What had everyone else been thinking as Kira acted erratically and jumped from danger to danger? It wouldn't be long before she found out. Hopefully she wouldn't end up in protective custody. "This is Lady Mechanic Kira of Dematr. Over."

A pause. "Repeat that. Over."

"I am Lady Mechanic Kira of Dematr. Captain of Lancers. The daughter of the daughter. My companion is Jason of Urth. Over."

"We are honored to assist you and the daughter, Lady! We'll have a team there as soon as possible. Over."

"Thank you. I am honored by your assistance. Out." Kira lowered the far-talker, seeing that Vina was watching her again.

The woman was trying to appear merely interested, but Kira saw skepticism and concern there as well. "Lady? Mechanic? Captain of Lancers?"

"That's right," Jason said, walking up to them, each step tentative. "And the daughter of the daughter. And a dragon slayer. Kira isn't being delusional. Not any more. That's who she really is. Doc Sino is going to be amazed that you did this, Kira. I feel a little weak, but that's it."

"Your body had to help," Kira said. "I think. I'm sure that Doctor Sino has seen better things on Urth."

"I doubt it," Jason said.

"Where exactly on Dematr is Urth?" Vina asked. "I've never heard of it."

"It's not on Dematr," Jason explained. "Earth is another world."

"Another world?"

Kira laughed. "At least we won't lack for things to talk about while we're waiting for those wardens to show up."

With hours to wait, Kira went carefully over the still-unconscious Stimon, finding nothing in his pockets or backpack that seemed unusual. Her search of Mage Ivor's body also turned up nothing.

She found herself looking down at Ivor. He was shorter than she'd expected. Frozen in death, Ivor's face held a Mage's lack of expression, as if even dying had aroused no feelings in him. It felt strange to realize that this man had been trying to kill members of her family since before they'd formed a family.

"Are you okay?" Jason asked.

"A little numb," Kira said. "It feels sort of unreal. Not in a Mage way," she added quickly. "I couldn't find anything useful on any of them."

"Okay if I look?" Jason asked, feeling around Stimon's backpack. "A lot of times in games they . . . hey, see how deep the bottom is on this?"

Kira looked. "That's the inside bottom? Why would there be that thick a bottom on a backpack?"

Jason dug around at the inside bottom, finally finding something that gave way at his tug. He lifted out a false bottom.

She looked inside, seeing a thin, rectangular metal case. Pulling it out, she examined it. "It's a waterproof dispatch case." No lock sealed it, so Kira used her knife to pry open the dispatch case.

Inside was a single piece of thick paper, folded over twice. Kira unfolded it, seeing three lines of writing. "Jason, look at this."

He leaned close, studying the writing. "Three alphanumeric codes. Passwords. Kira, this might be what we need to get into that place under Pacta."

"Do you think this is the only copy?"

"No, that'd be stupid. They probably made more copies. Remember, they need three people entering the codes simultaneously, so somebody like this guy Stomon—"

"Stimon."

"Right. He would have had to recruit two friends to help if he wanted to get in on his own." Jason studied the Senior Mechanic, who had regained consciousness but, his hands and feet securely bound, could only glare impotently at them. "You really did a number on this guy."

"He tried to force me to leave you to die," Kira pointed out. "You're the one who planted a knife in his gut."

"So we're a team again," Jason said, smiling at her as they walked away from Stimon.

"Yeah. Better than ever, forever." Kira carefully refolded the paper and closed the waterproof case again. "Why don't you carry this?"

"Okay, but when we get a chance we need to make a copy that we can hide on one of us."

What turned up a few hours later was not just a team of forest wardens with an emergency wagon, but also a full troop of Western Alliance cavalry.

Fully expecting that her "escort" would turn out to be keepers charged with bringing Kira back where she could be locked up somewhere safe, Kira was first surprised and then wary at their lack of worry over what she might do next. In fact, the captain in command of the troop asked Kira whether she wished to be escorted back to Cape Astra, making it clear that if she ordered otherwise he would comply. "What's going on?" she muttered to Jason as they waited for Stimon to be loaded into the wagon.

"I'll try to find out." Jason wandered over to some of the waiting cavalry crowding the small glade around Vina's cottage, expressing thanks and talking for a little while before rejoining Kira. "They think you're a genius," he whispered. "They think everything you did was designed to lure out renegade Mechanics and Mages, deliberately exposing yourself to danger just enough to make them think they could get you, but acting unpredictably enough to keep the bad guys busy trying to catch us so they couldn;t do anything else or hurt anyone else."

Kira stared at Jason. "They think I meant to do all that?"

"Yeah. They were actually out here looking for you in case you needed their assistance in taking down more bad guys. Your plan worked."

"Stars above, do not ever talk about that 'plan' again."

Jason shrugged. "Kira, you were either a genius, or you were crazy. We both know what it really was. What do you want everyone else to think?"

"I'm not going to lie to people!" Kira paused. "But if I told them the truth I'd have to talk about the, um, powers thing, and . . . What am I going to do?"

"Get back to Cape Astra," Jason suggested. "And from there get back to your parents with that stuff we found in Stimon's backpack."

"But—"

"Kira, in between the bad parts, and during some of them, you did some amazing, brave stuff. You fought the toughest battle ever inside yourself. You really did accomplish some important things."

She rubbed her face, feeling unhappy but unable to dispute what he'd said. "All right. But you're wrong about one thing. *We* did some amazing, brave stuff. *We* accomplished some important things." Kira deliberately raised her voice so the nearest cavalry soldiers could hear her. "I couldn't have done anything without you. We're a team. And without you, I'd have been dead somewhere along the way to here."

He grinned at her. "Want to get married today?"

She leaned close to whisper the answer in his ear. "We already did. It's too late for you to back out now." Then she kissed Jason, not caring who was watching.

Four days later Kira and Jason rode with a large cavalry escort toward the northern gate of Cape Astra. Kira was happy to be back in the saddle, but felt on display again, both because of the size of the Western Alliance force gathered protectively around her and Jason and because the three leading riders carried flagstaffs. One bore the flag of the Western Alliance, another the pennon of the cavalry unit to which the soldiers belonged, and from the third flagstaff Kira's own banner waved. She'd unsuccessfully suggested that her banner be furled, but the captain in charge of the escort had politely and respectfully demurred.

General Shun met them at the northern gate to the city. "Welcome back, Lady! You've done the Western Alliance a great service."

"I'm . . . glad," Kira said, feeling uncomfortable at the praise. People were gathering on the streets to stare and applaud. She felt her face warming with embarrassment and looked down, centering her gaze on the head of the horse she was riding.

She heard Shun speaking to Jason. "She's as modest as her mother, isn't she?"

"Yes, sir," Jason said, sounding proud.

"Lady Kira, I came to meet you in part because we've just received news regarding Lady Mari."

Kira looked up again, gazing at Shun anxiously.

The general smiled. "You have a brother, Lady. Both mother and child are reported to be healthy and happy."

"I have a brother?" Kira laughed, looking at Jason. "I have a brother!" Her elation tempered as another memory came to her. "I have *another* brother," she told the general. "My first brother, Danel, died at birth. This is my second brother, and I'm very happy about that, but I've had another brother who I don't ever want to forget."

"No," General Shun agreed. "Of course not."

Her escort, by now swelled to three troops of cavalry and a troop of dragoons, filled the streets, combining with the growing crowds to slow their progress. People were pointing and looking at her, and Kira, already feeling a bit different because she was married and because she had managed to save Jason with her powers, felt even more like an unwilling attraction in a show of oddities.

The column came to a brief stop, and as Kira sat her horse a woman hauling a boy in her wake darted toward her.

"Hold!" several of the cavalry shouted, moving their horses to block the woman.

"Please!" she called. "My son leaves on his first voyage soon. I only wish that Lady Kira touch his hand to give him good fortune against the sea!"

Oh, no. Kira gave Jason a helpless glance. She knew the superstition that her mother's touch granted sailors luck against the sea had also gained Kira as an object. But even though she wasn't happy about that, rebuffing the woman would be cruel. She nerved herself and nodded to the cavalry. "Let her through."

The woman came close to Kira, her son looking up at Kira with guarded wonder that further unnerved her. He looked to be perhaps twelve years old, the right age for a cabin boy set on learning the sea. "Please, Lady," his mother said. "You've faced the sea's wrath and won, and you're descended from Jules herself."

Feeling like a fraud, but not knowing what else to do, Kira leaned from her saddle to grasp the young man's hand. "Good luck. May you return safely from every voyage."

As the cavalry began moving again, leaving the relieved mother and her son behind, Kira lowered her head. "I am such a fake," she grumbled to Jason.

"It might really help," Jason suggested.

"How?"

"If people really believe something can make a difference, sometimes it does. The placebo effect, you know. Or the belief that your touch helps might help him do just a little more when it seems hopeless, maybe enough to survive something he wouldn't have. That happens, too."

"You make it sound like every person is a sort of Mage," Kira said.

"In that way, I guess we are," Jason admitted. "What we believe really can impact what we can do."

They finally reached the fort holding a good part of the garrison for the city, leaving the curious crowds behind..

Officials awaited them there, representatives of the city and the Western Alliance government who wanted to render their thanks. Kira, wondering why people kept thanking her for bringing so much danger to their doorstep, kept smiling politely and deflecting their praise for her courage.

Her courage. All she could remember of those weeks was being afraid, or of being so delusional and confident that it hadn't occurred to her to be afraid. Neither one seemed particularly courageous to her.

"There's a warship from the Bakre Confederation waiting in the harbor to take you back," one of the Western Alliance officials said. "We thought you'd prefer to get a good night's rest first, but if you want to leave tonight, that's your decision."

"I think I would like to stay here one night," Kira said, conjuring up her training on formal speaking from Queen Sien's court. "The Western Alliance, and Cape Astra, now have a firm place in my heart. I'll be sad to leave."

By the time the door to their rooms shut behind her, Kira felt exhausted again. Bracing herself, she opened the door anyway. "Is General Shun available? I have a favor I need to ask."

Shun responded quickly. "Anything, Lady."

"There's someone in Cape Astra that I need to talk to," Kira said. "But with as few people as possible knowing."

"We can bring that person here," Shun said. "Quietly and unobtrusively."

Kira and Jason were still eating a private dinner that seemed way too fancy and grand when Shun knocked on their door again. "Your visitor is here, Lady."

Kath came in, rushing to Kira. "I heard you were back! How could you scare me that way?"

"I'm sorry. Really, really sorry. But I'm all right," Kira said as they hugged. "I want you to know. It's all right now. *Everything* is all right."

Kath looked from Jason to Kira. "Everything?"

"Yes." Kira grinned. "Did you hear about Mother?"

"It's all over the place. Congratulations on your new sibling."

"Congratulations on being an aunt again. The Aunt of Opacity. I'm going to call you that from now on. You'll come to Tiae as soon as you can to visit, right?"

Kath made an uncertain gesture. "I wasn't planning on coming until your wedding."

"Oh. About that?" Kira leaned close to whisper in Kath's ear. "We already did it. Just the two of us."

Kath pulled back and stared at her. "Where? When?"

"In the Great Woods. A few days ago. Don't tell anyone!"

"You ran off to the Great Woods and . . . Mari is going to kill me."

"Why would Mother kill you for that?"

"She's going to think I gave you the idea!" Kath laughed. "All right. As soon as I can."

Kath stayed for a while, but saw how tired Kira was and finally left to be spirited back to her home.

Kira sat back, thinking. "If those codes get us into what's buried under Pacta, do you think you'll be able to tell how to disarm those weapons?"

"I don't know. I have to see them first."

"I guess we'll find out soon enough." She looked at their surroundings. "Fancy place, isn't it? I think I liked Vina's cottage more, though."

"There wasn't much privacy at Vina's cottage," Jason pointed out.

"Yeah. Pretty small." Kira looked around again, realizing something. "We've got separate bedrooms, but they're both inside this suite. So nobody will know if we . . ."

"I thought you were worn out."

"Not that worn out. Mess up the bed in your room so it looks like you slept there. Then come to mine. I'm sleeping with my husband tonight."

The Confederation, perhaps wishing to avoid further mayhem on its lands, and knowing that many of the Mages wanting to attack Kira had either been killed or captured, had ordered their warship to take Kira and Jason all the way south to Pacta Servanda. Kira had been just as happy to avoid another armored coach ride, while Jason had been relieved that they wouldn't be taking a train again.

The moment the warship was tied up and the brow across, Kira took time only to thank the officers and crew before racing to the pier. Her mother and father stood there, Mari holding a small bundle in her arms. Kira hugged them both before peering at the small face visible amid the wraps. "What's his name?"

"Andre. After Alain's father."

"Oh . . . that's wonderful. Jason, look! He's your brother, too."

Mari laughed. "Not quite yet."

Her father spotted Kira's reaction. "Is there something we should be told?"

"In private," Kira said. "There are a lot of things I need to tell you. How's Suka? Is he all right?"

"Of course he is," Mari said. "The Lancers say he's a little out of sorts without you around to spoil him, but otherwise your horse is fine."

The coach ride to their rooms in Pacta wasn't long, but it felt longer as Kira held Andre and felt her parents' desire to speak freely as soon as they could.

Once in their rooms, Kira reluctantly surrendered Andre to Mari again. "All right. So . . ."

Mari sat down, cradling Andre in her arms and eyeing Kira. "What the blazes happened, Kira? You had a pretty simple, straightforward job to do. Somehow that turned into a prolonged fight with our enemies that involved a lot of unexpected moves on your part. Mind you, I can't argue with your success. You managed to be unpredictable enough to survive their traps while leading them into your own traps. That was some brilliant planning."

Kira sat down with Jason, biting her lip. "Please don't talk about my brilliant plan. That was . . . Mother, Father, I owe you the truth. I was going insane. I did those things, in part at least, because I was out of my mind at times. If Jason hadn't been there—and he tried to stop me—but if he hadn't been there I'd have brilliantly planned myself into several deathtraps."

She heard the silence that filled the room, and looked up to meet the eyes of her parents. "And it was my fault. It was because of my powers."

"Kira," her father said. "Having powers is not your fault."

"No, that's not what I mean. It wasn't having the powers that caused the trouble. It was how I handled them, what I tried to do, how I refused to listen to anyone else, even refused to listen to myself! I nearly lost everything because I was so stubborn and wouldn't think and wouldn't listen."

"You're using the past tense," Mari said, her eyes worried. "Are you saying that's not the case now?"

"It's not. I'm all right. Father, look at me."

He came closer, gazing into her eyes. "There is peace where I saw turmoil before you left."

"Yes. Peace. Jason helped. Just like I thought he would. He saw things I didn't, and helped me find my path. I needed to walk that path, but without him I wouldn't have found it. Like how Mother helped you realize that people were real. Father, we need to talk a lot, but what it comes down to is, I needed to accept my powers, and give them . . . a separate place inside me."

"We will have to talk," Alain said. "You seem to have found a new wisdom on your own."

"I needed a new wisdom because I was the only person like me!" Kira looked down again. "Maxim is dead. For certain this time. I killed him."

"He didn't give her any choice," Jason rushed to say. "Kira couldn't kill him until he attacked her. And that lightning guy is dead, too."

"Mage Ivor?" Her father looked to her mother. "You are certain?"

Kira nodded. "I put six shots in him at close range. I was angry. He'd killed Jason." Mari and Alain stared at her. "He did. Jason's heart stopped."

Mari nodded carefully. "So you used HBR on him."

"Yes, but that didn't work. I . . ."

"She used her Mage powers to get my heart going again," Jason said.

Her parents were staring again, once more stunned into silence. Alain finally moved, coming to look closely at Jason. "I see what seem to be the faint marks of old injuries I had not seen before."

"He got burned by the lightning when it hit him," Kira said. "I fixed that, too. I don't know how! I trusted my Mage powers and they did it, and I can't tell you anything about that except maybe they understood what they had to do because I knew HBR and because you'd told me how you did it, Father. Maybe. But it's like I can't *know* how my Mage powers are doing things or I'll get irrational again."

"It did not harm you?" Alain asked.

"I was really weak. I had a lot of trouble handling Senior Mechanic Stimon when he showed up—"

"Stimon?" Mari said. "I haven't heard that name for a long time."

"Yeah, he said you'd messed up his life. Anyway, I was exhausted after saving Jason. I think . . . Father, I think it wasn't as hard on me because Jason didn't have anything broken or really badly hurt, he just needed his heart started and those burns taken care of, and because there was so much power there. Stars above, Father, you have to go there. Near Vina's cottage. The amount of power is awesome. It was like . . . Mother, you know how it feels when you're around a strong electrical field? Like the hairs on your arms are standing up? It was like that, only with Mage power."

Mari shook her head. "Stars above, Kira. Is that all? No other heart-stopping news for your father and me? Sorry, that wasn't a deliberate play on words."

"Ummm . . . one other thing. Jason and I need to tell you something."

"Again?"

"What do you mean?"

"I mean," Mari said, "that every time you and Jason are off alone for a while you come back and say you have a big announcement. What is it this time?"

"We're married."

Her mother gazed at Kira wordlessly for a moment. "Married?"

"We still need the license and the witnesses, but we said our promises to each other," Kira said, looking anxiously from her mother to her father. "I turned eighteen while I was gone, remember?"

"Oh."

"We were in the Great Woods. It was a really beautiful spot, and I wanted to! Because . . . wow, that's a really long and embarrassing story. Let's just say it helped us heal."

"I see," Mari said. "In the middle of everything else that was going on, you two found time to get married."

"Mother, how long did it take you and Father to get married?"

"All I recall," Alain said, "is that there was no time to explain."

"See?" Kira said. "And that was while, what, fighting the Great Guilds and assassins and dragons and being a pirate?"

"I was a pirate *after* we got married." Mari made a gesture of surrender. "Congratulations. You're both eighteen, so the decision was yours. Does anyone else know about this?"

"Just Aunt Kath. I had to tell her."

"Kath?" Mari gave Alain an aggravated look. "They talked to Kath. And then they ran off to the Great Woods to get married. How could Kath do that to us?"

"Mother?" Kira looked from Mari to Alain and back again. "Kath said you'd blame her. Why? She didn't tell us to do that. Are you angry with us?"

"How can I be angry with you?" her mother said, smiling. "It was your decision to make, and I think it was a very good decision. But really the only ones who have to be happy with the decision are you and Jason. And I think you are."

Kira grinned. "You wouldn't believe how happy."

"Yeah, I would." Mari looked at Alain, still smiling. "Kira, we'll keep your marriage secret until the official ceremony can be performed. I guess we'll have to set that up as soon as we can. I'm glad everything worked out. At least this time you didn't do anything to reinforce that Mara nonsense."

"Mara?" Kira hesitated, looking at Jason. "Ummm . . . well . . . actually . . ."

Her mother gave Kira a flat look, the smile gone. "Ummm well actually what?"

"I did . . . sort of . . . maybe . . . knock down a guy and bite his neck hard so he and his friends would think I was trying to drink his blood and was hunting them in the night."

Mari's gaze stayed on her, horrified, but Kira's mother seemed momentarily unable to speak.

"I didn't drink it, though!" Kira hastened to add. "I spat the blood out! Didn't I, Jason?"

"Yes," Jason said.

"And in my defense, I was a little bit crazy at the time. Wasn't I, Jason?"

"Yes."

"And we had to. If I hadn't done that, we might not have survived that night. Jason said that, didn't you, Jason?"

"Yes."

Mari finally managed to speak. "You bit a man's neck hard enough to draw blood?"

"Yes," Kira admitted. "It was disgusting. Really. I didn't enjoy it at all."

"I'm so happy to hear that. What happened to the man with your teeth marks in his neck?"

"I . . . don't know. I think his name was Bern. Wasn't it, Jason?"

"Yes."

"Bern of . . . ?" Mari asked. "Any idea where he might be?"

"He might be dead," Kira said. "Right, Jason?"

"Yes."

"I couldn't make out his accent very well, because he was screaming," Kira added, "but I think he sounded a bit like someone from around Emden or maybe Ringhmon."

"He was screaming." Mari shook her head. "You're trying to get the rest of my hair to turn white, aren't you, Kira?"

"Mother, we didn't have any choice! I don't want people thinking of me as the daughter of darkness any more than you want them thinking of you as Mara!"

"And yet somehow it ends up happening," her mother said. "Are there any other little details of your adventure that you haven't mentioned yet?"

"We should tell them about the other thing," Jason said to Kira.

"Oh, stars above," Mari said, "you're not already expecting, are you?"

"*Mother!* What is it with you and Aunt Alli and everybody thinking I'm going to get pregnant just like that? Jason and I are not in a rush!"

"You weren't in a rush to get married, either," her mother pointed out. "So what is the *other thing?*"

"We think we have the passwords to get into the buried facility," Jason said. "All three of them."

"Nobody tried to attack it while we were gone, did they?" Kira asked.

"Oh, we had a few problems," Mari said. "Nothing worth mentioning."

"Father? Why did you give Mother that look?"

"Jason will understand someday if he does not already," Alain said. "We can reach those weapons without setting off the terrible one?"

"If the passwords we have work," Jason said, "that door will open safely. It has to. They wanted to be able to access those weapons if they needed them."

"Then we will prepare to do that as soon as Mari and Andre are safely away—"

"Excuse me?" Kira's mother said. "We'll get Andre out of town. Bev's here. She'll keep him safe back at our place. But I'm not going anywhere."

"Perhaps Kira can take Andre. There is no need to risk her further."

"Excuse me?" Kira said. "Jason has to be here. That means I have to be here."

Alain glanced at Jason, who made a helpless gesture. "It seems Jason has already learned that battles of will with Kira or her mother rarely result in victory."

"Sometimes they do," Jason. "But winning is never fun, and I'm not eager to jump into another."

Kira's father nodded. "You are learning wisdom. I will tell the others we have these codes, so we can attempt this without delay. They should already be aware that Kira is back."

"Yeah," Kira said, "because of that banner the warship was flying! Mother, when did I get a banner?"

"That was yours? You've got a banner?" Mari asked. "Congratulations."

"I don't want a banner!"

"Neither did I, dearest. It comes with the territory."

CHAPTER EIGHTEEN

Kira stared around the excavation site at the damage done to the doors and walls. "It looks like a war was fought down here. What happened?"

"Nothing worth mentioning," her father said with a meaningful look at her mother.

"But if Maxim and the people with him had hit us at the same as this," Mari said, "things might have ended very differently. Your diversion helped a lot."

Before Kira could ask any more questions, the others began arriving. Mage Asha paused, studying Kira. "There is something different about you, Kira."

"Nothing worth mentioning," Kira said.

"How great is the danger?" Queen Sien asked Jason. "You are certain those in the city will not be hurt?"

"As certain as I can be, Your Majesty," Jason said, eyeing the doors leading through the walls to the exposed surface of the buried facility. "If the passwords we have work, then the door will open. If they don't work . . . the door won't open. The only problem would occur if we enter the passwords and they don't work and we keep trying. That might trigger some kind of defenses."

"You know this better than any other," Sien said. "I'll trust your judgment."

"Okay, I need two other people," Jason said. "Two people who can use the data entry pads on that door."

"That means Mechanics," Dav said. "I'm in."

Kira almost jumped in, but paused, thinking that others deserved the chance. "Uncle Calu?"

He hesitated. "I'm still mainly a theory guy. I'm not that good with understanding equipment. You need the best possible choice. Dav is one. I think Alli or Mari should be the other."

"I'll do it," Alli said. "Her daughterness shouldn't get to hog all the glory."

The doors in the protective walls were opened and pulled back, once again revealing the grayish permacrete, the actual door into the facility, and the three panels. "Mechanic Dav," Jason said, "here's your code. I'm going to activate the panel in front of you."

Kira, crowding forward, saw Jason touch parts of the panel, and saw it glow to life.

"They've still got power," Dav said in amazement, shaking his head.

"They've probably got a geothermal backup running in there," Jason said. "See the keyboard on the display? You just touch each word or number on the password in turn. Keep one hand on this other panel above the keyboard while you do that so the equipment knows a real human is entering the data."

"I can see the keyboard," Dav said, nodding. "When do I start?"

"Wait until I've powered up the other two panels and Master Mechanic Alli and I are ready," Jason said. "We need to all be doing it at the same time."

A couple of minutes later, the three of them were poised before their panels. "One hand on the panel above the lighted one," Jason said, showing the others how he set his palm flat on the surface. "It'll feel a little warm."

"It does," Alli said. Dav nodded.

"Okay." Jason took a deep breath and looked back at Kira. She smiled at him, and gave him a nod.

He faced the panel again. "Enter your code one character at a time, making sure it's the right one before you touch it. If you touch the wrong one, press that key marked with a crossed-out circle to delete it so you can enter the right one." Jason reached for the panel, one finger extended.

Kira watched, nervous, as the three pecked at their panels. She felt the tension in the others watching around her.

"Done," Alli said.

"Same here," Dav said.

"I'm ready," Jason said. "A command saying *enter* should have lit up on your panels. Touch that."

They waited, Kira imagining that white light appearing to engulf them all.

Instead, a mechanical thunk sounded from inside the facility. Kira watched as more deep sounds came, hoping they were the noises of massive locks releasing.

A dark line appeared around the door, more than a lance wide and more than a lance tall, growing larger as the door swung ponderously inward. Beyond, a harsh, strong light flickered into existence to illuminate the inside.

"Good job, Jason," Dav said, clapping him on the shoulder.

Kira inhaled, hearing everyone else around her doing the same.

"Now what?" Mari asked Jason.

"We go in." He advanced cautiously. "I don't see any more barriers. There's a wide, straight passage heading down."

The Mechanics all had tool packs with them, though what good those tools would do against the technology inside that facility was questionable. Kira saw Mari, Alli, Dav, and Calu also draw their pistols. She did the same, realizing at the same time that any danger inside that facility would likely be more than any Mechanic weapon known to Dematr could handle.

Her mother knew that, too. "Alain, Asha, have your spells ready. That's one thing we know the Urth people don't have defenses against."

"I should go first," Jason said, visibly nervous. "I have the best chance of spotting anything that might be trouble."

Kira lunged forward, past the others. She stopped beside Jason. "All right. Let's go."

Jason shook his head at her. "Kira, this is—"

"Jason, we both know how this argument is going to end. Let's save some time. To always stand beside you, remember?"

He looked around for support, but the others shook their heads, though the other women gave Kira questioning looks over her last statement, clearly wondering why she'd cited promise vows. "Deciding to accompany you is Kira's prerogative," Queen Sien said.

Jason pulled out a device that resembled an egg with one side flattened, the flat surface rippling with words and colors. "Doc Sino gave me this. It should detect dangerous gases or radiation so we'll have enough warning to stay clear."

"You think they'd use those kinds of traps?" Calu asked.

"No. But anything they left down here might have deteriorated and produced those kinds of dangers," Jason said. "Which is why I wish Kira wasn't insisting on walking beside me."

"You knew what you were getting," Kira told him. "Ready when you are." She and Jason started down the passage side by side, the others coming along a little ways behind. Jason moved slowly down the slope of the passage, searching the walls, the floor and the ceiling for any sign of trouble. Kira had feared the floor would be slick under her boots, but it offered good purchase.

The passageway ran at least a hundred lances before opening up into a large room with two other passages leading off from it.

In the center of the room, on a pedestal about half a lance high and a lance across, sat a box about the same size as a pig, gleaming with metal and other surfaces that Kira couldn't identify.

Jason approached the pedestal with small, careful steps, bending to read something on the side of the box. "Beta Field Generator. Model Five. Series Three. Caution." He stepped back, breathing deeply. "I've never been this close to something this dangerous before."

"Does it look like the ones from your games?" Kira asked, keeping her pistol up and canted toward the other two passages.

"No. Not at all. That's not surprising. Those deliberately avoided showing real stuff about the design of weapons of mass destruction. The games always had an easy-to-spot access panel on the weapons. But I can't see an access panel on this one."

Queen Sien had entered with the others. "Is this the weapon set to go off if the facility is forced? Can you disarm it?"

"It must be the one intended to blow up the facility," Jason said. "See those two green lights? I think that means it's active. It definitely means it's got power going to it. The power supply is probably routed through the pedestal. But . . . I've got no idea how to get at the inside of this thing. It might be set to go off if tampered with!"

"We can't just leave it there," Mari said. "Any ideas, people?"

Master Mechanic Lukas had been silent, staying back and observing everything. Now he walked completely around the pedestal, looking at the box from all sides. "Jason, is there any explosive in this thing?"

"Explosive? No. I'm certain of that. It's all electronics designed to create the beta field."

"No detonator?"

"No," Jason said. "I mean, some of the electronics might be dangerous to touch."

"Capacitors? Electronics like that?"

"Sort of."

Alli shook her head. "Lukas, are you thinking what I think you're thinking?"

"Probably," Lukas said.

"What are you both thinking?" Mari asked.

Lukas pursed his lips, nodding toward the box. "I'm thinking that if this is a box full of electronics, every component of which is important to the device functioning properly, then if our Mages make half of this box go away, we can rip out and break everything in the other half. The same sort of tactic that disabled the equipment the people on that ship from Urth tried to use against us."

Kira heard a choking sound beside her. She looked at Jason, who seemed to be having trouble breathing.

"That's—" Jason tried to inhale. "That's—"

Kira slapped her palm against his back. "Breathe."

Calu shook his head. "Jason seems a little bothered by your idea, Lukas."

Finally getting his breath back, Jason shook his head rapidly. "Um, no. No. I don't think we should do that. Like I said, even messing with the case might cause it to go off."

"Jason, we're not talking about opening it," Alli pointed out. "We're talking about making half of the entire blasted thing temporarily disappear. How could it work if we did that?"

"Alli's right," Mari said. "We don't know beta field generators, but we do know electronics. Nothing is made with half of the stuff redundant and not required to function."

"But—"

Lukas pointed to the device that Jason still held. "That thing Doctor Sino gave you. If Mage Alain made half of it vanish, would it work?"

"No," Jason said. "But the Invictus Drive. Remember? Kira made part of that go away, and the drive still worked."

"I thought you said that broke the drive," Kira said. "Because breaking the drive was the only thing that could cause the internal matrix to reset."

Jason stared at her, then reluctantly nodded. "That's right. The drive wouldn't work to save data while that part was missing."

"Jason," Mari said, "we're engineers. Engineers designed this thing. We may not know the technology they used, but we know how they thought when they were designing it."

Dav nodded. "Those engineers were thinking *Wow, this is going to be really cool when it goes off.* But also how to design it most efficiently."

Jason turned a pleading gaze on Kira. "What do you think?"

It startled her to realize that he trusted her judgment more than that of the others here. Trusted her despite everything that had happened. "I think Lukas and Alli are right. Can you think of anything on Urth, any device you used, that would work if half of it went away?"

He paused, thinking, before shaking his head again. "No."

"Is there a power supply inside there?" Mari asked.

"Maybe. It might have an independent power supply of some kind. A backup. Some kind of chargeable battery. That might not still be working, though."

"A power source that's fractured might still explode if something important is missing," Alli said. "But that would help break anything else in there."

Mari looked at Queen Sien. "Your Majesty, this is your call. We're in your kingdom, and that's one of your cities above us."

"Jason," Sien said. "As long as this device works, it remains a threat that could go off at any time. Is that correct?"

"Yes," Jason said.

Sien gazed at Lukas and Alli, then at Dav, Calu, Kira, and finally Mari. "If it is the judgment of the Mechanics present that this is the safest means to dispose of the threat posed by this object, then I say proceed."

Mari gave orders again, a role she fell into naturally after so much experience. "Let's minimize the chances of anyone getting hurt. Dav, how many pairs of heavy gloves do we have? Three? Alli, you put on one, Dav, you take the second. I'll put on the third."

"I'll put on the third," Lukas said. "You're the supervisor, Mari. That means you stand back and supervise."

Mari gave him a lowered brow but didn't try to argue the point. "Alain, you and Asha go to the other side of that box and walk as far from it as you can and still be comfortable that you can make half of it go away. Do we have enough Mage power for that?"

"Yes," Kira said along with Alain and Asha. She flinched. "Sorry."

"You'll have to hide your Mage senses in public a little better than that," her mother said. "Alain, Asha, when the Mage spell takes effect, Alli, Dav, and Lukas will move around to that side as fast as possible and start yanking out or breaking anything they can get at."

"Suggestion, honored Master Mechanic," Alli said. "There might be something in there that we can't break by hand or hand tools." She nodded toward Kira.

"Good idea. Kira, ready your weapon. When the rest are done, I want you to put bullets into anything that still looks intact. Everybody else stay out of the line of fire behind that thing in case any of her shots penetrate the casing and go out the other side."

"What should Jason and I do?" Calu asked.

"You two know more than the rest of us about how this thing might work. Watch for anything you think might be particularly critical or dangerous to make contact with. If you see something like that, call out and I'll decide what to do. And if something badly shocks one of the three putting their hands in there, use HBR on us." Mari's eyes went to Kira and then Alain. "You two also do what you can if that happens, but nobody dies trying to bring someone else back to life. Understand?"

"Why did you include Kira when you said that?" Calu said.

"Never mind. Let's get ready."

Kira held her pistol ready, the barrel aimed upward, while Alain and Asha walked past the other side of the beta field generator, getting about three lances away before stopping and turning to face it.

Jason stood beside Kira, muttering barely loud enough for her to hear. "In games you go in and you use micro tools to delicately manipulate tiny parts of complex circuits, doing everything just right and in the right order. And you guys are going to just break things."

"Every engineer knows sometimes you just gotta break things," Kira whispered back to him. She felt her father preparing a spell. "Stand by," she said, loudly enough for the other Mechanics to hear.

Her heart was pounding, wondering if the next thing to happen would be a bright white light that signaled oblivion.

From the angle she was watching, Kira could see part of the box vanish as she felt her father complete the spell.

She ran around to face the affected side of the beta field generator, keeping her pistol pointed upward as Alli, Dav, and Lukas dashed to the now open box. Kira caught a brief glimpse of small, shiny, boxlike objects fastened into arrays, of flat and round things whose surfaces glittered as if jewels were scattered on them, and of what looked like bundles of wires snaking through the other items. What had apparently been a spherical array of components in the center of the device was now a partial sphere, lights flashing on the remaining intact parts.

Then her view was blocked as hands in heavy gloves reached in, grabbing the wire bundles first and yanking them loose. Alli made a fist and punched at some of the other components, knocking some out of alignment and breaking a few free to dangle from bent rails. The neat partial sphere of components got ripped out, dropped to the floor, and stomped on.

"I cannot hold it much longer," Alain warned, his voice Mage-calm.

"Get back!" Mari ordered Alli, Dav, and Lukas. "Kira! Empty your magazine into that thing!"

Kira didn't try to aim precisely, simply pulling the trigger as she fired into the components remaining, seeing holes appear in them, worried about ricochets but the remaining innards of the beta field generator absorbing enough of the force that no bullets came flying back out. The outer shell was tough enough that no shots pierced it from the inside. The moment the slide stayed back on her weapon to indicate she'd fired the last shot in her magazine, she raised the barrel of her pistol and called out. "That's it!"

The rest of the beta field generator reappeared.

Kira waited, seeing the others doing the same, all tense as if they could leap into action and do something if the worst happened.

But nothing did.

"I guess it worked," Calu said.

"Let's do the other half to be sure," Mari said. "Same drill. Asha, you do the spell this time. Kira, do you have another magazine?"

"Duh," Kira said, reloading. "Aunt Alli taught me this stuff, remember? Do you think I'd do anything with you or with her and not have a lot of extra ammunition with me?"

"Maybe one of us should have taught you not to answer a question with *duh*," her mother said.

"I tried," Alli said. "Are we going to do this?"

This time when half of the beta field generator vanished there was a popping sound, and small fragments of something burst outward. But Asha maintained her focus on the spell long enough for the Mechanics to finish smashing and shooting the insides.

Asha staggered as the spell failed. "There is little power remaining near here," she said as Dav went to help her.

Alli pulled off her gloves. "We shouldn't need it. That sucker is broke."

Jason shook his head, laughing. "Mage talents save the day again. I wish I'd been able to use those in my games."

"Which passage do we check first?" Calu asked.

"That one," Sien said, pointing to the smaller one on the left.

Once again Kira joined Jason as they entered the passage, searching for trouble. She could see the end of this passage, a few hundred lances ahead, but it wasn't until they'd gotten closer that she spotted another passage jutting off to the left. A sealed door blocked access to it.

As they approached that passage, a high-pitched whistle sounded.

"What the blazes is that?" Alli demanded, looking around.

"The detector that Doctor Sino sent," Jason said, gazing at the device. "Radiation." He swung the device slowly before him, watching it all the while. "It's coming from the other side of that door."

"Can we get any closer?" Mari asked. "Enough to see what's in there?"

"Yeah. It says the intensity is low enough here that exposure for a short time shouldn't be dangerous." Jason walked forward slowly, his eyes fixed on the device, until he stood outside the sealed door. "Oh, man. It says we shouldn't spend more than a couple of minutes here."

"Is that one of the panel things?" Kira asked, pointing beside the door.

"Yeah. Let's activate it and . . . Camera! Maybe we can see what's inside."

Images appeared on the panel, as if she were viewing them directly. Kira called out to the others. "There's a heavy door of some kind at the end of the passage behind this door. Maybe a hundred lances away. It looks damaged, like . . . like something partially blew it out. And short of that, maybe eighty lances down the passage, there are other really wide passages on each side . . . no, those are rooms. Big rooms. I can see stuff in the parts of the rooms visible through the openings. It's equipment. Both of those rooms look a bit like the original equipment room in the librarians' tower. Lots of stuff in racks and shelves."

The device in Jason's hand wailed again, higher-pitched and louder. "Back!" he cried. "Everybody back!"

Jason touched something that made the panel go dark again, urging Kira ahead of him as everyone retreated all the way to the room holding the broken beta field generator. "This thing says there's a lot of radiation in there," Jason told the others. "Hard stuff. We do not want to open that door. The air itself on the other side is probably lethal."

"How did that happen?" Lukas asked. "Any ideas?"

Jason squinted in thought. "Like Kira said, that second door we saw inside was damaged, like something had exploded on the other side of it. I was paying a lot of attention to Doc Sino's device, though. Kira, did you see anything on the door?"

"Ummm . . . danger . . ." She tried to remember what else. "Something like a circle, but with, uh, sixths of it cut out. Like one sixth there, one sixth missing, one sixth there, and so on."

"What color was it?"

"Like black on yellow, I think."

Jason nodded, looking grim. "That's the universal radiation warning sign. They did make nuclear weapons. Or refined the materials to make nuclear weapons. Some of that must have suffered failures."

"I thought nuclear weapons did immense amounts of damage," Calu said.

"They do. But the nuclear material in them can, uh, sort of blow itself apart if safeguards fail. I think it's called a sub-critical explosion. Not a nuclear explosion, but enough to breach that door and scatter material."

"How dangerous is it?" Dav asked.

"According to Doctor Sino's device, anyone who goes into the hallway will receive a lethal dose before they reach that other door."

"They'd die before they even reach the end of the hall?"

"Uh, yes and no," Jason said. "They'd get a lethal dose. So they'd be dead at that point but they wouldn't be dead yet."

"Mostly dead?" Kira asked.

"Worse than mostly dead. They'd feel sick for maybe a day, then they'd feel fine for another day or so. That's called being a Walking Ghost, because everything inside that person is shutting down and dying. After that they die. No way to save them."

"Like poisoning," Calu said.

"Yes," Jason said. "It's called radiation poisoning. One hundred percent lethality guaranteed. Unless that Mage stuff can make a difference."

Kira looked to her father, who frowned. "I would not want to attempt to heal everything inside someone. Even healing a few parts is an immense effort."

"So we can't get at that room," Kira said. "What about the rooms to either side? There's a lot of stuff in them. Technology from the great ship."

Jason shook his head. "Those rooms are open. Anything in them has been exposed to the radiation. Everything will be hot."

"Hot?" Mari asked.

"Dangerously radioactive."

"One last thumb in our eye from the crew of that ship!" Dav said with disgust. "They saved that equipment for themselves, but because they built those other weapons and stored things carelessly, it's all useless to us even if it still works."

"What if we sent a troll in?" Alli asked. "Could a troll at least get something out? I mean, it'd die, but . . ."

"That something would be dangerous," Jason said. "That gear is not just surrounded by radioactivity. By now it's radioactive, too. And like I said, opening the door would release the air inside. We don't want to do that."

"Is there any way to make it safe?" Mari asked.

"Wait a few million years. Maybe longer. Personally, I'd stuff that open passage leading to the first door as full of fill as I could to keep in the radiation and keep any adventurers out. Rocks with lead in them. Stuff like that."

"One of the tech manuals," Calu said, "has information about building protective suits for situations like this. Maybe we can make something that will at least allow someone to look in that room at the end and tell us if any weapons are still intact and need to be disarmed."

"That's going to take a while, if that protective stuff is what I remember seeing," Lukas commented. "We still need to develop the means to construct some of the technology involved. And of course there's nothing in those manuals about those weapons. Those idiots in the original crew managed to destroy everything."

"That just means we get to rebuild it," Mari said. "Let's try the other passage."

This one was wider, leading a longer distance but staying level until it suddenly opened into a massive room. Kira stared around, seeing four rectangular shapes with curved edges and corners, each as large as a small ocean-going ship. "What are these things?"

"*Demeter*'s shuttles," Jason said, awe in his voice. "Actual colonization project shuttles. This is amazing."

"These things could fly?" Mechanic Dav asked. "They don't look like the ship that brought you here."

"This technology is centuries old on Earth," Jason explained. "Archaic to Earth. But it's way ahead of what Dematr has."

"Do they still work?" Mari approached the nearest shuttle cautiously, studying its exterior. "The outside looks a little corroded in places. Look there. That material is drooping down and disintegrating like some sort of rotted cloth."

"I think that's a synthetic material," Jason said. "Let me think. I did some virtual walk-throughs of shuttles like this on the way to this world."

"You haven't been in a real one?"

Jason gave Kira a sidelong look. "Nothing . . . virtual . . . is real."

"Did you tell him to say that?" her mother demanded of Kira.

"Not that," Kira denied.

Jason gave a small sound of satisfaction, walking to a spot on the outside of the shuttle and pushing something that gave way under his hand. "That should . . . it's not. Can somebody help me here?"

Calu, Dav, and Alli came closer, grabbing on to the crack that had appeared in the side of the ship, tugging until it widened and they could get a better grip. They staggered backwards as the opening suddenly fell outward, turning into a ramp that led to a dimly lit space inside the shuttle.

"That was supposed to come out under power," Jason said. "The lights are still working, but they're dim. The power supply on this shuttle must be almost exhausted." He led the way up the ramp, Kira rushing to be beside him, the others following.

The inside of the shuttle smelled musty and slightly tinny, like an empty piece of armor left buried too long. "Is this air safe?" Lukas called.

"Yeah," Jason said, holding up Doctor Sino's device. "This says there's safe atmosphere in here. If it goes off again that'll mean we've encountered toxic gases." Jason paused as he and Kira reached a place where the passage they were in met another running at right angles to it. "Okay, if I remember right, this should lead back toward the cargo bay and forward toward the command deck."

"Where are the engines?" Mari asked, looking around.

"Under us," Jason said, heading in the direction he had said the command deck lay.

A large hatch blocked them. Jason looked on either side of it, finally spotting what he was looking for. "This is normally a power-actuated hatch, but there's a manual release as a backup. Here. It's . . . wow. It's stuck. Kira?"

She grabbed the handle Jason was pulling on and strained to help him yank it down. The handle gave way as abruptly as the ramp had, almost making Kira and Jason fall.

"I'm not getting a good feeling about the condition of this thing," Alli commented.

Kira and Jason tugged the hatch open until it came to rest on a latch against the wall behind it. The room beyond was dark, but as Jason stepped in lights sprang to life, bright enough to reveal several seats positioned before narrow desks bolted to the floor.

"Command positions," Jason explained. "Like the pilot and flight engineer and stuff. When these controls were powered up, the displays would project above them." He studied one of the desks. "Okay. Flight engineer. That should tell us what shape this shuttle is in. Should I turn it on?"

Mari indicated Queen Sien, who everyone watched.

"Can it cause any harm?" Sien asked.

"No," Jason said. "See, this is the on/off. When the desk powers up, the other controls will light up, but nothing else will happen until I activate another command."

"Then do it."

Kira watched Jason push the button with the familiar on/off symbol on it. As they waited for something to happen, she leaned close to him. "I'm so proud that my man is the expert on this," she murmured.

He gave her a nervous grin before looking back at the desk.

Lights rippled across it, then to Kira's astonishment glowing symbols appeared in the air above the desk. "This is like that stuff inside the egg-shaped thing we rode when we were first heading off to hide the drive from your mother's ship," she said to Jason.

"The pod. Yeah. A few generations older, but yeah," Jason said. He turned to look at Queen Sien again. "This says 'ship status.' If I touch it, it shouldn't do anything but tell us how well everything on the ship is working."

"How can it do that?"

"It's like . . ." Jason hesitated, thinking. "The automated systems monitor all the other systems and see how well they're working. If anything isn't working right, they can tell."

"Sort of like Master Mechanic Lukas," Calu commented.

"I doubt they're that good," Lukas replied. "Basically, Jason, this is like someone watching gauges and dials and reporting whether everything is functioning well, but mechanized rather than using humans to report that. Am I right?"

"Yes," Jason said. "Basically."

Sien nodded. "You may do as you asked," she told Jason.

Jason reached and pushed the glowing symbol in the air just as if it were a real button. "Nothing is real," Kira said.

"Nothing is real," her father and Asha agreed, speaking together.

Red symbols abruptly appeared, and a voice began speaking in an accent different than Jason's but still understandable. Kira listened, awed to realize this was the voice of someone who had died centuries ago. "Danger. Critical system failure in primary lift. Danger. Critical system failure in primary maneuvering. Danger. Critical system failure in life support. Danger. Critical system failure in primary power. Danger. Backup power at less than one percent. Danger. Critical system failure in navigational sub-systems. Danger. Critical system failure in radiation shielding. Danger. Critical system failure in hull integrity."

The voice was getting quieter, the red glow of the symbols becoming fainter. Kira realized the lights overhead were also dimming further. She pulled out her hand light and clicked it on as the voice continued to fade.

"Dan-ger . . . critical . . . sys-tem . . . fail . . ."

The symbols above the desk winked out, the voice fading out completely, the lights on the desk itself rapidly dimming. Kira saw other hand lights coming on behind her.

The lights overhead flickered before settling into a dull glow that barely illuminated the control deck.

"Too bad it didn't tell us what still worked," Dav commented as he and the other Mechanics used their hand lights to study the now quiet and nearly dark room.

"I've got a feeling nothing still works," Alli replied. "Except that desk that told us everything was broken."

"Do you think there's any chance you could fix the broken parts?" Queen Sien asked.

"No," Lukas said, and none of the other Mechanics disputed him.

"Looking at what was inside that beta field generator, and the other things we've seen in here, we're a long ways from being able to fix any of it. We're a long ways from knowing how it works."

"There are four shuttles," Kira said. "Maybe one of the remaining three is in better shape."

But when they pulled open the ramp on the next shuttle they picked, everyone staggered away from the noxious smell that rolled out from the interior and Doctor Sino's device wailed a warning. "Something bad broke in there," Calu said as they muscled the ramp shut again.

"We're not going in that thing without trying to test the air and venting it out first," Alli said. "The other two are like these first two. You can see the corrosion on the outside of them."

Jason looked around, puzzled. "They must not have planned leaving these down here this long. There are ways to prepare stuff like this for long-term storage, and they didn't do it."

"How do you know they knew about those ways?" Lukas asked.

"That's how these shuttles were prepared for the trip here. They spent a long time on the *Demeter* before the ship reached this world. The crew had to bring them out of . . . I think it's called hibernation? Something like that. So they would have known how to put the shuttles back in that condition. But they didn't. Whoever was in here last thought they'd be back before long."

Kira gazed at the shuttles, broken monuments to the original crew. When had the last ones visited this place they had built to hold devices they denied this world but wanted safe in case they ever needed them? What had they been like, those men and women who had decided to suppress knowledge and technology so that they and their descendants could control this world? Had they looked and acted like Maxim or Stimon? Or would they have claimed false kinship with Lukas, Alli, Dav, and Mari?

They had been here, and they had left, planning to come back, and no one ever had. Pacta Servanda. Agreements Must Be Honored. But they had honored nothing, and left nothing useful to those they had sworn to protect and serve.

Mari sighed heavily. "It looks like they'll all be in the same shape, then. We're not flying to the moon in these."

"There's probably still a lot we can learn from them," Calu suggested.

"We'll see."

They walked all the way out, past the guards in the basement, sealing the door to the underground facility again to keep out anyone who might explore and be harmed by the radioactivity.

Outside, Kira breathed the open air with relief, trying to wash the dust of old treachery and greed from her lungs.

Jason gazed to the southwest. "There has to be some concealed hangar door over that way for the shuttles to use. If we opened it now, some buildings would probably fall in."

"The librarians will want to see what's in there," Calu said.

"I need to talk to the librarians about a number of things," Mari said. "That reminds me. Kira, I understand you declared war on Urth. At least, that's what the librarians told me you did."

"I told Urth that we were free, and they couldn't tell us what to do, and we would fight if they tried to control us or tried to take Jason. Did the librarians tell you that? Urth threatened Jason! They said they'd send a ship to arrest him and take him back to Urth."

"A ten-year trip to arrest him and another ten to get home?" Lukas said. "That sounds like a bluff to me."

Jason frowned. "That's not exactly what they said, though. Kira, I just realized. Earth said they'd send a message to arrest me to the *next* ship to arrive here."

Mari turned an alarmed gaze on him. "The next ship? You're sure that's what they said? That sounds like one is already on its way."

"I know others were being built when my ship left Earth," Jason said.

"Will it be like your mother's ship? Out to exploit us?"

"I don't know. Can I ask a big favor, Lady Mari?"

Mari looked surprised at Jason's use of her title. "What's that?"

"From now on, when we talk about Talese Groveen, can we just use her name? And every time we talk about my mother, can we mean you?"

"I think we can do that," Mari said, smiling.

"If there's a chance of another ship from Urth coming," Dav said, "maybe Kira and Jason should get married as soon as possible. Once they are, he'll legally be a citizen of this world. Urth won't have any basis for trying to arrest him, and we'll have legal grounds for fighting to keep him with us."

"That's a good idea," Kira's mother said. "Are you willing to do that, Kira?"

"Oh, I don't know," she said, acting put-upon. "I guess it'd be all right to get married soon. Jason?"

"Yeah," he said. "I'm good with that."

"They are already married," Asha said, her voice Mage-calm as usual. "I can see it when they speak of it. That is why Kira cited the promise vows to Jason."

"Aunt Asha!" Kira gave the others an apologetic look. "Yes, we said the promises. But it hasn't been officially, formally done."

"Then we'll keep it quiet until it's officially, formally done," Queen Sien said. "Who isn't here that we need?"

"Aunt Kath," Kira said. "And we need to set her up with some nice guy while she's here."

"I'll leave that to you," Sien said.

"Fine. But you need to get to know Kath, your Majesty. She has a very big heart. The biggest heart in the whole world."

Sien smiled. "I'll have to spend some time with Kath, then."

Jason gave Kira a disbelieving look, but she shook her head in warning to him not to say anything.

"My parents," Mari said. "And if it's all right with Kira, Sergeant Kira's family."

"Oh, of course it's all right!" Kira said.

As the others discussed dates and people who had to be invited, Kira led Jason off to the side. The street was nearly empty, still sealed off because of the access to the facility in the building here. The structures in this part of Pacta Servanda were old, only rising two or three stories, a wide swath of blue sky flecked with clouds visible above. She held him, looking up at that sky. "Do you really think another ship from Urth is already on its way here?"

"Probably," Jason said.

"The last one brought you. And Doctor Sino. Maybe the next one won't be all bad, either."

Jason smiled. "We can hope. Miracles happen sometimes. One happened to me. I love this dream I'm in."

"It's had its nightmare moments, hasn't it?" Kira laughed. "It's funny. We've come so very far from when we first met, but we're still right here in Pacta."

"I like it here," Jason said.

"So do I. Once I couldn't wait to leave it, to go somewhere else, anywhere else, but now I know how happy I am to have this place." She smiled. "To know that inside me this place will always be there with me, no matter where else I go. And you'll be with me, too."

"Always," Jason said. "No matter what."

"No matter what," Kira agreed.

"But I hope we don't have to take a train to get where we're going."

They heard a ruckus behind them and looked.

"Kira," her father said. "Mage Asha has just had a vision in which you appeared."

"Oh, blazes," Kira sighed. "Now what?"

ABOUT THE AUTHOR

"Jack Campbell" is the pseudonym for John G. Hemry, a retired Naval officer who graduated from the U.S. Naval Academy in Annapolis before serving with the surface fleet and in a variety of other assignments. He is the author of The Lost Fleet military science fiction series, as well as the Stark's War series, and the Paul Sinclair series. His short fiction appears frequently in *Analog* magazine, and many have been collected in ebook anthologies *Ad Astra*, *Borrowed Time*, and *Swords and Sadwdles*. He lives with his indomitable wife and three children in Maryland.

Don't miss the adventure that started
it all...

THE DRAGONS
OF DORCASTLE

PILLARS OF REALITY ❖ BOOK 1

JACK
CAMPBELL

NEW YORK TIMES BESTSELLING AUTHOR

FOR NEWS ABOUT JABBERWOCKY BOOKS AND AUTHORS

Sign up for our newsletter*: http://eepurl.com/b84tDz
visit our website: awfulagent.com/ebooks
or follow us on twitter: @awfulagent

THANKS FOR READING!

Printed in Great Britain
by Amazon